WERTHEIM FELLOWSHIP PUBLICATIONS

THE WORKER
SPEAKS HIS MIND

ON

COMPANY
AND
UNION

THEODORE V. PURCELL, S.J.

HARVARD UNIVERSITY PRESS · CAMBRIDGE · 1953

TO MY FATHER

THEODORE VINCENT PURCELL

WERTHEIM FELLOWSHIP PUBLICATIONS

In 1923 the family of the late Jacob Wertheim established the Jacob Wertheim Research Fellowship for ". . . the support of original research in the field of industrial coöperation . . ." The Fellowship was intended to enable men and women ". . . who already have expert knowledge of this subject, to pursue research that may be of general benefit in solving the problems in this field . . ." Fellowships are awarded annually by the President and Fellows of Harvard College on the recommendation of the Wertheim Committee.

The Committee undertakes to provide general supervision to the program of research of the Wertheim Fellow. When that research yields findings and results which are significant and of general interest, the Committee is authorized by the terms of the grant to Harvard University to recommend publication. The Jacob Wertheim Research Fellow alone has responsibility for the facts, analysis, and opinions expressed in this volume.

WERTHEIM FELLOWSHIP PUBLICATIONS

Theodore V. Purcell, S.J., *The Worker Speaks His Mind on Company and Union*, 1953

Lloyd H. Fisher, *The Harvest Labor Market in California*, 1953

Walter Galenson, *The Danish System of Labor Relations: A Study in Industrial Peace*, 1952

John T. Dunlop and Arthur D. Hill, *The Wage Adjustment Board: Wartime Stabilization in the Building and Construction Industry*, 1950

Ralph Altman, *Availability for Work: A Study in Unemployment Compensation*, 1950

Dorothea de Schweinitz, *Labor and Management in a Common Enterprise*, 1949

Walter Galenson, *Labor in Norway*, 1949

Leo C. Brown, S.J., *Union Policies in the Leather Industry*, 1947

Paul H. Norgren, *The Swedish Collective Bargaining System*, 1941

Johnson O'Connor, *Psychometrics*, 1934

William Haber, *Industrial Relations in the Building Industry*, 1930

Wertheim Lectures on Industrial Relations, 1929

J. D. Houser, *What the Employer Thinks*, 1927

FOREWORD

I know of no book of recent years that promises to be such rewarding reading for business executives, union leaders, or others who wish to understand the human problems of industry, as Father Purcell's.

There are two reasons why Father Purcell's book is particularly valuable. One was his success in getting close to the workers and finding out what they really think. This was possible because of his year and a half of living in the stockyards community. But it is not enough to know what is on the worker's mind. It is also important to know who thinks what — in other words, to discover patterns in people's attitudes and opinions. Are there significant differences in attitude between short-service and long-service workers, men and women, union members and nonmembers, Negroes and whites, foremen and nonsupervisory workers? The second reason why Father Purcell's book is particularly valuable is that his carefully selected sample enables him to show the patterns in attitudes and opinions.

Life always turns out to be richer and more complex than one expects it to be. Until one gets to know people intimately, one is almost certain to underestimate the variety of their interests, the multitude of facts that they take into account in forming their attitudes and opinions, and the many qualifications which they attach to their views. To me the most satisfying parts of Father Purcell's book are the numerous quotations from his interviews. These quotations make one realize that the Swift employees are not primarily employees of a certain company or members of a certain union, or even workers in a certain industry. They talked to Father Purcell about their jobs, their fellow-employees, their bosses, their company, and their union, but it is apparent that their interest in all of these matters was limited and greatly qualified by many particular facts in their lives and by their interest in other matters which were not related to their employment.

The interviews with Father Purcell have produced an abundance of challenging conclusions. For example, the interviews show that a considerable measure of allegiance to *both* the company and the union is not only possible but is, in fact, usual. Most of the employees had it. Most of them regarded the company as, on the whole, a good employer — better than the other employers in the Yards. This attitude predominated in spite of severe criticism among the Negroes of the company's unwillingness to promote Negroes to supervisory jobs.

The favorable attitude toward the company did not prevent the employees from having a considerable measure of allegiance to their union. Furthermore, this allegiance to the union persisted in spite of the fact that the union got them involved in a strike which failed and which most of the employees regarded as a mistake, and in spite of the fact that the local was temporarily dominated by Communists. Although the employees in general were favorable toward the union, there was very limited participation in union activities. The attitude of the employees was slightly more favorable toward the company than toward the union and there is evidence of competition between the two allegiances. It is significant that even the foremen as a group were favorable toward the union.

Father Purcell's interviews show that a number of widely accepted conclusions about workers and their attitudes are wrong. They show, for example, that it is not true that to most workmen the foreman is the company, and that a bad foreman causes the company to be regarded as a bad company. The employees distinguish clearly between the foreman and the company. Some of them may regard the company as a pretty good company even though they may not think much of their own foreman. Others regard their foreman as distinctly better than the company.

The interviews shed light also on what men regard as good supervision and what men regard as good jobs. One of the most important elements in good supervision seems to be the willingness and ability of the foreman to run his department without giving too much detailed supervision to his workers. Men like to be treated as capable of thinking for themselves, and the foreman who supervises with a minimum of direction is regarded as a particularly good supervisor.

Jobs which seem to the outsider to be rather humdrum and routine are found by the workers themselves to be rich in content, and to make demands on the worker that the outsider would not suspect. There was little complaint of monotony. But Father Purcell finds that subdivided, routine production on the whole destroys individual pride in work. It is true that he finds a goodly number of exceptions to this generalization. A worker who has a job in the soap house working with lye, a job that he has been doing for twenty-one years, gets a considerable measure of satisfaction from the job because "They say I'm one of the only ones who can do it." He even takes pride in the scars on his arms, but he does not hesitate to say that he thinks his job, which he finds important, should be more highly rated. He says he likes to work alone because he is not a good mixer, and he finds satisfaction in singing hymns while he works. Although the employees are generally favorable toward their jobs, the company, and the union, they wish something better for their children. Few of them wish their children to work in the Yards.

Managers will doubtless be impressed by the great importance which workers attach to plant-wide seniority, and the security which it gives the longer-service employees. The workers emphasize this advantage over the department seniority which is the rule in neighboring companies.

An important question is whether other persons reading the responses made to Father Purcell would come out with the same ratings on the scale of very favorable, favorable, neutral, unfavorable, or very unfavorable. Some readers of the responses might give more weight in general to the commendations and less weight in general to the criticisms. Other persons might do the opposite. It is not likely, however, that a difference of view toward the favorableness or unfavorableness of attitudes would change appreciably the *structure* of opinion — the linking of about the same degree of favorable (or unfavorable) attitude toward the company and the union, or the linking of a more favorable view of the workers toward their foremen than of the foremen toward their workers.

The kind of material which Father Purcell presents does not lend itself readily to brief summary. There is no substitute for carefully reading the book and especially for studying the interviews and the patterns of opinion. No manager, union leader, or student of labor problems can read these interviews without gaining new insights into American industry and the people who work in it. I repeat what I said at the beginning, that this is as rewarding a book on labor problems as I have had the opportunity to read in years.

Sumner H. Slichter

CONTENTS

TABLES

ILLUSTRATIONS

AUTHOR'S PREFACE

Five miles southwest of Chicago's Loop sprawls the meatpacking center of the world. In one square mile, now spilling deep into the surrounding neighborhoods, lies the heart and nerve center of one of America's basic food industries. It is a square mile of cattle, sheep, and hogs, the three great raw materials. It is a square mile of pens and buildings, smokestacks and railroad sidings, of windowless walls, overhead pipes, conveyor belts, loading docks and tramways. This is Packingtown. The northwestern half of Packingtown is the scene of this book — the mother plant of the leading meatpacker, Swift & Company, and the center of a key union of the CIO United Packinghouse Workers, Local 28.

"Hog butcher to the world" is the Chicago Swift-UPWA plant, producer of sides of beef for steaks and hamburgers, of bacon, lard, oil, margarine, wool, hides, glue, glands for insulin, soap, dog food, ham to be shipped to Boston or Toledo or London. This plant is a triumph of machines, for out of its pioneer disassembly lines, so legend has it, was born that second industrial revolution, the idea of mass production.

Yet more than machines, the Chicago Swift-UPWA plant is people. Negroes and whites, Poles, Bohemians, Greeks, Mexicans — people driving trucks, splitting breastbones, lugging beef, arguing a grievance, wiring motors, mopping the floor, washing aprons or tripe, stacking hides, pulling wool, directing a gang, running an elevator, or boning a ham. They come from the Back-of-the-Yards, or Bronzeville or almost anywhere on Chicago's Southside.

The story of these people is what this book is about — their thoughts concerning their work, their company and their union, their hopes and fears, their ambitions and satisfactions and needs. The top people of labor-management relations are described often enough in headline and in book. Here I am primarily telling the work story of the "little" people, the production workers. Theirs is a story less well known and just as important. Among other things, it is the unusual story of how these people lost control of their local union to the outside Communist party, and how in less than four years they won it back again for themselves.

After the rise of "vertical" unions in the 1930's, most American mass-production workers found themselves members of two partly overlapping, partly coöperating, often conflicting industrial organizations: their local union and their company plant. It becomes important to know how the dual and conflicting presence of company and union affects the attitudes and motivations of the worker who is between the two and a member of both; and how it affects his immediate superiors in each organization. Does the American worker offer a basis for converting the opposition of company and union into harmonious opposition? My main purpose in this book is to seek an answer to that question from the workers themselves.

In my search I went out and lived for a year and a half in Negro Bronzeville and in Back-of-the-Yards, getting to know the people there. But primarily I proposed to both the UPWA and Swift & Company a systematic plan for interviewing the workers and union members in the Chicago plant itself. Both Swift and the UPWA eventually agreed to coöperate fully. The UPWA was interested in how my findings might clarify its problems of organizing the unorganized, of race and ethnic-group relations, and of membership participation, while Swift was interested in the attitudes of its employees toward the company and in the functions and success of its foremen.

At the start I addressed the Swift supervisory force at the plant and the UPWA stewards at the Local 28 Hall, asking them to explain my plan to the 6000 men and women of the plant community. After that, the great majority of the Swift-UPWA people welcomed me into their midst. I went among them in a double capacity, as both psychologist and priest. If anything, this latter role apparently gave me a curious position of neutrality between company and union. At any rate, the people with whom I talked seemed to like their interviews and almost all of them relaxed and spoke freely once we were under way. Only four out of 303 production workers refused to come. For some of the workers it was perhaps the first time in their lives that they talked extensively to one who valued their opinions and simply listened.

Indeed, this is a book for those who enjoy listening because they see that it can lead to understanding. I would like to think that this is a workingman's book, with myself stepping in only to pull the interviews together into systematic conclusions. At the outset I wish to acknowledge my great debt to the men and women of the Chicago Swift-UPWA plant community whose coöperation and trust made this book possible.

I am obligated likewise to Mr. Harold North of Swift & Company and Mr. Ralph Helstein of the United Packinghouse Workers of America, for influencing their organizations to permit this research. Inviting an outsider into your family to inquire how its members get along with one another is a delicate matter, to say the least. Such courage and generosity of both company and union surely indicates their interest in advancing the cause of sound industrial relations. I must thank also the officers of Local 28 and of the Swift Chicago plant. Of course, neither Swift nor the UPWA is responsible for my findings.

Many other people have influenced the thinking that went into this book. I am deeply grateful to Gordon W. Allport, George C. Homans, Benjamin M. Selekman, Samuel A. Stouffer, and James J. Healy of Harvard University, to Peter F. Drucker of New York University, to Leo C. Brown, S.J., Director of the Jesuit Institute of Social Order in St. Louis, to Frederick H. Harbison, Joel Seidman, and W. Allen Wallis of the University of Chicago, to Vincent V. Herr, S.J., and Charles W. Anrod of Loyola University, most of whom have read the manuscript in whole or in part, and all of whom have given me many valuable suggestions. For her talented help in editing I thank Mrs. Ruth Whitman. And for its generous financial assistance I am very grateful to the Wertheim Foundation, its committee and its secretary, Mr. John T. Dunlop, who helped to steer this research from the beginning. Finally I want sincerely to thank Sumner H. Slichter of Harvard whose encouragement and inspiration led me to believe that there was a story here worth the telling.

Theodore V. Purcell, S.J.

Loyola University

Chicago, Illinois
June 6, 1953

PART

I

SETTING THE STAGE

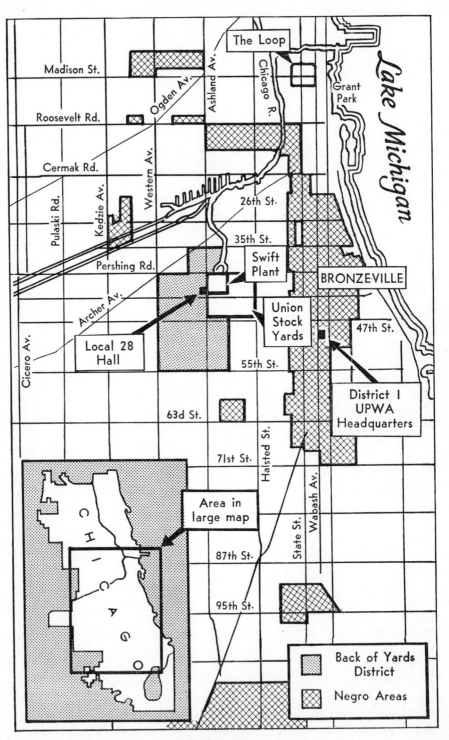

Madison St.

The Loop

Ogden Av.

Ashland Av.

Chicago R.

Grant Park

Lake Michigan

Roosevelt Rd.

Cermak Rd.

Western Av.

Pulaski Rd.

Kedzie Av.

26th St.

35th St.

Pershing Rd.

Swift Plant

BRONZE·VILLE

Archer Av.

Local 28 Hall

Cicero Av.

Union Stock Yards

47th St.

55th St.

District 1 UPWA Headquarters

63d St.

71st St.

Halsted St.

CHICAGO

Area in large map

87th St.

State St.

Wabash Av.

95th St.

Back of Yards District

Negro Areas

Packingtown

CHAPTER ONE

BACKDROP AND PROPS

THE PLANT COMMUNITY

The Chicago Swift-UPWA packinghouse workers form part of a true plant community. This fact is important. A community may be defined as a stable union of many people for a common end, using community means, with authority over its members.[1] The Swift workers, management and labor, foremen, stewards, and rank-and-file workers not only are in stable union — for the majority of them spend their lives in this plant — but they are working for a common end: namely the profitable production of meat and its by-products and the work satisfactions of wages, status, and so on. They are using common means, the buildings, equipment, machinery, raw materials; they give their labor, brains, and muscles, and receive a salary or wage under the authority of plant discipline.

For the vast majority of our industries, the plant community is the basic unit of industrial government and of social order. It is the smallest real governing unit in a large company[2] and is related to the rest of the chain as a municipality is related to the state. The larger units of both company and union build upon the plant communities below them. They both derive their leadership from these communities. They will have mutual harmony or lack of it in close proportion to the social relations existing in the various plant communities which make them up.

Perhaps the most important effect of the plant community is that it offsets to some degree the bigness of the new American big business and big unionism because it offers a comparatively small governing unit. While it is true that the River Rouge plant community of the Ford Motor Company with its 65,000 workers is large, this is the exception. In the packing industry, the Chicago plant of Swift & Company with its approximately 6000 people is exceeded only by the Armour Chicago plant with over 7000. The typical manufacturing plant in American industry, of the most productive establishments, employed 2500 or more production workers in 1947.[3]

Not all the people connected with the plant are strictly within the plant community — for instance, outside salesmen or truck drivers. UPWA Local Union 28 is part of the plant community, though there are functions of the local union which do not fall within the community, such as meetings at the local union hall, dances, picnics, and the various political and neighborhood projects of the union. Thus we do not say that the plant community is identical with either the company or the local union. But both of these, overlapping, fall into and make part of the plant community.

The plant community is not completely independent, of course. In a large company such as Swift it is dependent upon the other plants in the chain. Chicago, for instance, receives some of its meat already dressed from western plants; it does not sell all its production to the immediate area, but ships part of it to cities of the eastern seaboard and elsewhere. Also, Local 28 is dependent upon its own district and international UPWA organizations. Nevertheless, the local company plant and the local union may be said to have their own functions and specific unity within their own local plant community.

In plants which have a union, there is one important question to ask: can our definition of the plant community be verified in view of the traditionally opposed aims of management and labor? Is there one common end to be obtained? The purpose of the plant is indeed for one basic end, as stated above, gained only by the common effort of labor and management, using the equipment supplied from the capital of the stockholders. While it is true that any given worker may have various other motives for working in the plant community, yet he must also sufficiently accept and make his own the basic purpose of that community.

ONE COMMUNITY WITH TWO RULERS

The modern industrial plant community, viewed politically, is governed by two governments, the company and the local union. In the case of the Chicago plant of Swift & Company and Local 28, as in countless other plant communities throughout the country, there are, in fact, two organized governing bodies handling the affairs of plant discipline. Each has its own officials, union stewards, officers, bargaining and grievance committees on the one hand, and foremen, industrial and labor relations men and plant management on the other. Each has its own sanctions, with strike and lockout as the ultimate weapons.

The duality of government, of course, concerns only plant discipline, wages, hours, and working conditions — the matters explicitly or implicitly mentioned in the contract. Such matters are wage rates, holiday pay, hours of work, seniority administration, vacation administration, discipline, grievance procedure, and so on. As the Swift-UPWA contract itself states: "The management of the plants and direction of the working forces, including the right to hire, suspend, discharge . . . assign, transfer . . . increase and decrease the working force . . . determine products . . . schedules of production . . . processes . . . are vested exclusively in the Company; provided this will not be used . . . to avoid any of the provisions of this agreement." [4]

In case of unresolved conflict in the interpretation of the contract, the two parties agree to defer to an impartial arbitrator. In case of conflict about the very provisions of the contract, the parties may go to "war," by show of force in lockout or strike, to be resolved by capitulation of one or both of the parties or by government seizure.

It must not be thought that the local union governs in only a negative way. It is true that the day-by-day plant management is largely carried out by the foremen. Yet there are the annual changes in the contract at the international union level, and the daily interpretations of that contract by the local union. Thus, plant community government, in the form of decisions on wages, working conditions, and discipline, is constantly being administered as well by the local union as by local plant management.

We have arrived, therefore, at a unique political structure in the plant community. It is unique, at least, in modern times. Perhaps the only parallel, as Drucker[5] notes, is the medieval relationship between church and state. Instinctively we ask ourselves the question: Can a two-in-one government survive? Can it work for the common good of all people within it? In view of the opposition between its two parts, the union and the company, is it not basically a house divided against itself, which sooner or later must fall?

Clearly, the two governments are in some mutual opposition. First of all, their principles and objectives are different. The Swift "principles for enduring, successful business" are to:

(1) Deal honorably with all people.
(2) Operate efficiently.
(3) Research constantly to improve products and services.
(4) Pay equitable wages, provide opportunity for advancement, and maintain a sincere concern for the well-being of employees.
(5) Sell not only products but our good behavior as well.
(6) Earn a profit sufficient for the company to fulfill these responsibilities and to provide shareholders with a fair return on their invested savings.[6]

The "objectives" of Local 28, and, with slight changes, of the international UPWA, are as follows:

(1) To organize completely all workers in our jurisdiction eligible for membership in our Union.

(2) To establish for the workers of this industry and their families a higher standard of living by increasing wages, shortening hours, and improv-

ing conditions of work to the end that they will be assured a full and decent life.

(3) To secure legislation and support policies that will safeguard and improve our economic security and social welfare. To protect and extend our democratic institutions, civil rights and liberties and thus to perpetuate the cherished traditions of our democracy.

(4) To work with all like-minded groups to do all things necessary to accomplish these objectives and to advance the interests of the workers of the industry.[7]

We notice that four of the six principles of the company are concerned with the traditional problems of management: operations, research, sales, profits, dividends. The union mentions none of these as its objectives. The company is also interested in its employees, and effectually so, as will be shown later. The union, on the other hand, is aimed at building up its own organization (a sign of its own lesser security than that of the company), at improving working conditions and wages, and at securing social legislation, welfare, and reform. With the exception of wages, none of these are mentioned as objectives of the company.

The areas of interest of the two governments are also different. Management will tend to be most interested in production, efficiency, competition, and prices. The union tends to be most interested in wages, the wage-incentive system, hours, seniority, civil rights, politics. We do not mean to exclude the possibility of mutual sharing of interests. We simply mean that the emphasis which they put on their interests will tend to differ, as Bakke has brought out so well.[8]

Thirdly, both company and union have been and, to some extent, still are, in competition for the loyalties and allegiance of the worker. In the days before the CIO, Swift & Company had its own Employee Representation Plan and a very advanced personnel policy. At least one company spokesman admitted that some of the executives considered that this personnel policy was partly to make unions unnecessary and to keep them out, and since it had not done so, to that extent at least it was a failure. And a union representative admitted that especially in the early organizing days of the UPWA, the union would make extravagant charges against the company, charges which it knew were exaggerated, but which made it easier for the union to sell itself to the worker. This competition for allegiance has subsided, but it has not ceased completely.

While there is some difference and opposition between the company and union in their aims, interests, and efforts to gain supporters, this opposition must not be allowed to obscure the considerable area of coöperation. On the mutual solution of grievances, on safety programs, scrap drives, war production (first Swift plant to win Army-Navy "E"), and on some community projects there has been good coöperation. Moreover, in the day-by-day operation of the plant, a foreman will frequently enlist the aid of his department steward for passing along information or handling some human relations problem in his department.

Nevertheless, the presence of two governments in one plant community presents problems. There are three possible effects: First, a condition of "warlike opposition" between union and company, and therefore to some extent between workers and company, leading to an impasse resolvable only by government seizure and operation. This solution might ultimately involve state socialism.

Secondly, a condition of "antagonistic opposition" could result, involving a continual guerrilla sniping between company and union, or at least an aloof, noncoöperative relationship with ensuing loss of efficiency and peace, which in the long run would hardly help either farmer, management, worker, union, stockholder, or consumer.

Thirdly, a condition of "harmonious opposition" could result, with true coöperation between union and company, while each retained its own objectives. This relationship admits the differences, admits some opposition, but it also recognizes the great areas of common interest within the plant community, and it is willing harmoniously to settle differences in friendly give and take.

To achieve harmonious opposition it will be necessary to prevent the allegiance of the plant community from being split off from either organization and transform it into an allegiance simultaneously given to both organizations. As Drucker well says:

> Society cannot stand the "split allegiance," the enterprise cannot stand it, the union cannot stand it. Above all, the individual member cannot possibly stand it. . . .
> "Split allegiance" puts the worker into an unbearable conflict of loyalties. In the long run it can only undermine his allegiance to both enterprise and union. It demands of him continually that he takes sides, that he declare himself for one allegiance or the other. But he must give his allegiance to both. If he abandons allegiance to the enterprise, his job must become repugnant and meaningless and something done only because he has no other choice. His own self-respect demands pride in the job, pride in the work, pride in the company he works for — and that means allegiance to the enterprise. By giving up this allegiance he turns himself from a "self-respecting worker" into the "*Lumpenproletariat*" of Marxism. But if he gives up allegiance to the union he gives up the assertion of his own interests, needs, and purposes against the interests, needs, and purposes of the enterprise . . . and this too means abandoning his self respect. . . .
> What is necessary therefore is to convert the "split allegiance" of the members of the plant community into a bearable and functioning "twin allegiance." [9]

DUAL ALLEGIANCE AND THREE BASIC QUESTIONS

What do the workers, the stewards, union officials, and company foremen and managers so intimately involved in this new social structure have to say about it? Do we have any basis for twin allegiance in the Swift Chicago plant? With these problems in mind, we may formulate the three basic questions we are asking in this book:

1. Will the average worker actually have dual allegiance to, and find the satisfaction he requires from, both company and union?

2. Will the worker have allegiance which is necessarily dual, in that he says his wants can be satisfied only by both organizations?

3. Will the worker's allegiance to one of the two organizations in the plant community pull him away from the other organization, thus straining his dual allegiance? Or will the allegiance he gives to one organization not noticeably affect the allegiance he gives to the other?

These questions are interrelated and complementary. The most important are the first two, in which we are concerned with the basic fact of dual allegiance. We shall infer allegiance from the worker's various statements of satisfaction with the "company as an institution," all of which may be quite compatible with certain things he does not like, for instance, his foreman or his pay. By union we mean the "union as an institution" also, aside from its leadership, dues, and so on. In the second question, we ask whether the worker believes that the union is a necessary organization and fulfills a function which the company cannot fulfill. That the company is a necessary organization and fulfills a function which the union cannot fulfill is obvious to most workers. The third question inquires more deeply into the competition of the two organizations for the worker's loyalty, to see if the one tends not only to attract to itself, but also from the other. It asks whether or not the two allegiances of the workers are under stress.

These questions are fundamental and important. They are often asked but rather too easily answered without adequate consideration of the working people concerned. Consider, for instance, these remarks by a trade unionist, a business executive and two university professors. Solomon Barkin of the Textile Workers, in his recent challenge to the Harvard Business School personnel philosophy, states: "Some management spokesmen, perhaps with excellent intentions, have argued that loyalty to the company and to the union can be maintained concurrently, without contradiction. Unfortunately this well-meant concept does not stand up under even a cursory examination." [10] While Barkin's major objection is that the union should be treated as a "handmaiden of employer policy," to make his point he states that dual allegiance is impossible.

A Swift executive implies that allegiance given to the union is somehow taken away from the company: "I don't understand why the workers have gone back to the Union in such numbers after the [unsuccessful] strike of 1948! What is it about the Company that they don't like?" [11]

Finally, Carroll Daugherty and John Parrish solve the dilemma by asserting that the workers really give their whole allegiance to the union: "Each House [the House of Labor and the House of Management] . . . needs the loyalty of the workers if it is to prosper; hence there may be competition and conflict rather than coöperation and good will between the Houses. The workers conceivably could be torn apart mentally by the opposing pulls; *but most of them avoid this unhappy result by giving the union most of their affection.* This resolution of the dualism is not unnatural, for after all, the union is the workers' own organization." [12] For the Marxists, of course, the impossibility of dual allegiance is an essential part of their dogma, the principle of the inevitable class warfare.

At least one businessman, however, Robert Wood Johnson, believes that dual allegiance is quite possible and not abnormal: "There is no basic conflict between workers' loyalties to their company and their allegiance to their union. Life is full of multiple loyalties which can be adjusted by common sense. Only in abnormal cases do these situations involve conflicts . . ." [13]

If there is to be harmony in our industrial life, with unions and managements working together for the common good, it will be possible largely because there is dual allegiance among most constituents of the plant community. Furthermore, if our social science theory is to be meaningful, it must be based, at least in part, on the ordinary relationships of people in the most ordinary of their daily functions, their work in the plant community.

Other questions can be asked which will throw the three basic ones into sharper relief. Regarding attitudes toward the company, it will clarify the worker's views if we know also what he thinks about his chances for the advancement within the company, whether or not he wishes his children to come and work here, how he likes his job and foreman, what he thinks of his pay and the wage-incentive system, what he thinks of the *Swift News,* how he gets along in his "gang," his position on the questions of race relations and discrimination, what he thinks of working conditions and what improvements he might suggest. Regarding attitudes toward the union, it will help to know not only what the worker thinks of the union as an institution, but also what he thinks of his local leadership, why he joined in the first place, what he thought of the important 1948 strike, how much and in what way he participates in union activities by attending meetings, voting, accepting office, using intermediation of his steward, reading union literature, discussing union affairs, attending union social events, and so on.

Many horizontal studies have been made in which just one thing has been taken, e.g., the wage-incentive system, or the foreman's problems, or the grievance procedure, and investigated in many plants. Our view, however, is a vertical approach examining all these basic relations and problems in order to see their interrelation in one plant community. It is a "global" method of studying the plant community, as the neurologist Goldstein suggests for studying personality. While this approach is primarily social psychological, it also enters the fields of industrial sociology and labor economics, for many of the important facts and problems of the plant community do not follow along academic lines.

SELECTING THE SAMPLE

Since it was impossible to interview all the Swift-UPWA workers, the problem was to choose a representative sample of them, at random, with no systematic bias. Snedecor's Table of Random Numbers provided a list of selections. Each employee had a check number ranging from 1 to 20,000, from which it was simple to draw up a completely random sample of about 350 production workers.

After many preliminary conversations around the Yards, it became apparent that the workers agreed or differed among each other in their attitudes, depending especially upon whether they were men or women, colored or white, with short or long service. These key variables: sex, race, and length of service, emerged as the most important strata for analysis of variance among the production workers.[14] The design for the production-worker sample looked as follows:

Male-Negro Short-Service	Female-Negro Short-Service	Male-White Short-Service	Female-White Short-Service
Male-Negro Middle-Service	Female-Negro Middle-Service	Male-White Middle-Service	Female-White Middle-Service
Male-Negro Long-Service	Female-Negro Long-Service	Male-White Long-Service	Female-White Long-Service

Here the sex and race variables are evident. Length of service is as follows: Short-service: 2 through 7 years. (Plantwide seniority begins only after two years. It usually takes that long for attitudes to congeal and we therefore did not take employees under this time of service as we did not consider them to be representative of the regular Swift-UPWA workers.) Middle-service: 8 through 15 years. Long service: 16 years and over.

Of course there are many other variables that could affect attitudes: age, skill, status, education, nationality, religion, income, and so on. It would be unwieldy to handle all these variables mathematically though we shall point out their influence later. In the analysis of variance, we can hold two variables constant, for instance, sex and race, and see how the workers vary in their attitudes by their length of service alone. In this way we can control the influence of sex and race, and get a better understanding of why the production workers think what they do, and how they may differ among themselves according to what strata they occupy.

To obtain a complete picture, it was necessary also to hear the story of the stewards (also production workers, of course), the foremen, union and management leaders at all levels, and other plant workers not in the CIO. The distribution of the completed interviews is as follows:

Interviews

Random sample of all production workers (about 6% of population)		303
Stewards (about 20% of steward body)	34	
Interviews used in rank-and-file stratified sample and treated quantitatively in analysis of variance	192	
Extras, not in CIO bargaining unit, electricians, truck drivers, etc.	14	
Extras in the bargaining unit	63	
Random sample of foremen (about 20% of line foremen)		31
Union leaders at all levels (in addition to those in random samples)		26
Total union leaders (all key people interviewed)	32	
Management officers at all levels (all key people interviewed)		20
Neighborhood and community leaders		5
Total Interviews		385

HOW THE INTERVIEWING WAS DONE

The use of a questionnaire did not seem appropriate here, though that method is useful for detecting simple attitudes of people accustomed to questionnaires. But for the deeper understanding of what the workers felt, expressed in their own words, the interview method seemed most effective.

Nondirective interviewing seemed to be best suited to finding out what the workers really felt and believed about their company, their union, and the industrial relations of the plant community, for it encouraged them to express their feelings spontaneously, in their own words. On the other hand, there were a certain number of definite questions on which the interviewee's opinion was essential, such as his attitudes toward advancement, the incentive system, and so on. The interviewer therefore used the nondirective approach for the first fifteen or twenty minutes of the interview, and after that, if necessary, focused the interview on the specific questions.

Most important of all, however, the interviewer must have the confidence of the men and women he interviews. Intelligent interview techniques are important, but mutual respect and trust are an absolute *sine qua non*. A number of workers commented quite spontaneously on the whole idea of the interview program. For instance, elevator-operator, Sam Couch, 36, colored, Local 28 Union Steward, began the interview as follows:

> It's a good idea for you to be here. Get a load off your mind. You stand for the right thing. You not for the union, you not for the company, you for the right. Men are not always lazy. You might have sump'n botherin' you you want to get straightened out. Get a load off your shoulders to talk it out. You oughta be here.[15]

Most of the Swift-UPWA workers showed real acceptance of the interviewing work. There were, however, a few exceptions, and it might be well to take a glance at one of these.

Old-time butcher, Al Ewart, 47, up from a Kansas farm, a nonunion man very dissatisfied with the 1948 strike, but apparently satisfied with Swift, made this remark to a checker in his department about the interview:

> Why the hell did they ask me? I don't want to be a "case." I couldn't tell him nothin'!

This was a poor interview. Possibly Ewart was in a state of anxiety. He said that he was constantly borrowing money, was $1000 in debt and had seven children. There was trouble in his family; he had also been given several disciplinary layoffs by his foreman.

During some interviews, of course, the interviewer was tired or inadequate. Occasionally the workers were dull or suspicious personalities. On the whole, however, an atmosphere of trust and friendliness was usually established.

WHY BE QUANTITATIVE?

Some sort of numerical treatment of the interview was necessary if we wanted to summarize and compare them. Each interview of production workers and stewards was therefore evaluated on a basis of six categories, including five attitudes:

Company Allegiance
    attitude toward the job
    attitude toward the foremen
Union Allegiance
    attitude toward the local union leadership
    participation in the union

The foremen interviews were evaluated on the basis of:

Company Allegiance
    attitude toward the job
    attitude toward the employees
Union Allegiance
    attitude toward the union leadership

Other subjects which came up in the interviews, such as attitude toward the Standards System, toward having one's children work in the Yards, and so on, bear upon the main question, but for simplicity's sake we did not treat them quantitatively in the analysis of variance design.

1. The Chicago Swift-UPWA plant community looking west from the stockyards.

By permission of the Chicago Aerial Survey Company

2. The Chicago stockyards. In the upper left can be seen the Swift plant; in the lower left, part of Back-of-the-Yards is shown.   By permission of the Chicago Aerial Survey Company

3. A portion of the union stockyards looking west toward the Swift plant.

Each of the five attitudes was then graded on a scale of five possibilities:[16]

Very favorable	1
Favorable	2
Neutral or "I don't know"	3
Unfavorable	4
Very unfavorable	5

Attitude scaling is not perfect, but if we are aware of the pitfalls, it is thoroughly worth attempting. There was a slightly different system of grading and a new set of criteria for participation in union activities. Attitudes were determined from the worker's answers to such questions as: "What do you think of Swift & Company? Do you need a union here? What do you think of the UPWA? Also essential to the determination of general attitude was the total interview impression the interviewer gained of the worker's allegiance. As Allport well says:

> Much investigation in social psychology is conducted through interviewing. Now it goes without saying that replies to questions will be determined by the way the respondent perceives the questions asked.[17]

The danger of leading questions or misperceived questions can be greatly offset by considering also the total interview impression about the attitude in question.

Do the interviews validly measure "company allegiance" and "union allegiance"? To know whether or not we have validity we must know what we mean by allegiance. We shall defer discussion of this to Chapter Four. As for reliability, do our scales give the same results consistently and would another interviewer rate the worker at the same point of the scale as the present interviewer? While we do not have a precise test for such reliability, since the interview was private and only a sound film of it would enable the reader to judge the worker exactly as the author did, yet the interview data can be inspected by others. Actually, a fair sample of the interview records was submitted to the judgment of company, union, and university people to see if their grading agreed with that of the author. Judgments were very close in most cases.

HOW FAR CAN YOU GENERALIZE?

The over-all observations of this research cover a four-year period from 1949 to 1953, and packing plants and unions outside of Chicago. In addition, we explore the history of relations between company and union. Nevertheless our essential facts were sought at a limited time and place: in 1950 at Chicago. Therefore are these findings safely applicable to other times and places? Can these findings help us arrive at general principles and conclusions of social science and industrial relations?

First, let us see how time affects this research. Are the attitudes and feelings of the workers constantly changing? Would not the attitudes we found in 1950 be different in 1947 or 1954? However interesting the findings may prove to be, are they not of only momentary value? The answer is: No. The workers build up their basic work attitudes over years of experience. Their attitudes change, of course, but not greatly if we take the work force as a whole.

One fact is important. The year 1950 was the low point in the brief history of Local 28. In 1948 the UPWA lost a costly strike. After the strike, Local 28 led a rebellion against the International UPWA. In 1949 Local 28 leadership was captured by the Communist party. By 1950 the people of the plant community were confused and bitter and dissatisfied with their radical leaders. Yet these people had clear allegiance to their union as an institution, as we shall see. If the interviews for this book had been made in 1947 or in 1954, it is very probable that the workers would have had more union allegiance than we actually found.

As for company allegiance, the majority of the rank-and-file union members are not much affected in their attitudes toward the company by the fortunes of their local. The company allegiance of some older workers might have been adversely affected by the Chicago plant retrenchment program in 1951 and 1952. But they are a minority.

In a word, time will have some minor influence on our principal findings; namely, it may well bring a greater union allegiance and therefore a greater dual allegiance. Of course, attitudes toward local union leaders will change with time, since those leaders themselves are changing every few years.

Secondly, how does place affect the findings in this book? The Chicago Swift-UPWA community has certain leadership personalities, a large number of packinghouse operations, a larger number of Negroes on the work force than whites, a sizable part of its workers (the Negroes) living in a crowded, high-rent section of the city. None of these variables will be present in the Swift South St. Paul-UPWA community for example, in precisely the same way, where there are different personalities, almost no Negroes, a lesser number of operations, a newer plant, and so on. Many variables, however, will be common to South St. Paul, Chicago, and almost all packing plants. Finally, there are many variables more or less common to all large mass-production plants in America today: working on an hourly pay basis, foremen over workers who are a long way from top management, shop stewards, assembly lines, layoffs when work is insufficient, grievance committees, the ever-present task of getting people to come to union meetings, and so on. Many of the conclusions are valid chiefly in the Chicago Swift-UPWA plant community, yet these findings will doubtless be suggestive of conditions in other plant communities, especially where similar sets of variables are operating.

With proper caution and awareness of its limitations in time and place, we can still find a genuine transfer value in such a case study as this. As we gradually add independent case studies together and study their common conclusions, we build up a body of industrial relations theory which has genuine validity, since it is based on real familiarity with the plant communities and the thoughts and feelings of the people who work there.

CHAPTER TWO

PARENT PLANT AND WORKER POPULATION

THE PERSONALITY AND INFLUENCE OF SWIFT

From midwest abattoir to world empire of food and by-products in seventy-five years — this is Swift's dramatic history of growth and development, parallel to the growth of industrial America itself. This history is indelibly marked by the personality and energy of Gustavus Franklin Swift, who translated Horatio Alger from fiction to real life, and, along with Rockefeller, Carnegie, and Vanderbilt, became a leading example of that American contribution to the world, the business genius.

Starting with no money, no powerful friends, without even a high-school education, and ending with millions, great personal influence, important benefactions to the University of Chicago, Swift left behind him the foundations of the largest food corporation in the world. As a young man he progressed rapidly from butcher to cattle-buyer to meat-packer, and finally, in 1877, formed the Swift Brothers Company in Chicago.

Swift's only surviving son, the present chairman of the Board of the Company, gives this remarkably fair appraisal of his father:

> The most energetic man I ever knew was my own father. He was a prodigious worker. He died when I was eighteen so I was never in business under him. . . . Father talked and thought business most of his waking hours. He had three great interests: his family, his business, and his church. He was affectionate and fond of us; he left the children's care pretty much to mother. His business took most of his time. We would have breakfast together. Father came home to lunch. We would have supper together. Evenings, he looked over the office mail and prepared for the next morning's dictation at home. As for church, both my parents were Methodists and ardent church people. Father was reputed to have been responsible for the building of our church in the stockyard neighborhood.
>
> Father was nervous, high-strung, quick-tempered. We kids were afraid of him more or less. We knew he loved us, but we kept out of his way when he came home tired at night. . . .
>
> I have heard reports that while he could be unkind at times, he was

always just; he might be harsh and critical, but he was fair. I think father was a genius. He had great vision. He knew what he wanted to do. He tried awfully hard to do it. Our country was not served properly in its meat supply. Two-thirds of the cattle were raised west of the Mississippi; two-thirds of our meat consumption was east of the Mississippi. My father tried to bring them together. . . . He was very conscious of wastage in freight. 1000 pounds of steer was only 60% meat, so to save freight charges the refrigerator car was originated.[1] Father went west from New England, to Albany, Chicago, Kansas City, Omaha, St. Paul, thus always going to the source of supply and saving freight. He was "hellbent" on the economics of operation. . . .

There is a parallel between my father and Mr. Rockefeller. They were born in the same year, one in Massachusetts, the other in Ohio. Both were pioneers. The evolution of each business was very similar. Only Mr. Rockefeller made more money. They were pretty much the same kind of men. John D., Sr., had the same three interests my father had. Both saw the economies of big business and therefore both tried to increase their business so far as they were able to do so. Were both callous and constantly trying to ruin their competitors? This was not true of my father, nor do I believe it was true of Mr. Rockefeller. Father did buy some unsuccessful companies because he thought he could manage them properly, but I don't think father wanted to ruin a competitor. . . . Both were industrial geniuses. Both used trial and error methods.

Some of my father's efforts were socially unsound and had to be abandoned. Father had no social philosophy. He worked sixteen hours a day. He was not sorry for those who worked ten hours. It was unfortunate that in those days people didn't have the same social vision as they had industrial vision. But they didn't. There was a lag. . . . It amazes me, however, to count their successes against their failures.[2]

During the panic of 1893, Swift was perilously close to bankruptcy, for he had always needed money and had borrowed heavily. One day at the Chicago Board of Trade, the ticker tape carried the message that Swift & Company had failed. Within half an hour, Swift strode in angrily, banged his fist for silence and said: "Swift & Company cannot fail!" Then he went across the Loop to a meeting of his bankers who were planning to call his loans, and said: "I'm sorry, gentlemen, but we have to have more money, not less!" He left the meeting not only with deferments but with additional loans as well.[3] The company has been far from financial danger ever since.

At the turn of the century consolidations were in the air. The United States Steel Corporation had been formed. Swift, seeing the possible savings, formed the National Packing Company with Armour and Morris in 1902. Later, because of public opinion, the combination was dissolved, but Swift never lived to see it. He died in 1903 at the age of sixty-three.

After his death Swift's influence was carried on through his sons and traditions. That influence is present today especially in higher Swift management circles and is one cause of the "morale" or "family-mindedness" of Swift executives.

THE COMPANY TODAY

Swift's sons, under the leadership of Louis, the eldest, ran the firm for over thirty years. The first ten years of this century and of their leadership was notable for the "trust busters" with spirited "Teddy" Roosevelt as president. Ida Tarbell painted a sensational picture of Rockefeller's Standard Oil. Upton Sinclair's *The Jungle* in 1906 made the Chicago stockyards famous all over the world. Sinclair, the socialist, was aiming at people's heads with his ideologies, but he hit their stomachs instead. The net result of his novel was pure food laws and sanitation reform with not much advance for socialism. But a period of poor public relations for the packers had gotten well under way. One of the charges was monopoly.

Since 1902, the Federal Government has brought twelve different antitrust suits against Swift & Company (including the current pending one), and two against the National Packing Company in which Swift had an interest. All the past cases have been dropped by the government. The company has not been legally proved to have violated any antitrust laws. The National Packing Company was unquestionably a combine. But the jury did not find it guilty of monopoly. It was voluntarily dissolved.

In 1917–1919, the Federal Trade Commission made an elaborate study of the packing industry and came out with an unfavorable report. The packers replied that the investigators had misunderstood the business, had not substantiated their charges, and that the federal grand jury had brought no indictment. In 1920, the important "Consent Decree" was handed down by the Supreme Court of the District of Columbia, which was an agreement between the packers and the Attorney General under which the packers agreed to give up their holdings in stockyard companies, food canning (except for meat foods), retailing and cold storage activities (except storage in their own plants).

In 1919, the American Meat Institute was founded (then known as the Institute of American Meat Packers) to "bring about a clearer understanding of the economic place that the packing and allied industries hold in the life of the nation and how they may function to the mutual good of the industry of agriculture and the country at large." [4] Since the 1920's, the industry has enjoyed better public relations, but doubtless there will always be someone to complain about the price of meat. This modern period is also marked by the rapid growth of the so-called "independents," Rath, Morrell, Kingan, Oscar Mayer, Hormel, and so on, smaller companies but doing a brisk business, usually in a few specialized products. Their presence is a warrant that competition does exist in the meatpacking industry today.

When John Holmes became president of Swift & Company in 1937, the operating management of the company passed out of the hands of the Swift family for the first time. Today the family does not control the corporation. In 1951, the Swift family held 227,982 shares, or less than 4 per cent of the total outstanding common stock — six million shares.[5] Yet the Swift family spirit remains, in the presence of Swift's youngest son, Harold, chairman of the board of directors, and in the attitudes of most of the present officers, who under the Swift policy of promotion from within, were trained by the family. One of Swift's grandsons and one great grandson are now with the corporation in executive positions. Another grandson is a director.

With the demands of the second World War, Swift continued to grow, doing over two billion, three hundred and sixty million dollars of business in 1948, its biggest year, and constantly experimenting with new production and marketing methods, new products, new research, following old G. F. Swift's motto: "Still I am learning." Today, Swift & Company is the largest of the "Big Four" meatpackers and the pattern setter in many ways, especially in the terms of union contracts. By dollar value of annual sales, it is one of the ten largest corporations in the world. It is in a very secure financial position with a ratio of current assets to current liabilities of 3.45 to 1, in 1950, and a net worth of over three hundred and thirty-eight millions. It is almost independent of the banks in its financing.

Swift's strong financial position enables it to do things such as handling a liberal pension program, which many other packers cannot afford to do. While Swift's profit margain on the sales dollar is low, around 1 per cent, this is fairly typical for the food industry, though lower than the heavy-goods industries. Swift's profit, as figured on its net worth, however, compares favorably with other industries, ranging in recent years from 5 to 10 per cent. This is not spectacular, but such profits are steady. Even during the Great Depression, for instance, Swift operated successfully, foregoing dividends only in 1933.

Swift operates fifty-seven meatpacking plants, two hundred and ninety-four branch houses, one hundred and forty dairy and poultry and ice cream plants, thirty-one cottonseed and soybean mills, seven vegetable oil refineries, twenty-three plant food (fertilizer) factories, a total of over five hundred establishments in every state of the union except Wyoming and in most sizable cities, as well as in Canada.

The Chicago plant had reached its peak during the first World War in both pounds of output and size of labor force (see Tables 1 and 2). While the decline of pound output does not appear to be marked, these are shipping figures and do not indicate that a good part of the meat output of the plant is slaughtered elsewhere and only partly processed here. The actual productive operations of the plant are gradually being retracted. For instance, one of the two beef-killing floors was recently

TABLE 1

Total number of people in Chicago plant
(*Supervisors and employees*)

1877–1885	A score to several hundred *
1885–1910	Several thousand *
1910–1917	6000–7000 *
1917 (May 19)	7,775
1917 (Sept. 22)	8,440
1918 (May 18)	9,973
1918 (Sept. 31)	11,072
1918 (Dec. 14)	(maximum) 12,938
1919 (May 17)	9,998
1919 (Sept. 21)	11,357
1920 (May 15)	7,771
1920 (Sept. 18)	8,734
1930	4,907
1940	5,100
1945	6,300
1950	5,734
1951	5,777
1952	5,336

* Indicates estimates.

TABLE 2

Pound output of Chicago plant

1877–1915	No figures
1915	871,000,000
1918	(maximum) 1,275,000,000
1920	1,048,000,000
1925	902,831,000
1930	871,470,000
1935	958,364,000
1940	972,746,000
1942	(war) 1,098,171,000
1945	783,932,000
1950	832,698,000

abandoned, as well as one of the two sheep kills. Likewise, the cheese, glue, fertilizer factories, and wool house have been moved elsewhere. In 1952, the famous hog-killing department was deactivated. Some departments are expanding, of course, such as the Table Ready Meats Kitchen, but the over-all trend is toward gradual retrenchment. Likewise, the number of workers has dropped remarkably — half in the second World War of what it was in the first, though, due to improved machinery and work simplification, the workers' productivity has increased. However it declines, the Chicago plant will probably always be a major Swift plant because of its proximity to raw materials, markets, and transportation.

The plant has many modern departments. Yet the age of some of its buildings affects not only the efficiency of its employees but also employee relations. A building like the sixty-year-old wool house (deactivated in 1952) can hardly compete with a bright new plant in plumbing, lighting, cleanliness, comfort and cheerfulness. Working conditions have indeed changed greatly since Upton Sinclair's descriptions in *The Jungle,* written in 1906, and they compare favorably with other manufacturing industries. Better lighting, ventilation, and sanitation have been installed, along with shower baths, locker rooms, and cafeterias. Safety equipment has made the safety record of the plant remarkably good.

On the other hand, there are certain inescapable drawbacks to working in a packing plant. The dressing floors of necessity involve blood and animal heat. Meat must be kept under refrigeration and coolers are cold. Tank rooms smell bad. Soap is dusty. There is also a general prejudice among many against working in the Yards. Working in the Yards is associated at once with "sticking pigs," although only one department out of 173 had the function of killing and dressing hogs. Swift has both a public relations problem here and the problem of competing with the new mechanical industry plants on the south and west sides, such as the new Ford aircraft plant. Perhaps competition for labor will bring Swift and the other packers to spend larger amounts toward the improvement of working conditions.

HOGS AND SEASONS

There is another factor affecting the employees' working conditions besides the age and physical characteristics of the plant, however, and that is the seasonal nature of the packing industry. This seasonality is due to both the supply of cattle and hogs and the habits of consumers. Most marked is the seasonal production of hogs. The majority of hogs come to the Yards during the "hog run" from November to February. As a result, the Pork Cutting Department, for instance, may cut 700 hogs per hour with a gang of 175 men in November and be down to only 300 hogs per hour with a gang of 80 in June. Thanks to the current practice of "plant-wide seniority," the men displaced are transferred to other departments as far as possible. From about two-thirds to three-fourths of the hourly-paid workers get (or could get) fifty-two weeks of work a year.[6] Most of the people who are laid off are those who have not yet obtained this plant-wide seniority, people usually under two years' service. Roughly 80 per cent of the work force have plant-wide seniority. The other 20 per cent are a cushion of workers coming and going with the seasons. Inevitably these are the most recently employed workers. Because they have such instability in the beginning of their career with the company, they tend to go elsewhere and so it is difficult for the company to hold new workers, even though they might be good workers. Of the recent influx of "DP's" to the Yards (1949–1950), for example, not many stayed.

Swift & Company has taken a lead in trying to persuade farmers and cattle-growers to market their crops evenly throughout the year. Yet a perfectly even supply of the three basic packing raw materials — cattle, sheep, and hogs — will doubtless never arrive. Those materials are too closely connected to the agricultural industry which will ever be tied to seasons and to uncertain weather.

Also there is seasonality in consumer demand. People want turkeys at Thanksgiving and Christmas, hams at Easter, pork in the winter, lighter meats in the summer, more meat in the cold weather, less meat when it is hot. The large packer, like Swift, thanks to the variety of his products, can turn from one product to another and thus steady his operations. For instance, Swift has built up a large "table ready meats" trade in the summer of frankfurts, pork sausage, and so on. Yet a rush order from the A & P for 100,000 pounds of freshly dated bacon may force a foreman suddenly to double his gang, only to lay off the next week.

The fact that meat is perishable greatly affects this seasonality and, indeed, modifies the entire industry. Delivered cattle, even though alive, cannot be stockpiled like coal or iron ore because of the feeding expense and lack of space. But especially once the animal is killed, speed is imperative. In spite of all our modern refrigeration, meat deteriorates in quality if it is held too long, or at least loses its "bloom" and thus depreciates in value. Only an infinitesimal amount of the total meat product can be economically deep frozen. Thus the workers cannot produce in the summer much of what will be held for the winter or the time when the market is suitable.

HOW THEY OPERATE

Most of the Chicago plant departments are small, with fifty to one hundred men, working in moderate-sized rooms, often without windows because of the refrigeration, and artificially lighted, connected by heavy, heat-proof doors. In the beef, pork, and lamb divisions, the killing and dressing rooms are at the top of the building, so that the different parts of the animals can be conveniently dropped down through chutes to be further processed on the floors below.

Although the Chicago plant is not large compared with the iron and steel industries (20,000 men at the Indiana Harbor works of Inland Steel, for instance), yet it is more divided, and probably has more work and storage rooms. As a result, the department, as the basic unit of work organization, takes on a considerable importance. Here the worker makes his acquaintances and has his contacts with the management. The department is sometimes "the company" to him. There are many workers in the "East End" of the plant who have never been in the "West End" and indeed would get lost if sent there, and vice versa. But plant-wide seniority tends to offset this departmental isolation, for many workers do get transferred to neighboring departments and even to a completely distant part of the plant. Plant-wide seniority may make for inefficiencies, since under it a foreman may have to lose some of his best-trained people and take on a new set of untrained workers because the next department is laying men off and those men, having a higher plant-wide seniority than his own men, come in to displace them. Many foremen complain of it. On the other hand, it helps the foreman to know that his men are still in the plant and that he can easily call them back when he must build up his department again.

Plant-wide seniority means a good deal to the workers, as will be seen later when we report the interviews, for it gives security against being repeatedly, though temporarily, out of a job. Not the least of its advantages is that it does get the worker out of his own department, acquaints him better with the total meatpacking process, gives him one more skill, and paves the way, at least, for his greater identification with and participation in the total work of the plant community. There may be disadvantages, if his transfer involves a cut in pay, unfamiliar work, change of shift, going from a "clean" department to a "dirty" one, or from light work to heavy work. For these reasons, sometimes a man will rather take a layoff than a transfer, but on the whole, for most workers, the advantages outweigh the disadvantages.

The following is a list of the major operating divisions among which the worker may be moved during the course of his career:

Major Operating Divisions in Chicago Plant

(1) Beef, Lamb and Veal Dressing and Cutting Division. Contains fourteen departments for yarding the cattle, killing, dressing, cutting, boning, cooling, inspecting, packing, shipping, etc.

(2) Fresh, Cured, and Smoked Pork Division. Contains twenty-two departments for driving, killing, dressing hogs, for warm "fancy meats" (up to 1952), coolers, cutting, trimming, packing, shipping, box factory, grading, pickling, boning ham, dry cure, smoke house, vein curing, salting and exporting, sliced bacon, sliced beef, ham washing and smoking, wrapping and tying, packing and shipping, "sealtite," etc.

(3) Table Ready Meats Division. Contains nineteen departments for the chopping, stuffing, smoking, curing, spicing, packing, shipping of cured sausage, bologna, cooked hams, frankfurts, canned meats, dog food, etc.

(4) Mechanical Division. Contains fifteen departments including masons, scale shop, paint shop, oilers and elevator operators, millwrights, carpenters, planning department, wood mill, etc.

(5) Steam and Power Division. Contains six departments: power plants, refrigeration plants, pipe shop, electrical shop, boiler shop, etc.

(6) Machine Shop, Division. Contains four departments: machine shop, blacksmith and welding shop, tin shop.

(7) Protection and Laundry Division. Contains three departments: laundry, fire department, police department and watchmen.

(8) Truck Garage Division. Contains eleven departments: truck garage, auto and tractor repair shops, employees' garage, intraplant truck drivers, yard cleaning, paper baling, Michigan City Terminal, cafeterias, restaurants and employees' market.

(9) Oil House, Tallow and Grease, Tank House, Animal Feed and Bone House Division. Contains six departments.

(10) Lard Refinery, Industrial Oils, Hydrogenation, Margarine, "Swiftee" Cooper Shop Division. Contains twelve departments.

(11) Soap, Glycerine, Adhesive Products and Gas Plant Division. Contains 11 departments: soap boiling, framing, toilet soap making, cleanser making, canning, shipping, glycerine, adhesives, soap fat hydrogenation, etc.

(12) Car Switching, Freezer Storage, Car Icing, Casings Division. Contains around 12 departments for switching and icing refrigerator cars, a complete cold storage plant including frozen meatpacking departments, hog, sheep and beef casings cleaning, grading, testing, inspecting, packing, shipping.

(13) Car Loading, Tramway, Beef, Fancy Meat Sheep Cooler Division. Contains seven departments.

(14) Wool House Division (abandoned in 1952). Contains five departments for wool pulling, grading, drying, baling, sheep skin house, shipping, etc.

(15) Hide Curing Division. Contains two departments.

(16) Standards Division. Contains one department with time study men and checkers covering all departments that use the Standards System.

(17) Time Office Division, Safety Division, Camera Analysis Division, Work Simplification Division, Stores Division, etc.

In addition to these operating divisions there are also the usual staff departments, industrial relations, auditing, bookkeeping, livestock buyers, purchasing agent, credit, sales, and so on. In studying the operating divisions, one is struck by the fact that so many divisions do no meat butchering or packing at all, but service the meat divisions, for example the Mechanical Division, or handle their by-products, as does the Lard Refinery.

1. *The Status System.* There are seven levels of authority, or status, in the Chicago plant:

Superintendent
Two assistant superintendents
Division superintendents

General foremen
Foremen
Assistant foremen
Work force

Actually there is one more top level, the plant manager, who normally does not interfere in plant operations except when a major decision must be made. He reports directly to the president, while the superintendent reports both to him and to the general superintendent under the vice-president in charge of operations for the entire Swift chain. (This double routing to the president was established to facilitate communications, especially in sales.) The seven levels may be augmented by an assistant division superintendent. However, seven levels are usually the maximum, and in several divisions it is less.

It may seem that a status system of seven levels is highly complex. The Ellwood Works of the United States Steel Company, for instance, had only four.[7] However, it is probable that the unusually complex nature of a packing plant, as we have seen, requires such a system. It is difficult for a plant superintendent or even a division superintendent to master all the operations under him without assistance.

2. *Communications.* The system of communications is closely related to the status system and, in fact, helps to define what the actual status system is, as opposed to the formal organization chart. Here we note that in communications down, there may sometimes be four levels, the three "assistants" being temporarily by-passed. Indeed, the plant superintendent and assistants have face-to-face contact with all levels for they normally spend many hours a day on the plant itself going from department to department. But most formal orders are passed down the regular status channels. There are weekly division meetings in some divisions. And there is a monthly meeting which all supervisory levels attend. In general, communication down seems to be ready enough.

Communication up is quite a different thing — and not as good. As we shall see, a foreman would rarely by-pass his division superintendent to the plant superintendent in spite of the open-door policy. To some extent, the industrial relations department is a "listening post" passing complaints, information, and so on, upward. Since we are principally interested in the relationships between the hourly paid workers and the management, we note that the foreman plays a role of key importance in the status and communications systems. Likewise, the stewards and the grievance procedure are of great importance in facilitating communications upward. Both of these will be treated in later chapters where status and communication will be linked to attitudes.

3. *Job Requirements.* Just as we have seen that the Chicago plant produces an encyclopedic list of products, so we may imagine that the number of separate operations necessary to produce them must be vast.

The division of labor is complete so that the "operation" becomes the "job" and the number of jobs runs well into the thousands. These jobs can be fairly well classified either as craftsmen, butchers, or unskilled. All the crafts are represented. In such a large plant, with constant repairs and new building, these craftsmen are busy most of the year and not dependent upon the weather, as in the building trades, for instance. Then there are the butchers, pork, beef, lamb. Incidentally, as one company representative stated: "The mechanical gangs tend to look down their noses at the butchers." Finally there are the many unskilled and semiskilled conveyor belt operators, elevator operators, janitors, and so on.

While it is not easy to draw lines between unskilled, semiskilled, and skilled jobs, roughly one-third of the work force falls into each of these categories. In 1951 Swift developed a new system of classification defining "unskilled" as common labor plus one wage bracket, "semiskilled" as the second through the eighth wage bracket, and "skilled" as the ninth wage bracket and over. By this system the work force of the Chicago plant in 1951 was 23 per cent unskilled, 47 per cent semiskilled and 30 per cent skilled.

In the modern packing plant only a minority of the workers are skilled. Among the unskilled are janitors, truckers, clean-up men, and so on. Among the skilled are most of the crafts, electricians, engineers, mechanics, and so on. Top butchering skill is of a different nature. For instance, the "floorsman" on the cattle killing floor is one of the aristocrats of butchering skill. His job is to loosen the hide of a beef carcass preparatory to separating it completely from the body. He is a skinner and he must be very careful not to score the hide, thus lowering its value, nor cut too deeply into the "fell" (flesh below the skin) thus lowering the value of the carcass. A first-class floorsman is a marvel to watch in speed and dexterity. As one said: "My knife knows where to go even when my eye can't see it." Yet a floorsman could not do a complete butchering job on a steer. He might know the other jobs in his own Beef Dressing Department, but chances are he would not know how to butcher the entrails on the floor below. In a word, he is highly skilled, but his skill is confined to a few operations. The butchering craft, unlike the mechanical crafts, has been so subdivided that there are probably few butchers left who could handle an animal from slaughter to cooler to cook. Evidently the modern packinghouse meat-cutter is a far cry from the village butcher of one hundred years ago.

It is an important question as to whether or not the extreme operation-specialization of the conveyor lines in the Chicago plant has destroyed craft skill, pride of workmanship, and thus a sense of status coming from one's job. We shall treat this question in a later chapter. See the almost microscopic job specialization in the Pork Dressing Department which until recently received live hogs, dressed them, and sent them to the Cooler Department:

Pork Dressing Department Jobs

Live hogs receiver and counter
Live hogs driver and penner
Assistant to Bureau of Animal Industry Inspector to detect cripples and suspects
Hog-driver into shackle pens
Shackler
Sticker (precise knife thrust into throat of hog)
Tubman — dropping hogs into tub of warm water (scalding)
Hog-locater in tub, and passer to tub chain feeder
Tub-conveyor chain-feeder
Tongue protector inserter
Hog-feeder into U-bar scraper (automatic dehairing machine)
Hand-puller of hog bristles
Hog-straightener on roller table
Tongue protector remover
Gam cord exposer
Gambrel stick putter-in (a stick is placed beneath "tendons" of both hind legs and is then hung on trolley from which hog is suspended for the rest of operation)
Hang off man — from roller table to rail
Toes-puller
Carcass-shaver and eyelids-cutter
Head-dropper
Brisket-opener (breast splitter)
Belly-opener
Bladder-pizzle or pig bag cutter
Aitch-bone-cutter
Bung-dropper
Eviscerator
Retaining Room Man (carcasses with condemned parts)
Feeder of trolleys and sticker into magazine
Dressed hogs grader
Head-cutter and tongue-remover
Splitter (precise cleaver cut down the middle of the spinal column)
Bruises-trimmer
Sterilized neck-trimmer
Kidneys-exposer
Leaf lard-puller
Leaf lard-scraper
Trimmer and carcass finisher
Neck-washer
Hams-facer
B.A.I. stamper (on carcass)
Wiltshire selector (a special English cut)
Wiltshire singer man
Wiltshire scraper
Back-marker (continental style)
Back-beater (continental style)

Pick-up man for fallen hogs from floor
Trolley-cleaner
Janitor
Hand trucks puller or pusher
Kidneys cutter
Spermatic cord cutter and remover
Suprarenal glands remover
Splitting-chain feeder and belly-spreaders inserter
Hog singe man (with hand operated torch)
Pork tongues washer and scraper
Sterilized heads worker
Front feet and shoulders cutter (from heavy hogs)
Hoister of shoulders to rail
(After this, trolley takes carcasses to coolers, entrails to fancy meats department on floor below, lard to refinery, ears to rendering tank room, and so on)

Of these fifty-eight different jobs, three are very skilled, such as the sticker, splitter, retaining room man (who is a general butcher). Some jobs are semiskilled, such as the head-dropper, breast-splitter, belly-opener, bung-dropper, eviscerator, and ham-facer. Twenty-four jobs are unskilled. The skilled men are generally able to do any job on the conveyor line. These fifty-eight jobs give us a closer look at the anatomy of the mass-production revolution: keen efficiency and minute worker specialization.

PEOPLE OF THE PLANT COMMUNITY

A revealing fact about the people of the Swift-UPWA plant community is the constant historical ebb and flow, the persistent departure of the old, established employee groups to other jobs elsewhere, and the arrival of new groups, especially new nationalities, to take their place.

The first ethnic group to work in the Chicago stockyards was the Irish in the 1870's. From 1880 to 1886 [8] there followed American-born workers, and Germans, famous for their sausage-making and butchering and thus outnumbering the Irish,[9] and a few Scotch. The strike of 1886 brought a decrease in Americans and Irish, and the first of the Poles, who monopolized the unskilled and common labor jobs, only to be superseded by the Bohemians, Lithuanians, and Slovaks. There were virtually no Negroes except for the brief period during the 1894 strike, when Negro strikebreakers were brought up from the south.[10] It was not until the 1904 strike, however, that the Negro strikebreakers continued to work in the Yards.[11]

Many national groups were suspicious of their traditional European rival, who might be entrenched in the very next block. Little Italy, Norde Seite, Kilgubbin, Canaryville, Swedentown, the Ghetto, Pilsen, Little Poland sprang up. It was a union organizer's nightmare, as we shall see. By 1911 the Immigration Commissioner's report put the percentage of foreign-born employees in the meat industry at 60 per cent. Then the first World War began the great Negro migration from Mississippi, Louisiana, Tennessee, Alabama, and Georgia.

> Within a period of eighteen months, in 1917–1918, more than 50,000 Negroes came to Chicago. . . .[12]

> Prior to 1915, there had been little to encourage plantation laborers to risk life in the city streets, now there were jobs to attract them. Recruiting agents traveled south, begging Negroes to come north. They sometimes carried free tickets in their pockets, and always glowing promises on their tongues. For the first time, southern Negroes were actually being invited, even urged, to come to Chicago. . . . As each wave arrived, the migrants wrote the folks back home about the wonderful North. A flood of relatives and friends followed in their wake. A bewildered South had visions of a land left desolate for lack of labor.[13]

Some of these Negro migrants found jobs in the steel mills and other munitions plants. Great numbers came to the Yards, took the common labor jobs in place of the Poles, Lithuanians, and Bohemians who were moving up or out, and the old round of the substitution of nationalities began again in the Swift Chicago work force.

The great and sudden Negro migration to Chicago not only supplied a source of additional labor, but also created racial tensions and desperate housing problems. Did the packers encourage this wave of migration? The Chicago Commission on Race Relations, established to investigate the great Race Riots of 1919, gives conflicting reports. One testimony before the Commission concerns a Bronzeville leader, Richard E. Parker:

> Parker stated that Swift and Co. and Armour and Co. were expecting a strike at any moment and are prepared to fill the strikers' places with Negroes sent from the South. . . .
> He [Parker] said that he went South last winter for Swift's, Armour and Co. and the Steel Trust and imported more Negroes than any man in Chicago . . . and now any time a Negro wanted work, he can give him or her a note, and they will be given work in the stockyards, but if they join a union, they can't.[14]

But the final report of the commission states that:

> during the course of its inquiry, statement was frequently made to members of the Commission or to its investigators that large employers of labor in Chicago, and particularly the packers, had imported many Negroes from the South. Although the Commission made a thorough investigation of such statements, no evidence of any value was discovered to support them. The general superintendents of the Armour, Morris, Swift and Wilson plants who attended conferences, declared emphatically that their companies had not engaged in any encouragement of migration. . . . The fact remains that labor leaders insist that employers, in the Chicago district, imported Negroes from the South notwithstanding their inability to cite facts in support of this belief.[15]

In the early 1920's the Mexicans came to join the stockyards melting pot. They may have displaced a few Negroes, but they were never very numerous. Although like the Negroes before them, they started at the bottom of the ladder of skill, yet since there was little prejudice against them, they began to advance more rapidly.

Meanwhile, many Polish, Bohemian, and Lithuanian workers had advanced into supervisory positions. The Irish and Germans had almost entirely vanished from the nonsupervisory work force, a small minority remaining in the mechanical crafts. The Negroes had become nearly a third of the work force in Swift Chicago. The Great Depression of the thirties reversed the trend, slightly, but only temporarily. The second World War, with its tight labor market, brought a strong increase in the Negro participation in the Chicago stockyards. In 1942 Swift Chicago, along with the other Chicago packers, was probably the first basic, mass-production plant in the north to employ over 50 per cent of Negroes on its work force. At that time, the supply of able-bodied men was limited and the defense industries attracted the more skilled so that only Negroes could be persuaded to work in the Yards.

The last nationality influx occurred in 1949 when Polish, Lithuanian, and other displaced persons came to the Yards. But these immigrants, unlike their predecessors, were well educated and trained, and thus were not satisfied with unskilled packinghouse work. Also, because the system of plant-wide seniority at Swift meant that DP's would be subject to seasonal layoffs in the first two years of their employment, most of them went elsewhere.

If immigration laws are liberalized, it is possible that other Europeans will come to the Yards. Possibly Puerto Ricans will come. But it is most likely that the Negroes, victims of limited educational opportunities and persisting discrimination in craft work and office work, will bear the brunt of the labor for many years to come. This result will not be a benefit either to white or Negroes. The continued high employment of Negroes and the refusal of whites to work in the plant may make the plant community virtually a segregated Negro community, a situation which neither group desires.

Few sons of white workers come to join their fathers at the plant. As will be seen from the interviews, especially those of the short-service whites, the young Poles, Lithuanians, and Bohemians avoid the Yards, at least for nonsupervisory work. The Irish and Germans never give it a second thought. If Swift Chicago wishes to retain a sizable proportion of white workers, it will have to improve working conditions, raise wages, and above all improve its community relations in conjunction with the other packers of the Chicago yards with whom (perhaps unfairly) it is joined in the popular mind.

THE PEOPLE AND STATISTICS

The total number of people operating the Chicago plant in 1950 was around 6000, including office workers and supervision. During the winter peak of 1950–1951, 5455 employees were in the CIO bargaining unit. Of these, 3789 were actual union members, about 69 per cent. In studying the Service Profile of Table 3, note that the number of white men has decreased over the years, while of the colored men the reverse is true.[16] A fairly similar situation will be seen to exist with the women workers.

TABLE 3

Service profile of Chicago plant workers

(Random, unstratified sample of 202 workers by service, race, and sex: 1950)

Service	Men		Women	
	Colored	White	Colored	White
Short (2–7 yrs.)	26%	2%	7%	2%
Middle (8–15 yrs.)	13%	11%	1%	3%
Long (16 yrs. and over)	11%	20%	under 1%	2%

The bargaining unit is around 85 per cent male and 15 per cent female, and 55 per cent Negro and 45 per cent white (1950). Over a third of the employees have been with the company over sixteen years. As we shall see later, this is due in good part to satisfaction with the whole job situation.

TABLE 4

Average years of schooling of Chicago plant workers

(Random, stratified sample of 192 workers by service, race, and sex: 1950)

Service	Men		Women	
	Colored	White	Colored	White
Short	8.1	7.1	10.8	7.9
Middle	6.9	8.3	9.3	9.0
Long	5.1	6.6	7.5	7.4

The young colored women are the best educated in the plant, but due to racial discrimination in office jobs both in Chicago's downtown Loop and in the Swift office, they are forced to come to the plant to work. White girls with an equivalent amount of formal education (some high school) would probably be working in offices. The long-service colored men, most of whom were educated in very inadequate southern schools, have the least education in the plant. They are, however, among the best workers and are often highly skilled.

As to skills, we see in Table 5 that service obviously makes a difference, since most beginning workers have to go through a training period. Often older workers are unable to do heavy skilled work and are put on lighter and lesser skilled work, such as a janitor's job. This fact accounts for the decline in percentage of skilled workers among the long-service white workers at least. Also we note a difference between the sexes. No women appear in the sample as skilled workers.

TABLE 5

Skills of the Chicago plant workers

(*Random, stratified sample of 192 workers by service, race, and sex: 1950*)

Service	Men		Women	
	Colored	White	Colored	White
Short				
Skilled	8%	29%	0%	0%
Semiskilled	46%	54%	38%	63%
Unskilled	46%	17%	62%	37%
Middle				
Skilled	8%	52%[a]	0%	0%
Semiskilled	59%	44%	75%	25%
Unskilled	33%	4%	25%	75%
Long				
Skilled	26%[b]	38%	0%	0%
Semiskilled	69%	45%	25%	77%
Unskilled	5%	17%	75%	33%

[a] One half mechanics.

[b] Butchers, not mechanics.

Finally, there is a difference between the races. Only recently has the Negro advanced into the skilled mechanical trades and crafts, though he has long been among the top categories of skilled butchers. Among the men, the most skilled group is the white men of middle service and the least skilled, the colored men of short service. Among the women, the most skilled group is the colored women of middle service. As we saw earlier in our discussion of skills, the proportion of skilled workers is not large, except in the "mechanical gang." Here we see how race, sex, and service affect that proportion.

Is degree of skill an important influence on attitudes and motivation? Skill is connected generally with longer service and also with higher earnings. But as we said, it affects colored and white differently — the white more likely to be skilled mechanics and the colored more likely to be skilled butchers.

As to age of the employees, the rather advanced age of the short-service men workers is noteworthy. (We see that the parallel groups of our cells are not parallel in the age variable.) None of these short-service men has been with the company more than seven years, many less than that time. This means that the colored men came to the company after the age of twenty-six and the white men after thirty. Evidently the white workers have had various other jobs before coming here, even though they may have had time in military service. This is an indication of the mobility and perhaps the instability of some American labor. The rather inconsistent age pattern among the women indicates the lesser stability and continuity of female labor. Some women would come to the Yards for a few years to make some side money. They might leave, break service, and return.

TABLE 6

Average age of Chicago plant workers
(*Random, stratified sample of 192 workers by service, race, and sex: 1950*)

Service	Men		Women	
	Colored	White	Colored	White
Short	34	37	35	38
Middle	44	41	35	34
Long	52	51	51	43

As to time of starting service with the company, the short-service men, both white and colored, are almost all postwar workers. The colored men of middle service came mostly during the war boom, whereas the white men of middle service came mostly before the War, during the end of the Depression.

The saying goes around the plant that a number of the better foremen came to the plant during the Depression when they could not get work elsewhere, and simply stayed on. Swift, of course, being a basic food industry, operated at fair capacity right through the Depression, unlike the more cyclical heavy-goods industries. The long-service employees had a wide span of starting years, the eldest employee in our sample had a service record of over forty years, going back to 1909.

In Table 7, we see that workers of Polish birth or descent are the major ethnic group among the white workers, constituting nearly a third of the white group. Some of the Americans are likewise of Polish descent. The Poles have retained for many years their relative importance among the white men, for one reason at least because the Back-of-the-Yards area is largely Polish. There is no other major ethnic group, though the Lithuanians, Mexicans, and Slavs are next in order. There are very few German and Irish among the production workers. Are nationality or ethnic groups significant influences on attitudes? Very probably. We shall see later how our findings suggest great differences in unionization between the Poles and the Lithuanians.

TABLE 7

Ethnic background of Chicago Swift-UPWA workers

(*Random, stratified sample of 192 workers by service, race, and sex: 1950*)

Service	White		Colored	
	Men	Women	Men	Women
Short	11 Polish 3 Mexican 3 Italian 2 American 2 Lithuanian 2 Jugo-Slav 1 German	2 Polish 2 American 2 Lithuanian 1 French 1 German	(Almost all American born. A few from West Indies. Almost all long- and middle-service workers southern born.)	
Middle	7 Polish 4 American 2 Lithuanian 2 Slav 2 German 2 Irish 1 English-Irish 1 Czech 1 Italian 1 Bohemian 1 Hungarian	5 Polish 1 German-Bohe- mian 1 Slav 1 Irish		
Long (mostly foreign born)	7 Polish 5 American 3 Lithuanian 3 Mexican 1 Czecho-Slovak 1 German 1 Swede 1 Italian 1 Irish 1 Scotch	4 Polish 3 American 1 Lithuanian		

The turnover of the work force gives us an additional clue to the habits of the people who make it up. A moderate turnover rate can be a good thing since it brings new blood into the company and it gives the worker a chance to move about until he finds the job best suited to him. But a high turnover rate not only is very costly to the company in new employee training, but it indicates instability on the part of the workers, brought on either by dissatisfaction or restlessness. The turnover rate at the Chicago plant is fair, neither very high nor very low. In recent years it has been dropping. Forty-eight per cent in 1950, it is lower than Swift St. Paul (93 per cent), Swift Omaha (76 per cent), all Swift plants (80 per cent), but higher than Swift Fort Worth (38 per cent), and Swift Cleveland (40 per cent).

TABLE 8

Chicago plant turnover

(Salaried and hourly paid workers)

	1947	1948	1949	1950	1951	1951 (hourly paid only)	1952 (hourly paid only)
Quits	38.3%	27.7%	14.4%	11.5%	11.4%	14.2%	8.4%
Discharges	16.4%	16.8%	5.9%	4.8%	6.1%	7.2%	12.4%
Layoffs	9.5%	7.7%	17.5%	28.7%	29.2%	35.2%	35.6%
Retirements and deaths	2.6%	1.6%	1.5%	3.1%	3.4%	3.4%	3.8%
Average work force	6330	6369	6251	6254	5777	4789	4589
Turnover	68.8%	53.8%	39.3%	48.1%	50.1%	60.0%	60.2%

Swift & Company figures turnover by dividing the total number of "exits" (quits, discharges, layoffs and retirements or deaths) by the average number of employees on the payroll for a given period, e.g., a year. While this method is simple to figure, it gives a result that is not highly meaningful unless it is interpreted. Evidently some of the quits and most of the layoffs will return to the company, perhaps within a few weeks and surely within the year. Thus the turnover figure will be too high, if we are considering old faces going and new faces coming. For instance, in 1949, of the 3294 returns to the work force, 1522 were people who had never worked at Swift before, but 1772 were Swift employees most of whom had kept their service record intact and were only briefly laid off.

The number of quits and discharges has been reduced. It was high immediately after the War because of the poorer quality workers who had come to the plant during the War. It is still, no doubt, higher than would be desirable. Regarding layoffs, as we saw, two-thirds to three-fourths of the hourly paid work force are not much affected. Every effort is being made to stabilize employment for the remaining third or fourth who have not achieved much seniority. What do we learn from these turnover figures? We find that turnover is lower among the skilled and semiskilled workers. These figures apply mostly to the short-service, unskilled workers and give further evidence of their ceaseless mobility, and doubtless, in many cases, of their instability and lesser job satisfaction.

In Swift Chicago, as in most plants, absenteeism was a serious problem[17] during the last war. No figures on it have been kept since that time. Judging from the workers in our sample, however, who worked fifty-two weeks in 1949 and those who did not, we can get some idea of the working habits of the people.[18] These figures are not precise, but only suggestive. They are correct where big differences between groups are concerned. These figures suggest practically no differences among the men, except among the middle-service men who are definitely more likely to be colored. Among the women there is a sharp racial difference, however, the colored women having a very high absentee record. Also the middle-service group predominates. The higher absentee rate among the colored workers is to be explained, especially for the women, by

TABLE 9

Estimated absenteeism in Chicago plant

(*Partly stratified sample of 199 workers by service, sex, and race who worked less than 52 weeks in 1950*)

Service	Men		Women	
	Colored	White	Colored	White
Short	28%	25%	58%	25%
Middle	35%	17%	100%	33%
Long	20%	20%	43%	25%

poorer health and home conditions and more family obligations. One foreman stated, whose department had mostly women workers: "The Negroes are not so healthy in our gang, they're more touchy than the whites, and they want to go home more readily if they're sick." [19] Moreover, the Negro worker, forced to live in the so frequently inadequate housing of Bronzeville, is more likely to ask for a leave of absence so he can take a trip south to see his relatives or at least to escape the harsh city neighborhood for awhile. About 10 per cent of the work force is consistently off sick — 500 to 600 people as a daily average. This figure goes up in winter and down in summer. Likewise the day after payday brings a large number of absences. Home, neighborhood, and family conditions and customs have a considerable effect upon work habits.

Sometimes it is said that packinghouse workers are a rough lot, handling knives, butchering, walking in blood, as some of them do. In 1948, for instance, a Chicago plant belly-skinner knifed his foreman. And a few years before, in the Pork Dressing Department, a hog-butcher went berserk and stabbed several people before he could be seized. But these are exceptions. The total record is good, there being only one disciplinary case involving fighting with knives, in 1949. As one plant police officer said: "In some departments, each man has a whole scabbard full

PARENT PLANT AND WORKER POPULATION   37

of knives. Those men know what sharp knives will do. They respect
them." Organized theft rings are rare. Intoxication is also a moderate
problem. It appears not so much as a disciplinary case, but as a "sickness layoff" or as simple absenteeism. Since many men work in cool
temperatures, there is a desire to carry a flask in order "to keep warm."
Since nine out of the ten store fronts on Ashland Avenue between 42nd
and 43rd Streets near the west gate of the plant are taverns, the source

TABLE 10

Chicago plant disciplinary cases
(1949)

Charge	Number of cases	Penalty	
Theft	112	Discharge	30%
Fighting	20	Disciplinary layoff	53%
Intoxication	8	Reprimand	17%
Smoking	27		
Miscellaneous°	102		
Total	269	(about 4% of total work force)	

° Includes city arrest warrants served at the plant, complaints, gambling, etc.

of "warmth" is not inaccessible. However, there is an Alcoholics Anonymous chapter in the plant which has been able to make considerable improvement in both cure and prevention. In sum, the total number of
police discipline cases in the Chicago plant is small, involving only four
per cent of the work force in 1949.

Wage assignments tell us something about the habits of the people.
They are usually, though not always, an indication of imprudent install-
ment-buying and of living beyond one's means. They also show the
marginal savings of so many workers, who are often living from weekly

TABLE 11

Estimated Chicago plant wage assignments
(1949–1950)

Total	(about 120 per week)	6240
Number of employees assigned who have already had previous wage assignments		90%
Number of employees assigned for first time		10%
Number of assignments affecting white workers		5%
Number of assignments affecting colored workers		95%
Number of workers getting assignments (about one-fifth of work force)		1000–1500
Average number of assignments per assignee		5
Maximum number of assignments per assignee		22

payday to payday, sometimes unable to meet an unexpected expense as low as $25. The number of wage assignments tends to go up in the summer time and at holiday times such as Christmas. Most of the assignments come from firms selling clothing, jewelry, loans and automobiles. Not a little blame for causing workers to live beyond their means must fall upon the advertising and credit policies of these companies.

From these figures we see that only a minority of the workers is much affected by wage assignments and that this minority is mostly repeaters and mostly colored. A certain type of colored worker in the plant, by no means representative of the colored workers as a whole, is improvident and spendthrift. He seeks an escape from the ugliness of his ghetto and the degradation of being a second-class citizen. He has not yet been able to build a family tradition of saving for home owning and the education of his children (found so strongly among the Polish and Lithuanians), either because he is too recently out of an easy-going plantation life, or because he thinks discrimination makes saving fruitless. Therefore, he buys expensive clothing, cars, jewelry or television sets, instead of saving for decent housing, education, and unexpected needs.

BACK-OF-THE-YARDS

Since this study is a "global" study of the Chicago Swift-UPWA plant community, we are naturally concerned with the neighborhoods of the workers, but only insofar as those neighborhoods affect the industrial relations of the plant community itself. Inevitably there is an important mutual relationship between the plant and the neighborhood, as Hart found in Windsor.[20]

Most of the white workers live "back-of-the-yards" in a square mile and a half immediately west and southwest of the Union stockyards and the Swift plant. At the turn of the century, Back-of-the-Yards, though not Sinclair's *Jungle*, was undoubtedly a disorganized slum with overcrowded homes, muddy streets, "Bubbly Creek," disease, crime, and poverty.[21] Back-of-the-Yards does have some "patched-up shacks and cavernous tenements, sheds and boxcars, viaducts and fences, bricks and cobbles and dirt in gutters, dominated by the smokestacks of factories and the spires of churches . . . [with] . . . colors . . . dirty brickred and gray, [with] sounds of the grinding steel of streetcar wheels . . ."[22] but it also has bright, clean-looking homes, cheerful gardens for flowers as well as vegetables, streets and alleys as clean as a breeze, parks and parkways and backyards with graceful trees, friendly corner taverns where jukeboxes play lively polkas and the talk at the bar is in many languages . . . people who are happy and purposeful, proud of owning their homes, glad to be where they are. On the whole, it is a decent and modest workers' community, for which a share of the credit must go to the Back-of-the-Yards Council.

The BYC represents the 125,000 people living back-of-the-yards. It is not really an organization but rather a "title summing up the pooled efforts of the many organizations and groups of the district" [23] — over 185 of them. The Depression, the old nationalist rivalries, juvenile delinquency, all created problems which the people themselves needed to deal with, and in 1939 the Back-of-the-Yards Council created the spark to ignite that self-helping coöperation. A loose organization of all the neighborhood groups, clubs, churches of all faiths and nationalities was formed with Davis Park director, Joseph Meegan as executive secretary, sociologist Saul Alinsky as technical consultant, and Catholic Bishop Bernard J. Sheil as honorary director.

Since 1939, the BYC has had a stormy, controversial and productive career. It supported the UPWA in the fighting days of organization during 1939 and 1940. It tangled with the Park District and city political machine — and won. It struggled with the big Goldblatt Department Store at Ashland and 47th — and won. It fought a battle for a school-lunch program all the way to Washington. It supported the UPWA in both the 1946 and 1948 strikes. It conducted programs for neighborhood improvement in the following areas: infant welfare; employment office; nutrition for school children; health; housing (where it campaigned ceaselessly against gross violations of building and zoning codes by careless landlords and the small packers and truckers); traffic safety; youth recreation, delinquency; credit union; coöperation with labor unions, local merchants, and so on; and personal counselling. Naturally such a fighting organization made enemies.

Let us consider briefly the relationship between the Swift-UPWA plant community and the Back-of-the-Yards neighborhoods. In Back-of-the-Yards, the BYC has been an important center of influence, along with the Catholic Church, the unions, the various national organizations such as the Polish National Alliance, the politicians, the schools, and so on. The BYC attempted to marshal all the groups to support the new drive to organize the Yards. It succeeded with most, not all. The Catholic priests of the Back-of-the-Yards along with Auxiliary Bishop of Chicago, Sheil, supported the UPWA practically from the start as a good and necessary organization for their people. Herbert March, former District Director of District One of the UPWA and a member of the National Committee of the Communist Party (who, incidentally, has never concealed his membership in the party) stated in 1945:

> When the UPWA-CIO first tried to organize the stockyard workers, we met with the antagonism of all the so-called respectable people, including the Catholic Church. . . . But we kept up the organization

drive. . . . The Back of the Yards leaders knew the people were entitled to higher wages and better working conditions. Their people were largely our people. So they mobilized the support of the whole Council behind the union, including the churches. At one of the first meetings (around 1939) it was a priest who presented the resolution that the packing houses should recognize the union and avoid a strike. . . . The Catholic Churches stood behind us in a block. . . . Nobody in the union can say enough about the value of the Back of the Yards. . . .[24]

Thus two leading centers of influence in Back-of-the-Yards, the Catholic Church and the BYC (uniting almost all groups and churches) had an intimate relationship to the UPWA part of the Swift Chicago plant community. (The union saw the need of this, for it remembered how failure to secure much community coöperation had hindered the AFL efforts years before.) In recent years, since many of the Chicago district UPWA union activities have been moved to the Packinghouse Workers Labor Center away from Back-of-the-Yards and in the heart of Bronzeville, and since the Chicago locals have become more overtly communist in leadership, as we shall see presently, contacts and coöperation between the BYC and the UPWA have diminished. Naturally, relationships between the packers and the BYC were strained, since the Council had supported the UPWA in its organizing and in both its strikes. Only Swift & Company of all the packers has maintained a membership in the BYC. Beyond this token relationship, Swift Chicago plant management have not participated in Back-of-the-Yards affairs. At the annual BYC ball game, besides the local BYC members, the Chicago newspaper writers, politicians, and members of the managements of the Chicago White Sox, the Chicago Junction Railway, Goldblatt's, and so on, are represented. But no packers. In commenting on this omission, Joe Meegan said to me: "It seems if you can't *win* 'em, it would be a smart thing to *join* 'em!" So far, in their community-relations programs, the packers, including Swift, have not seen fit to "join" to "win 'em."

BRONZEVILLE

Most of the Negro workers of the Swift-UPWA plant community live in Bronzeville. Bronzeville, also called the Black Belt, the Black Ghetto, and Black Metropolis, is Chicago's Negro "city" (over 400,000) within a city. Beginning years ago just south of the Loop, Bronzeville pushed itself further southward as each new Illinois Central trainload of migrants arrived. South it thrust like a dark finger, down along the elevated tracks and South State Street, down through the former wealthy white section, edging the Swift mansion, now standing empty at 49th and Ellis, down past Washington Park, all the way to 71st Street. The Negro neighborhoods get successively better the farther one goes south from the Loop. Like the city, Bronzeville has its suburbs too, such as Altgeld Gardens to the south, and Morgan Park to the west. But there the resemblance stops. For Bronzeville is a city of social disorganization.

There are thousands of Negro families in Bronzeville, it is true, living happy, balanced lives at a good standard of living. There is some excellent housing, homes as fine as the best in Chicago's wealthy suburbs. Yet the over-all tone of this Negro city is the depressing tone of social disorder. If the American family generally is in crisis, Bronzeville's Negro family is in greater crisis. Again and again, in our interviews it would be: "My husband drinks, I am the sole support." "I am a widow" (often meaning, simply, that her husband has "gone"). "We are separated." "No husband and six kids." "My wife don't care about the kids." Crime in Bronzeville's Fifth Police District is high in the nation for an equivalent area, with dope traffic as the newest problem.

The biggest difficulty is housing. Crowded kitchenette apartments, often with a whole family living in one room, are common among the lower and even some of the middle class. The European immigrants to Chicago could move away from an undesirable neighborhood if they saved their money. But the Negro, because of caste discrimination against him, has no place to move. The result, especially among the middle classes, is "mixed neighborhoods," with excellent families having to live across the hallway from degenerate ones, thus slowing down the entire advance of the race.

High rents are commonplace, one Swift worker having to pay (in 1949) $100 per month for a single basement room! According to Philip Hauser, University of Chicago sociologist, "Chicago Negro families pay 94 per cent as much for housing as white families do, but on only 65 per cent as much family income."[25] As will be seen (Appendix III; How Well Are They Paid?), the Swift Negro worker makes less, on the average, than the white, due largely to his greater share of unskilled jobs. With that smaller check he must outlay more for rent and even for groceries. In Bronzeville the class distinctions are roughly 5 per cent upper class, 30 per cent middle class, 65 per cent lower class.[26] None of the upper class works in the stockyards, of course. Swift Chicago workers are probably evenly divided between the lower and the middle classes.

Unlike the white neighborhoods such as Back-of-the-Yards, Bronzeville as a neighborhood has considerable influence upon the Negro worker in the Swift-CIO plant community. The marvel is that most of the Swift Negro workers are the good and steady workers they are. It is a testimonial to their capacity to adjust and to wait, to both their sense of humor and their faith in God.

Some of the centers of influence in Bronzeville itself are the press, *Chicago Defender* and Chicago Edition of the *Pittsburg Courier,* the churches, mostly Baptist, the National Association for the Advancement of Colored People, the Urban League, the Democratic machine, the "policy" gambling syndicate, social clubs, the unions, and so on. While there has not been as close a relationship between any of these centers of influence and the Swift-CIO plant community as existed in Back-of-the-Yards, still there has always been a definite relationship.

Back in 1919, Negro preachers, politicians, and leaders were suspicious of organized labor and some actively campaigned against the AFL's efforts to organize the Yards. The Chicago Federation of Labor charged the packers with subsidizing these men. We shall treat this question more fully in the following chapter on the history of unions in the Yards. In the CIO Swift organizing days, in 1941–42, two Bronzeville leaders spoke out vigorously for the new union, Rev. J. C. Austin, pastor of the Pilgrim Baptist Church and Alderman Earl B. Dickerson[27] of the Second Ward. Since then there have been various contacts between both company and union and the Urban League, the National Association for the Advancement of Colored People, neighborhood improvement associations, but not of the same degree as the union-BYC relationships. Swift & Company has supported such Bronzeville institutions as the YMCA, Urban League, Provident Hospital, the South Central Association. One Negro leader stated: "We can't afford to fight against Swift to get Negroes into their front office. We need their contributions to Provident Hospital." [28] One cannot conclude, however, that Swift's motives are simply to "buy off" opposition, because it is their national policy to give support to charitable institutions. A sincere concern for community welfare seems also a plausible motive.

The UPWA in turn has always tried to stay close to the community problems of its members. The various Chicago locals, including the Swift local have had "union counselors" at various times to give social help to their members. The International Union has recently proposed to build an inter-racial housing project southwest of the Yards. The unions have often campaigned against discrimination, for better housing, local political projects, and so on. But since the District One Headquarters have been moved to the old International Workers' Order hall, now called the Packinghouse Labor Center (see next chapter), under the aegis of the Communist party, the efforts of most of the big locals in District One to influence Bronzeville have been constant, noisy, and not very effectual. For instance, they supported packinghouse unionist Sam Parks for Congress on the Progressive party ticket in the congressional elections of 1950 with poor success. They are constantly getting out handbills, seeking signatures, having rallies, making speeches, picketing this and that. But Bronzeville, like "Ole Man River," just keeps on rolling along, not very much concerned.

CHAPTER THREE

UNIONS PAST AND PRESENT

There unions compete with each other in the packing industry: CIO, AFL, NBPW. Such competition is rare in most American industries and is not found in this divided form in such fields as steel, autos, or rubber. The nearly seventy-five years of union-company relations at Swift have been marked until recent years by mutual distrust, union factionalism, strike violence, scabbing, espionage and black listing, and six major strikes, five of which were lost by the unions.

WHEN KNIGHTS OF LABOR FLOWERED

In the 1880's, youthful America was flexing its industrial muscles. Immigrants were streaming in and production boomed. At this time America's first great labor organization, The Knights of Labor, now nearly 700,000 strong,[1] with over three-fourths of all organized labor, came to organize the Chicago stockyards in February, 1886, with good success. At that time their rival, the Federation of Organized Trades and Labor Unions, the incipient AFL, was beginning a nation-wide campaign for the eight-hour day. The Swift Knight-Butchers sympathized, and threatened a strike under John T. Joyce of the cattle-butchers. With surprising speed, the eight hours was granted and more packinghouse workers at once joined the Knights.

Meanwhile Chicago labor and the American labor movement received a severe blow in the form of the Haymarket affair, which seriously prejudiced public opinion against unions in general. Samuel Gompers remarked that the eight-hour movement was set back at least ten years by the Haymarket bomb discharged by the anarchists at the Haymarket rally.[2] In that boiling summer, P. D. Armour, heading the Packers' Association and later joined by Swift, led the packers back to the ten-hour day and stated they would employ no more Knights in the future.[3]

The Knight-Butchers struck on November 2 and were on the point of winning, the packers having rescinded their ban, when they received orders from Terence Powderly to return to work. Powderly, resentful that the eight-hour movement came from his rival Federation, thus broke the strike.[4] After that the Knight-Butchers declined to almost nothing. For fifteen years no man would dare to organize in the open again for fear of his job.[5]

But the Knights of Labor had not yet completely died, and in 1894 the new and small (1600) Chicago Stockyards Butchers' Union answered the call for a general strike to support the American Railway Union.[6] Thus began the second great strike in the Swift plant community and among the other Chicago packers, one not between workers and packing management (though officially the workers protested a recent pay cut), but a sympathetic strike for the remote aims of Debs.

> The strike was characterized by lawlessness and retaliation. The yards swarmed with workers of every nationality seeking employment. From 2000 to 8000 disappointed laborers were kept moving at the point of fixed bayonets through the streets of "Packingtown." Destitute women with canvas sacks followed the men to the yards, picking up small pieces of meat that chanced to fall to the ground at the loading platforms. The general cry was for vengeance against non-union men and especially Negroes. As a protective measure, strike breakers were housed in the meat packing establishments.[7]

The 1894 strike marked (even more than in 1886) the great disunity of the workers, and now, for the first time, on racial lines.

> Incendiaries fired the wholesale meat warehouse of Nelson Morris and Company. . . . In the warehouse there was a refrigerating plant and during the fire the ammonia tanks exploded. This started an every-day . . . scare. By the light of the roaring flames an effigy of a Negro hanging from a telephone pole was brought out in relief. Across the breast a placard was pinned with the words, "N----r scabs" in big black letters.[8]

Since the American Railway Union barred Negroes from union membership[9] it is not surprising that Negroes had little sympathy for a sympathetic strike.

In view of the fact that the packers often presented a common front to the public, it is interesting to see the role played by Gustavus Swift:

> Despite his masterful handling of the bankers in 1893, the strike of 1894 found Swift weak, and some of his pay-roll checks were being turned down at the tellers' windows. Swift called in a committee of the butchers to settle the strike, and Nelson Morris was willing to go along with him. But Armour was adamant against any settlement and there was no prospect of peace unless he consented to go along with Swift and Morris.[10]

On July 7, Debs and the other officers of the A.R.U. were indicted and arrested for disobeying the federal injunction against the strike. The moral effect of Debs' indictment, plus the arrival in Chicago of U. S. troops sent by President Cleveland over Illinois Governor Altgeld's protest, scotched the "revolutionary general strike." By August first, the

4. The Swift-UPWA Local 28 Hall, 4306 South Ashland Avenue.

5. Howard Pratt (right), new president of Local 28; Hugh Currie (center), executive board member; and Russell Snodgrass (left), new grievance chairman, in front of the local hall. These men helped free Local 28 from the Communist party.

6. Andrew Pitts, president of Local 28 in 1948, plans union strategy with fellow-officers in the local hall.

packinghouse workers were back to work, their strike lost and the Knights of Labor finished forever in the Yards.

What lessons did labor learn? "First, that nothing can be gained through revolutionary striking, for the government was sufficiently strong to cope with it; and second, that the employers had obtained a formidable ally in the courts." [11] Also, they learned that if organized labor was to succeed in the Yards, it must embrace all skills, all nationalities, all races; it must have unity and good sense in its leadership. Swift management learned, among other things, that "fight when you have to" brings results, and that if strikebreakers were needed, the great pool of Negro labor in the south might be tapped. It did not learn that the basic social problems beneath the unrest in the Chicago plant community were problems of the worker's insecurity, his right to have some voice in the government of that community, his right to organize, his dignity. It would take many more years, more conflict, and more federal laws before that lesson would be learned. Nor did the labor leaders of the day learn how to unite the polyglot world of the packinghouse melting pot, nor even how to unite their own internal factions and temper the hotheads in their midst.

THE AMALGAMATED ON THE SCENE

In 1896 the Amalgamated Meat Cutters and Butcher Workmen of North America was organized and received its charter from the AFL the following year. At first organizing had to be done underground, but by 1901 the new union was so successfully launched that it dared to come out in the open in Chicago. It is important to notice that the Amalgamated was trying to be an industrial, not a craft union. It wanted to organize everybody who handled meat and by-products, from hog shackler to retail meat clerk. Also, to its credit, it began a deliberate interracial policy.

The Amalgamated objectives, as expressed by Homer D. Call, its first secretary-treasurer, were "to avoid strikes and settle difference with employers by arbitration." [12] Further, it was not union policy to interfere with management, but simply to reform and improve plant working conditions and hours and wages.[13] The new union secured greater regularization of the work day by which overtime without pay was abolished for the cattle-butchers, the right to observe four legal holidays in the year, and a kind of seniority system designed to prevent foreman favoritism. It helped to ameliorate the evils of casual work and the resultant undermining of family neighborhood life.[14] It worked as an important force toward Americanization of the immigrants, bringing them in touch "with English-speaking men for a common cause and . . . preparing them for self-government." [15]

In May, 1904, walrus-moustached Mike Donnelly, Amalgamated's

President, submitted to the packers a combined wage scale demand for all departments and all classes of labor. The packers were against including the unskilled. Finally they agreed, but refused to meet Donnelly's eighteen-and-a-half-cent demand. The union began a nation-wide strike on July 12.

This strike was not only a strike of the skilled on behalf of the unskilled underdogs, but it was a strike of Irish, German, and Bohemian Americans on behalf of Slovaks, Poles, Lithuanians, and Negroes. Cooperation had finally been achieved. This was an important social fact, but as we shall see, it did not last. The men were out for only eight days when the packers agreed to arbitrate. The union agreed. A contract was signed saying the reëmployment of strikers would also be arbitrated.

Then, the tragic mistake occurred. Most of the packers did not discriminate much in rehiring the strikers. There may have been isolated cases of discrimination and several strike leaders were not immediately rehired at their first appearance. The union had contracted to arbitrate these cases. But certain hot-heads forced Donnelly to call out the strike all over again thus clearly breaking their signed agreement. Now the war was on! The packers threw down their old gauntlet — the importation of strikebreakers, which meant, this time more than ever, the Negro strikebreaker.

Twenty-thousand men from the Chicago Yards were on the street, including 4,500 from the Swift plant. There was a minor depression in 1904 and labor was plentiful. Then there was the constant stream of immigrants. A "phantom train" from Ellis Island was pulled right into the Yards — south Europeans with bundles and boxes still bearing their custom house stamps.[16] Finally, there were the Negroes, hundreds of them, knowing nothing about unions or strikes, brought up from the south and smuggled into the Yards, where one agent who collected them for Morris and Company at 35th Street and Armour Avenue, received a dollar a man.[17] For safety's sake, the Negroes were lodged in the plants, where conditions were hardly ideal.

After six long weeks, with racial hostility, worker against worker, and moderate picket-line violence, President Donnelly called off the strike. The strike was lost, the union utterly routed, membership dropping from nearly 75,000 to 7,500. The hope of industrial unionism, the bilateral labor-management coöperation that had burned brightly for three years, was quenched with astonishing rapidity and thoroughness.

If there was one lesson the union should have learned as a result of the 1904 disaster it was this: unless you can overcome the factions and above all, the hot-heads in your own ranks, you will never build a solid union. According to Commons, however, the union's "mistake was natural. It followed a history of grievances on both sides and a conviction on the part of the workmen that the packers were determined to destroy their union." [18] It was the old story of each side adding fuel to the other's fires. Packing management did not want the institution of unionism in its plant community or, at least, it failed to convince labor that it did. This begrudging of organized labor's right to exist in turn helped some labor leaders to become resentful, overly aggressive and even violent, thus making their union institution still less desirable in the eyes of management. It is hard to break a vicious circle.

At this time, Swift management-thinking was changing. Preoccupation with wildly increasing production gradually yielded to greater and genuine concern for the human beings who made that production possible. While in 1904 the worker had few of the personnel benefits he has today, and, although after the strike, seniority was supplanted by foreman preference, still a beginning was made. Swift had established a medical office in the plant community back in 1900. In 1907, an employees' benefit insurance association was started, followed by a series of real improvements in working conditions (see Appendix IV), cafeterias, restrooms, compensation and accident insurance, safety programs, and so on. In 1912, Swift led the entire packing industry by stabilizing employment with the guaranteed weekly wage (or guaranteed hours of pay), and again in 1916 with a noncontributory pension program for all employees better than many negotiated today, and again by providing one-fourth pay to hurt or sick workers in 1917. Common labor rates in the Chicago plant, however, remained frozen at seventeen and a half cents per hour from the 1904 strike to the 1914 outbreak of war. Meanwhile, Swift national sales more than doubled (200 millions to 425 millions), as well as earnings (4 millions to 9 millions) and dividends (2 millions to 5 millions). During this same time, wholesale prices had risen about 13 per cent; retail food prices around 30 per cent.[19] Considering those figures, the fact that worker-productivity was probably increasing, and the fact that the Chicago plant unskilled workers were living in poor conditions, a wage raise during that ten-year period (besides the helpful fringe benefits) was surely justifiable. Was it because there was no union pressure that management failed to give such a raise?

With the coming of the war and the increase in production, the packers needed men desperately. Moreover, they wanted no strikes or slowdowns. Under the influence of the new labor philosophy of the democratic administration under President Wilson, who had created the Department of Labor, the entire labor movement grew without precedent, and the "dead" Amalgamated revived from 7,500 members in 1916 to 100,000 in 1919.

By November, 1917, the various labor groups at Swift and in the Yards felt strong enough to demand increased pay, the eight-hour day and union recognition. The packers categorically refused to have any dealings with the labor leaders, and Swift's Libby, McNeil and Libby fired two men for belonging to the union.[20] A strike was threatened. Washington set up a President's Mediation Commission under which the parties agreed to submit their differences to Federal Judge Samuel Alschuler as arbitrator. The report of the President's Mediation Commission is worth quoting:

> In December, a strike radiating from Chicago threatened the meat packing industry. . . . As is generally true of large industrial conflicts, the roots of the labor difficulty in the packing industry lie deep. The chief source of trouble comes from lack of solidarity and want of power on the part of the workers to secure redress of grievances *because of the systematic opposition on the part of the packers against the organization of workers.* The strike of 1904 destroyed the union, and for fourteen years the organization of the yards has been successfully resisted. . . . More important than any of the specific grievances, however, was the natural desire to assert the power of the union by asking the packers for union recognition, at least to the extent of a meeting between the packers and the representatives of the unions.
>
> This the packers refused to do. They refused to meet eye to eye with the union leaders because of the distrust of those leaders. It cannot be gainsaid that the absence of a union organization for fourteen years, the increasingly large per cent of the non-English speaking labor, and the long pent-up feeling of bitterness all tended to make some of the men in whom the leadership for the time being rested, somewhat devoid of that moderation in thought and speech, which come from long experience in trade negotiations. On the other hand, refusal of the packers to deal with those leaders tended to encourage and intensify those very qualities which dissuaded the packers from industrial contact with them. . . . Unfortunately, the refusal of the packers to meet the union leaders deprived the packers of the opportunity of explaining away, if possible, the belief entertained by the men that the packers were profiteering. . . . The two important specific grievances involved low wages and long hours. . . .[21]

Judge Alschuler held hearings and gave his first award in March, 1918, in which he decreed a basic eight-hour day (instead of ten), pay for overtime, wage increases, and guaranteed time which Swift had put in six years before. One packinghouse worker, later both an AFL and CIO leader, thinking perhaps mostly of Wilson and Company where he had been a butcher writes:

> The Alschuler award was but a dream for the workers, it meant so much to the average man and woman. As a packinghouse worker looking back over thirty-three years of packinghouse experience, a panorama of much that was terrible in those early days passes before my eyes. There alone was that question of sanitation. I can recall the hell holes of filth that were ours to labor in; the toilets, not fit for the beasts of the field to sit on. No respectable wash-up facilities; dressing rooms a mockery on decency, with roaches as thick as ants in the lockers. The wages paid per hour in those days compared to pin money today. Sundays and holidays meant very little. If work was there, you worked, and at straight time. Seniority rights, there were none. The pets got the best jobs. That

was thirty-three years ago. That is the reason why we organized in 1917. We got together for a common cause so that our children may gaze upon the sunlight of opportunity. . . .[22]

But in spite of the Alschuler award, the unions began to have their old internal factional troubles all over again.

> Intrigues, inexperience and incompetence, a bit of dishonesty here and there — all these wracked the union and fed the flames of factional trouble — factionalism broke out into secession and the Amalgamated split into several competing groups. A weakened union . . . ($4112 in cash) had to meet a deliberate offensive of the packers, who used the 1920–21 depression to smash the union.[23]

Still another plague returned to infect the body of healthy bilateral industrial relations; the old plague of white man against black man. Some union men remembered the lessons of 1894 and 1904; most did not. Twenty of the craft unions in the Stock Yards Labor Council were plainly Jim Crow, and a typical AFL solution of separate locals was suggested. Only the Amalgamated, keeping to its constitution and the ideals of Mike Donnelly, did not discriminate. Negro organizers were put on.

> Many Negroes joined unions, but on the whole, the organizers were disappointed in the response of the colored workers. It was estimated that among northern-born Negroes, 90 per cent became union members. Few southern-born Negroes joined, however, and at the height of the drive only about a third of the Negroes employed in the Yards became affiliated with any union organization.[24]

The Negro did not see equal opportunity in the unions, and especially the southern migrants had not thrown off the servility with which they had been forced to look upon owners and managers. Many of their leaders were cold to unionism. And a certain Richard Parker, a Negro "Uncle Tom" set up the American Negro Protective League to keep colored workers out of the labor movement, giving out handbills reading:

BEWARE THE STOCK YARDS UNION

All Colored Working Men in the Stock Yards —
Do Not Join Any White Man's Union
Save Your Jobs

Come Tonight to 35th and Forest Avenue, Corner Restaurant, hear the Protective League Speakers. R. L. Jackson, Chairman.

R. E. Parker, President[25]

Swift management, however, was determined to stop the growing unionization of its workers, either white or black. In 1917 Swift sent out instructions to its Denver plant to dispense with the services of certain active union members, handling the discharges "so as not to force a strike," and finding "cause other than being members (of) labor unions . . ." This plant reported back that "we shall start at once to increase the percentage of colored help in the plant with the intention of getting it to 15 per cent or higher as soon as we possibly can." [26] Clearly, both the company and the unions were competing for the allegiance of the Negroes. By 1919, Swift was one of the largest employers of Negroes in the Chicago area, with over 3200 Negroes, or 26 per cent of its work force. By 1920, Negroes were 29 per cent of the Chicago work force.[27] The situation was greatly aggravated by the race riot of July, 1919, which set back unity and coöperation in the Yards at least ten years.

1921 — ANOTHER DOOMED STRIKE

After the first World War, with the marked decrease in business and production, Swift wished to substitute an Employee Representation Plan (previously tried experimentally) for the Alschuler Arbitration setup that had been operating for the last four years. Swift, like managements in steel, autos, and so on, had seen the need for some kind of grievance procedure in the plant, some way the voice of the workers might be heard yet, in a way, could be kept "contained," as an independent union like the Amalgamated could not be "contained."

The postwar depression had struck. Swift had a net loss of nearly eight millions. In December, 1920, Swift unskilled workers got the first in a series of wage cuts. The Amalgamated refused and called a national strike the following cold winter of 1921. It was a tough strike, and Clemen claims that Swift workers did not want it.

> It was not an action representative of the majority of the employees. In the first place, less than one-third of Swift and Company's employees, for example, belonged to the unions, and in the second place, the number of employees who came to work when the strike was called, was so great as to furnish good proof that the employee representation plan action had the indorsement of the workers.[28]

Although Clemen might be considered partisan as editor of *The National Provisioner,* yet part of this opinion is corroborated by unionist Kampfert:

> Then and only then [summer, 1921] was a strike vote taken by the membership, but nine months too late. No real support came from packing house workers in Armour, Morris and Company or Swift's in Chicago. Several of the International Unions did not sanction a strike vote, mainly those in the mechanical trades and motive power. The Teamsters' Union in Chicago had their own agreement for years with the packers and would not strike in sympathy.
>
> The workers from Armour, Morris and Swift plants did not respond as had been expected, but with thousands of workers on the picket lines, it was dangerous to attempt going through.[29]

As the strike dragged on, picket violence increased, though the Swift plant was operating almost at capacity.[30] Mobs formed and police riot squads were ordered to disperse them. Newspaper headlines read: "ONE DEAD, 26 HURT IN STOCK YARDS RIOTS." "NINE SHOT WHEN POLICEMEN AND MOBS STRUGGLE. WOMEN FIGHT BY SIDE OF THEIR MEN." [31] Charges and countercharges of mob irresponsibility and police brutality were hurled, and both were doubtless true, in part. Judge Sullivan granted an injunction limiting picketing. The police went further and broke up a union meeting at AFL Columbia Hall, 48th and Paulina.[32] It was a mean winter along Ashland and Halsted and 47th and Racine. Violence did not help the workers' cause.

For the third time in stockyards history, Negroes were used for strikebreakers. Their influence was important: the plants could hardly have operated without them. Richard Parker, alleged tool of the packers, head of the new American Unity Labor Union, said:

> We did not believe that striking at this time will help the cause of labor, as there were thousands of men out of employment. We will refuse to coöperate with the Amalgamated Meat Cutters and Butcher Workers' Union in any way and will not strike.[33]

Many Negroes, it is true, were not yet union-minded, were suspicious of AFL Jim Crowism (despite the Amalgamated), were subservient to packer paternalism, were desperately in need of work and thus helped to break the strike. This was not true of all Negroes:

> The use of the Negro as a strike breaker seems to have led the white unionists to forget that the Negro also played his part in the conflict as a striker. "Our union workmen," said the *Chicago Defender,* the largest Negro paper in the country, "obeyed the dictum of their superior union officials and did exactly what their white brothers did — struck. The packers scoured for non-union help and in the dragnet many of our group were found.[34]

It soon became evident that the strike was lost, and that it was working great hardships on the workers. On January 27, 1922, the Amalgamated Meat Cutters gave in. For the second time in their short history, they took a terrific beating, dropping from 100,000 members in 1916 to 5000 after the strike. The strike was a bad failure for at least seven reasons: (1) the Teamsters and mechanics were against it; (2) the Amalgamated was internally disunified; (3) the plant was only partly organized; (4) Swift had a plentiful supply of labor — those of their workers who were against the strike, plus Negro strikebreakers from Bronzeville; (5) the postwar depression made men desperate for work; (6) the Amalgamated had not organized many retail meat markets and got no help from them; (7) violence of the strikers alienated many.

What lesson did the Amalgamated learn this time? It learned that it had failed to learn the lesson of 1904: unless you can overcome the factions and, above all, the hot-heads in your own ranks, you will never build a solid union. What lesson did Swift & Company learn? It thought it learned a new formula for industrial-relations peace — the Employee Representation Plan — which would keep unions out while seeming to bring them in. Was the lesson sound? We shall see.

N.I.R.A. — WHY DID AMALGAMATED FAIL TO LAND BIG FOUR?

By 1933 the Depression had seemingly become a bottomless pit: capitalism had "failed." Men jumped out of windows or just leaned numbly on shovels and picks. Then, hope was revived. The nation's Chief Card-Player had dealt a New Deal, and when the packinghouse workers picked up their hands, they found blue eagles flying, but more, they found a little clause, 7a, which (for the first time in federal law), protected the right of their independent unions to exist!

Swift Chicago and the Yards buzzed with union talk. Four unions began to organize. The Amalgamated Meat Cutters eyed the Yards. Martin Murphy came back to revive the Stock Yards Labor Council. The Communists descended upon the Yards to form the Packinghouse Industrial Union, with Herb March as its secretary. March was also a member of the Council. The Socialists (or perhaps company-minded Harry Floyd) started the small United Food Processer's Union. The merry-go-round of union disunity was turning again, with each group spurring on its own hobby horse. The music was cheerful and hopeful, but the riders ended up pretty much where they had started, as happens on merry-go-rounds. Nevertheless, union talk over bars and conveyor belts was developing a nucleus of union leaders in the Swift plant community.

In spite of its nearly forty years' off-and-on experience, its industrial structure, its former and reviving power, the Amalgamated failed to capture the Swift plant or the Big Four. The first reason was the 1921 strike. "If you mentioned Dennie Lane to the old timers," said a former AFL man, "they'd frown and say: 'No good, no good!'" Fairly or unfairly, the Amalgamated was blamed for that strike. The second reason was the Negroes' distrust of AFL unions. As we saw, the Amalgamated had a declared policy of nondiscrimination. (How that policy has been carried out has not been investigated.) Policy or no policy, however, to the Negroes, the Amalgamated was simply AFL. Also, there were other reasons. Amalgamated's Secretary-Treasurer Dennis Lane did not see eye to eye with CFL's President Fitzpatrick on policy. Again, Lane did not trust the Stock Yards Labor Council left-wing element. He had not forgotten William Z. Foster's extremism of 1918. The result was apparently too much top-down, outside-the-Yards direction. There were sensible leaders in the Council too, but the Amalgamated failed to develop them. According to Kampfert:

> The leaders of the local unions worked in the plants and did know what the workers were thinking and talking about. They also knew the

problems of the workers much better than those who had not worked in the plants for many years. The Amalgamated did not realize that democratic participation by rank and file is the strongest basis for organization.[35]

Though the Amalgamated failed to win the Big Four, it succeeded in winning the Independents such as Oscar Mayer, Illinois Packing, and also chain store butchers, such as in the A & P. In a few short years, under Secretary-Treasurer Patrick Gorman, Amalgamated would soar to nearly 200,000 members and a treasury of over $5,000,000 in 1950 — a tightly organized business union. But the packing industry would be split in two, between two major industrial unions. For the CIO was soon to enter the scene.

PWOC-CIO

In February, 1937, the infant CIO auto workers had won a victory over General Motors. In March, the steelworkers got a contract with Big Steel, and the letters CIO spelled new magic and enthusiasm to the nucleus of AFL-trained, union-minded men in the Yards. That same month the Big Four gave a nine-cent raise, partly, no doubt, to offset the rising tide of unionism. In April, the Supreme Court declared the Wagner Act constitutional and outlawed company unions. Swift's Employee Representation Plan was stopped at once and the "Employees' Security League" was established. This was a new kind of company union, attempting to be legal under the Wagner Act, but still somewhat company-influenced and not quite independent.

In October, 1937, John L. Lewis formed the CIO Packinghouse Workers Organizing Committee under the chairmanship of coal miner, union veteran Van A. Bittner, followed by J. C., "Shady," Lewis, with Arthur Kampfert as Chicago Area Director. (Ever since, the packinghouse workers have had many bonds with the miners.) The PWOC concentrated first on Armour and the smaller plants as the easier targets, and finally got a contract with Armour in 1941, after threatening a strike.

Meanwhile, in Swift Chicago, Henry Schoenstein, Herman Lage, Refugio Martinez, "Red" Knutson, Joe Kinch, Ralph Gantt and others, especially in the pork block, glue house, and cold storage plant, were actively sowing union seeds and buttons. In the spring of 1937 Local Industrial Union #340 was formed under a CIO charter and competed with the Security League. How did Swift & Company feel about this *enfant terrible*, this new independent unionism, struggling to assert itself with the protection of the Wagner Act? And what did the key union leaders think that Swift felt?

It seems certain that Swift top management policy wanted scrupulously fair dealing with the new unions. Here are Harold Swift's instructions of April 21, 1937:

TO MANAGERS AND SUPERINTENDENTS:

The Supreme Court decisions [upholding the Wagner Act] will have a considerable effect upon our methods of dealing with our operating employees in the future. . . .

Some of our people may think that with our method of bargaining changed, the company's attitude toward its employees will change, but this, of course, is not the fact. Whatever our methods . . . of bargaining with employees shall turn out to be, we still want to maintain a cordial, coöperative attitude, with our ideals the same as heretofore, and with a very definite desire to have a fine spirit of coöperation and mutual respect and regard.

Please make every effort to see that this shall be understood throughout all our organization. Please reply.

H. H. Swift[36]

It is probable, however, that fair treatment for the CIO organizers was not universal at the plant and lower supervision levels. We must remember that labor law in 1937 was still being formulated and the rights and duties of union organizers were still in process of being defined by a series of Labor Board decisions. Swift Chicago by no means welcomed the CIO into its plant community, but rather clearly favored the Security League and hoped that this would develop into a certified independent union under the Wagner Act.

Six key PWOC organizers describe these early days as follows. Hank Johnson, a Negro, later to become Assistant National Director of the PWOC organizing drive said:

Swift has a system and it is pretty neat [1937]. But the closer you look, the better you understand it. It is to fight union without fighting union. They pay a few cents more, and always allow workers to discuss their problems. They never fight organization openly, but buy off or weed out the more aggressive leaders. . . . Now the union is the biggest force towards brotherhood of the different races. National prejudice melts away when people see men and women of all nationalities standing together bravely and winning better conditions for all.[37]

And Owensby Lee, former Swift old-timer and second President of Local 28, describes his own organizing efforts:

We really needed a union. We had to wait five years for one week's vacation. And I've seen men work four and one-half years and then get laid off, to break seniority and then get rehired. Once we were trying to get a foreman's pay for a fellow who was really doing a foreman's job. The company told us: "Up to now we don't have any Negro foremen."

Interviewer: Did the company intimidate the unionists?

Lee: Yes, but so cleverly you'd hardly detect it. They would go around and talk to key workers and poison their minds against the union. One day I was alone and trimming meat and three men came and asked me about the union. They were from the Security League. The foreman said to me: "I see a lot of people coming to you. You'd better watch yourself!" I said: "Why?" I was on my job doing my work, wasn't I? . . .

The fellas [rank and file] fought us too. They'd whistle: CIO, CIO, CIO, throw 'em out! . . . There was fear. . . . The Employees Representation Plan maneuvered to get smooth men as representatives, men who always favored the company. . . . The company still tried to recognize the Security League and build it up in the minds of the workers. But it was just the old Representation Plan revamped.

Interviewer: Were there any firings for union activities?

Lee: Swift & Company was very clever about it. They'd make you believe they wanted a union in the Yards. I was never fired. Always kept my skirts clean! [38]

Joe Barrett of "West House," another key organizer in the plant, continues the theme: the union organizer's desire for a really independent union, and his suspicion of the company-favored Security League:

As chairman of the grievance board of the pork division of the Employees Representation Plan, during the last three of the six years I worked at Swift & Company's stockyard plant, I came to some very definite conclusions. I realized the workers would never settle any real grievances or achieve any real demands under such a company union plant.

When the Wagner Act was upheld, I knew that the CIO for the first time had the chance of success which it deserved; long before this, all of us who had given any thought to it, had realized it was our real hope to better our conditions. I began organizing Swift workers into CIO; now I have some real help.

We are anxious to show the workers of Swift's that the Security League, which exists in Swift & Company, is the same old Employees' Representation Plan with a new pair of pants. The only difference is that you get nothing for nothing under the old plan, and now you get the same thing for fifteen cents a month from the company-dominated Security League.[39]

Local leader Ted Kurowsky (fictitious name), a fiery man, to say the least, tells of the hazards he found in organizing.

In '37 and '38 I was laid off twenty-one times! Why? They wanted to demoralize me. I was building the organization in the plant. If there was a crowd in the Employment Office, I'd be the last to be hired. Men would never want to go into the Employment Office with their badges on. But I did. A steward's badge looks so big. But in the Employment Office it looked soooo big. [Gesture] They gave me the tough jobs. *But they never fired me for union activities.* There was the Wagner Act. But they got many men if they ever overstepped the bounds. You'd be fired at once.

Interviewer: Did you ever get any disciplinary layoffs?

Kurowsky: No. But in rehiring, you'd get hired last. And on layoffs, you'd be the first to get laid off. If they'd need ten men, you'd be the eleventh.

Interviewer: Wasn't there seniority at that time?

Kurowsky: Seniority? There was no contract. The seniority lists were not published. . . . Fear for your job — that was our biggest enemy. Men would hide their union buttons in those early days.

Henry Schoenstein, for many years the International UPWA's wage-rate specialist and a key Swift organizer, continues a similar theme:

The company gave a raise in 1937, after the Steel raise, *in order to keep unions out.* As though to say: "The company gives freely. You don't need a union." It's like this: This Armour Local was not satisfied, and tried to get an additional five cents an hour in August (1937) from Armour plus the Conciliation Service. But Swift & Company jumped the gun and also gave a flat raise, but even one day ahead of Armour and before PWOC negotiations, as though to say: "You don't have to have a union. You can get five cents without it."

Interviewer: How do you know they gave the raise just to oppose the union: Maybe it was because they wanted to keep up with Steel?

Schoenstein: Well if the raise they gave in 1937 [and again in 1941] was just to keep up with Steel, then why did Swift fight the UPWA contention before the War Labor Board that Steel and Packinghouse rates had always been historically the same?

Then, too, there was that layoff in the Pork Trim Department in 1937 *with no regard to seniority.* Mostly union people were laid off. Red Knutson was a leader and the company was after him. It wasn't the foremen who did it. They had orders. ——— [a foreman] said: "I've got orders." The PWOC protested. It went to a hearing under the Wagner Act. The hearings officer was in the Loop. The union won. The men were reinstated with back pay.

When the Wagner Act was declared constitutional, the E.R.P. dissolved and the same officers became officers of the Security League and the company recognized *them* as bargaining agents and bargained with them and not with the Industrial Union #340, CIO, even though they had had no election. . . . The foremen would take up grievances with the Security League but refused to recognize the stewards of #340. We'd have to go over the foreman's head and go to the General Office and use pressure. [It is significant that Schoenstein felt free to do this.] We'd say: "If you let Security League men walk around the plant, we could too."

Then there was the *Flash* versus the *Tribune.* The company said: "The Government says you can't bring the *Flash* or printed matter into a department where there are food products." Their purpose was to stop the *Flash.* I said: "Therefore you'll have to keep the *Tribune* out!" The result was that they let us bring in the *Flash.*

The foreman tried to stop the stewards from talking unionism to the men while they were working. Therefore, I said, we can't talk about baseball or anything else. Once the foreman told me if I didn't stop talking about that union stuff I'd get fired. I said: "Is that a threat or a promise?" He said: "Don't you talk unions to the people or you'll 'get your time.' If you talk about work, it'll be all right." I said: "If I get my time for talkin' about unions, you'll have to fire everybody for talkin' baseball or if you've been out with your wife or girl friend last night." — It was the baseball season. — And besides I wasn't stoppin' work. Our gang all make their B's. The foreman said: "That doesn't pertain to work neither." So I went over to ———, the Division Superintendent, and he says: "Forget it, Hank! Come on and have a cup of coffee!"

The top echelon knew better. It was the little guys who tried to scare you. Of course they might have had orders and the Big Guys hiding

behind them and letting the little guy take the rap. I don't know. . . .
But I guess at the top, you get justice.

Then they would never transfer me on Department Seniority out of
my department. [You see, if they were short some day, they had a practice
of loaning people out.] But they never loaned out Hank! . . . I used to
have a police escort that followed me. They were trying to catch me
signing guys up on the job, on company time.[40]

Finally, an illuminating quotation from top unionist Arthur Kampfert
will help round out our picture of company-CIO relations in organizing
days:

> After the union came out in the open, the company put up a sign:
> "No soliciting or organizing on company time or premises." Phil Weight-
> man, Lawrence [Red] Knutson, and Hank Schoenstein had a police escort
> whenever they left their departments.
>
> The company tried to bar the *Flash* . . . from the plant under the
> federal health regulation against bringing in printed material. The union
> countered that the company *Arrow* and the *Tribune* couldn't be brought
> in either. So the company compromised by giving the union a box to put
> the *Flash* in.
>
> The union won another round when the company refused to recognize
> a grievance committee of five men. Sixty-seven women in the hog trim
> department had grievances. Each woman selected a personal representa-
> tive and 134 of them marched to the General Office. To this the company
> objected very strenuously. From that day on, the company was glad to
> deal with small committees.
>
> In the fall of 1937, the Swift local wrung four very important conces-
> sions from management. During the depression, when jobs were scarce,
> Swift had started to weed out Negroes. Because they were the last hired
> and the first laid-off, very few Negro workers accumulated seniority dur-
> ing the first half of the thirties. The union told the company that it ex-
> pected Negroes to be hired according to their proportion in Chicago's
> population.
>
> Since 1929, Swift had hired no Negro women. [This is not entirely
> correct. Two women in our random sample alone were hired during this
> period.] The union's position convinced the company to hire Evelyn Wat-
> ford and to continue hiring Negro women.
>
> The PWOC local union also won a seniority plan which is still the
> envy of other local unions. Seniority was to be department-wide for pro-
> motions and plant-wide for layoffs.
>
> Finally the company agreed to pay stewards and committees for time
> spent in handling grievances. . . . Although no NLRB election took place
> in the Chicago Swift plant until 1942, from 1937 the PWOC was an or-
> ganization to be reckoned with. While fighting the Security League and
> pushing for 100 per cent organization in the Chicago plant, the union had
> an informal working agreement with the company. . . . Swift & Company,
> which everyone predicted would be the hardest of the Big Four to or-
> ganize, had yielded better than expected. However, from the experiences
> in the G. H. Hammond plant in 1933 and 1934, one could not under-
> estimate their strategy. . . . Swift's labor policy was shrewd and its work-
> ing conditions were slightly better than the other big packers.[41]

Despite the comparative mildness of Swift Chicago's attitude toward the union, the union leaders felt they were operating under considerable odds, against clear management opposition operating in many small ways, especially in its favoritism for the Security League. Yet these leaders were not anticompany men, as we shall see more clearly later. Henry Schoenstein says:

> We couldn't fight the company on rates, or on being a "bad Company." But our fight was for seniority. Especially in the pork block. Seniority didn't mean so much to the mechanics. They had steady work.[42]

To the union leader the Security League was important competition. To Swift management the League was also important, as the ERP had been before it. Many of the Local Security Leagues that had evolved in the Swift chain from the old Employees' Representation Plan did in fact resist the CIO and AFL and formed their own independent (largely Swift) union, the "Swift Brotherhood," or the National Brotherhood of Packinghouse Workers, as it is known today.

Whether or not the NBPW locals are "company unions," as some UPWA men call them, or whether they are quite free of indirect Swift influence, the author is now investigating. At any rate, they are legitimate unions certified under labor law. In 1952 the Swift chain had 10,000 of its workers in seven NBPW locals, or 25 per cent of its packing plant work force. The CIO had some success in winning a few NBPW locals to the UPWA, but many have stayed in the Brotherhood. This situation is perhaps unique. Most of America's big industries had Employee Representation Plans in the 1920's. There are very few, such as those in the oil industry, that preferred to resist the CIO and AFL and maintain their own almost exclusively company-wide independent union. All this is convincing evidence that Swift workers were generally satisfied with company treatment and the Security League. Of course, in fairness, we should also mention that the Security League started off with the blessings of Swift & Company while the UPWA did not. Indeed, the CIO brought unfair labor-practice charges against Swift in Denver, East St. Louis and South St. Paul for attempting to influence its workers against the CIO and for the Security League.

In addition to the NBPW about 13 per cent of the Swift chain is in the AFL Amalgamated Meat Cutters. This makes a triple unionism in Swift which is a very important factor in collective bargaining and other labor-management relations, as we shall see. At any rate, in Swift Chicago the PWOC steadily gained ground and three years later, in April, 1940, it stood alone. Charges were filed before the NLRB [43] by Local 340, then called PWOC Local 28 that Swift was favoring the Security League. Swift agreed to withdraw recognition from and disestablish the Employees' Security League, and in the future in no way

"To interfere with the formation or administration of any labor organization" in the plant. It posted notices to this effect on Chicago Swift bulletin boards.

Toward the end of 1941, Federal Wage and Hour Administrator Fleming won an injunction against Swift before U. S. District Judge Igoe, restraining the company from violation of the Fair Labor Standards Act. The PWOC and its counsel Arthur Goldberg had also urged the injunction as a test case and had filed a brief supporting it. Local 28 leaders testified in the hearings. After the injunction Swift volunteered to pay back-pay to its employees. Because the PWOC and Local 28 shared in this suit, they naturally gained prestige in the workers' eyes.

This prestige helped the local in its important certification election that followed soon after, in January, 1942. Against "no union" and the Independent Swift Union, CIO Local 28 won by an unquestionably large margin, and was thereby certified as the exclusive bargaining agent for the workers of the Chicago plant.[44] Bilateral labor relations had begun at last. On April 1, 1943, the first Swift-PWOC master agreement was signed for all the PWOC locals in the Swift chain, retroactive in some respects to the fall of 1942. In 1943 the CIO gave the PWOC independent status and the United Packinghouse Workers of America began their existence as an international CIO union under the presidency of Lewis Clark.

Why was there a delay of five years (1937–1942) before Local 28 was certified as an officially recognized local union? Because the campaign had centered on Armour rather than Swift, and because Swift workers were known to be quite satisfied and company-minded and therefore harder to organize. Owensby Lee, second president of Local 28 gives the following reasons:

> The company tried to recognize the Security League and build it up in the minds of the workers. It was indelibly marked in the workers' minds. Also the workers were afraid of union organization. [Perhaps they remembered the Republic Steel May Day violence in 1937. Or perhaps were afraid for their jobs.] Two certain gift-of-gab Assembly Representatives opposed the union bitterly. . . . Even if you had been out listening at a union mass meeting, all eyes were on you when you came back to your department. . . .[45]

Henry Schoenstein, a key Swift organizer, gives a different reason:

> Some of the International and District people wouldn't support us. Left-wingers Hank Johnson and Shaw disrupted our meetings and called us company stooges because they couldn't control us. The Communist Party was against us because they couldn't control us. We had only a few commies in our crowd. [Note: Communists had infiltrated, but did not control the PWOC staff.] Company opposition was only a minor point in the delay. The key reason was the communist boys. They wanted the prestige of signing up the Armour local first, and also since they couldn't

control us, they opposed us. They always said we were too "company-minded." [46]

TWO MORE STRIKES

By 1946 the young UPWA was beginning to feel its strength. The second World War was over. The National War Labor Board, which had overseen labor relations in packing and other industries, was bowing out of the picture. The National Labor Relations Board remained. Fringe benefits had been given during the War, but beyond some flexibility under the Little Steel formula, wages and prices were more or less frozen. A thaw was not long in coming. On January 16, 1946, together with the Amalgamated, the UPWA called a strike for a raise. A federal fact-finding board recommended a raise of sixteen cents. In only ten days the strike was over and won — the first and unique victory of the packing unions. It was won both by strike pressure and the aid of the government, for President Truman, acting under the War Labor Disputes Act, ordered the Secretary of Agriculture to seize and operate the packing plants. The strikers returned to work, and soon the wage increase of sixteen cents recommended by the fact-finding board was put into effect by the government over Swift management's head.

By January, 1948, the UPWA was ready to push out in front of other industries on the third round of postwar wage increases. In wage-re-opener negotiations, the union demanded a raise of twenty-nine cents per hour. Then the important point of strategy occurred. The AFL Amalgamated and the NBPW accepted Swift's final offer of nine cents. Thus, 40 per cent of Swift's workers were in agreement with the company. But the UPWA decided to go it alone and called a nation-wide strike for March 16. Unlike 1921, there was very little roughness in the Chicago stockyards this time, thanks partly to left-winger Sam Parks' speech at 42nd and Marshfield a few days before the strike deadline:

> If you see any damned police around, do not pay any attention to them. Do not worry about the police. We will take away their guns. We will take away their stars. We will take their clubs and rub their heads with them and rough them up. If they send in the Army we'll bump heads with them and take care of the soldiers too. If President Truman does not move our way, we'll take care of him also.[47]

Ironically, a violent speech may have helped to prevent violence. At any rate, there were almost as many police at the yards as pickets.

The strike wore on; Swift refused to arbitrate. This weakened its public-relations position because many people had come to believe that if collective bargaining arrives at an impasse, and a serious strike occurs threatening the common good, at that time it was fair and just for the parties to invite some expert and impartial board to step in and settle the matter. The company stated:

Arbitration in the present circumstances is unacceptable to the company. We believe that our negotiating officials and representatives of our employees are in the best position to know the facts and to reach a mutually satisfactory settlement of wages. This is true regardless of how well-intentioned the arbitrator may be.

Collective bargaining will inevitably break down whenever there is a possibility of third party intervention such as imposing an agreement by arbitration.[48]

Two facts affected the UPWA's public relations position: First, two labor unions, the AFL and the NBPW, had already accepted the nine cents. Second, although President Truman had appointed a Board of Inquiry, the union did not wait for its verdict, but called the strike anyway. UPWA President Helstein replied that "maintenance of the *status quo* suggests sacrifice by one party and only one party . . ." Knowing that the Board had no power of recommendation, he stated that such a Board would not be likely "to produce any change in the adamant attitude of the packing companies . . ."[49] Nevertheless, these two facts gave the UPWA a weaker public relations stand than that of the packers. Moreover, the Board of Inquiry, while not making explicit recommendations, found that "the companies' offer of nine cents per hour wage increase was a substantial offer" and that it was "adequate to compensate for changes in the cost of living since the last wage increase."[50] Incidentally, the Board clearly asserted the propriety of the UPWA's cost of living, budget approach.[51]

One of the most interesting findings of the Board of Inquiry touches on the question of double unionism or, in the case of Swift, of triple unionism:

> In any realistic appraisal of the reasons for the impasse, the fact that the companies must negotiate with three competing unions is of inescapable significance. Despite the fact that they regarded nine cents as a fair offer, the companies might have taken a more flexible attitude toward the UPWA demands, had there been only one union to consider, or had all three unions been bargaining with the companies jointly, or had not the companies previously settled with the Amalgamated and the NBPW. On the other hand, the UPWA might have accepted nine cents an hour as an adequate increase under all the circumstances, rather than strike, had not the companies previously settled with the other two unions at nine cents.[52]

Another noteworthy point in this strike, as in all the other five major strikes in the history of the meatpacking industry, is that all the Big Four or Big Five (unlike the steel or auto industries at least before 1952) held out for the same terms and the strike went on as against one unit.

The 1948 strike was crucial in UPWA history, and it is worth knowing the role that Local 28 played in it. A strike vote was taken in January with not over half, perhaps only one-fourth of the members voting. There is some dispute about this vote, but the local apparently voted to empower the International UPWA to call a strike if necessary. The whole picture changed between January and March. At that time the Local 28 officers were against the strike and tried to stop it, along with many other locals, at the strike strategy meeting at the Hamilton Hotel, saying: "The packinghouse workers do not want a strike at this time." The evidence from our interviews later will confirm this attitude. But the International Strike Strategy Committee voted for the strike.

The strike then dragged on for ten long weeks. Many workers, unable to stand the loss, came back to work, 250 by April 13, 764 by May 5, and 2068 by May 21 (around 40 per cent of the union members and 35 per cent of all in the bargaining unit). Finally, on May 21, the UPWA called off the strike and the men took the nine-cent raise without retroactivity. It was a costly strike — the workers losing $500 to $700 each (one-fifth of a year's pay) and the UPWA going into $100,000 debt to the United Steelworkers. Although a number of the workers were bitter about the strike, yet the marvel is that the UPWA was afterwards able to make a comeback, and that the AFL has not succeeded in raiding many UPWA plants.

What lessons did the union learn from this strike? It learned that in a triple-union industry, a national strike against the Big Four without the AFL and the NBPW is bound to fail. Swift could operate at half capacity at least (though some unionists felt that a UPWA strike against one company might succeed), and the Independents (being mostly AFL) could do a roaring business. What did Swift learn? The strike probably confirmed Swift opinion that the way to deal with radical union leadership is by a showdown fight, provided you believe yourself to have the general support of your employees.

LOCAL 28

So far in this brief history of labor relations in the Chicago plant community we have talked mostly about relations at the top-union top-management level, about bargaining and strike strategy. Yet it is the local union we are primarily interested in, and here we get down to the job of giving an airplane view of its structure, functions, and history. We are brief because we devote three chapters to the local later on.

(1) *The Officers.* Local 28 has had eight presidents,[53] of which five were colored and three white, three were Communists and five were not. Often the secretary-treasurer and the chief steward are also important officers. An outstanding fact about the officers is their turnover. It is hard to be a local union leader because of the sacrifice of sleep, peace of mind, family life, and even money, except for the secretary-treasurer and recording secretary, who get a modest expense account. Neither the officers nor the stewards are paid, and the rewards of prestige or privilege are not extraordinary. The drive to self-sacrifice for the cause of labor

welfare is a powerful motive for many Local 28 officers and is not to be overlooked. But union politics are rough and tough, and the number of men willing to sacrifice themselves on such an altar for more than a few years is not many. The turnover in officers is also caused by turnover in the industry — four of the eight presidents no longer work for Swift! It is also caused by upward movement in the union. Local 28 has given several leaders to the International and the CIO. But turnover was hard on the local, for it brought inexperience and constant relearning by the costly method of trial and error. In 1949, for instance, when the left wing got control, almost the entire steward body was replaced, with poor results for the grievance procedure.

(2) *The Committees.* Local 28 has eight standing committees: Organizing, Activities, Legislative, Grievance, Bargaining, Membership, Educational, Budget. These have varied in size, importance, and activity. Other committees of importance are the Resolution and Strike Committees. Most important is the Grievance Committee. Very little bargaining is done.

(3) *The Grievance Procedure.* One of the most important local functions, it will be treated in Chapter Ten.

(4) *Communications.* The *Flash* is Local 28's weekly newssheet and has varied in journalistic quality from excellent to poor. Other communications methods between the leadership and the membership are union meetings, mass meetings, leaflets, cafeteria conversations. The department steward is the key intermediary. As will be seen from the interviews later, communications leave a lot to be desired. Many of the rank and file know little about the officers and activities of their local.

(5) *Meetings.* There are monthly membership meetings, monthly stewards' meetings, occasional dances and parties, occasional mass meetings with other locals of the Yards, an annual picnic. Participation of the members in these meetings will be treated in Chapter Nine.

(6) *Local Hall.* Local 28 owns an excellent hall for its purposes located near the West Gate of the Yards at 4306 South Ashland Avenue, with adequate office space, hall, bar, and kitchen. All the normal social functions can be accommodated there (several hundred people). But large political or strike gatherings would overtax it, as happened once in 1949.

(7) *The Dues.* The dues have been raised to $2.50 a month. This is about the same as the Amalgamated, though more than the NBPW. It is, of course, lower than many other AFL unions. The UPWA is not a high-dues organization.

(8) *Union Security.* Local 28 is not a union shop. Nor are many other locals in the UPWA chain. Once in, members may not leave the union except during a short interval at the time of contract renewal. While there has been no strict "maintenance of membership" in the Chicago

plant bargaining unit since 1948, yet the fact that the dues checkoff is irrevocable for one year or for the life of the contract and is automatically renewable unless the worker utilizes the "escape clause," does give Local 28 some measure of union security.

At times, the local has had a large membership:

TABLE 12

Trend in Local 28 membership

Year (December)	Eligible (in CIO bargaining unit)	Number in Local	Percentage of unit in Local
1946	5522	4638	84
1947	5706	4735	83
1948	5954	5118	86 (Max.)
1949	5518	2483	45
1950	5455	3763	69
1951	4971	3877	78
1952	4240	3554	84

The sharp drop in 1949 was due to discontent at the 1948 strike, a split in local politics and the fact that the Taft-Hartley Act had required new union cards to be signed. Even at best, however, neither Local 28 nor the International are easily secure.

LOCAL AUTONOMY, RACE, AND COMMUNISM

A few Communists had come into the union during the Depression, and by 1937 had wormed into the PWOC and even into high positions. Left-winger Herb March, a former Chicago Area Director of the PWOC, was elected in 1943 to be District One Director of the UPWA. He resigned in 1948, refusing to sign the Taft-Hartley affidavits. There were also some Communists in the International and in other districts such as New York and Boston, but the focus of concentration was the Chicago District One. Local 28 had its share, but according to one local leader, a former party member himself: "We weeded them out. By 1942, the Communists were pretty well gone. Most of us who were Communists thought the Party so corrupt we got disgusted and got out." [54]

In 1943, when the PWOC became the independent UPWA and Herb March its Chicago District Director, the Communist party set out to organize cells in each of the big Chicago plants, for here was the heart of the food industry, vital for defense. The big Armour plant with its Local 347 and the Wilson plant Local 25 were soon captured. But Local 28 was too tough a nut to crack; it had its Communist members, but they did not like outside dictation, and the battle was on. Local 28 moved out of the District Headquarters and bought a hall of its own.

In 1945 the Communists decided to take over the CIO Chicago Industrial Union Council. Michael Mann, the Council's secretary was hard put to it for awhile, but managed to keep control. As a result, the Armour, Wilson and satellite locals withdraw from the Council. About this same time three key 28 leaders left the party or were expelled for disobedience. The break between Local 28 and District One was widening.

The 1946 strike after the war was a sincere effort for a decent wage. During the strike, Local 28 tangled with March on strike strategy and strike relief. Result: March labeled 28 as the only "weak spot" during the strike, and threatened to drive its leaders out of the union.

"L'Affaire Criley." The party's strategy was almost clever. Soon after the strike, a clean-cut young man by the name of Richard Criley applied for work at Swift and for membership in Local 28. He worked only twenty-six days and then quit. At once he sought leadership in Local 28 and was given some responsible work to do. Later March also gave him the important post of District Education Director. Local 28's officers were suspicious that this smooth-spoken young man was not much like a packinghouse worker. They found that he lived in well-to-do Sheldrake Hotel. They further found that he was a college graduate, a Communist "intellectual," and a former President of the California Young Communist League. Criley was an obvious "plant" to capture the local for the party. It was not long before his party line appeared. Among other things, he agitated to get the local to disaffiliate from the CIO Industrial Union Council. This was too much for Local 28. They held a formal trial and expelled Criley. Said Ralph Gantt, an officer of Local 28:

> We are not concerned about any person's belief as such, because within our organization we have worked harmoniously with communists, Trotskyites, socialists, democrats, republicans, and so on. . . . We are disturbed when any group outside our local union interferes with our autonomy.[55]

The whole affair got much publicity and spread Local 28's name throughout the UPWA as a spearhead in the fight for unionism against communism. By this time Local 28 had broken with District One and stopped its per capita payments to it.

The Communist issue became more acute in 1947 when the question of signing the Taft-Hartley affidavits arose. The UPWA International Executive Board decided to sign, which put the Communists in a poor light. In order to recoup, and also to help sabotage the Marshall Plan (meat would build up noncommunist Europe), the Communist element in the UPWA led in the agitation to call the ill-fated 1948 strike. This strike was not uniquely a Communist affair, for many noncommunists supported it, too. But the party was the strike strategy's catalytic agent. Local 28 and many other locals opposed the strike, as we saw.

Next came the UPWA 1948 Constitutional Convention in June and July, at which time the left wing strengthened its position. Soon after the convention, several right-wingers were discharged from the International staff. Likewise several important members of the International openly supported the left-wing Progressive party's Wallace-for-President campaign in direct opposition to national CIO policy and to a UPWA Resolution of the recent convention "to endorse and support" that policy. They were not publicly repudiated.

Local 28, seeing the increasing anti-CIO and leftward movement of the International, decided it could sit back no longer. As leader it summoned a rump National UPWA CIO Policy Caucus for all UPWA right-wing locals at Cedar Rapids, Iowa, on August 15, 1948. This caucus began a minor insurrection at a time when the whole UPWA was at the weakest point in its short history. The caucus charged the International mainly of not following national CIO policy, but rather the Communist party line:

(1) The July issue of the communist *Chicago Star* carried President Helstein's picture and statement approving the policies of that newspaper. [Mr. Helstein, however, privately denied the statement and said it had been published with neither his knowledge nor his consent.]

(2) Two prominent members of the UPWA, one from the International and one from the Chicago District participated in Communist-supported Progressive Party convention in July at Philadelphia, contrary to the convention resolution against Wallace and the third party. They received no public repudiation.

(3) The International had "purged" five right-wingers, Godfredsen, Bollard, Mooney, Gates and Kinch, under the guise of "economy" while rehiring avowed Communist Herb March and retaining noted Communists Jesse Prosten and Les Orear.

The Policy Caucus made other charges against the International and then finally took the extreme measure of immediately withholding all local union per capita tax payments to the International. To the trade union movement this was revolution. The sixty delegates at the unofficial caucus represented over a third of the UPWA.

Clearly the UPWA was in a crisis. It had badly lost the 1948 strike. It was deeply in debt. For months it would fight a bitter duel with recalcitrant Wilson and Company. The Amalgamated had begun its raids. For one reason or another, around thirty-three NLRB elections were required. And now there was a threatened revolution led by 28.

Charges and countercharges flew thick and fast. The International seized Local 28's treasury in the Amalgamated Bank. But Local 28 got a Superior Court order directing the bank to turn back the funds to the local, thus upholding the local's autonomy against the International. At the subsequent Estes Park Convention in 1949, the UPWA constitution was changed, giving the International more power over local unions.

In the meantime the locals who had withheld their per capita tax gradually began to pay up, all except Local 28. An administrator was appointed to govern Local 28, but the local refused to accept him, as unconstitutional. As a result, to the average worker in the Swift-CIO plant community there appeared to be two unions in the plant. Two sets of stewards appeared in some departments. The *Flash* competed with the *Official Flash*. The company was in a dilemma as to which group should receive the sizable monthly dues check and finally settled by holding it in escrow. Local 28 offered to pay its per capita if the International would get Swift and the bank to release the funds. The International refused. The result to the worker was confusion and chaos.

The duel became hotter. Local 28 was not seated at the 1949 UPWA convention. Local 28 remained loyal to the CIO, of course, and did not bolt either to the AFL or the NBPW. But the situation in the plant had become intolerable. New contract negotiations were approaching and a temporary *modus vivendi* was struck between the local and the International, by the local accepting an administrator, with checkoff dues to be paid through him, a special election of officers to be held in July.

The election was held after a short campaign. The right wing lost. At last the Communists gained control of the powerful Swift local. It must be noted, however, that not all the new officers were Communists, but only some key officers who would be able thereby to control the Local Executive Board. Such mixing, of course, is an old party strategy. It is also noteworthy that hardly a third of Local 28's members came out to vote in this crucial election, indicating their discontent with both the 1948 strike and the union confusion in the plant. Philip Weightman, former Local 28 President, and UPWA Vice President defeated largely by the left wing at the 1948 convention, currently on the National CIO staff, sums it up:

> My conviction was then and is now, that I am unalterably opposed to Communist infiltration of our union. . . . I helped clean this [Illinois State Industrial Union] Council out and helped make it the Council it is today. Since that time, however, the commies have made further inroads into my beloved union. They have now taken over my own local union. . . . My local union, I know, consists of some good people, and I hope within the very near future that local union, Local 28 UPWA-Swift Chicago, will again be reaffiliated with this Council.[56]

Why did the right wing lose? Because the left had a great deal of District and some International support, because the right wing itself was split, because of overconfidence, and finally because of general apathy. The revolt of Local 28 was finally over. What judgment should we make upon it?

(1) The local had a right to protest the obviously leftward, anti-CIO trend of some individuals and some policies of the International.

(2) The local used methods perhaps unwise for the trade union movement, by starting a virtual revolution at a time of crisis in the UPWA.

(3) On the dispute as to the constitutionality of Local 28's methods we make no statement. The facts are highly complicated. Their appraisal is not necessary here.

The Party versus the Negro. In the autumn of 1949, the Communists were expelled from the CIO trade union movement. This move angered the man then behind the throne of District One. Said Herb March, in the Armour newssheet, *The Cleaver,* pulling hard on the class-warfare "stop":

MURRAY MESSING UP CIO

The CIO convention, now going on in Cleveland, is most harmful to the CIO. . . . Now when all of Labor should be UNITED, Phil Murray and others are kicking out the so-called "Left Wing" Unions . . . and splitting CIO.

We're afraid that Murray is trying to make the CIO "respectable" in the bosses' eyes. The AFL has been that way a long time — and it hasn't done the workers a bit of good. Respectable unions make the bosses happy. . . .[57]

With no support from the labor federations, it was necessary now for the party to intensify its Negro campaign. The dialectic of class warfare was easily twisted to race warfare, though Marx and Lenin had said practically nothing about race. The manifold injustices to the American Negro gave plenty of material. A DuSable (Bronzeville) edition of the (Sunday) *Worker* was planned and would soon come out (February, 1950). The party would talk as though it alone were concerned with Negro welfare, though the CIO had always fought for civil rights and would continue to do so.

In October, 1949, UPWA District One took an important step. It moved the District headquarters from Back-of-the-Yards to 49th and Wabash, the heart of Bronzeville. They took over the financially distressed Communist International Workers' Order building (known as the DuSable Community Center) where there was plenty of space for offices, bar, store, and very large auditorium. This would make an excellent community center from which the party could carry on its drive to convert Bronzeville to "the dictatorship of the proletariat," conveniently financed by workers in the Swift, Armour, Wilson and other packing plants.

The fact that the Packinghouse Workers' Labor Center, as it was now called, was nearly two miles from the Yards and was in a neighborhood where white workers (almost half of the UPWA bargaining units) would hesitate to go, at least at night, and that there were other buildings available nearer the Yards, made no difference. Once again the motive of "economy" was alleged, though the I.W.O. building was rather run down and cost around $45,000. (While it may be true that an outside real estate agent coincidentally recommended purchase of the I.W.O.

Hall, in view of the other facts, the conclusion is overwhelmingly forced upon us that the move of the District Hall to its new location was primarily motivated by the Communist party to serve its own ends.) The Wilson and Armour locals held almost all their meetings at the new Labor Center, and the Swift local often met there, even though it had a good hall right at the plant gates. Thus the Chicago locals became more and more "Negro unions" getting little or no white participation. While in fairness we must admit that this trend had begun long before the move, yet the move greatly accentuated it.

Now the red lid was off in Bronzeville. It is interesting to note the left-wing zeal of District One and Local 28 at the new Labor Center:[58]

1950, February

> Lodge 751 of the Lincoln Douglas Society of left-wing International Workers' Order has offices at District Packinghouse Center.
>
> *Daily Worker's* press banquet at District HQ.

April

> Progressive Party convention at HQ.
>
> Armour local officer a leader in Chicago Labor Conference for Peace (CP).

June

> (Left-wing) National Trade Union Conference for Negro Rights endorsed by Local 28 and held at HQ and attended by expelled CIO unions:[59] UE-FE, Mine, Mill, Smelter, FTA, Longshoremen, etc. (This was violating UPWA Resolution No. 18 [60] of the 1950 convention which endorsed CIO policy in expelling these unions and promised support against them.)

July

> CP Stockholm Peace Petition circulated by Local 28 in plant.
>
> Local 28 employs office-girl member of United Office and Professional Workers, one of the expelled unions. (Violation of Resolution No. 18.)
>
> Local 28 begins to use District HQ more and more for parties and meetings.
>
> Local 28 takes up and follows (along with District) the exact party line on the new Korean War.
>
> District joins in "peace" rally with UE-FE, Mine, Mill and Smelter unions, etc.
>
> Sam Parks, Secretary-Treasurer of District One is candidate for Congress in Bronzeville area for the Communist supported Progressive party.

October

> Local 28 votes funds to send Charles Proctor, its Chairman of Grievance Committee to CP. International Peace Conference, moved from London to Warsaw, including "conducted tour" of Moscow, etc.
>
> Local 28 supports Parks for Congress — Progressive party ticket.

November

Progressive party cabaret party at HQ.

December

Midwest Bill of Rights Conference at HQ. Gil Green, one of 11 national CP leaders, talked along with Herb March.

1951, February

Robeson concert-rally at District HQ.

District One Communists planned a half-day walk-out in Yards to picket Chicago Wage Stabilization Board. This was in violation of union contracts. President Helstein called it off, despite District One.

March

William Z. Foster Birthday Ball at HQ. (Foster is national chairman of CPUSA.)

Labor Youth League-CP-Dance at HQ.

CP strike talk to force Wage Board action.

May

Ernest de Maio, District Director of expelled UE and Lester Davis, Secretary of Illinois Civil Rights Congress (CP) talk at HQ.

Testimonial dinner for Claude Lightfoot, new member of National Committee of CP at HQ.

May Day Rally: Elizabeth Gurley Flynn, top CP leader, and Herb March, UPWA District Organizer, speak at Ashland Auditorium.

June

All Nations Salute Rally with Negro Labor Council (CP supported) and Midwest Committee for Foreign Born (CP supported) along with expelled CIO unions at HQ.

Entire executive board of Armour Local 347 support big (CP supported) national conference for Peace Rally at Coliseum, the "cultural events" of which were held at District HQ, July 1.

Clearly, the Packinghouse Labor Center had become a nest of Communist activity, and only incidentally a trade union hall. District union leader H, when asked about Communist activity at the Center, stated:

We need money. We rent to anybody, Twenty-second ward Republicans, Democrats, Communists. We don't believe in discriminating.

If the Ku-Klux-Klan, the racist White Circle League, or a Fascist group should apply, this union leader quite possibly would discriminate. However, he would not think of discriminating against the Communists, their "brothers under the skin."

This Communist misleadership succeeded in accentuating the decline of white participation in Local 28. After the 1948 strike and the Communist seizure of the local, Local 28 became predominantly colored in membership — 72 per cent colored, though the bargaining unit was only

55 per cent colored. This was a serious problem for the local, since a healthy union needs to get all eligible members signed up, and needs to tap all sources of leadership and responsibility.

In the AFL organizing days of 1917–1921, Negroes did not want to wear a union button in the Yards, but in 1951 the tables were curiously reversed. The whites were the ones who hung back. Said Tony Bachacci, a white worker of short service, a union member, and a craftsman, who participates rarely in union affairs:

> The union is for the colored. Forty per cent of the whites are out. Only n——s are in the union. Lewis [the union president] holds dances. That's out! Also they ought to keep the union out of politics. Then they have their meetings over at Indiana Avenue. [District Headquarters at Wabash Avenue.] The colored — you can't trust 'em. Yet they're all right in the gang. . . . I do believe in the union and I don't believe in it. Ain't done much for a man. Takes the poor man's money. . . .

Back in 1920, it was just the opposite. "J.L.," a foreman in a box factory stated to one of the Chicago Commission on Race Relations interviewers:

> Unions ain't no good for a colored man, I've seen too much of what they don't do for him. I wouldn't join for nothing — wanted me to join one at the Yards but I wouldn't; no protection: if they had been, the colored men who belonged might have worked while the riot was going on: only thing allowed out there then was foreigners. If a thing can't help you when you need help, why have it? That's the way I feel about unions. I tell you they don't mean nothing for me.[61]

The Communist party in its efforts to win the Negro packinghouse workers, was willing to sacrifice bi-racial participation in the Chicago locals. In spite of all their efforts the Communists failed to capture the Negro packinghouse workers or for that matter American Negroes generally.[62] But they did capture the leadership of the big Chicago locals. By 1952 much of the Communist activity in the Packinghouse Workers' Labor Center had gone elsewhere or quietly underground. The International UPWA was much cooler to such activity, and the party line of 1953 was one of coöperation rather than opposition.

Local 28 Conquers the Party. Right-wing forces in Swift Local 28 were still trying. Immediately after the Communist victory in 1949, Local 28 leaders formed a new right-wing coalition, called the "New Committee for CIO." This did not include former President Pitts or Chief Steward Gantt, leaders of the Local 28 revolt, who had withdrawn in disgust to "wait and see," and who would not touch this new effort with a ten-foot pole. The International, however, stepping into this new internal fight in Local 28, opposed the New Committee as "disrupters" and supported the left wing. Failing to win the important "election committee" elections, the New Committee also failed in January, 1950, to recapture the leadership of Local 28. The left wing won again by a narrow margin. The party was now entrenched in Local 28.

The 1950 Minneapolis convention of the UPWA was host to Philip Murray and Allan S. Haywood of the CIO, both of whom strongly urged the current CIO purge of Communists who were attempting to use the trade unions for their own ends of world revolution. It was evident at this time how curiously complicated and ambiguous was the political structure of the International UPWA. But it is not our purpose to discuss the International UPWA except insofar as it had dealings with the Swift-CIO plant community.

The right-wing opposition in Local 28 had now seemingly collapsed. In the next local elections in January, 1951, the left-wing officers won easily with almost no opposition. But the right-wingers never gave up. In spite of factionalism in their own ranks, they began an intensive campaign to win back their local from the control of leftist District One. They were aided by the mistakes of the left-wing officers themselves who made exaggerated demands and claims in the plant community. In addition there were charges of misappropriation of local union funds. Finally some of the fellow-travelers among the officers caught on to the real objectives of the Communist party and deserted the party line. For these reasons, along with the fact that the International UPWA kept hands off and the Local 28 leftists could get help only from District One, the right-wing group did the "impossible" and won a majority of offices in the January elections of 1952. The election itself was disputed, but the run-off election gave the right wing the edge of control.

Ever consolidating their position, the Local 28 right-wingers were able to win a clean sweep in the elections of January 1953. Thus in less than four years the pendulum swung from right to left and back to right. This is a rare occurrence in American trade unionism, for once the party gains control it is very difficult to dislodge, sometimes requiring a dual union to be formed. (Witness the failure of the steelworkers to win back the Mine, Mill and Smelter Workers.) The credit must go largely to the good sense, hard work, courage and CIO-mindedness of the various groups of right-wing leaders and workers in Local 28 itself. Their example may encourage the right-wingers in the big Armour and Wilson locals in Chicago. For these locals are still firmly in the hands of the Communist party.

The long struggle over the governance of the Chicago plant community demonstrates three prominent facts. First, the hardy and persistent desire of the workers for self-organization around their jobs. The Knights of Labor rose and fell, but the Amalgamated came in their place. The Amalgamated had a roller-coaster career, yet it perdured, with its last loop up. Local 28 suffered a crisis — the 1948 strike, the fight with the District and International, the two unions in the plant, the influx of Communist leadership, the problem of white participation, yet the workers of the Swift-CIO plant community still want a union, as the interviews clearly show.

The second fact is this: Swift's historic opposition to bilateral union-ism, as we have seen, along with that of almost all American manage-ment, tended to make that very unionism itself more aggressive and mili-tant. Most of the original PWOC and Local 28 organizers and leaders can remember company opposition to the AFL of the first World War days, or at least have heard the tradition about it. And almost to a man, they faced keen opposition and suspicion, at least at the foreman level, in their first CIO efforts to organize the Yards.

The third fact is the persistent presence of disunity and radicalism among packinghouse union leaders. Factionalism has often dogged the footsteps of American labor. Some of it can be a good thing, providing challenge. Too much of it can mean simply union insecurity which so easily leads to overaggressiveness or wasteful jurisdictional rivalry. As for radicalism, some of it was necessary to overcome the entrenched opposi-tion of management. But the excesses hurt, not helped. The Haymarket anarchists only hurt the incipient Knights of Labor in the Yards. Debs' radical European-modeled general strike of 1894 only forced labor un-derground. It was the hot-heads who forced Mike Donnelly to reopen a strike that was almost won in 1904. It was Foster and his I.W.W.'s who split the Yards against the Amalgamated in 1919. Finally, it was the Communist "trigger unionists," who, loving agitation and scorning "busi-ness unionism," for nearly four years brought class warfare and disrup-tion into the Swift Chicago-UPWA plant community. Indeed, these left-wingers still threaten the unity and security of the UPWA today. Again we may speculate what the present would be if factional hot-heads could have been controlled by "labor statesmen" in the past. The chances are the Amalgamated would be the unique union in packing today.

What about the future? If Swift management grows in acceptance of the UPWA, not just as a powerful nuisance "here to stay," but as a kind of partner — at least in the governing of the plant community — and if, in turn, the union can eliminate its Communist agitators and develop trade-unionist leaders in their stead, then labor-management relations at the plant level will greatly improve. At the international-chain level, relations are already rather good. As we shall develop later, these pro-visos may eventually mean stronger union security provisions for Local 28. They might also mean the fusing of the Amalgamated Meat Cutters and the UPWA, though this juncture is unlikely at present. As we shall see, the workers in the Swift-UPWA plant community do have "dual allegiance" to both company and union. So why can't they have local-union-company relations of "harmonious opposition"?

PART

II

WORKER AND COMPANY IN ACTION

CHAPTER FOUR

THE COMPANY AND THE MEN

COMPANY ALLEGIANCE

Company allegiance is, of course, an abstraction. Each worker who possesses it does so concretely and in his own way. But one can abstract from each interview the common factor of allegiance, interpreted in this way: allegiance means "general satisfaction with the company as an institution," or "an attitude of favorability toward the company as an institution," or "general approval of the company and its policies." [1] Although the word allegiance may not perfectly describe these attitudes, it comes closer than such words as approval, loyalty, attachment, endorsement, or identification, and we must ask the reader to stretch his own conception to include our definition.

Allegiance does not mean complete satisfaction with every aspect of the company, with the pay, job, wage-incentive system, with plant leadership and foremen, with chances for advancement and opportunities for one's children, with the harmony of the work gang, nondiscrimination, and general working conditions. These things will influence a worker in his attitude toward the company as an institution, but they do not constitute that attitude. The worker can and does make the distinction, for instance, between his attitude to the foreman and to the company. Dissatisfaction with some of the above categories is still compatible with a favorable attitude toward the company.

Secondly, company allegiance does not necessarily mean loyalty to the company in the sense of strong volitional or emotional attachment, or ego-involvement in the affairs of the company, as Gustavus Swift certainly had and as many of the present executives have. This brings up the important question: what is the relationship between a worker's approving attitude to the company and his behavior toward the company?

Not all attitudes affect behavior in the same degree — much depends on the volitional and emotional content of the attitude. In the following interviews it became apparent that attitudes toward the company varied from slight emotional-volitional content at one extreme to real loyalty or ego-involvement at the other, with most of the workers distributed evenly between the two extremes. As described in Chapter One, the workers were graded for their attitudes of favorability or unfavorability, a grading which inevitably involves some emotional-volitional content. Though workers who are very favorable or very unfavorable will have a higher emotional content than those who are neutral, with consequent greater effect on their behavior, company allegiance affects the behavior of some workers in the plant community very little, of others, very much, and of most of them, only partially. The interviewer did not grade the workers on such company behavior as punctuality, discipline, coöperation, etc., but there was over-all information about the sample and the work force from statistics, observation, and comments by foremen and fellow workers.

In general, company allegiance is a factor affecting better workmanship, but even this cannot be stated as an inflexible rule. Take Jorel Byron, for instance, a middle-service beef-butcher, who states:

> Swift & Company is one of the greatest industrials in the world. It has grown up from just a little red wagon. You can praise Gustavus Swift. I have nothing against Swift company as a whole. I am only against the management and superintendents who don't understand the people. But the Swifts themselves have been great people. They have 45,000 stockholders. . . .

Byron was one of the most complicated personalities interviewed. While he could be rated as having a very favorable attitude toward the company as an institution, he dislikes both his job and his foreman and is known as a trouble-maker in his department. He is an efficient worker, but his company allegiance does not make him a very coöperative one. He is exceptional, however, rather than typical. For Byron, his company allegiance is offset by his attitude toward his foreman and job.

The second reason why it is hard to pin down the effect of company allegiance on company behavior is that no single attitude, like company allegiance, is enough to explain all behavior toward the company. For this reason we have established a method of investigating other important variables such as attitudes toward the job, foreman, and union, and also the influence of race, sex, service, as explained in Chapter One, in order to weigh our general conclusions more precisely.

Letting our random sample speak for the plant population, the over-all attitude of the work force toward the company is between favorable and very favorable, 1.6 on our scale. Such results were not unexpected. Our preliminary investigations around the Yards made them seem probable. Company allegiance is a fact.

The workers vary among themselves, of course, in degree of company allegiance.[2] We see from Table 13 that men and women, long-service and short- and middle-service workers differ from each other. And we know

TABLE 13

Workers' attitudes toward company

(Random, stratified sample of 192 workers by service, sex, and race: 1950)

Men			Women	
Negro	White		Negro	White
1.90 (least)	1.52	short service	1.25	1.38
1.58	1.77	middle service	1.25	1.63
1.48	1.42	long service	1.13 (most)	1.13 (most)

Totals (Weighted in proportion
to population)   Attitude Scale

Men	1.62	
Women	1.32	
Negro	1.66	1.0 Very favorable
White	1.52	2.0 Favorable
Short service	1.73	3.0 Neutral
Middle service	1.64	4.0 Unfavorable
Long service	1.43	5.0 Very unfavorable
Union members	1.60	
Non-union members	1.60	
All workers	1.58	

from our statistical analysis of variance that those two differences would almost never happen by chance. In other words, they are statistically significant. Just why women and old-timers should have more company allegiance we shall see presently. There is no significant difference between the attitudes of the colored and white workers. The most favorable groups are the white and colored women of long service. The colored men of short service are the least favorable relative to the others, though they too are clearly favorable. It is interesting to note that there is no difference in attitude toward the company according to union membership. In other words, being on, or off, the union checkoff does not affect company allegiance.

TABLE 14

Distribution of attitudes to company

(Unstratified random sample of 202 workers: 1950)

Very favorable	1.0	☐──────────────────────────────☐ 85
	1.5	☐─────────☐ 25
Favorable	2.0	☐───────────────────☐ 68
	2.5	☐──☐ 9
Neutral	3.0	☐───☐ 13
	3.5	▮ 1
Unfavorable	4.0	0
	4.5	0
Very unfavorable	5.0	▮ 1

A frequency distribution of the attitudes toward the company shows remarkably few dissatisfied workers: 187 out of 202 workers, or 92 per cent, of the random sample have some positive allegiance to the company. Only one per cent are clearly unfavorable.

The objection might be made that such a remarkable record of allegiance does not really indicate approval of the company as an institution, but simply an unconscious or conscious means of ego-defense, since the worker, being chained to the company for life, is driven to love his chains. For instance, if the worker said: "I hate the company," he would be admitting that he was chained to something he hated and was living a frustrated work life. He would be admitting his inadequacy, his failure to get a job or find a company that he liked. But being afraid to admit his failure, he pretends to like what he really hates.

Our answer to this objection is to recall our definition of allegiance. It does not mean that this 92 per cent are completely satisfied with everything on their jobs, but simply that they are satisfied with the company as an institution. This distinction will become clearer when we quote the actual interviews. Any such latent content as an unconscious or conscious company "disallegiance" as a means of ego-defense is not evident for the great majority of the people, judging from this part of the interviews and from their total interviews.

The manifest-latent distinction of interview content is important. In the next chapter on the man and his job this will be evident, and in Chapter Eleven on the company wage-incentive system, it will be clearly asserted, where the worker's latent discontent with being an assembly-line robot emerges fully. But here there is little evidence to support a latent discontent with the company as an institution. The company allegiance we find in these interviews is extraordinary and testifies to Swift's progressive and successful personnel policy.

TABLE 15

Attitudes toward the company
(*Special sample groups: 1950*)

Group	Degree of Company Allegiance
Foremen	1.6
Right-wing Union Leaders	1.6
Steward body	2.0
Left-wing Union Leaders	2.3

When we consider other groups in the plant community such as foremen and stewards, we notice a difference at once. Note that both foremen and right-wing local union leaders have the same degree of favorability toward the company as the work force in general, 1.6, between very favorable and favorable. Apparently being a foreman or union leader does not affect one's allegiance beyond simply being a worker. But the steward body (partly left-wing), and the left-wing union leaders are significantly less favorable. This is what we would expect, either because of their greater identification with the union or because of their class-war bias. On the average, however, these groups are also favorable to the company as an institution in spite of any doctrinaire position that some of their members may hold. Of the steward group, 12 per cent are unfavorable to the company. Significantly, the entire 12 per cent consists of Negroes who consider they have been discriminated against and who feel very strongly about the race question.

Long-service employees and women employees seem to be strongest in company allegiance, as they are weakest in union allegiance. There are three main factors which affect the picture of the "simple-hearted loyal old-time employee": (1) the old-timers' longer opportunity for experiencing fair company treatment; (2) the dropping out of unfavorable workers through the years; (3) the old-timers' greater age, conservatism, maturity, lesser formal education, and frequently, foreign or southern birth.

Likewise, five main factors seem to affect the company allegiance of women: (1) the women have a comparative pay advantage at Swift over jobs outside, especially the clerical jobs so common to women; (2) since women do not wish advancement into supervision, there is no frustration at lack of promotion; (3) the early afternoon quitting time (3:30 P.M.) means more to the women than the men, since they are usually concerned with home management as well; (4) women in general do not have the jobs with difficult work conditions; (5) the foremen may often be more polite to the women than to the men.

To put flesh and bones on all these factors, let us listen to four workers of the plant community. First, Elizabeth Washington. Mrs. Washington works in the Lard Refinery feeding cans in a conveyor line. She comes from Oklahoma, is well up in her fifties, and has been with the company over twenty-five years. She says:

> I found Swift & Company to be all right in every respect. . . . It's one of the top rank concerns. They're more for their employees than any other company. They try to do the right thing for them. They are a leading company — they pay more.

> *Interviewer:* How is your pay, Mrs. Washington?

> It's okay. I don't go out much. I lead a simple life. Always can save something. . . . About the bonus system, they have no bonus elsewhere. Yet they work as hard as we do. Other companies don't have it.

> *Interviewer:* How do you feel about your foreman?

> Both are pretty nice. Both are G.I.'s. You have to understand them. I know. I had a son who would get nervous at times. Everything works out

all right. The whole thing is truth. If you coöperate, everything's all right.
. . . There was a man burned out last week. [Fires are a constant
menace in crowded Bronzeville.] His name was Jacob Riddell. He went
to the [local] union for help, but ———— told him: "We have no money
for that kind of thing." The Industrial Relations tried to help him right
away. Other companies don't do that. People should appreciate that —
the little things. They should know they are working for one of the best
companies. I'm not saying it just because I work here either. A couple
of times I was sick. A lady from the Industrial Relations came out and
asked me what I needed. . . . They bring coal to people who need it.
When you're sick you get half-pay and E.B.A. [insurance]. Other companies haven't got that. Armour hasn't got nothin' like that. We're privi-
leged to talk to the superintendent. At Armour you got to have a committee.

It was evident to me that Elizabeth Washington has a high degree of
company allegiance — even real ego-involvement and loyalty. It casts
some light on the relationship between allegiance and behavior to hear
Mrs. Washington say she had gotten up at five o'clock every morning for
twenty-eight years to get to work on time. She was against the 1948 strike
and returned to work before the end of it even though she was stopped
twice at the picket lines. Her attitude toward the union is ambivalent;
she is trying to be loyal to it. We shall return to her union views in a
later chapter. The case of Jacob Riddell, which had happened shortly
before the interview, impressed Mrs. Washington greatly. The time-tried
concern of Swift & Company for the welfare of its people was one of the
leading reasons for her high company allegiance.

Next, Hermann Birkenhauer. Mr. Birkenhauer is a skilled mechanic.
He was born in Germany, is now in his sixties and has been with the
company over thirty years. He says:

I'd like to work here or I wouldn't be here so long. I raised five children
by Swift & Company. . . . There have been changes in those thirty-two
years. Oh, yes! It's like an office now. The plant is clean. For the butchers,
things are more sanitary than ever. They used to have only nails on the
partitions for your clothes. Now they got lockers and showers, and cleaner
toilets. . . . I was a harness maker. I learned upholstering, varnishing and
painting in Germany under a master. I've enjoyed my life.

Interviewer: How about your pay?

I'm satisfied. I make $1.62 an hour. I own my home. It's all paid up. I
can't kick. My wife likes to work in the garden. . . .

Interviewer: How do you get along with the foreman and the gang?

I'm satisfied with my foreman. He doesn't misuse me or nothing. Of
course, you have to step on the gas. If a man doesn't produce, the company couldn't make money. . . . The gang is fine. I get along with
anybody — colored or no coloreds, it's all the same to me. The colored
people are not like white people — they take their time — but they're all
right.

Interviewer: Do you like your job?

Oh, yes, I like it. I repair smokehouse machinery. My feet bother me sometimes. Blood don't circulate the way it should. I've had no layoffs though. I'm always interested in my job. . . . I don't think there can be a better company than Swift & Company. And I've worked in different places. Their sick benefits are good. . . .

Mr. Birkenhauer, who is very close to retirement, gave me the over-all impression of being a conscientious workman, very content with the decent living he has made, and quite satisfied with the company as an institution. Like Mrs. Washington, he is a union man, but against the 1948 strike. He returned to work before its end. Mr. Birkenhauer is a good example of our picture — the loyal old-timer. No doubt, most of the factors we listed above have influenced Mr. Birkenhauer to his high degree of company allegiance.

Next, Mary Radak. Miss Radak is an unskilled salami packer. She is in her forties and has been with Swift just seven years. She was born in America and finished seventh grade at school:

Interviewer: Where did you work before you came to Swift's, Miss Radak?

I worked in a beauty shop for awhile. Then at Western Electric.

Interviewer: How did you like it at Western Electric?

Well, there was more position work there. More strain on your eyes. Your posture was cramped. I was coil winding. It was tense. I was there nine years. [She was there during the field work of the Roethlisberger-Dickson research of 1925–1934.] You felt like you were in jail. If there were any words, you were called into the office and called down. They were very strict — so much discipline. Here, there's more freedom. . . . Here I feel right. Their personnel [foremen] are very nice. It's one of the best places in the Yards to work. And there are more benefits.

Interviewer: What job do you have here?

I'm a packer. I pack salami. It's very nice. I like it. Easy, not hard work. And clean. The bosses are pretty nice.

Interviewer: That's good. So you've got a pretty good foreman?

There are all kinds of foremen. They've got to understand different human beings. Women are different from men. I worked before at Armours as a girl. Now the personnel [supervisors] are more intelligent. . . . The lowest type of people worked in the Yards in those days. Not any more. You used to be ashamed. But there are intelligent people here now. I'm not ashamed to tell people I work in the Yards now. . . . Billings [her foreman] is one of the nicest fellows. I don't think I could find a better foreman than him. He understands you. He's a quiet person. You have your own personal things to tell him. And he looks at your point of view. He is very helpful. . . . It's not your people higher up — they're there on merit — they're trying to make this a good place. It's the intermediate, smaller bosses — trying to get ahead — the ones who don't know how to treat people, especially women. They should treat her like a *woman* even though she does work in the Yards.

Interviewer: I'd be interested to know what you think about your pay, Miss Radak.

I make $1.09. The pay is much better. The Yards are paying better than places outside. I have to help support my mother.

Interviewer: Can you save anything?

Oh yeah. Of course, you have to live on a budget. You should always save. . . . I get a pretty fair salary for a woman. [She made around $2500 in 1949.]

Mary Radak has a strong company allegiance due to her satisfaction with company policy, her job, pay, and most of the supervisors. Gentlemanly treatment by the foreman is an important point in her mind. Her attitudes are similar to those of many of the women workers and help to explain their somewhat greater company allegiance.

A final example, Mary Ellen Jones. Mrs. Jones is an old employee, being with the company twenty-five years. She is fifty-five, of little schooling, unskilled, doing utility work, such as washing pans, in one of the sausage departments:

Interviewer: How are the bosses around here, Mrs. Jones?

For my foreman's part, he is very nice. He's all right. If you go to work, you don't go to sit down. I'm satisfied. I *like* evvybody. . . . As a girl in Georgia, I brake corn stalks.

Interviewer: What's your job now?

I washes pans and do utility work. I like it fine, I do it right. Things should be clean.

Interviewer: Indeed they should. How's the pay for your job?

I gets $1.04 an hour. My idea is I ought to get more. I can save only now and then. [She made around $2400 in 1949.] . . .

Interviewer: What's your opinion about Swift & Company, Mrs. Jones?

I love Swift & Company. I love my foremens. Evvybody knows me. Sometimes I wash and iron shirts for the foremens. Also I help the foremens' wives. I've went to their houses. . . .

Perhaps Mrs. Jones belongs to another generation. Doubtless many younger workers would differ with her. But there are not a few long-service workers like her. She is devoted to the company and devoted to her job. Company allegiance comes naturally to her. She helps us to understand why the long-service employees have such a high degree of company allegiance.

THE IMPORTANCE OF JOB SECURITY

The workers give many reasons for liking Swift & Company: fair treatment, better foremen, more pay, pensions, sick pay, insurance, cleaner plant, convenience to home, but the reason most often mentioned, apparently most important of all, is steady work — Swift gives steady work, and that is what the worker wants. This prime desire is no doubt founded on the worker's bitter experience of the Depression, and especially of the constant layoffs, plant shutdowns and plant openings that especially bedevil unskilled laborers. Many of the unskilled packinghouse workers live an almost nomadic life. "Labor mobility" to the packinghouse worker, who often has small savings and large bills, who must support his family in the short run as well as in the long run, means frustration, discouragement, anxiety, and even bitterness.

Surprisingly, almost all the workers who mentioned security of employment were Negroes, especially of short service. The colored worker knows the meaning of that phrase: "Last to be hired, first to be fired." Also the short-service worker is closer to his insecure days before he earned enough service to have plant-wide seniority at Swift.

John Oswald, 40, three years north from Mississippi, loader of freight cars with steel drums, trying to support a family of six on "common labor" rating ($1.15 an hour in 1949 plus premium pay), says:

> Swift & Company is a good place to work. In the ———— House, where I work, they don't lay off much. It's pretty *steady*.

Says Robert Jackson, navy veteran, shipping supply man, 27, whose wife works at Armour though they have two young children (watched by the lady next door during the day):

> Swift is a very nice company to work for. There's a pension plan — they have been havin' that a long time. And when the union goes in for a contract, Swift is one of the first to sign. . . . My wife has been six years at Armours. My wife said Swift was one of the best packinghouses out here. You get better breaks. She wishes she started at Swift. They have no *plantwide seniority*. Swift does. It's a good system. It's nice.

Some middle-service men[3] state: "Swift & Company is one of the best. They go by *seniority*. You can always make a little money here." . . . "The company is a good place to work. It's better than Wilsons and Armours where my in-laws work. You got *steady* employment here" . . . "It's a pretty nice system, this *seniority*. They transfer you to other departments. At Armours it's a rough system. Swift is much better. I advise my friends to come here."

We notice how often company allegiance and job security are expressed in a comparative way, the worker compares Swift with other firms such as U. S. Steel, Harvester, Crane, Wilson and Armour. Most of the "mobile" packinghouse workers have had several jobs before they came to Swift. And since (perhaps uniquely in American industry), the different packers are concentrated in one part of Chicago, around the Union Stock Yards, what goes on in one firm becomes known to the workers in the next plant. When Swift workers claim their company as the best in the Yards, this could be due to "natural pride" in the place to which they have committed themselves. But these statements are so over-whelmingly frequent that they are doubtfully due to mere "company pride," especially since many Swift workers have actually worked in the other companies or have relatives now working there. (We did not test whether workers in Armour or Wilson would make similar statements about their companies, but judging from the few of such workers we did meet, it is improbable.)

Some of the old-time colored workers continue this same theme about security of employment. Tractor driver James Ratcliffe, who had only one year of schooling years ago in the south, is fairly satisfied with his long years with Swift, though he finds his $1.33 an hour (1949) thins out on the $20 rent he pays weekly for one room in Bronzeville:

> Since 1917 I been here. By that I must have liked the job. Only had one *layoff* in that time. . . . Swift is about the best company I've worked for since I been out here. Armour and Wilson don't give a man a break as good as Swift does — lay a man off after years, or to keep 'em from getting a vacation.

Dignified Philip Elder, ham-pickler in his sixties and near retirement, looks back over a quarter of a century to say:

> I first knew Swift & Company in Alabama. There was a small branch house there. I had my first job with Swift in 1916 in New Jersey. I broke service for eight months to work with McCormick Foundry. In June, 1921, I came to Swift here. . . . It's about the finest place I've ever worked. I don't look to take the boss' job. I do my work. If I stayed here, I had a job *steady*. So no use to change.

Not all the workers who are concerned with job security are colored; there are also a few white workers who mention it. Take, for instance, Lithuanian immigrant, Mary Mikalauskas, 50, a pork-trimmer. She has to support her two children, since her husband drinks. Neither son wants to work in the Yards. Mrs. Mikalauskas is very company-minded:

> I never find a better company than Swift. It's the best company in the Yards. I was work at Armours. I no like. I get *laid off*. Bosses different there. Everybody different there.

Stephanie Ogwicz, another long-service pork-trimmer echoes the same sentiments: "Swift *don't lay off*. Armour lays you off. Also they give you a pension at Swifts; they don't at Armours." Elevator-operator, Rudolph Zema, with Swift only seven years though fifty-five years old, well enough off financially to retire, says:

> Swift 'bout the best company in Chicago, I been try all over. Armour is rotten place — breaking *seniority* all time. Wilson same thing. You can ask any employee. Swift better. . . . At Steel, they put awful high pressure on you. Always behind you. After three years no good. . . .

Not every worker, however, finds that Swift & Company has provided the stability he wants. Elder Drake, 52, shipping clerk in the sausage factory, says:

> I'm fifty-two. To me, Swift is a good place to work. If I was twenty-one, I would try elsewhere. For a very simple reason — nothing seems to be stationary out here. Never know if you going to make forty hours [a week] or twenty hours. 'Course you got a guarantee [of thirty-six hours]. But no peace of mind. It's not the fault of the company. It's the way conditions are. You get forty hours this week, thirty-six hours that week, then a layoff.

> *Interviewer:* Under plant-wide seniority, don't you get transfered to another department?

> Yes, but some have to go out on the street. I honestly think the company likes it no better than I do. But they can't change it. In the steelmills, conditions are about the same.

The UPWA deserves partial (though not exclusive) credit for the important seniority benefits introduced into the Swift-UPWA plant community. Local 28 organizer, Mr. Henry Schoenstein laments: "The union helped to build up company allegiance because it got and helped seniority — so vital to the people — and for which people now give credit to the company. Seniority didn't mean nothin' until it had been policed." The distinction between what happens on paper in the general office and what happens between people in the plant must not be forgotten. At the same time, Swift must be given credit for spontaneously beginning a definite seniority program as early as 1924.[4]

FAIR TREATMENT AND OTHER FACTORS

After job security as the important factor in company allegiance, we find a variety of other factors, also important, but following no special pattern and varying with individuals. The foremen, of course, play an important role in bringing about company allegiance. This connection is not often made explicit in the interviews. But some workers bring it out. Wilbur Reidy, elevator-operator and truck-pusher, mentions it:

> I would say Swift Company is pretty nice. . . . A lot of things happen and a fella brings it on himself. . . . The foremen are pretty nice. If you want a favor you can get it. If you go along, nine out of ten fellows go along with you. . . . The foremen are pretty good to the mens in a way of speakin'.

Francis Buda, 36, a father of four, middle-service check-scaler, is not too satisfied with his foreman, but has company allegiance because he feels he can go over his foreman's head:

> My foreman? All he's got on his mind is *production*. He never compliments anybody. He's trying to get ahead too soon. If you're doing all right he

just looks in and goes. Praise never hurts anybody. But if you're behind
he drives! I don't talk to foreman much. Get into arguments. There are no
compliments for him around our department. . . . Swift & Company is
a good place to work. No trouble. Sometimes they are not responsible
for their foremen. But if you go over to the office, they'll treat you okay.

Many other factors influence company allegiance. And we must remember that such allegiance is not at all incompatible with dissatisfaction
about some aspects of the job. George Hahn, 59, utility man in one of the
rendering tank rooms, dissatisfied about Negroes' chances for advancement says:

> I find Swift to be one of the *fairest* companies I've ever worked for. . . .
> [Yet Mr. Hahn distrusts the company monthly magazine, *Swift News.*] I
> very seldom read it. They're always talkin' about costs, labor costs and so
> on. I can't be bothered. They figure to keep people satisfied. To console
> the help. To keep 'em thinking they're gettin' some place an' they're not.
> [Advancement ceilings for Negroes.] [5]

Company concern for the welfare of sick workers is a repeated factor
in forming company allegiance. Fair treatment and sincere charity at
such a time of crisis in one's life generally make a deep and lasting impression, as we saw before, for instance, in the case of Elizabeth Washington. Oswald Zemrad, fire box repair man, 40, European-born, was
impressed with the treatment he received:

> Swift is a pretty nice place to work. I was sick a couple of times and the
> company treated me pretty good. I got half pay. I kept my job.
>
> *Interviewer:* So Swift is a good place to work?
>
> It's good for me. I also got better treatment here than on the Chicago
> Surface Lines [where he previously worked]. There the foremen stay
> on your back all the time. 'Course maybe they're better there now.

Cheerful Carlos Robledo, 43, happy in spite of considerable need for
money, pork-butcher, gives the same reason:

> I want to say, Father, Swift, eet is good place to work for. 'Course some-
> times . . . I got nine kids. One in service. Just came back from Korea.
> Sometime ago I started to slow down. One of my boys can help me a
> little now, but I'm afraid he may get drafted. . . . It's another good
> thing about Swift Company — they help their men when they get sick.
> Last month I was sick. Twenty days off. Blue Shield, Blue Cross — all
> that helps. . . . It's a good place to work. I like to work here. It's seven
> years since I came here. No trouble.

Canned-meat machine-operator, Emma Lee, short-service employee, continues the same theme of satisfaction with kind treatment:

> I used to work for a baking company. But my boy friend worked at
> Armour's so I stopped in here. It's the best job I've had. I love working
> for Swift & Company. It's the greatest company there is. I wouldn't quit
> for Wilson or Armour. Swift are first one always to do the best thing.

They're nice to their people when they're sick at home. . . . At the Employment Office they're nice and kind. At Armour's they bite your head off.

Joanne Haywood, bacon-packer, 45, four years with Swift, making good money and quite generally satisfied, states:

> I like working for Swift — very much. If you're ill, they treat you nice. If you call for their physician, they'll send him out. I broke my wrist once. Swift was nice. They sent a doctor and I got nice care. . . . Once I was a ladies' garment worker. Bad on my eyes and nerves. Had to come here. Another nice thing about Swift, they give you eye examinations and take care of your teeth. They'll extract them free. . . . I'm very satisfied, very much satisfied. Of course, everybody has different opinions.

Mrs. Willamae Potter, 29, pork-trimmer, says:

> Swift is a good place. I'd rather work at Swift's than any other place in the Yards. I got a cousin at Wilson's and friend at Armour's. It's bad over there — way she talks. *Swift had an Open House in 1947.* The food was free. It was very nice. They had soap flakes mixed up for decorations in one place. You could let your family see where you work. I worked that day and got double pay.

On the other hand, Louella Scott, sausage-roper, has quite a different reason for her company allegiance. She is thirty-two, quite well educated, having had some college, and a former union leader. She is not satisfied with everything, especially with a recent grievance she lost. Yet she says:

> Swift is an excellent place to work. You couldn't find a better place. During negotiations, Swift's *bargaining committee is the best to deal with.* We ought to have a union of all the Swift workers alone, without the Big Four. Swift always agreed, but . . . Armour and Wilson would hold out. . . . I believe in organized labor. If it wasn't for organized labor, the common workingman wouldn't be anywhere today.

Francis Connell, 44, long-service man, has clear though not enthusiastic allegiance for several reasons:

> With my limited education, my best bet is with Swift & Company. I've been seventeen years here. I've been treated fair. I could *talk to the bosses.* [Connell next told about his reaction when his foreman once assigned him an unpleasant job.] I can go higher than you [said Connell]. We had a friendly discussion. Not hot, but firm. I was going over to Swift's Industrial Relations to present my case. I had a feeling I could go all the way up in the general office. . . . I came here as a mechanic. We were a big family, and strangers. The Depression hit hard and as foreigners we could not get relief. My brother was here at Swift's. So I came here. I was a checker first. I tried later to get in the mechanical gang. There was a long delay, but after the war shortage of help I got in. . . . ———, my boss, told me: "You're wasting your time here. Go out and get a good job and make some money." I said: "No, half a loaf of bread is better than none." Insecurity was in the back of my mind. I was thinking of the Depression.

Middle-service checker and scaler, Mary Weidemann, 28, single and supporting her family, gives a different reason for her attitude toward the company:

> I worked at the dime store and at American Can. It's very nice here —
> much better. I will bring Kathryn, my sister, here to the general office for
> a job. I took shorthand and typing once. It was boring. I wanted to *get
> out where I could sing and shout. Education don't mean nothing.* [She is
> a high-school graduate.] I didn't like the Pork Trim [Department]. It's too
> "icky." In Sliced Bacon, they don't have as much fun as we do. I scale.
> I love to scale. I take keys out of a box with numbers on 'em. I stamp
> the numbers on the package. You can move around. I like my work. I
> don't like to stay at home.

Middle-service bacon-packer, Anna Pulaski, who came to work for Swift nine years ago at age twenty, favors the company in spite of the prestige problem of working in the Yards:

> I looked for an office job, but I had no experience and there were no
> opportunities. I worked at ———— Company for awhile. My brother works
> here and *I live near here,* so I came here. I can walk to work. I like it
> here pretty well. . . . Swift is good if you don't mind working in the
> Yards, if you're not proud. I'm not proud. My friends think it is funny to
> work in the Yards. They work in offices and dress nicer.

PENSIONS

As we have seen, Swift has had an outstanding noncontributory pension program for its plant workers ever since 1916. This is unique among the Big Four and rare in the entire industry. Neither the UPWA nor the Amalgamated Meat Cutters have as yet been able to spread pensions throughout the industry as the auto workers and steel workers have done. Thus the workers in the Swift-CIO plant community enjoy a pension benefit worth several cents an hour which the workers in the neighboring plants do not enjoy. Moreover the air is filled with pension talk these days. Under the circumstances, we might assume that pension benefits would be a considerable factor in bringing about preference for, and company allegiance to, Swift & Company. Such, however, is not the case. Few of the workers mention pensions as a factor in their allegiance. And in this case at least, we are entitled to argue from their silence. For pensions are something remote, rather abstract, and entirely unexperienced by the worker who is still on the job. Moreover, the pension issue has not been discussed much by the UPWA on the plant; there has been little publicity about it. Only a few employees mention pensions (we have seen some already), and they, naturally enough, are mostly long-service workers near pension age.

William Krawchuk, 63, millwright, says:

Swift & Company are the best place in the Yards. They have a pension. Wilson and Armour don't have it. [He does not know how much pension he will get.]

Bill Kaunas, 62, with Swift for thirty-three years, puts pensions first in talking about company benefits:

Swift is pretty good. From what I hear it's better than Armour's. We have pensions, Blue Cross, insurance, accident pay at one-half. . . .

Old-timer Henry Dvorak, 60, has spent forty-two years with the company, coming from Europe not so long after Gustavus Swift died. He says he was never laid off and never quit, and once a night foreman, he is now ending his service on a light janitor's job. His allegiance clearly merges into deep loyalty. Pensions are only one factor:

I like Swift's. . . . It's the best place in the Yards. Better than Armour or Wilson. [These comparisons continually crop up!] Armour pays no *pensions*. [Armour agreed to a pension program in 1952.] I never worked Armour or Wilson. But I hear that Swift is best. . . . I belong to company and company belongs to me. If anybody breaks anything, I don't like it. It's like my own home. . . . I don't like to argue with the foreman. He's got a boss too.

Alexander Thompson, 51, shipping clerk, well informed about company and union affairs, dissatisfied about chances for Negro advancement states:

Swift is very fine — tops of the five big packers. I'd tell anybody that even if they were going to shoot me the next minute. At Swift's you got *pensions,* compensations and liberal insurance. . . . Everything I own, I owe to Swift & Company.

On the other hand, we have the following, interesting, and atypical view of Kingsley Bennet, 59, middle-service mechanic, home-owner, of Irish and English descent:

I don't believe in pensions. I believe a man should work up to the end. Some can't stand pensions. They should have some jobs after 65 — inspectors, etc. They could have a separate department. Then the old-timers wouldn't be lonesome. I *may* get a pension. But I may have to go out and get a job. . . . Too much idleness is not good. [Bennet then brought up the question of work hours.] There used to be a twelve-hour day as against the eight-hour day we now have. I think we were just as well off then.

We see that for a few of the older workers the prospect of a pension is a definite factor in their company allegiance. But for most of the workers this is not the case. Although each worker upon his entrance into the company receives a booklet describing the pension program, the company has apparently not sufficiently advertised that pension program to its workers so that the program becomes important to them. Apropos of this, it is interesting to note that the Steelworkers sufficiently vitalized the remote pension issue with their members in 1949 to be able to call an industry-wide strike over it.

The leaders of the Swift-CIO plant community, the foremen, stewards, and union leaders, do not differ greatly from the other workers. But because of their positions of influence, and because of those differences they do show, we shall study their company allegiance separately.

The Foremen. The foremen mention fair treatment, consideration to the sick, pay, and security as factors in their allegiance. A significant minority mention treatment of the sick. Foreman James Drucker, for instance, came to Swift during the Depression; interested in his work and satisfied, he says:

> Swift is the best place I've ever worked. In 1949 I had *appendicitis.* They just left it up to you. "Whenever you feel like it, come back." The company has always been very *fair* with me, and I with them. . . . Security is the main thing. People are still afraid of another Depression.

Foreman Tommy Wallace was impressed with Swift's policy to the sick. Although his wife wanted him once to set up his own meat store, and he himself says he wouldn't come to Swift's if he had it to do over again, yet he says:

> Oh, I like Swift's. I was off *sick* once. And my pay came in just the same. They asked my wife if I needed help. My brother-in-law is coming from Ireland. My wife says: Let him get a job at Swift's, a job with security, E.B.A. etc. . . . Swift is one of the best packers.

Peter Mills, 54, over twenty-five years a Swift foreman, says:

> Swift's I don't think could be any better. As I get older, I read about my friends [outside] who get dropped. Here the boss transferred me from the ——— department. They are very democratic. Harold Swift started the Employee Representation Plan. He would sit on your desk and chew the rag with you. People speak to each other. I think they're real lenient with you. If you feel you can't come back [having been sick], they say don't come back. Or, sit at your desk and don't run around. It gives you a good feeling. . . . I had my first *sickness.* The company treated me very nice. Industrial Relations was very nice. They visited me, sent doctors, etc.

A younger foreman, Oliver Keighley, 34, who has advanced rapidly, and who is dissatisfied with his work force, the pay policy, and the "open door policy" (he says: "If you open your mouth, they'll open the door!"), is nevertheless quick to say:

> Still I say Swift & Company is an awful good place to work for. For instance, the way they've *handled old-timers* — like old Harris — helping him the way they did. And there are also other cases. Yes, if I had it to

do over, I'd come here again. [Harris was an intermediate supervisor who was quite sick for a long period and helped very much by the company.]

The Union Leaders. The right-wing leaders of Local 28 do not differ from the general work force in their degree of allegiance. Frank Goff, long-service skilled Swift worker, held a position of considerable influence and always refused to become a foreman. He has fair company allegiance:

> Swift likes to be thought respectable. They are hard to organize. They do have a moral standard. If you don't measure up, you don't get anywhere with them. . . . What do I think of Swift & Company? Well, I think enough of it to stay there. Is it very good? I wouldn't go that far. But the Swift administration isn't second to any. [Goff is very familiar with the organizational set-up of the Chicago plant.] . . . The foremen? The foremen are of no higher intellectual level than some of the workers. I could name some fine guys who are foremen. But the key guy is not the foreman. The operating superintendent is the key guy. Also the plant manager — it's a new job — who works for the president.

> *Interviewer:* What about your son, Frank? Would you want him here?

> No. The Yards have "tough elements." Who wants to be a butcher? Who wants to work in a cooler? The race question doesn't help it any. [Goff has done much to help Negro-white relations.] But who wants to work beside "jitterbugs"? You go down to their level.

An old spark plug of Local 28 leadership, Ted Kurowsky, dead set against some things like the bonus system, and a lover of controversy, says:

> What do I think of Swift? I'll tell you. It's the best of the packers. They've got a very shrewd management — very smart. Much shewder than Armour's. Armour's is run by Wall Street bankers. [Young Armour did lose out to the banks after the first World War.] Swift is still a family. They got family pride. It's a good company.

Harold Waite, 50, long-service man, skilled butcher, union leader, dissatisfied about foreman ceilings for Negroes, has some allegiance:

> Swift beats all packers, but not all industry. They try to be one step ahead of their employee. They're nice to him at one end, and dirty to him at the other.

Left-wing leaders are harder to assay in their company allegiance. At times they will talk as though the company were not really so bad after all, and then, as though suddenly realizing that such liberality is not according to Marx, they will quickly bring up some company fault that will secure the class-warfare dogma. Their dogma tells them that since capitalism is to be damned, the company must be all wrong. Their experience tells them differently. The result is a curious ambivalence that often intrudes upon their conversations about the company. As we saw, the case of Jorel Byron illustrates this. It is important to notice that these so-called "left-wing leaders" are not a monolithic group. While there are some convinced communists and fellow-travelers among them, there are also others (by no means sympathetic to communism) who are temporarily interested or just apathetic about the real intentions of the Communist leaders. These people "go along" with the key Communist leaders but do not take on their attitudes.

Tom Wade, another dynamic local leader, is about neutral in his company allegiance, though his behavior is consistently anticompany. He says:

> The head men of the company, Holmes and Richardson, are all right. They don't tolerate the foreman doin' the wrong thing. It's some foremen, the nasty little guys who are trying to get ahead!

Wade's motivations and attitudes are highly complex. If he did not have at least an attitude of neutrality toward the company as an institution, very likely his anticompany behavior would be even greater.

Hardly very enthusiastic is Jasper Collins, 47, long-service man and union leader who is just "going along":

> In my opinion, Swift is *slightly* better than the other packers. But like all the others, they're in it for all they can get out of it.

District union leader and leftist, Jake Vickers (who never worked for Swift) is more orthodox. He states:

> Swift wants to win its people. So it gives 'em a carrot instead of a club. [He is referring to Swift's wage-incentive system.] But Swift works its people harder than Armour or Wilson. I think the Swift worker is more *exploited*. So you see Swift gets it all back! [Vickers is a crusader against all forms of bonus system and of "speed up."]
>
> During the last strike [1948] Swift was 80 per cent in production by the end of the strike! The folding of the Swift plant demoralized the others. Armour workers saw the Swift workers going in the gates and on the "L." They had only a token picket line. They were demoralized. . . .
>
> Swift is paternalistic. They got sick leaves and pensions better than a lot of CIO plans. But Swift doesn't lose! They get more work out of their men. They pull stunts. If there's a good bonus on a certain job, they re-time-study it and cut it. Oh, there are a lot of loose ends at Swift's!

The Stewards. The stewards, some of whom go along with left-wing local leadership, while some oppose it, in general have company allegiance, though to a lesser degree than the work force in general. Steward Bill Ryan, 38, semiskilled in mechanical work, aggressive on grievances, states that:

> Swift is pretty good about layoffs. For the company itself, I'd rate it pretty good. But your foremen and general foremen — you run into good ones and bad ones! [He dislikes his general foreman.] Swift is better than Armour and Wilson. They go along with the employee and give him a break.

[Ryan doesn't want his son to work here.] I don't want my kid to work for any corporation. You're just a cog. A part of machinery. I want to give him a college education if possible.

Benjamin Evans, 44, janitor and rather slow of wit, new at being a union steward, has his own very human reason for company allegiance:

> Swift is a very good place to work. I used to be at a foundry with heavy lifting work. You expect that. I'll say this: Swift has convenience for the employees. That foundry didn't have no locker rooms. Things wasn't just like they should be. A man couldn't wear a nice suit to work. Had to get on a streetcar with your dirty clothes. Here you come to work *presentable*. People don't mind sitting beside you.

William Tarbuck, 45, high-school graduate, middle-service pork-handler, returns to our old theme for allegiance:

> Swift is a good place to work. More than one person says it's the best around here. If you're off *sick*, or get hurt, you get insurance. If death, the insurance is $4000. You get half pay if sick.

Short-service drum-filler, Jack Oates, 34, finding his pay swallowed up by high Bronzeville rents, is sold on the union movement. This influences his allegiance as follows:

> Swift is a pretty good company to work for. It's my pick among the four packers. I worked in Steel, and a freighthouse. It's 'bout the same there. Swift is better than Wilson. I can't see a company that don't want a union. [At this time, as a result of the 1948 strike, Wilson and the UPWA were in deadlock with no mutual contract recognized.] 'Course it's the people. They're afraid of their jobs. I wouldn't want my job that way! The union don't hurt the company. Union protects the workers, that's all.

The Top Union Leaders. The top union leaders (and we include the Amalgamated here along with the UPWA) have not worked in the Swift-CIO Chicago plant community and thus their attitude toward Swift is based on top-level bargaining and grievance experience, rather than on plant experience. Of course, their attitudes affect the plant community greatly, though indirectly. Therefore it will be interesting to see what sort of company allegiance they have, if any.

Top leader A, a man of long experience in the packing industry, favors Swift in one sense, although it makes organizing more difficult:

> Under Van Bittner, the PWOC concentrated on Armour's. Swift had a keen industrial relations policy. They treated their people with a smile, with a pat on the back. They were harder to organize. You wouldn't tackle a giant like that when you could work on Armour and Wilson. . . . Is Swift different? You bet! At Armour the standards are such that you must make it [output]. At Swift's, you can work over the standards and you get a bonus. . . . You felt part of the company there. They did build up good employee relations.

Top leader B, another union veteran, reflects on the past to say:

In the old days, Swift, along with the others, did try to break the Union . . . [but] the Swift boys were good. Around the Yards in Chicago, they knew the people. They would fight on either side of a fight at a bar. . . . Swift is the best of the Big Four. . . . But Swift was worse than Armour in the old days!

Top leader C states:

Swift is the best of the Big Four. They are tough, but honorable. They've got principle. They're paternalistic. Try to win their employees' loyalty. We have a tough time trying to set a Swift employee against the company. With an Armour employee you can do it at the drop of a hat. [C then cited the personal promise of ———, a certain Swift executive, to rectify conditions in a number of plants. He said he would never take such a personal promise from a certain other packer.]

Top leader D evaluates Swift very much in terms of his own high degree of union-mindedness:

Swift seems to be trying to capture its peoples' loyalty. I often ask myself the question: How far has Swift really accepted unionism as a *good* thing? Maybe they say: "If it is an evil, let us try to control it." Swift people are of high calibre, honest and honorable. But they have an *esprit de corps*, unconscious maybe, that "the company can do no wrong." Their judgment is "better" than ours as to what is good for the employees. In a sense, they may say, we don't need a union around here. We'd be better off without it. They do not accept the union as an equal. Are they bargaining just because the law requires it?
[Top Leader D goes on to make a highly significant remark about fear of union-management coöperation based on union insecurity, an insecurity which a union-shop would help relieve.] Labor-management coöperation? It's okay. But you can't get too cosy with the company! We'd become a company-union! Not long ago, Mr. ———, a Swift management man, moved nearby me. His daughter and my daughter, aged seven, are friends. I don't know what that will lead to!

Top leader E comments that:

Swift is way out ahead of the others in industrial relations. They have had a pension plan for thirty years which is superior to the one just negotiated by the UAW. They've got integrity. You can't horse-trade with Swift. They stick to what they believe is right without budging. For instance, once there was a stoppage on the beef kill in a plant of ——— Company because a man was suspended. The union put in a long-distance call. The man was taken back, and the gang back at work within an hour. They were afraid of spoilage.
Now Swift would never do that. If they suspend a man he stays suspended. Immediately they would have called all the foremen in to move the beef and keep it from spoiling. But ——— Company is unpredictable. Mr. ——— [a Swift executive] is a good man. . . . I'd rather deal with Swift. When the chips are down, Swift is tougher. But you know where you stand. Swift never does anything petty or mean. . . . You always need a letter with ——— Company. Must get it in writing! Never with Swift. Their word is enough.

In these remarks by top union leaders we can find a common theme. Swift has had an advanced and successful personnel policy. Swift is a fair and honest company to deal with. Most of these leaders really do have a "general satisfaction with the company as an institution." In other words, they have "company allegiance."

COMPANY DISALLEGIANCE

The anatomy of company allegiance will become clearer in our minds if we examine the attitudes of those workers of the plant community who fail to have it, who are not just neutral, but who positively have "disallegiance."

The Foremen. A few foremen, less than 10 per cent, are dissatisfied with the company as an institution. Jack Toby, 41, nearly 25 years with Swift, is long dissatisfied. He is a college man, while the average foreman's education is second-year high school. Maybe that is a clue:

> I was an assistant foreman for years, and thought of as "no good." I resented this. I would not have come back to Swift & Company [after his term in the service] except that I just did so. In fact I would have quit before the War but for the Depression. The death of my previous foreman finally gave me a foremanship. After twenty-three years' service! They should have fired me or promoted me.
>
> [He is dissatisfied about not getting raises or answers on his requests.] They oughta let me know if I'm too hot-headed or this or that. Then let them tell me. The policy of the company is fine, but the way it works out is not so good. . . . *The job of a foreman is a nervous strain.* Not so much from the men. [He thinks he has the finest work force in the plant.] *But from the supervision,* especially the "Stockyards Aristocracy."

Likewise, Charles Buresh, 49, twenty years a Swift foreman, is not happy about many things and as a result fails to have company allegiance: he says he has high blood pressure, is hot-headed and sometimes says things he regrets. Doubtless his health is a cause of, but also an effect of his dissatisfaction. Difficulty in advancing rankles him:

> If you don't belong to the clique and wear the right ring, you don't get a chance. ———, only three years here, got a job that was promised to me seven years ago! All the key positions, division men, general foremen, etc., go to the clique. They don't promote according to seniority or ability, but according to cliques and who you know. . . .
>
> Then, too, raises are not automatic. The only time you get a raise is when the CIO goes out on strike! . . . We had a Foreman's Association here once with forty members. I was active in it. The foreman was absolutely alone. . . . The problems as of that date are the same now. The things the FAA were supposed to correct are *not* changed. . . .
>
> Any job connected with shipping [Buresh is a shipping foreman] is a headache. My men are all over the building. *I got to worry* about time sheets, phone calls, Standards Department bonus sheets, wrong orders to correct. . . .
>
> Why don't they work a gang long hours and not hire a second gang?

Don't change the size of your gang! The employees will be more satisfied. The superintendents will be more satisfied. ——— had sixty men laid off at Easter. They will never see them again. They're losing money this way. You get a green man. You need a teacher. You get less output. On Saturday I had twenty-two borrowed men in my gang — all green. It's a waste of time. Those DP's don't know beans from applesauce. . . . *They tell you you're part of management. Then they ought to let you run the department as you see fit!* "Why should I worry about these things, they don't belong to me," that's what a foreman will say. . . .

In these men we see that the feeling of lack of recognition and approval as shown through advancement, praise, or spontaneous raises are the most important factors in their lack of company allegiance. Also health, difficult work, and "overeducation" are involved.

The Stewards. About 12 per cent of the stewards are anticompany. And in most cases the stewards involved are colored and embittered about discrimination, "race men." We must hasten to note that many Negroes and members of other minority groups might mention discrimination in the plant community as something they resented, and yet would have withal a basic company allegiance. But for these men and women, this 12 per cent who gravitate naturally into stewards' jobs, their race so modifies their attitudes toward the company as to destroy allegiance.

For Steward Willard Smith, 36, who had one year of high school and ten years with the company on a can-filling line, discrimination is not a major issue, but lack of recognition is:

> The company is all right, but the people who operate it are not always so good. The people in the general office are prejudiced. They think the people who work in the stockyards are dumb! Many are not dumb. They just can't get a job elsewhere . . . Negro psychology — they try to work that on the men. [Smith is also dissatisfied with the foreman. He has been continually feuding with his own foreman about "too much work."]

Harvey Taylor, 26, war veteran high-school graduate, short-service utility man, is an active union man and steward. He is affable and a good talker. The race issue seemed to color most of his thoughts. Although we shall discuss this complex question later, we bring it in here without comment as it is necessary in order to understand Taylor's attitude toward the company.

This attitude is representative of a number of Negro workers:

> Swift is a nice company. But when they hire, they discriminate against Negroes. Mexicans and whites come back when Negroes are not there. It's technical. You can see it, but you can't put your hands on it. . . .
> The foreman I used to have was one of the fairest men I met on the plant. No partiality. But now my foremen do have it. I know discrimination. I see it. I live it every day. I don't have a complex. Some folks have one, but I don't. There were several cases of discrimination last month. . . . What anyone wants is to be satisfied on his job. It's better for the

company and the union. . . . I had a run-in with ———— [his fore-man] recently. The average white man acts superior. I didn't like the way he [the foreman] approached me. I was talking about social and union business. I said to him: "I don't want you to talk to me as a child. You can't demand respect from me and treat me as a kid!"

[Taylor now mentioned an incident that irked him. He was recently leaving the plant by the 41st Street gate which is not supposed to be used by plant workers after 4:30 P.M. and he was stopped.] The police at the 41st Street gate stopped me. . . . But they let the whites go through. The guard said that they work in the general office and [Union Stock Yards] Exchange Building and that he couldn't stop *all* of them. [Office workers were permitted to leave after 4:30.] But how do I know whether they were office workers or not. They did let me go through, but they kept other Negroes back. If they had stopped *everybody*, I wouldn't complain. [The dilemma of the guard was obvious; he knew that Negroes were not office workers, but he could not tell about the whites since all the workers dress pretty much alike en route home.]

Swift discriminates in a big way. The foremen, general office, truck drivers, police — there are no Negroes on these jobs. You don't need no high I.Q. for some. Look at ———— [a local union leader]. He's got two years' of college and doing a common job! A lot of fellows know their job better than the foreman. But there's no advancement for them! If they thought they could advance they'd work harder — set a record, accomplish something, qualify. But there's nothing to look forward to. They lose hope. Their morale is low. If a white doesn't get ahead, there's somethin' wrong. He's got all the chances. But the Negroes are the last hired and the first fired. . . . It's the same routine, day in and day out. They could have colored in the office. It would help morale. They could have colored cops. People all over the country would see colored policemen here. . . . But advancement in the union — that *is* possible! . . . I feel proud when one of my race advances, Bunche, for instance. Even though *I* may never have a chance to get there myself. Swift is a pretty good place as a whole. The only bad thing is discrimination. If there was no discrimination, I wouldn't want to work at a better company.

Aggressive stewardess Lily Leonard, 30, who has continually fought discrimination and perhaps developed a chip on her shoulder as a result, is neutral or unfavorable to the company:

Swift & Company is as bad as it is good. . . . I don't have much chance for advancement. I have gone as far as I can. Once I applied for social-service work [Swift has two full-time workers] to see sick employees. There are a lot of colored workers. We don't have a colored social service worker. They denied me. . . . The suggestion system is a lot of malarky. I put in a suggestion. "We had that in there already, so we can't pay you," said the company. That's not true. It's because I was colored they said that. The company have a slick way of getting away with what they want to do. . . . The *Swift News?* That's good for the company. Not for the employees! It's just somebody playing a big part for supervision, not for the employees. There was a company policy [a former, but not current policy] that Negroes can't be photographed handling meat. They were taking a photo on our line once for some newspaper. They took the colored girls off the line for whites. I felt bad.

The race question evidently modifies most of Miss Leonard's attitudes, and keeps her from having a company allegiance which she might otherwise have.

The Rank and File. A small minority of the ordinary plant workers are dissatisfied with Swift as an institution. Their reasons differ: lack of future advancement, an accident blamed on the company, bad working conditions, "overeducation."

George Lake, 30, highly skilled pork-butcher, new father, satisfied with his foreman and gang, might be expected to have company allegiance, but he hasn't:

> Swift & Company are just a fair place to work. Not so good. In the long run, you *injure your health.* It's real damp. It's cool.

Tom McClellan, 33, semiskilled machine-operator, one of the few Irish on the work force, is neutral to unfavorable in his attitudes toward the company:

> I came here through Dad in 1936. Dad liked it here, but he didn't want me to have no part of the Yards! But it was tough then — the Depression. So I came. Dad saw no future for me here. Men are here twenty-five years and get nowhere. There's an example of a man — after long service, he opened a door from a hot steam room to a cooler, and he lasted three weeks. He died. . . . As far as my future is concerned, it's just a *job.*
>
> *Interviewer:* Have you had a chance to get ahead?
>
> I've been offered a gang leader's job. But for all that responsibility, a little extra per hour — $2.00 per day — it's not worth it.
>
> *Interviewer:* Do you think you could get to be a foreman?
>
> No, we have an abundance of foremen in our department. There's no opportunity. Only a long chance. [McClellan likes his foremen and his gang. However, he had recently lost a grievance on work-load and wage incentives that irritated him.] . . . Swift & Company are "in between" [between good and bad]. If I could get something better and get out, it would be a lot better.

Semiskilled machine-operator, Jonathan Jackson, about 30, well-spoken, apparently quite intelligent, who went two years to college, and now studies music education at night, is probably misplaced in his job:

> I like it more or less. It's not interesting. But there's no time to be bored; there's too much to do. But on a quiet Saturday it can be quite boring. . . . Most people think the worker hasn't a brain. They try to push you around. The foreman doesn't say anything to me unless he *has* to. He won't listen. He'll listen to everybody *but* you. . . . Swift & Company are all right. But not as a permanent job. Should I be here 35 years doing *this!*

Barney Edwards, 30, short-service beef-butcher, father of three, had been recently injured and this incident modified all the rest of his thinking:

I was hurt by a falling trolley — my right eye. The doctor worked on my eye for weeks. It did turn out to be a permanent injury. My vision was now only 20–50. But I had an exam of my eyes before I came to work here and they were okay. The company says the defective vision in my right is a normal accretion and not due to the accident. The union suggests I sue the company. . . . I feel the company was rotten in the whole deal. I was losing time to go to a Loop doctor. I was docked for the time, not paid.

Edwards goes on to say that his foreman is rotten, the wage-incentive system is bad, the pay could be more, and so on. He referred to the eye incident repeatedly in the interview. It was evident that this accident was a kind of traumatic experience for Edwards, and the major factor in his antagonistic attitude toward the company as an institution.

We learn from these interviews that there is some attitude — call it company allegiance — common to a remarkable majority of Chicago Swift-UPWA people. The general attitudes revealed here — the goals and dissatisfactions of the worker in relation to the company — are already well known. We have not discovered them. But the anatomy of these goals, their composition of attitude and motive, their variation from man to man, the way they are influenced by service, sex, race, leadership, and union membership, their hierarchy — these things we can well afford to dissect in greater detail and thus learn to understand with greater comprehension.

CHAPTER FIVE

THE WORK AND THE MEN

It has been said that mass production has destroyed the worker's creativity, pride, and status in his work. Some even claim that the worker is quite content to be a machine tool, if he is bribed with good pay. The worker's attitude toward his job intimately involves such factors as working conditions, pay, advancement, foremen, gang, and so on;[1] his favorable attitude may mean that he actually likes his work, or simply that he is glad of the fact that his present job is dry and warm while his previous one was damp and cold. It does not necessarily indicate real love of work or pride in it.

Nevertheless, the worker's answer to the question: How do you like your job? is significant, for his job is an important part of his work life in the plant community and his attitude toward it affects and is affected by his company allegiance.[1]

TABLE 16
Workers' attitudes toward their jobs
(Random, stratified sample of 192 workers plus stewards and foremen: 1950)

Weighted Averages		Scale	
All workers	1.79	Very favorable	1.0
Stewards	2.30	Favorable	2.0
Foremen	1.90	Neutral	3.0
Men	1.84	Unfavorable	4.0
Women	1.46	Very unfavorable	5.0

Why are the women the most favorable? Patently for the same reasons we gave in the last chapter on company allegiance, namely, high relative pay, no advancement frustration, afternoon quitting time, easier working conditions, more polite foremen. Why are the stewards less favorable? As leaders of a partly opposing organization, they are more critical of the company's jobs. Some men who are dissatisfied with their jobs are more likely to gravitate toward the steward body than those who are not. It is noteworthy, however, that the stewards as a whole are not unfavorable or even neutral toward their work.

Once again now, we shall let the worker tell us about his work, what he likes about it, what his job means to him. One interesting factor emerged in a minority of interviews: the worker liked his job because he knew what to do and his superiors left him alone. For instance, James Drew, 35, well-adjusted short-service man says:

> I likes my job. I never have any trouble. I'm a shipper in the cooler. I fill orders and *there's nobody to bother me.* I like it very good. I only see the foreman once a week. I'm *on my own.* I really likes my job.

Oliver Calvin, 54, middle-service utility man is fairly well satisfied with his job:

> I'm a janitor. It's all right. *I know what I have to do.* I can get everything ready. . . . If a G. Man [Government Inspector] tags a machine [meaning it must be cleaned before it can be used] I clean it. I like to do good work. I get here early, 6 A.M. Only been late three times in five or six years. . . . It's pretty agreeable work. Once I had a hernia in the East Lamb Department. Had an operation. But this work now, this is not too heavy.

Old-timer, George Hahn, whose company allegiance, mixed with dissatisfaction about Negroes' prospects of advancement, we have already seen, says:

> I'm on a utility job. I like it, I been doin' it so long. *Nobody got to tell me what to do.* I'd rather be there than elsewhere.

Highly skilled mechanic, Terry O'Boyle, 38, is very craft-conscious of his trade, likes it and says of his job:

> I studied at the ———— Trade School. You must have theory in mechanics. I think machine work is the best in the world! . . . . It doesn't pay as much as elsewhere. But conditions are ideal. *Nobody bothers you.*

Youthful mechanic, Tommy Zorach, only two years with Swift, says:

> As for my job, I like it very much. I work on hydraulic pumps, steam, etc., around the plant. It's a job outside. *The boss is not on your neck so much.*

As we shall see in the following chapter, one of the factors in satisfaction with the foreman is the fact that "he doesn't stand over you all the time, he leaves you alone." Evidently the workers just quoted do not like to be considered machine tools or cogs. They like to be allowed to take personal responsibility for their work. They do not like to be constantly told what to do. They have initiative and it satisfies them to use it.

Venerable old Henry Woodell, 58, Mississippi migrant, nearly thirty years with Swift, who thinks enough of the company to say: "Swift & Company thanks you for every hour you works here," describes his job:

> I got one of the toughest jobs in the Soap House. Work with lye. They say I'm one of the only ones who can do it. Been doin' it twenty-one years. See these scars on my arms. [He rolled up his sleeves to show me his arms.] I don't lay down. *I'm interested in my work.* But I think my job

should be higher rated. Especially compared with other fellows I know. My work is much harder, yet I get less. But I can't afford to quit, I'm too old. [This was Woodell's one major grievance. Besides this he is satisfied.] My foreman and general foreman all say I should have the raise. But it has to come through the union. Nothin's been done. I been asking for ten years. . . . Working conditions are hard. I got one of the worst jobs in the soap house. You got to wear boots against the lye. The job is all right. They've made improvements on dust collectors, etc. But — . They'll find me on the job. I work alone all the time. I'm a poor mixer. I like it. I sing hymns.

Woodell is doubtfully favorable to his work. He likes some things about it; being alone, being the only one who can do it, being interested in it. Yet the working conditions are hard. Probably his major problem is his rate raise. If this were handled, Woodell would have an unambiguous satisfaction with his work.

The following workers bring up differing factors regarding their jobs, but all are in general satisfied:

Edna Stepac, Bacon Department: I'm a tally-girl. Sometimes there's a lot of grief. I should get paid twice as much! . . . But the job is suited for my need. I'm active. Bacon packing is monotonous and too nerve wracking to me. They're always wanting to make that rate! *My job has change.*

Mary Mikalauskas, Pork-meat-wrapper: I like my job very much. There are *only two of us.* Women are all too talkative and arguing. I really enjoy it here.

Alec Stimac, Wool-grader and puller: I'm a grader and wool-puller and all-around man. Things are slow in our department now. Graders have to be careful. Have to be company men and watch what they're doing. Graders look out for profit. . . . *If I no like my job, I no stay.* The Wool House is okay for old-timers. New ones, they don't take it. . . . Grading is the best job, but it's tough. You hold a twenty-pound pelt and grade it four hours a day. Tough. Too much walking back and forth.

Fred Riedl, Millwright: I've been at the same department for the last fourteen and a half years. I work at night adjusting the conveyors and cleaning and putting in new parts. I'm alone a lot. I enjoy it. It's skilled work, not labor. *There's somethin' new and different* all the time.

William Thompson, Ham-boner: My job? I likes it. I got nothing against my job. It took me six to seven months to learn it. You can *talk and work* at the same time.

Irene Penner, Bacon-packer: I likes that job. It's better than any job I had. You can *sit down.* And when you go home, you're *not too tired.*

Louella Scott, Sausage-tyer and roper: I like the job. *It pays more money.* After you get used to a department you hate to get out. Only thing I don't like — it is wet. I had a kidney removed. And I thought the dampness would affect me.

We have seen that the stewards are favorable to their work though less so than the rest of the workers. Their reasons for satisfaction do not differ from other workers. Steward Frank Daniels, for instance, 35, un-skilled tractor driver says: "I like the job; it's the best job I've had since I've been on the plant." And Steward Hugh Scott: "My job is to cut off tripe. I likes it pretty nice. *I knows it*. It don't worry me."

As for the foremen, they, too, like their work. Clarence Strachan, an old-timer with the company, after proudly showing me all around the different sections of his department, said with evident satisfaction: "I like my job. It's one of the *most important departments* in the Yards. It's 80 per cent of everything. All departments depend on our department!"

As we seek better understanding of the men of the plant community and their work, we come naturally to those who do not like their jobs. They are a decided minority, less than 10 per cent, but they can clarify the subject.

> *Kingsley Bennet, millwright of middle service, who has drifted into many jobs:* I do pipe-fitting in the ———— Department, fixing valves and leaks. I don't like the work. But it's absolutely necessary. *I gotta work.* It's the best I can do.

> *Amos Maker, Hog-lugger:* Workin' here is both good and bad. The coolers are *damp*. It's easy to get a cold. For me it's a no good place to work. It's the only thing I have now. I will better myself elsewhere if I can. *I catch colds easy.*

> *James Jackson, Hog-pusher:* I had ten years' experience in shoe repair. But the AFL shoe union was a kind of racket. Hard to get jobs. So I came to Swift's. I like shoe repair better than hog pushin'. *It takes a long time to learn shoe repair.* I don't want to push hogs all my life! . . . I don't like it. But it's a job. You got to keep the chain full to keep the butchers busy. *Anybody can push hogs.* You can learn it in two days. The only skilled part is handlin' the switches.

We have said that young white men do not want to work at the Yards. David Kniznik, 27, grammar-school graduate, short-service repair handyman, gives us a clue to the attitudes of these men. He has high company allegiance but is dead set against the working conditions and apparent lack of future of the plant:

> I'm learning a carpenter job and I like it. On our gang you learn about roofin', concrete, brick work. And in the shop if you ask any questions, they're pretty good about answering it. I will learn to fix windows and screens. I'll get all around the plant. I like that. *I get tired of one place.* . . . [Kniznik likes his foreman very much but dislikes the wage-incentive system.]
> *There's no future here.* My brother has a job in an aircraft parts factory. He tells me I'm silly to be working here, why don't I go out and get a *good* job somewhere! He gets $2.00 an hour plus overtime. . . . There's no future in the Yards. I know a man in the coolers — sixteen years. He told me if he wasn't too old, he'd get out. My father's been here twenty-seven years. He said: "If I was a young man I'd go get a good job." He says I'm a fool for working here. . . . *The jobs smell!* When you get

home you gotta take a bath. 62 House has a terrific smell. **And Rendering** — I was in there once! When I get through nobody will stay by you. Even when you come back to ———— House, the fellas will say: "Don't touch me!" "Don't rub against me!" You wash here. And when you go home you stand in the door and all move away. You take a bath. Even then you can smell your hand. . . . They don't clean the showers here. You get stuff on your feet. . . .

Advancement? Trying to be a foreman in the stockyards is very hard. You might wait sixty-seven years! Then they bring bosses in from the West End or the Standards Department. There's *no chance for me to be a foreman.*

The fellas I know at Crane, for instance, say they'll never go back to the Yards. *They make more money.* I figure I may go out and get a different job next year. I worked at Armour for two days. There was water in the sausage department. They would give me no boots so I quit. . . . Swift is one million times better than Armour. I heard a lotta fellas say that. Armour is a bad place to work . . . filthy. They got iron tires on their wagons. Swift is trying to paint the place up and put rubber tires on the wagons. I take Swift any time — *if* I'm s'posed to work in the Yards. . . . The gang are swell guys. But even *they* tell me I'm foolish to work here.

The union stewards with the least job satisfaction of all are worth hearing. We come back to Jorel Byron again, the highly skilled beef-butcher who has company allegiance mixed with sheer job dissatisfaction:

My job? It's only a matter of makin' a living, not a matter of liking it! Mechanical work is rated higher. *Butchering* is underpaid and *underestimated.* You got to stop your knife — not to cut the hide, or make "black eyes." You don't do that from seein' but from feelin', from the inside [of the hide]. A nervous man is not as good as a calm man. That job never has been properly rated. A man with education doesn't bother with butchering. . . . The manure [on the hide] eats into your nails. [He showed me his hands and stunted fingernails.] If you wear a glove, that creates a germ. You can't use gloves. *It's tough on your hands.* Any man will say that. . . . Peoples come in who look over the job. But to actually put out the work? They don't know it! It's hard to work on a job if the bosses don't know as much about it as you. . . . Butcherin' works on your nerves. You can strain yourself for life. You can get hernia broaching the cattle over. The floor is slippery, wet and greasy. You can slip on the floor, and that's dangerous with a knife. You might cut another. . . .

The dressing room facilities are not what they should be. No tables for lunch. You're worked up to the last minute. You've got filth and it takes considerable time to clean up. Your hands may have TB germs. You sit down to lunch and the germ may get in your system. There's not proper time, in a one-half hour lunch-hour. You're wet with sweat. You passes through drafts on the way to lunch. You might get rheumatism or "arthuritis." The company gets a reduction on dirty cattle. But the gang gets no reduction. And it's harder to skin them. . . .

Steward Jack Oates, 34, unskilled, says:

My job is fair. *It's not too good on health* if you stay there too long. There's no fresh air, it's stagnating. But the rules are that the doors must be closed to keep the temperature steady. It's always wet.

These two stewards made much of difficult working conditions. For those who are dissatisfied with their jobs this is a common complaint. The white men of short service seemed to complain the most. One such worker, Tony Bachacci, 43, a skilled craftsman says:

> It's a good company as a company. But they should improve the plant a little better. Fix up the killing floors. The company is behind the times. In Rendering, in 62 House, they could put in a vent to suck the dead air out by motor. It would cost money. But it would be a better place to work. And they'd get more work out. [When I asked why he didn't put in a suggestion to that effect, he said he did not believe in suggestions.]

Complaints are mostly about the cold and damp, rarely about the hot jobs. Danger from knives or elevators is mentioned, occasionally also, complaints against locker and dressing rooms. Some old-timers mentioned great improvements in working conditions over the years.

MONOTONY AND PRIDE OF WORK

These are vastly important though elusive topics. Since they are not at the focus of our research but rather at the periphery, we did not attempt to cover them thoroughly in all the interviews, nor did we set up any special test or make any special observations to explore them, but in the course of the interviews certain facts emerged.

Monotony. There are few complaints about monotony. When asked to discuss his job, the worker rarely brought it up spontaneously. If specifically asked about monotony, some did complain of it, many did not.

On the other hand, a semiskilled machine-operator, who states that the incentive system is his pet peeve, says:

> My job isn't bad. It's all instrument work. I keep the steam at the right pressure and temperature. It's an easy job. You don't break your back. But it's monotonous. *The same thing over and over every day!* Every morning I can tell what I'm going to do.[2]

But a skilled millwright says:

> On the work I'm doing, *everything is different*. It's not the same thing over again. That's why I like it.[3]

Terry O'Boyle, the very highly skilled mechanic whom we quoted above, is extremely proud of his work and says:

> You've got to work hard outside the company. There, there's monotony. Here, there's new work. . . . Swift is a good place to work, if you know what you're doing. But if you don't have much experience when you come here, you get a rough deal. Some of the tough jobs are the hide cellars, the hog shacklers, and the hog kill . . . I'd hate the monotony. *On my job there's always something new.*

We must note, of course, that production-line jobs — assembly and disassembly lines — where monotony would be most common, make only a part of the total number of jobs in the plant. But the fact that monotony is not a common overt complaint does not mean that there are not covert evil effects flowing from a repetitive work that demands no skill or responsibility, gives no status, "job prestige," or play to the initiative and creative powers. It simply means that the average worker does not talk about it. The workers' comments on the satisfaction of knowing their jobs, being somewhat independent of the foreman, their frequent dissatisfaction with the wage-incentive system; their evident union-mindedness, are all highly suggestive that monotony of work, lack of dignity, and pride in work are important, though disguised, factors in the plant community.

Pride of Work. If anything, our tentative findings bear out the claim that mass production destroys individual pride in work. Foreman Archie Ferris, 45, twenty-five years with the company, who to the best of my knowledge is not race-prejudiced, says:

> The old-time white worker was proud of his work. Proud to do a job right and cause the least trouble and move up a step in ten years. Take butchering, for instance, they used to have *contests* for the best skinning around the Yards in Chicago. And picnics for the best butchers who could do it best and fastest. The Germans and other races did it. . . . But after the Depression the colored came in. Out of a hundred colored, there are only four or five operators who are proud of their jobs. Who are trying to do the job at all times. Who have pride in being butchers, pride in working for Swift and Company.

Butchering has been steadily losing prestige as a craft, partly because of its subdivision into operations, and partly because of the rising prestige in the last twenty-five years of the mechanical crafts. While Ferris' remarks refer only to one department, and his percentage figures may be exaggerated, his conclusions cannot be ignored.

Skilled craftsman, Eugene Heilhacker, 47, however, blames the foremen:

> A job is a vocation. It's like yours, Father, you got to have your heart in it. A lot of men are just out for the money. They got no pride of work. Now I like my job. But Swift doesn't want pride in work. *They want quantity not quality.* I don't mean Swift *and Company,* I mean, the *supervisors.*

Another skilled craftsman, Tom Schlos, 22, with craft pride, speaks in a similar manner:

> I can truthfully say I never had a better job in my life. They don't kill you. Every day is interesting. Not the same thing. Not a production line. I'm on an outside gang. I wouldn't trade for a million dollars. . . . I been doing this job since I was 15. I don't need trade school lessons. I love it. . . . You enjoy it. You like to come down. But they shouldn't give two jobs to you at the same time! Produce! The company don't want beauty. I don't believe in that. I'd rather do ten minutes longer. Not just

7. After the hog has been thoroughly bled, it is placed in a scalding tank so that the hair can easily be removed. Here the hook-out man is removing a hog by placing a conveyor chain around its hind leg.

8. The gutter eviscerates the hogs as they pass on the conveyor chain or "disassembly" line. The viscera are then placed in one of the trays behind him.

9. The pituitary gland, which is sold to the drug industry, is here being removed from the skull of the hog by the gland picker.

10. These men are loin-pullers in the Pork Cutting Department. They separate out the pork loins by pulling a curved draw-knife through the side of the hog.

11. The pork-loin trimmers, of whom the dissatisfied Richard Rex was one, remove the excess fat from the loin. The steel mesh glove is worn to protect the left hand.

12. As the sides of the hog come past on the conveyor belt, the belly-trimmers trim and square them to be cured for bacon, and place them back on the conveyor. The man with the button on his cap is a union steward.

13. The belly-graders must be able to judge many kinds of meat.

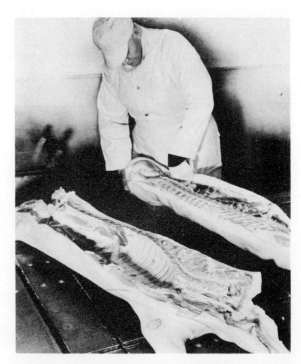

14. The ham cutter-off, shown here, is removing the hams from the sides of the hogs, which move along on the conveyor table.

15. In the curing cellars, this man weighs and grades green hams. The average weight will determine the curing and smoking time.

16. Like peas in a pod, these hams are packed in a curing vat.

17. The ham-washer scrubs hams which have been removed from cure. Now the hams are ready for the smoke oven

18. The smoke-house man is here seen pulling a smoke house. The hams are hung on trees and smoked and are then ready for inspection and wrapping.

19. "Pigs' knuckles and sauerkraut" begin with this pork-foot trimmer.

20. The bacon and hams have just been removed from the smoke house by the hanging-room man who lets them become tempered here before they are wrapped.

21. Girls wrapping slabs of bacon in the Wrap and Tie Department.

22. After the bacon is sliced, it comes to these girls for grading scaling, and wrapping. This is the Swift "show department." The fast operators sometimes make $40.00 a week bonus above their regular pay. They consistently make more than office girls.

23. The sausage-stuffer fits a long casing onto the nozzle of the stuffing
machine and blows out several yards of sausage.

24. The men stuff sheep casings with Brookfield sausage, while the women twist the filled casings to a
uniform length.   Both operations are semiskilled.

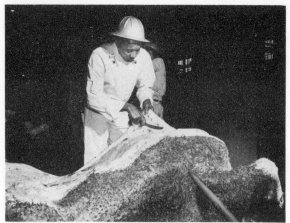

25. This man is a floorsman on the beef-dressing floor, removing the hide from a carcass. He is the aristocrat of all the butchers in the plant and is highly skilled. Should he nick or score the hide, its sales value is greatly lowered. This was Jorel Byron's job. For his description of it, see Chapter Five.

26. Amid a cool forest of white carcasses, the beef-brander rolls his wheel on the side of the beef. The forequarter, partially cut away, will be cut through and carried to the refrigerator car by the husky beef-lugger on the left.

27. Skilled butchers cut sides of beef into wholesale cuts.

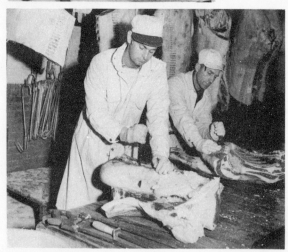

8. Here we have the veal luggers loading the refrigerator car. The man on the platform removes the carcasses from the gambrel stick on the trolley and the lugger carries them to the car.

9. In the damp hide-cellars, these men salt the hides which come down a chute from the Beef Kill several storeys above. They spread rock salt on the hides and pile them in layers.

0. After the cure, these men fold and tie up the hides for shipping to the tanneries.

31. As the sheep go by on the conveyor chain, their pelts are severed by the pelt-remover. As with the beef floorsman, his is a highly skilled job and depends on keeping his knife sharp. Note his scabbard of knives.

32. The pelt-pullers complete the job of removing the pelt from the sheep.

33. The sheep are then split by the breast-bone splitter who cuts through the breast bone by pounding his knife against it.

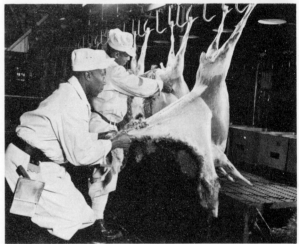

34. This man washes the sheep carcasses as they pass by on the conveyor chain.

35. A member of the shipping gang loads the refrigerator car with dressed lambs ready for distribution to branch houses and dealers.

36. The wool-puller removes the wool from the sheep pelt and grades it. He is a highly skilled worker as he must be able to distinguish up to sixty different grades. This difficult job "is okay for old-timers," says Alec Stimac. "New ones, they don't take it." (Chapter Five.)

37. This truck-pusher works in a freezer where the temperature is about 20 below zero, although the general temperature for storage rooms is 2 or 3 below. The frost on the walls and pipes must be scraped off at regular intervals.

38. A semiskilled workman operates a machine which forms margarine into one-pound "prints" and wraps it in parchment paper. The margarine goes into the machine in the form of noodles which, previously chilled, have been pressed through a "hasher plate." This machine wraps per hour about 2,250 one-pound prints which come out of the machine at the lower right.

39. This man is a filling-machine operator in the Dog Food Department. With his left hand he controls the feed of the material into the filler.

40. The retort cooks receive the cans of dog food that have been filled and closed, and lower them in baskets, as the man to the right is doing, into large vats. Here they cook in order to eliminate any danger of spoiling.

41. The operator holds open the shipping box, while the automatic machine lines up forty-eight cans of dog food and pushes them into it.

42. A slab-cutting machine operator pushes a frame of soap through the machine which cuts it into slabs. The slabs are then further cut into the proper size for bars. The frame weighs approximately 900 pounds.

43. A worker attends and adjusts when necessary this soap-wrapping machine. The soap is fed in on a conveyor belt, and as it passes through the machine, a wrapper is placed around it and sealed.

44. This girl is operating a machine which stamps out the metal circles for the top and bottom of cleanser cans. The tin is fed into the machine in strips which are held by the operator.

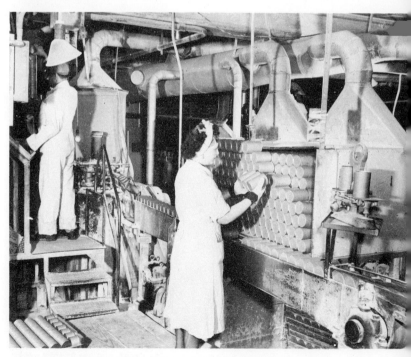

45. As a cleanser-can inspector, this girl rejects any cans which show leakage. She also check-weighs to be certain that the cans contain the correct amounts.

46. The operator makes certain that all is well while the machine automatically fills boxes with soap.

47. Every craft is represented in the Swift-UPWA plant community. Sparks fly from welder Ted Gierlawski's torch.

48. Here the blacksmith is at work.

49. There is pride in the work of the machinist. Terry O'Boyle, Tommy Zorach, and Tom Schlos indicate their feelings about it in Chapter Five.

50. Careful adjustments are made by the pipe-fitter.

51. An auto-mechanic is seen servicing a "thermo-king" refrigerating unit attached to one of Swift's large fleet of trucks. These trucks are refrigerated in order to carry perishable products during the summer months.

cover over a split. But get penetration. *I believe in quality over quantity.* . . . Then we ought to keep the same pairs. Get to know one man. You can talk about fishing, etc. When they change you, you get this or that.

During the 1948 strike, many of the foremen and staff men had to pitch in and work on the production gang itself. Old-timer foreman Richard Babbit says that when the foremen came to work in his department the only thing they asked was: "How much money, and where is the toilet, and when do we go to spell?" Babbit comments dryly: "Maybe that's the view of the worker often enough."

To continue this pattern, mechanic Stanley Grodzki, 31, middle-service welder, unmarried, has little pride or joy in work:

I can't honestly say I like or dislike my job. It's the money. If you have enough money for your pleasure. . . . As for the job, it's just you *got to do it.*

Of course, some men do have real pride of work. For instance, butcher Edward Alberquerque, 56, whose service record was interrupted several years, says:

Yeah, I like my job, I skin parts of the cattle. I keep my knife sharp. I had a good job with Inland Steel, on the open hearth. Sometimes you do nothing there but watch. I like it better here. . . . The chain doesn't go too fast. I keep my knife sharp. [He then showed me his knife and said rather proudly that he sometimes shaved with it.]

Union leader Jack O'Brien, who knows the plant from long years of service and many contacts, and whose judgment is sound, believes that there is pride of work:

The butcher will want to pull those spare ribs right. The mechanic who fixes a pump will come back the next day to listen to it and see if it's right. There is pride. It's not expressed, but it's there.

This may be pride in the sense of self-esteem, but pride of work in a job well done is not too common. It is found among some workers, of course, especially among the mechanical craftsmen. But to the others, operation specialization, lack of confidence in the suggestion system or in advancement, oversupervision, tend to discourage it. Here is a real challenge to the Swift-UPWA plant community and to our industrial system generally. Intelligent men in the role of machine tools are not likely to make for a very high development of either industrial relations or personality.

ADVANCEMENT

What a man thinks about his chances of moving up into a better job or perhaps even into supervision may be a significant factor in his job satisfaction and company allegiance. It is unquestionably a factor in his union allegiance, as we shall see. From our interviews with the people of the Swift-CIO plant community we find that by no means do all workers want advancement. Some feel that advancement is not possible because of their own inability or lack of education. Others feel that favoritism or discrimination hold them back. It is for these latter, especially, that the question of advancement becomes an important factor in company and union allegiance.

As a whole, the women workers do not bother much about advancement. For them there is not much place to go. They have few job and pay grades. Women are not made supervisors, except in the cafeterias. Moreover, most would probably not want to work for a forelady. Says Mrs. Edna Stepac in a department with many women and not a few factions:

> A forelady for women would never work. I wouldn't work for her. If a woman gets authority, she forgets she was in the gang. A woman is not kind to women. Women will work better for a man. ———, the assistant foreman, has a job. When he goes home at night he doesn't care if his wife does go out. He's so glad not to see any more women!

Negroes have long been top pork-, beef-, and lamb-butchers, but in spite of the nondiscrimination clause of the old Employee Representation Plan, Negroes in the past have not been promoted to mechanical jobs (except in dribbles) or to policemen, firemen, salaried checkers, standards men, or supervision.

There are, however, a few interesting exceptions to this. James Johnson, a Negro, was made a foreman in the Soap Framing Department away back in 1911, was highly successful, also, in handling white subordinates, and was pensioned in 1950. Says Mr. Johnson about his early experience:

> I was thought of as Polish when I first came. The superintendent said: "See if you can handle a gang." I did and succeeded. There was lots of trouble at first. Some of my fellow-foremen sniped at me. They tried to get me to blow up. But I never did and they were ashamed. They learned better. You had to be level-headed. . . . I think that having Negro foremen will work. I think it should be done. It's a matter of justice. [Johnson then suggested several possible candidates.] If there's one thing such a fellow must be, it's level-headed. That's the big virtue. . . .[4]

Some Swift foremen are doubtless prejudiced against a Negro joining their ranks, so that a Negro candidate would have to be able to stand the gaff.

The United Packinghouse Workers, CIO, have unquestionably done great work to promote Negro-white harmony, the elimination of discrimination and the advancement of the Negro worker. Thanks to the nondiscrimination and plant-wide seniority clauses of the UPWA-Swift contract and the union's watch-dog enforcement of the contract at the plant level,[5] Negroes have now advanced into choice departments such as the Sliced Bacon Department for women, and the various mechanical departments for men. While it is true that in the past, mechanics were hired from outside with few Negroes applying, and that Negroes as a group were perhaps not yet as well qualified as the whites, still there were certainly far more qualified Negroes waiting for the better jobs in the plant community than Swift actually used.

Partly because of Swift & Company's failure to show aggressive, far-sighted leadership toward the Negro's advancement, and the betterment of interracial relations, the Negro workers have strong union allegiance. Swift's personnel policy has been so definitely advanced that its blind-spot in the face of American basic industry's greatest contemporary social problem, the integration of the Negro worker, is a confusing inconsistency. One top executive stated: "We don't want to go ahead of other companies in this regard, but we do want to keep up with them. This is not a policy of our directors. It is the people who work here. . . ." [6] Yet in other personnel and in production and selling matters, Swift has wanted to go well ahead of its competitors and has succeeded in doing so. And in many matters, such as attitudes against socialism, Swift executives have tried to lead, not follow, the attitudes of their employees, as for example, the "Freedom Forum" lectures given to the entire Swift personnel in 1950.

Now let us see what the Negro workers have to say about this question of advancement. "Shortage man," Al Lamb, shows a reasonable attitude:

> I've got no hard feelings about races. [He hesitates.] Naturally things are more rapid for the white race. Swift & Company doesn't give the colored race a chance for school as it does for the white race. Young men should get a chance. It might mean dollars and cents to the company in the long run. . . . I'm going to be frank with you. If we had more highly educated workers — high school and college — it would be easier for the colored to be foremen. But the college man doesn't want to start at the bottom in the gang. It would make a difference. . . . I ran the gang for four months once. It worked fine.
>
> *Interviewer:* Do you think you could be a foreman?
>
> No. My education is insufficient. There's quite a bit to a foremanship. More than people think. . . . [But with Negro foremen] it would create a better relation between the workers and the employers.

Arnold Lonsdale, 37, high-school graduate, who has indifferent company allegiance started the interview spontaneously as follows:

> We're all on labor. *To be perfectly frank, why can't we take part in the educational program for foremen and general sales — how to prepare for a foreman's job?* Not any colored boys take part in them. I asked about it. They told me I could take a mail order course in it. . . .

Shipping man, Elder Drake, 52, who, as we saw before, is dissatisfied about job security, may well have advancement frustration as his root problem. Notice how this affects his views toward having his children come here to work:

> For my people, there's not much chance for advancement. There are jobs where the white man gets a break in advancement — to supervision. If a man is in the plant twenty years, and capable of it, he should get it — especially a young man, I don't mean me, looks to be a foreman. *You stay twenty-five years. You know the work from top to bottom. You never go any place!* . . .
>
> I will honestly state that I would try hard to *keep my children from the Yards. If there was a chance to advance, I wouldn't feel that way about it.* For the amount of colored who works in this plant, they should have some in supervision. As for education, we have some who have education equal to a foreman's. . . . I've been in my department for years longer than my foreman, yet I'm down [gesture].

Machine-operator, Tom Wright, 38:

> *Advancement is not for colored people.* The cook is tops in our department. *I've seen colored fellows more qualified than the foreman.* I was a sergeant in the army and once I cooked for a living. . . . I know how to handle people. I've seen fellas made foremen who couldn't handle seven men! I believe there is a colored foreman in the plant. Armour's has a few [this is an error]. But Swift is a better company than Armour. . . . I've thought of being a foreman. Don't take long to catch on. I was a battalion mess-sergeant with 1000 people to look after. I always got along. You use certain techniques on certain fellows. I've had ninth grade. It don't call for much education for being a foreman. They got schools anyway. . . . I don't carry a chip on my shoulder. . . . The union has helped about discrimination. They can't put you on a job by partiality. You got job rights, seniority.

To return to George Hahn:

> Advancement is not for the colored. You come in as a laborer. You leave as a laborer. *It's not by ability. I don't see it.* Some colored are mechanics. That's all thanks to the union. There are no colored foremen that I know of. Gang leaders, yes. I should think a man would have to prove himself. *A lot of war jobs came to colored only because the company was forced to do it.* The need for men — oh, I should say the union has helped in discrimination!

The interviewer received the following statement from a Swift worker during the course of a casual conversation one evening on the Indiana Avenue Elevated Station:

> I had four years at Englewood High School. I took an exam for a checker's job. The foreman told me I failed. *Another fellow got the job, a foreigner who could hardly speak English. He didn't take the exam.* I didn't say anything to the foreman. I just took it. I got to work with him, after all. I got a sense of humor. Don't let it bother me. Just keep on working at $1.24 an hour.

Because of the union's help, union allegiance comes easily to an old-timer like Jacob Riddell whom the company helped when his house burned down, as we saw in the last chapter:

> So far as the colored man is concerned, there's not very much advancement. In the last three or four years a few colored fellows have gotten jobs they didn't used to have, like millwrights, mechanics and electricians. *The union helped to bring it about.* The union is a good thing to have — provided it is carried out one-half the way it should.

Another old-timer, Wallace Read, with two years of college, has good company allegiance and likes his foreman, but because of the advancement problem, he continues the same theme regarding the union and placement for his children:

> Race has a lot to do with it. It's pretty hard for a Negro to get a better job. *The foremen and the scalers have a school. Negroes are not admitted.* My foreman tried to get me in, but they turned me down. . . . All Negroes are blamed for one. When I first came here, I was ambitious. . . . A colored foreman would have more trouble with his own people. The new generation are more liberal.
>
> *Interviewer:* How do you feel about all this?
>
> How? You got to take it. Our race is so trampled. . . . In the next century, there won't be any labor. It'll be all machinery. . . . I tell a young man there's no future in this place for him. My son is going to be a doctor. I'm not satisfied to have my son slave all his life. For the "old man" to rot out here is enough. Two-thirds in the general office were office boys. Mr. ——— [a top executive] was an office boy. Color means a whole lot. The union has helped the race. You know the Negro is the last hired and the first fired.

Shipper, Alexander Thompson, another old-timer, whose company allegiance we saw, states a problem for a Negro foreman (sometimes heard, rarely substantiated), although, perhaps inconsistently, he wants Negro foremen:

> People from the Islands [Jamaica, etc.] are different. We listen to each other. Americans [Negroes] don't do that. I once knew a gang leader and he did all right with the whites, not the coloreds. He couldn't understand 'em. You can't be a leader if you can't be heard. This hurts the chances of a colored man being a foreman. [The objection that *whites* will not work for a Negro foreman is more often made and no better substantiated.] . . . My theory is that it is hard for a colored foreman to get obedience from American colored. It's the same in the army, I've seen it. . . . Another thing. We educate our girls in the best of schools. There is a nice intelligent young lady who should get an office job. We have some girls in our department with college degrees! I know a man with a college degree who cleans the toilets!
>
>   One thing you may not understand. But if you were in my stead, you would. I know a fellow who came from Austria years ago. He can't even speak English. They made him an assistant foreman. ———, he can't

hardly write his name. With ———, a German, as foreman. Older men resent that! But what can you do? Who can you go to? It's really unjust, it really is. [Thompson then quoted his own general foreman.] "As long as I am general foreman, I'll never have a pollack as foreman!" If he thinks that about him, what does he think about me? I heard him say that in the office. There was a group of men there. I got up and walked out mad! They put all Germans in there, like Irish on the police force. I have a relative on the [city] force. He has an Irish name. That helped him. They should break those things down. *There'd be better relations between workers and management.* I don't say give *every* colored man a chance. In every race, there are good and bad. It's like driving a nail in a plank. One may be faulty. Try another. Keep trying. Don't just stop if one man doesn't work.

Steward Jasper Collins, 47, makes a point about Negro advancement that we consider very important; namely, that a Negro would take more interest in his work if he had opportunity to go up:

> I don't think there are any full-fledged colored foremen here. You can't get colored into those departments where you can become a foreman. *A number of fellows would take more interest if they had a chance to be foremen.* It would make for better relations between a man and the company. *He'd feel he's a part of the company rather than a tool.* He could improve his condition as the company does.

Resentment about advancement ceilings among middle- and long-service Negro workers is quite common. Less so, among the short-service workers. Seniority now gives them equal chances for most plant jobs. They are too new to be thinking much about supervision. Skilled butcher, Frank Pine, 25, for instance:

> I think there's a great chance for advancement here. I started at seventy-nine cents as "labor," now I'm a splitter at $1.48! I've never been laid off yet. From labor I went to pole man, boner, then splitter. Do I think there's a future here? I really do. . . .

Young White Workers and Advancement. Many white workers feel that they have a good future. But a considerable minority of whites feel that chances for advancement are inadequate. Like working conditions, lack of advancement is a factor that deters some young white men from coming to Swift. Tom Winkowsky, 24, single, high-school graduate and veteran, doing clerical work, sums up the views of this minority:

> I feel I have no future here at all. I came here only as a part-time job. I was offered a job as assistant foreman, but I didn't like the hours. [He evidently wants advancement on his own terms.] Also I was offered a job in the general office. I put in an application at the Ford [Aircraft] Plant as a mechanic. It's okay, but I don't like to get grimy. Still my Dad does it . . . I got a clean, easy job and good hours. But it's cold! There's some effect on your health. It's interesting work, I meet all types of people in different situations. But it's a small department. You can't advance far. At Ford, it's larger. They got more foremen. So you got more chances.

Many people are here who I think are pretty smart. They've been here twenty years and get nowhere. It's mostly foreign-born and colored here now. You don't find many people here my age. . . . Guess it's the hours why I don't like to leave. [He works from 10 a.m. to 6 p.m.] People ask why I stay here — I can't give a decent answer. My friends tell me I wasted four good years here. I could be an apprentice somewhere. I figure I can go out and get a job like my job any day in the week. My Dad and sister, Jackie, Red, Tommy, Billie, and Dave, all have worked in the Yards at one time or other. And all have quit. I tell 'em the *hours* is why I stay.

[Incidentally Winkowsky has clear company allegiance.] Swift is the best of the big and small packers. Their pay is best. They treat employees fine. My job is fine, but others aren't. . . . There's blood or grease or soap in your lungs. . . . If others punch in late they're sent home, and they get only a fifteen-minute break spell period. But I can come in late. I can go out for 'coffee and . . .' for a half-hour anytime.

[The lower prestige of the Yards is perhaps Winkowsky's big problem.] People don't come to the Yards unless they're desperate for a job. There's lower pay here. I'm the lowest wage in my neighborhood. There are less skilled jobs. And they're dirtier except for the office and printing jobs. . . . Once I went out on a date. My boyfriend's girl asked me where I work. My girl said: "Tell 'em, Tom. Tell 'em you slaughter hogs!" So I did. If I go to a dance and they ask where I work, I change the subject. If you work in the stockyards, it means you're lower grade or somethin'. . . . I would never send my kids here.

Not all young white workers agree with Winkowsky. Ford Bartlett, 28, up from an Oklahoma farm, with six years of schooling, says: "I've got a pretty good chance for a foreman. I will get it pretty soon. Maybe next January."

The Foremen and Advancement. A majority of the foremen think they have a chance to advance if they wish to. A significant minority do not, and are dissatisfied with their opportunities. Foreman Tom Moore, twenty-two years with the company, and well satisfied, says:

Advancement goes back to education [Moore had no high school.] I feel very well satisfied. I don't look for advancement. All I want is to do a better job and make better ————. I like to get to work in the morning. I never knew a more honest sup. then ————. He's about as good as they come. The old man is okay, too.

On the other hand, Archie Ferris' basic dissatisfaction goes back to lack of advancement:

Swift & Company don't recognize their first-line foremen enough. Because of ability on the job, they keep 'em there. . . . I blow my top a lot. I talk too much. They've promised me a mountain. . . . I'm not satisfied. I've lost ten years. I'm made for better things. Stay two years only, they said. I'm in my department twelve years now! . . . I do the best I know how. *But if I do, I stay there, and if I don't, I'm satisfied!* I'm a dissatisfied customer. . . . I've wanted to quit often.

Craft foreman, Philip Kostka, old-timer near pension age, likes his chances:

I always found advancement very good. I've got two sons here. I've always had a chance to talk to supervision. . . . Would I come here over again? I think I would.

In sum, we see that advancement means different things to different segments of the work force. For many it is a minor problem only. But for the more skilled Negro worker it is a severe problem indeed, and an important factor in allegiance.

DO THEY WANT THEIR CHILDREN HERE?

The answer is: No. Out of a sample of sixty-six employees, nearly four-fifths did not wish their children to come to the Yards. Their reasons are as follows: They want their children to get a better education and get a better job elsewhere. Many colored want their children to be doctors or lawyers. They dislike the difficult working conditions and the large amount of unskilled and semiskilled jobs in the plant, but they often say that they would not mind their children getting a good mechanical job or better yet, a job in the general office. Like most people, these parents are enticed by the prestige, often undeserved, of the white-collar job. Of a subsample of twenty-four long-service men, both white and colored, only three wished their sons to come to the Swift plant community. The foremen are more favorable, yet at least half of them wish their sons to go elsewhere.

We listen to the workers themselves. We have already heard Elder Drake and Wallace Read say they would not bring their sons here because of advancement ceilings for Negroes. William Krawchuck, Polish old-timer and millwright says:

Youngsters these days want an easy job. They don't want to work in the Yards. Those who come from the Army don't want to come to the Yards. They want to run their own gas station or store. Only the colored will work here.

Clemente Orozco, 47, twenty years with Swift, has company allegiance, but says he got rheumatic fever on a dock-loading job and was given a janitor's job. He states:

I don't believe I want my boys to come here. I can't write English. I can't talk good. I can't get good jobs. But my boys — I want them to get some place where they don't have to push trucks. Maybe if they were a checker or scaler, might be all right. I don't want them to have to work hard like me.

And the following:

Colored pork-butcher, Robert Huston: My son's taking mechanics at Tilden High. He's got big ideas. Doesn't want to come here. He wants to make a better showing than the old man did.

White pork-butcher, Paul Gedansky: The younger generation don't want to come here. They want to get a better job. They don't want to work as hard as their fathers did. I had one son in the war. Said he had enough of killing and didn't want to work on the hog kill with wet and blood on the floor.

White hog-casings-cleaner, Matthew Bruozis: My son works at the airport. I tell him: "You're lucky you don't work in the stockyards." And he says to me: "I don't know why you work in the stockyards." [This man is favorable to the company, job and foreman, however.]

Colored pork-trimmer, Richard Rex: No, there's no future for my sons here. No advancement here. I don't want them to come here. It wouldn't be nothin' but a lot of hard work. . . . One's interested in commercial art and the other television. . . . I wanted to be a doctor or a lawyer when I was a kid, but my father made me quit school when I was fifteen. I lacked a couple of months of the eighth grade.

On the other hand, Mrs. Elaine Ducharme, beef-packer, short-service, says:

I tell my son — he's a sophomore at Mt. Carmel High — : "I'll bring you over here to work with me."

The fact that a man doesn't want his children to follow his footsteps in the Swift-UPWA plant community does not primarily mean he himself does not have company allegiance, and job satisfaction. It means he does not want this community for his children. But his attitude does show us the perspective in which he views the plant community against jobs and professions elsewhere.

HOW THE RACES WORK TOGETHER

The harmony and teamwork of the work gang are an important factor in job satisfaction, productivity, and good industrial relations. The Roethlisberger-Dickson-Whitehead study of the Chicago Western Electric plant brought out concretely the importance of the informal work group. Since the Swift-UPWA plant community is nearly half white and half colored, we are primarily interested here in the racial aspects of how the work gangs work together. This race question will come up again when we discuss it with reference to the foremen and the union. In general, there is excellent harmony in most of the work groups between colored and white (as also between Pole, Lithuanian, and other nationalities).

The Attitudes of the Colored Workers. Most of the colored workers think their gang "a fine group," "nice," "coöperative," with maybe "a little playfulness now and then," with maybe one or two "characters who make for 'confusion,'" but on the whole a "nice bunch." Very rarely do they show any antagonism toward their white fellow-workers in the interviews. Was this because the interviewer himself was white? I do not think so. For the Negro workers did not hesitate at all to talk unfavorably about white foremen whom they did not like, or about the policy of white management. Says James Drew, 35, shipper in a gang divided evenly between colored, white, men, and women.

> Our gang is pretty good. It's very nice. Both colored and white get along very good. 'Course there's always some one who causes some trouble. But we're one nice happy family.

Amos Maker, 28, semiskilled loader in a small department two-thirds colored, says:

> The gang is okay. They play around and kid like babies. You pass away the time. Keep your mind off the time. Then it's almost time to go home.

Semiskilled meat-handler in a sausage factory department, 70 per cent colored, Harrison Wallace, 38, states:

> We get along swell. If a man gets sick, the gang takes up a collection for him! I don't think many others do that.

Jasper Hartford, 43, unskilled, who has high company allegiance, says:

> Our gang is very nice. They're "mixed up." [He means that they are both colored and white. Such circumlocutions to avoid mentioning race as such, or color as such, are not infrequent among the colored workers.] We're all supposed to be one. All should get along. . . . I just want to be recognized.

A few workers mention the jealousy and hurt feelings that sometimes crop up in a department. Old-time beef-butcher, Luke Daniels, 52, in a large department nearly 90 per cent colored says:

> Generally they do get along. Colored people at that level are more jealous of each other. If the foreman sends a man on an easy job, with more salary, some think the boss is doing him a favor. I don't. But some get sore. It's impossible, in my opinion, to treat everybody equal.

Harmonious racial attitudes are more predominant among the women than among the men, as we shall see. Mrs. Ella Robinson, in a large evenly divided department, says:

> The white and colored girls have a club. A Christmas savings club. And we give wedding anniversary gifts. . . . We all coöperate well.

The Attitudes of the White Workers. These must be distinguished between men and women. The women are more favorable. The white men have more adverse remarks about the colored, about half are favorable and half are not. Those who are unfavorable frequently distinguish between the older colored workers whom they call excellent and some new, younger workers, the "jitterbugs," whom they criticize.

The White Women. Barbara Siwicki, 33, a scaler, shows how attitudes can be ambivalent. (This gives us a warning of how careful we must be in making generalizations summing up attitudes.) Says Mrs. Siwicki:

In our gang, some are okay, some no good. Some of the colored are loud, trouble makers, lazy. The colored take it easy, but yet they get the same bonus. [Gang bonus.] But we get along okay. To tell you truthfully, some colored girls are better than the white girls.

Old employee, Mrs. Mary Mikalauskas says:

We gotta lotta black ladies. One black lady is very nice. She buy me a present. She grab me by the neck every morning and calls me "Mama." She gives me a nice present at Christmas time. Colored and white? Tha's all right.

Short-service worker, Mrs. Edna Stepac, 34, in a large department, says:

On the whole, our gang averages well. The colored are all right. Once a colored woman complained to the foreman: "I think you're pickin' on me because I'm colored." But the foreman answered: "I think you're picking on me because I'm white." Everybody laughed.

Two workers in the pork division:

We get along well. Some of the colored are nicer than the whites. They are kinder, I guess.[7]

The colored women are okay. Better than the white. I needed to get a bond cashed once. And a colored woman at my bench agreed to do it for me. She did.[8]

The White Men. Eugene Heilhecker, skilled craftsman, who wants to have pride in his work as we saw above, says:

There are about five colored in our gang. I been with a colored lad for four years. I wouldn't trade him for a white fella! He's trustworthy. I broke him in.

Polish old-timer, Jim Osuch, says:

The colored are all right. I'd sooner associate with a colored person than a white person. . . . But the colored *right* from the south — maybe they're hard. The colored we have now are really nice to work with. I don't talk to no DP's, even when neighbors.

And even David Kniznik, whom we saw to be dissatisfied with his future and the working conditions of the Yards, likes his colored coworkers:

The gang are swell guys. You'll always find one gappy guy in a gang of course. . . . The colored are all right. They'll help you out. They'll give you money for coffee. There are five colored in our gang now.

Another short-service white worker, Everett Stasiowski, 28, states:

Boys are okay. Colored are a nice gang. We sit together at spell time. They talk sensible. We tell each other our troubles.

Most of those whites who are somewhat unfavorable to the colored do make distinctions. Very few condemn the colored race as a race. Most give hopeful evidence of an effort at least toward fair judgment. Here is an interesting example of how a man's conscience, and "racial incidents" can pull his attitudes in opposite directions. Joseph Kulbis, 41, old employee says:

> I hate to say it, but I'm not in favor of colored. The colored will try to make a fool out of you. . . . They'll steal pieces of meat. My work partner was fired for that yesterday. To tell you the truth the colored don't put out a fair day's work. They try to step on you. The old-timers are all right, though.
>
> So help me, I always believed they should be treated like a white man. Not now. I've changed my mind. I know the Catholic Church says all men are equal, but — . Why the way the colored pushed people around on streetcars! It's a shame. My brother-in-law was robbed on a streetcar by a colored man with a knife. He could do nothing about it. And recently here in the plant, two colored men pulled knives on me. I carry a trimming knife now. . . . It was 80 per cent white before the war. It's 80 per cent colored here now. The colored went along fine before the war. Since the war I've changed my attitude. It's hard to work with those guys in the gang. I was a gang leader, the only white with forty colored. [Mr. Kulbis asked for a raise as gang leader. Said he wouldn't run gang for only seven cents more than gang. Says company stalled. He is now back in gang. He says he read that company wanted college men for foremen. And he figures that he is a workingman, hasn't got a chance. This may be his big difficulty.] They have no respect for matrimony. Their morals are down. Those jitterbugs are like a canary out of a cage!

Husky Jim Stowa, 28, skilled machine-operator, veteran and appearing highly intelligent, makes a distinction between attitudes and behavior:

> They [the whites] *talk* about racial prejudice. They call dirty names. But they work, eat, associate and drink with Negroes!

Salvador Gomez, 44, old-timer in a department nearly two-thirds colored, says:

> The colored people, especially the young are hard to get along with. Too many smart-alecks. [Then he talks about participation in union affairs.] I'm afraid of the colored. They want to start a fight. I never want to be close to 'em. I don't trust 'em. Work together with the colored — that's okay. But after work, I go home, where I belong. [We see the roots of neighborhood segregation in that remark.] I don't like their shoving on streetcars. Especially the young, those new from the south. Union dances — once they asked me to bring my family. I said no. My family is at home. It has nothing to do with the union.

Veteran night-watchman, John Roucek (not in the bargaining unit), is extremely anti-Negro. His bigotry is brought out by his exaggerations and distortions:

> The colored people are awful lazy. Got to watch 'em, especially the ones from the south. They had a fight yesterday in the beef kill — two colored with knives. I remember other incidents in the hog kill. Oh, those colored people from the south! From the north, they're okay. Two "fruits" talk about their women during the War. Colored are funny people especially

when they get a few drinks. They'll borrow $300 to buy a fur coat for their sweetheart. Does their wife know it?

Another thing. They talk awful bad. No wonder people hate them. They talk bad especially in the dressing room and at spell time. You couldn't live with them. They got Communists' ideas. The colored buy a lot of cheap jewelry from the Jews. Overcharged. They're really lazy. If you watch 'em, they work. You can't tell 'em anything.

During the War they thought they owned the place. The union was stronger then. The union is weaker now. . . . *The CIO is nothin' but Communists*. I've been in Russia [Kiel]. Seen people starving. I say: "If you like Russia, go back there!" *Who got in the Commies? The Democrats! Who brought the colored up from the south? Kennelly!* [Mayor of Chicago.] To get more votes. So they could live like white people! On the relief line for one white there are twenty colored. Too lazy to work. They got dirty housing. How are you going to live with them. Nothing but morons. White men won't work in the stockyards. Wanted defense jobs during the war.

[Yet Roucek brings up this curious exception to his own bigotry.] I know a colored fellow on Blue Island [Avenue]. He's got twelve kids. Real nice fellow. Got two lots. Nice fellow. Got to give him credit. He's a beef-brander. He gave me a cigar lighter when I took my vacation to Poland. He hates the south. He's an old-timer of twenty years' service.

An unpleasant incident between the races tends to solidify attitudes as is brought out by the following anecdote told by Anthony Kudsma, 42, semiskilled, middle-service worker:

Our gang? Some are nice, some nasty. . . . Once I told a colored girl how to fix some cartons. I thought she understood. I went away and later came back and saw it was not fixed. As I came back I was thinking out loud: "Of all the nincompoops!" I shouldn't have said it. But I did. She figured I called her nigger. We had a discussion with the supervisor and it was settled. But she doesn't speak to me to this day. . . . The colored, I'd fire the lot of them. All they talk is dating and such on the job.

The distinction between old-time colored workers versus new ones is commonly made, especially by the foremen, as we shall see in the next chapter; also the distinction between northern-born and southern-born. Though these differences tend to be stereotyped, there are undoubtedly differences following geography and service. Two workers bring this out. First James Rendak, 46, with the company for twenty years in an evenly divided department:

The gang is okay. . . . It's mostly colored. [Just half colored.] During the war it was five to one. The whites say: [regarding the union] why should I fight for those guys?. . . . But colored and white work together all right. Except the new guys from the south. They're wild. The old-timers are all right.

And William O. Coyne, 39, skilled craftsman, in a department mostly white:

In my opinion, to be truthful, the colored got too much seniority over the whites. They don't want to work and compete with the whites. They act dumb. In our gang we got some darn good colored men in there. But the new colored help — they're like a bubble anyway. Here today and gone tomorrow. But the colored old-timers, here for years — even they are against the jitterbugs, types come in from the hills.

In sum, working harmony between the races is quite good. Mutual attitudes are fair. The colored are mostly satisfied with their white companions, though many are dissatisfied with advancement opportunities. The attitudes of the whites are so full of distinctions that it is difficult to summarize them.

The Swift-UPWA workers have shown us in this chapter that most of them like their work, that most are concerned (overtly) with neither the monotony nor the pride of their work, that advancement is a problem for some, that few wish their children to follow their footsteps here, and that most work well with other races and nationalities, although with mixed mutual attitudes. Their attitudes are not simple, but complex, and studded with many distinctions, interrelations, and sometimes contradictions. There is an area, however, in which we find a surprising amount of agreement, and this is general satisfaction with their work in the plant community, a large factor in company allegiance.

CHAPTER SIX

THE MEN AND THEIR FOREMEN

In the Swift-UPWA plant community, the foreman, while not a "master and victim of double-talk,"[1] is nevertheless the "first line of management." He hires his employees in conjunction with the central employment office. He can fire, discipline, and, ideally, settle grievances at his own level. The average worker's contacts with Swift management are with the foreman or his assistant. Almost never does he deal with the general foreman, the division superintendent or the plant superintendent. Thus the foreman is a key man in the work life of the men and women in the plant. Moreover, the foreman, being close to his men, ought to have a pretty good idea what the people of the plant community are like. His ideas about their working habits, their attitudes and motivations will give us a fresh point of view, provided we sift his opinions carefully before accepting them.

We ask two questions in this chapter: What do the men think about their foremen? What do the foremen think about the men? The workers distinguish between the foreman and the company. A worker will say, "It's not the company, but the people," or "I can go over the foreman's head to the general office," or "I can talk to the Industrial Relations Department."[2] Again and again we notice that the worker, either because of transfers to different foremen or because of contacts with the Industrial Relations Department, comes to recognize that there is a company policy affecting his welfare, as well as a foreman doing so. Further, he sees that sometimes in the grievance procedure, company policy may override a foreman. Thus, while the foreman is important, the worker does not take him as the company itself. Indeed a scatter-diagram of the attitude scores of our interviews, plotted on one axis as attitude-to-the-foreman, and on the other, as attitude-to-the-company, shows no significant association between the two. Most workers are favorable to both. But too many are favorable to one and unfavorable to the other for clear association or correlation. While the foreman is an important factor in company allegiance, he is by no means the only one. Proponents of foreman training programs as the unique key to successful industrial relations will find no support in our findings. Foreman training is important, of course; but good company policy is equally important.

On the whole, the Swift-UPWA workers like their foremen. Only about 5 per cent of the work force and 18 per cent of the steward body clearly and positively dislike their foremen.[3]

TABLE 17

Workers' attitudes toward their foremen

(Random, stratified sample of 192 workers plus stewards, foremen, and union leaders: 1950)

Weighted Averages		Scale	
Women	1.48	Very favorable	1.0
Men	1.92	Favorable	2.0
Stewards	2.30	Neutral	3.0
Union Leaders (right)	1.60	Unfavorable	4.0
Union Leaders (left)	2.30	Very unfavorable	5.0
All workers	1.76		
(Foremen toward workers)	2.40		

In Table 17 we see a significant statistical difference between the men and women. The colored women of middle-service are the most favorable (1.25) and the colored men of short-service are the least favorable (3.04). The reasons for this sex difference are about the same as stated in Chapter Four, page 81. We might have expected that the colored workers would be less favorable since the foremen are white, or that the old-timers would be more favorable since they have more company allegiance. Such, however, is not the case. There is no significant difference by race or length of service. But there is significant difference between the steward body and the workers as a whole, the stewards being clearly less favorable to the foreman (though still favorable). The right-wing union leaders are about the same as the average work force. The left-wing union leaders are the same as the steward body, less favorable. This follows the general pattern we have already noted as to company allegiance and attitude toward the job. As an analysis of this pattern, we shall discuss later the opposing pulls of the union and company on the worker's allegiance.

WORKERS SPEAK OF FOREMEN

The workers of the Swift-UPWA community give many reasons for liking their foremen: he is "understanding," "not too strict," "not too easy," "not hot-headed," he "talks nice," "has no favorites." But two reasons emerge as far more important than the rest: (1) "He doesn't bother you," that is, he leaves you alone, and (2) "He listens to you," that is, you can talk to him and reason with him. Both these reasons express the worker's desire for a certain measure of independence and responsibility, and, more basically, his desire for dignity as a person. He does not want to be constantly told what to do, or checked upon as to how he did his job, like a schoolboy. We have already seen that this is a factor in his attitude toward his job. Also the worker wants his opinions and arguments listened to with respect and attention, even if the foreman must later differ with them. It is no discovery to say that what the worker wants most of all in his foreman is to be treated as a responsible person with dignity. But it is a fact constantly being forgotten; therefore one that must be constantly relearned. The importance of this fact will become more graphic as we see it expressed in the workers' own words.

Charles Sucholdolski, 56, short-service night-worker in the pork division, whose service record at Swift was interrupted for work elsewhere, likes to work on his own:

> I got a new foreman now. I worked for four years in the sausage room. My foreman's not bad. Our job is a night job. Everybody knows what to do. I do my job. *Foreman no bother me.*

Jim Stowa, whom we saw as a highly intelligent machine-operator, would not want to be a foreman himself because it involves "too much responsibility for the money you get; and the foreman's just a stooge anyway . . ." But Stowa is:

> pretty well satisfied. My time is free. . . . I believe P——— Q——— is my foreman. We take orders from four or five different foreman above us. I hardly know who *is* my foreman. *We all know our work and we do it.*

Old-timer Al Barre, grader in the pork division, high in company allegiance, is satisfied with his foreman:

> I've been very successful on gettin' along. Been late only once in six or seven years. I do my work alone. *I never see the foreman* much. We three or four men work together and I keep the boys straight. The foremen are fair enough as a rule. . . . It ain't what a man says, it's how he says it! We get along very well on the job. *They trust me,* for some reason. We're mostly old-timers — Polish, Mexican. I speak some Polish. [Barre is Negro-American.]

Jasper Hartford, middle-service worker likes both the company and his foreman:

> My foreman? I never worked under a better man. . . . He's an old foreman. Been here forty-nine years! He is very nice. I have no complaints. *He leaves us alone.* He knows a man. The younger foremen, they talk down to a man: "Go here!" "Do that!"

These workers do not mean, of course, that the foreman should omit necessary instructions, but they feel that they should be left alone to carry them out. Some foremen may growl, upon reading this, "If you don't stand over them, they don't get the work out!" But these workers reply: "We'll get more work out if you are nice, and if you leave us alone." Supervision is necessary, obviously. But oversupervision is not.

The second major quality stated by the Swift-CIO workers as the mark of a successful foreman is that "he listens." Terry O'Boyle, whose pride of craftsmanship we saw before, gives that reason for satisfaction with his foreman:

> Things are going pretty good in our shop. We have few grievances. And *you can talk to the foreman.* . . . The foreman has been "right" with me. And the former division man, ———, would stop and talk anywhere with you.

Old-timer Maurice Decker, 47, semiskilled machine-operator, dislikes one of his foremen because he fails to listen. Incidentally, he makes a clear distinction between the foremen and the company:

> The company itself, as a corporation, is a wonderful thing. Only some bosses aren't all they should be. . . . One of my foremen is pretty good. One is very nervous. He knows it all. And he don't know nothin'! "Why don't you tell me?" he says. But if I try to tell him, *he won't let me tell him.*

Back-of-the-Yards man, Walter Stuczynski, young war veteran, doing a skilled job on a meat-production line, is satisfied with the foreman:

> My foremen have got a job to do like everybody else. It's hard to be a foreman on our floor. It's a job on a chain. For instance all can't go to the washroom at the same time. Two or three relief men can't relieve all. Some abuse the privilege and stay down a half-hour. [The foremen had been protesting this.] But the foremen are pretty nice. They have treated me fine. *You can argue with them.* And you could always go to the general office; Swift & Company is not the kind of a company to say the boss is right always, and you're out.

As we saw, Stanley Grodzki does not like his job very much, but he has company allegiance and continues the same reason for liking his foreman:

> Tom's all right. He's reasonable. *You can argue with him.* You can talk to him like a confessor.

Scotch mechanic and old-timer, Alex McLean, 63, has high satisfaction with company, job and foreman. He says:

> I have really a swell foreman. Indeed all have been pretty fair men. *I can talk to him and he will reason with ye.* . . . There's an old sayin': "A mon can make a foreman. A mon can break a foreman."

Middle-service worker on one of the loading docks, Stanley Stowe, 41, has had only about two foremen since he came with the company. He says:

> Not everybody feels the way I do. I been working here fourteen years. Never had any trouble. I been working with Jack Sherman, my foreman, for twelve years. If any trouble comes up I just go to Jack or Bill [the

general foreman] *and talk*. Industrial Relations man, Mr. ———, came around a lot and I could talk to him. . . . The foremen treat me fine. I got no kick at all.

Semiskilled grader, Covell Pearson, 50, old-timer, and home owner, has fair company allegiance, though not satisfied about Negroes' chances. He likes his foreman:

He's a good foreman. It's pretty hard to understand him. He don't talk much. He's Irish. Though white fellows talk with him. *But he'll listen.* He's one of the best foremen we've had in this department. He is smart, an ex-Bedaux man.

And truck-washer, John Sharry, 37, quips:

Well, I got a good foreman. *He looks and listens.*

Mrs. Willamae Potter, who liked Swift's Open House as we saw, states:

Oh, I got a nice foreman. He's real understandin'. *He listens to you.* When my father passed, I had to go south. I just called up, I didn't have to come down to work. They took up a collection and sent me flowers. . . . The foreman lets some girls get their check earlier in the week. . . . It's a bunch of girls, of course. But if we tend to our business, it's okay. We get along nicely.

Swift-UPWA workers mention many other reasons for liking their foremen, for instance, that he is "understanding." Robert Jackson, supply-man in a Table Ready Meats Division department, whose company allegiance is clear, says:

My foreman is real nice. He's one of the best. He seems to *understand*. He treats us just like he wants us to treat him. Some try to ride you. Everybody likes him. He's one of the best foremen Swift & Company have. . . . It's the way you tell a man! You can't do nothing but do it!

Washington Hubbard, 45, in the same department and talking about the same foreman continues the same theme, but also mentions another important quality, namely that the foreman knows the work, for he once worked in the gang himself:

I came to the ——— House in 1946. I like it here better than in the ——— Division. Here I get the hours. And the bosses are more *considerate*. My foreman has been on labor hisself. *He knows the work.* He's pretty good. The superintendent rides him. But you can reason with him. We don't have many grievances.

Most superiors find they like certain of their subordinates more than others. But if they permit these likes to develop into partiality by the allocation of choice jobs and rewards to their favored few, they will soon alienate the group. Such favoritism is made impossible by the seniority clauses of the Swift-UPWA contract. The worker wants a foreman to treat all the gang equally. Nick Pellegrini, 52, semiskilled shipping and traffic man, brings this out and then returns to the two major qualities of a good foreman:

> My foreman? You couldn't want any better. What is a good foreman? He treats his men all alike. *He don't show no partiality.* If a little grief comes in the family, he gives you a break. He's like a father with a brood of chicks. A poor foreman? He's a pig-headed man. Take a foreman *you can talk to* — he's fine. Two-thirds of your trouble is if a foreman won't listen. . . . If a foreman goes along with the men, *he don't have to stand over us.* I was a foreman once in construction work, over 125 men. . . . Swift & Company treated me wonderful, treated me okay. It's pretty good for the working man. It depends on your foreman. Supervision is the head. [According to Pellegrini, the foreman is a key factor in company allegiance.]

Youthful clerk, Tom Winkowsky, who, as we saw, has company allegiance, though he is sensitive about "working in the Yards," wants his foreman to be "fair":

> My foreman's got a funny disposition. If he's got troubles at home, or there's irritation in the plant, it's hard to work with him. But he is very *fair.* He's not very strict. He will listen. Once somebody pulled off one of the doors in our office. They were going to fire me. But he listened to me. I didn't do it. It was okay.

The small number of workers who are dissatisfied with their foremen do not form a simple pattern, but they bring out negatively all the points we mentioned before, each man with his own emphasis. Several mention that their foreman never has any praise for his men. Only two of the seven men we shall quote as antagonistic to their foremen fail to have company allegiance. Short-service janitor, George Stompert, 47, New Orleans migrant, fifth-grade educated, has clear company allegiance, but has five or six complaints against his foreman:

> He's not so good. You can't talk or reason with him. He puts you on one job, then on another job. Then he comes up and says: "Why you haven't did so-and-so on the first job!" He gets all *mixed up.* He's forgetful. . . . He seems to want you to do more work than you can do. I will do my work. But I don't like to be *ridden.* He never said to me: "*That's a good job.*" Others say the same. . . . ———— and ———— [higher foremen] are fine. You *can talk to them.* But ————, he doesn't talk to you like human. You'll do more work for a good foreman. He should talk to you in the right way. He knows you do the work as he asked. But if he jumps on you for work not did, that's bad.

We have already seen that Barney Edwards, beef-butcher, has no company allegiance, primarily because of the traumatic experience of an accident to his eye in which he felt the company was unfair. This experience has affected his estimate of his foreman:

> We got a new foreman. And just like the company, he's rotten! I've seen many things. He's caused good men to quit. He wants a man to run on the job. . . . If a man goes out to the bathroom, he goes out after you.

He runs too much; all in the cooler call him "Seabiscuit"! You *can't talk to him.* He just says: "Go home." 'Course the Employment Office knows about him. He's caused old-timers to quit. You can't get men to retransfer back here.

It is interesting to note, however, that the other three men interviewed from this same department all approve this foreman:

He's very nice. He's reasonable. I know my work and I do it.[4]

It's a tough job to be foreman. . . . He's a nice fellow. I hate to see him go, the former foreman. He'd get you a discount card for merchandize. Our present foreman seems pretty nice too.[5]

He don't say much. But he's okay. What's a good foreman? If you do something, *he let you go do it.* He don't stand and say: "Do this! Do that!" [6]

Fred Pike, 24, high-school graduate and father of four, whose home is one room in Bronzeville, comes in contact with many foremen throughout the day. He has mixed views about his foremen and assistant:

As a whole the company treat you all right. A few foremens don't understand. They expect a new man to be no good. They're looking for trouble. My straw boss [the assistant foreman] is kinda hard. If you do something wrong, he's right on you. But he never praises you of his own accord. *A man kinda likes to be complimented.* [We must note that Pike had had a run-in with this assistant foreman just before the interview.] But my foreman is an all-right foreman. He will listen to you. . . . The assistant foreman goes around hoping he'll find somethin' wrong. . . . A foreman should not boss me, not beg me, but *instruct* me. Now ———— [another foreman], he'll talk to you. If something gets behind, he'll ask you, without jumping on you. But that straw — he uses a *belligerent* tone. He wants to let everybody know he's foreman. You can be strict without that. In fact the foreman is stricter than he is. There's no sense in asking questions, unless you wait for the answer. "I don't like your attitude," he says. I'd like to just sit down and tell him: "Shut up and *listen* a bit!"

Craftsman Eugene Heilhecker considers his job a vocation, as we saw, and likes Swift & Company very much, but he seems not to favor his foreman. He sees a "wall" between management and labor and offers a suggestion:

The big bosses from the general office should go around the plant dressed up like a regular workingman in the plant and talk with the men. The men'd be willing to talk to them. It would create a good feeling. They used to do it before — so I heard. There's kinda wall grown between them and us. We don't tell them much. They should walk among the men and women, colored and white. *Ask 'em about their jobs.* They shouldn't come around like a banker though. Should even have overalls on. . . . A foreman should *understand the trade* before he's made foreman.

Interviewer: How about your foreman, Mr. Heilhecker?

Let's skip that, Father! [He plainly did not want to talk about his own foreman. I had the impression that he disliked him. Though Mr. Heilhecker was very pleasant and talkative during the interview, he was concerned about my taking notes and was afraid his name might be used. I reassured him, and ceased taking notes. At the end, he said he would have enjoyed talking longer. His name, of course, is not Heilhecker.]. . . . A good fore-man will *take the workingman's ideas.* I see so many things around the plant! But I'd never turn in suggestions. The workingman's afraid of rate cuts, and two or three men losing their jobs.

Long-service butcher, Carl Berger, 36, stout and smooth spoken, likes the company and his job, but not his foreman:

> I handled the department once as assistant foreman during the war. The office was on my neck. The plant was on my neck. You're better off as labor. . . . My foreman is a crazy pollack. He's too *nervous.* He fires and then he doesn't follow through. He *rides* the men. He goes behind my back.

Shipping clerk, Joe Pohle, 38, though he looked much older and was nervous, over twenty years in the same department, also has company allegiance but says:

> My foreman is good at times, but he can be real *nasty* at times, a real slave-driver. . . . Louie [one foreman] kids around. They'll work for him. But ———— [the other foreman] he's all business. His only friend is money. He *never praises you.*

Everett Fuller, a packer in the same department as Pohle, has a different reason for disliking his foreman. Fuller, 30, and supporting a family of six in a crowded Bronzeville apartment on a rather unskilled job, fre-quently homesick and appearing not too alert or robust, has secured a part-time job at night in a tailoring school where he also receives in-struction. Getting to bed late, he frequently comes to work late. This is his major source of friction with his foreman. He likes neither his job nor the company:

> At times, my foreman is kind of tough to get along with. I came late this morning. I was just sleepy-headed. If you come late two times, he sends you home. There isn't anybody in the department care anything about him. . . . I guess he's sore because I'm going to school. Coming to work on time, that's my trouble. He said he'd see the division boss if I came late again. Sometimes if you come late, he'll kid with you. I just didn't hear the clock. I get out of school at 11 and get to bed at 11:30, five nights in the week. . . . Me an' the foreman will probably fall out pretty soon any-way. I'll be late again. Gettin' to work on time, that's my biggest problem. But I likes to get to work on time. . . . One day me and the foreman had a big run-in. I was supposed to close some boxes. The foreman said: "If you can't do the work, go on home!" I got angry. He said he was kidding. The assistant foreman can get more work out of the men than ———— can. He don't holler at men the way ———— do. He treats everybody the same. I'm goin' to try to stay here as long as I can and get to work on time. *My trouble is I have quite a bit of sickness in my family.*

> *Interviewer:* What do you think about the company, Everett?

It's pretty good, but other places are much better places to work. Their *rule* — I've never seen anything like it before. You come late a couple of times and they send you home. Other places, if you're five minutes late they'll okay your card. Here, if you're three minutes late, if you get here at 7:03, you have to wait till 7:30 to start. I was sent home once for being late. . . . Another thing — when you go to the washroom, you have to tell the foreman you're leaving the floor. Shouldn't have to tell foreman. Some can go out without asking, the old-timers. Therefore all should.

The foreman over Fuller and Pohle is Charles Buresh whom we have seen earlier to be dissatisfied with the company and his job. He says about his gang:

It's a very good gang. A little absenteeism, but good punctuality. It's one of the best gangs in the ——— House. . . . But punching in in street clothes is no good. The stockyards gets the trash of the labor market as compared with other plants. For instance, they had a joke about the Yards just last night on the radio. When college boys work here one summer and we ask 'em will you come back here next year, they say: "Heck no!"

The union stewards are less favorable to their foremen than the general work force, and for different reasons, usually union reasons. This minority of dissatisfied stewards (18 per cent) usually feel that the foreman is not fair to their union activities. Richard Rex, who is a generally dissatisfied man, due largely to his feelings about discrimination, says:

In our department, *our foreman has fought the union* in every way possible. He has, definitely! In '46 and '47, the foreman gave me a rough time definitely usin' every method he could, without coöperating. For example, I couldn't pass out union cards to the men on my time after I punched out. The contract, paragraph ten, says you can't "disrupt the work." But just distributin' those cards wasn't disrupting the work. . . . It's a company policy to fight the union, because the company always backs up the foreman.

Steward Bill Ryan likes his foreman, but not the general foreman:

Interviewer: How do you like being steward?

I do and I don't. I've been steward a little over a year now. It's hard when a bulldozer like ——— [the general foreman] tries to be right all the time. He adds more work. He turns his head away from me when I come up. [Ryan then discussed a *grievance* case where two men had been by-passed on promotion for which he had trouble with the general foreman.] This case agitates the fellows. Eight have joined the union since the case started. . . . But the foremen are pretty nice. They're strict about some things in here. But they'll give you a break. If you're smoking, they will look the other way. They're younger men. They will listen and will pitch in with you.

Another new steward, Upton Roberts, 37, one of the most amusing talkers interviewed, gave the interviewer the impression of being a troublemaker in his department. Both personal and union reasons set him against his foreman:

Since I got to be steward [eight months], it seems like they don't want me around there. . . . Once I came back five minutes late from lunch from Ashland Avenue. They sent me home for the rest of the day. But I see a lot of others late, and they didn't do anything about it. . . . *The fo'hman don't want to talk to me.* We had a *grievance* an' he wouldn't let me handle it. "What you doing over here! Go on back and go to work!" he said. Same as you a dog, an' not a man. . . . Once I went to the wash-room ten minutes early. The fo'hman pulled my card and said: "Where you been the last half-hour?" Then he bawled me out in front of the whole crowd. . . . They don't want you to tell 'em nothin'.

Steward Joe Calder, 38, semiskilled machine-operator, thinks the foreman is all right, provided he keeps busy as steward:

When I was first hired, I got a book of regulations. But lots of things go on here that are not in the book. Things that the top Swift & Company don't know about. The company is fine. It's the *peoples!* . . . The foreman is all right, so long as the steward keeps after him.

Finally, Willard Smith. Smith, we saw, feels he doesn't get recognition. He lacks company allegiance and has been constantly in feud with his foreman:

The foremen try to force too much work on the men. It's speed-up. And the foremen should be more considerate. . . . The foremen don't co-operate with the employees like they should. There's too much work. It's too hard. We could have a third man on that machine. The foreman *won't listen* to you. He will walk away. Once a man was gone to the washroom five minutes and the foreman sent him home for three days. We have as many as three *grievances* a week. . . . They have a lotta good foremen. But the majority of the foremen, the men don't like them much. They try to frame up on a man. They force a man to do *too much work.* [This is Smith's major complaint against his foreman.]

The left-wing union leaders are about as favorable to the foremen as the steward body in general. (We recall that not all these leaders are Communist sympathizers.) Not all are against the foremen by any means. But these three leaders are. First, Jorel Byron, who has company allegiance, but much dislikes his job and foreman. His main problem is that he believes the foreman does not really know the work itself:

We haven't got a qualified foreman. They haven't got experience in the work itself. . . . Peoples come in who look over the job. But to actually put out the work? They don't know it. ——— is the only foreman who worked from the gang up. It's hard to work on a job if the foreman doesn't know as much about it as you. [This is no doubt the base of Byron's resentment. He feels that management does not understand the difficulty of the work. We remember that he dislikes the work. And also he feels that management does not understand the standards output pace on which he has been disputing with the foreman.] . . . *Some of us were here before this foreman came.* We have more experience. We take exceptions. He plays favorites to get them to control the gang. It causes confusion. The gang is upset. The foremen are better now from what they were.

Don't curse so much — thanks to the gang being better organized. . . . A foreman should be intelligent and have integrity to understand men, to get the work out of them without treating them like beasts. But this man don't want to talk. He ignores you, gives you the run-around. "I haven't got time, I'll see you later," he says. . . . *He insists that you get the work out, but he can't do it himself. He don't know the cost to human flesh or body.* The foreman is concerned about what the office thinks of him, not what the men think of him. It causes slowdowns and stoppages. But he don't tell why the people stop.

Byron's complaint is not typical, but it does bring out the important point that a foreman usually gains more respect from the gang if he has had experience in the gang himself. Most Swift foremen have. But since the gangs are often predominantly colored, if white "outsiders" are brought in, instead of the colored promoted from the gang, the foremen will not have this gang experience. It is a good guess that if Byron, who is a natural leader, had been promoted to a foremanship, colored though he is, much of the trouble he is alleged to have caused and much of his own dissatisfaction would have vanished into satisfaction and greater productivity. Incidentally, the four other men interviewed from this department all approved of this same foreman.

Local leader Tom Wade, neutral in his attitude to the company, has had different experiences with various foremen. But except for one foreman, he too is quite critical:

Some foremen are nice. But others act superior to the workers. They rawhide the workers. Now ——— was all right. He'd never rawhide you. He'd come up to you in the morning and say: "Tom, I got a lot of work to get out today, will you help me?" You *work* for a man like that! He'd never bother you. He'd never stand over you. Sometimes, before we had spells [relief periods] he'd say: "Wade, go upstairs and take thirty minutes' rest. You did a good job!" I'd go and come back and hit it! [Wade now tells of another foreman. He has had many.] He was a southerner and a rat. He say: "Hey you! get on over on that packing machine!" I say: "I don't like that!" He says: "All right, goddam you, get over here. No back talk!" I say: "Don't you swear at me!" He says: "How many years are you here?" I say: "Twenty-three years!" "That's twenty-three years too long!" Then I go over to the superintendent. *Every* day we had a fight. He'd shake his finger in my face. I thought if I hit that guy I'll beat hell out of him. But I gotta wife and sister to support. When the union came in, we gave that man hell every day. He called Negroes "darkies." If I'd go to the washroom, he'd say: "Tom Wade, get back downstairs again!" The superintendent was going to fire him.

In view of Wade's ideological position against capitalism and management, it is surprising to see the praise he has for some foremen, thus not showing complete loyalty to the class-warfare dialectic. But such lack of perfect orthodoxy is not surprising at the local union level, since the leaders at that level do not have the training and discipline which the Communist party insists upon at higher levels.

Finally, Tom Metzger, who is no Communist sympathizer. Metzger constantly rows with his foreman, often about conducting union affairs in the department, yet he admits that the foreman is not too bad:

> My foreman? I knew him from before packing days. He's not too bad a guy. One day he's okay. The next, he's not! You got to live with him. But he drinks. . . . And our foreman is too strict on adequate time off for rest periods, especially for the women workers. [These rest periods had been abused by some workers, which accounts for the tightened discipline.]

In sum, we see that a minority of stewards and left-wing union leaders oppose their foremen partly for union reasons, partly for the same reasons as that minority of the general work force does. Some of these men, of course, are dissatisfied for reasons other than the foreman, such as the company or the job. Some are at fault themselves. Others are up against an inadequate foreman. But the qualities which they seek in their foreman are about the same as those sought by that large majority of the Swift-UPWA workers who are satisfied with their foremen, namely that he "leave you alone," and that he "listen."

FOREMEN SPEAK OF WORKERS

The second major question of this chapter is: What does the foreman think about the people of the plant community? He is their closest observer and his opinion is important. Briefly, the Swift foremen think they have a fairly good work force under them. A few are unfavorable, about 20 per cent. The majority, about 75 per cent, are favorable including some who are very favorable. The foremen are significantly less favorable to the employees than the latter are to the foremen.

Now let us hear what the foremen themselves have to say. Old-time foreman, Peter Mills, we saw to have high company allegiance. He has a small veteran gang in one of the craft departments and thinks highly of them:

> My gang is very good. *The newest man has ten years' service;* the oldest, thirty-three years. We have almost no absenteeism or tardiness. And there's no drinking that I know of. At times we have rush jobs. Then I will say: "Mike, I've got a rush job. I'd appreciate it if you'd help me out." But I don't do that for all. If a man is slow, I give him time. . . . We haven't had a grievance since 1923 when I started the gang. [A remarkable record.] There are no union men in the gang as far as I know. [The mechanical and craft departments used to be the stronghold of the union. But since the 1948 strike, they had mostly dropped out. Later they began to return.] . . . You got to know the men. There are not two alike, I've found. One needs a pat on the back. Another needs a kick in the pants. I play no favorites. Sometimes I keep their pay envelopes for them. And every Christmas, I send a card to the whole gang.

Foreman James Drucker, 46, over a moderate-sized department, mentions the length of service of his gang as we noted both Mills and Gibravich to do. The foremen constantly rate the old-timers over the new-comers. This is related to our previous finding of greater company allegiance among the long-service groups. Drucker states:

My work force is *mostly old-timers* now, with fifteen years' service. They're all good men right now. They go ahead and do what they're told. During the war we worked twelve hours a day. And to train an all around man in our department takes a year. We couldn't get the men. The colored made our big problem and our life miserable. There was absenteeism, tardiness, and the quality of the work was poor. But we weeded out all the undesirable workers since the War. Now our gang is about 60 per cent white and 40 per cent colored.

Interviewer: Is there any difference between the colored and white?

The white will do more and go out of their way for the company. The colored do just what they have to do. You have to prod them more than the whites. But we don't have much absenteeism or tardiness now. And all the workers average a 70 B-Hour in my department.[7] [This is a good productivity record]. . . . Each man is a different individual. You've got to use diplomacy, psychology and common sense. . . . Five or ten of my gang can't read or write. These are mostly colored. I don't understand why they don't go to school. I talk to 'em, try to get 'em to night school. One fellow went right through eight grades. . . . We haven't hired a white man in ten or fifteen years in ———— House. We had four recently, but they didn't want to stay.

Interviewer: Why was that, Mr. Drucker?

Well, it's hard work. A lot of it is hard and heavy. The plant is well over fifty years old. Working conditions — that's the main factor. Even pay don't attract them. They'd rather work elsewhere for less pay in better working conditions. Ventilation, light and layout, those are the three main factors. It's dark, and the ventilation is no good. Unless they *have* to work, they don't stay. People don't want to work in ———— House. Now take that new plant of Johnson and Johnson out in Clearing on Cicero, south-west of the Airport. You would work for less money to be able to work in a place like that. . . . I'd never have come to the stockyards unless I was forced to. [He came during the Depression. He does like his work, however; and he has company allegiance.]

The foremen who are unfavorable to their work force come from a variety of departments, but none from craft or mechanical departments. Their gangs are all at least two-thirds colored. Their attitudes follow a surprisingly uniform pattern. We note how they mention the change from white to colored during the second World War. For these foremen, the colored workers are a major problem. It is hard to tell how much of their unfavorable attitude is due to the poor workers they had to supervise under difficult war-time conditions, how much is due to sheer prejudice, how much is due to the actual record of their present workers, and how much is due to poor foremanship. All these foremen have company allegiance and most like their jobs.

Foreman Archie Ferris, whose keen dissatisfaction about his own advancement we have seen, says:

> My gang is quite radical. It's a hot bed. It was 65 per cent white, ten years ago; it's most colored now. . . . Because of seniority, I can't get whites, except at "labor." What are they going to do for supervision ten years from now? And why shouldn't the colored be trained for foremen? There'd be no trouble. The backbone of the company is the colored boys. They couldn't operate without 'em. . . . The average white guy won't work here. He has to start as a laborer. He has to buck seniority. He has to wait twenty-five years to be a butcher. If I had to come here as a butcher, I wouldn't stay here five minutes. *By scalers or checkers, is the only way to bring in prospective foremen.* But then they never have know-how in the gang. [We remember how Jorel Byron, who works in this department, spoke about the need of a foreman knowing the work of his gang.] . . . It's hard work in here. A man wears out his hands. If Swift pays him $1.87 an hour [1949], they get it back! . . . It's hard to force a man to do something you yourself thought wrong. The gang doesn't want to make a 70 B-Hour. They will do a 60 B-Hour only. I don't like to force it down their throats.

Foreman Tom Hall, 52, thirty years a supervisor, is now over a large department, 82 per cent colored. Hall does not seem to be a highly successful foreman. He shows prejudice, perhaps due in part to his dissatisfaction with a number of things:

> The help has changed since the War. It was a pleasure to work in this department before the War. There were almost all white employees then. Now it's mostly colored. . . . The colored will lie direct to your face and don't even know it. They throw hooks into you. Absenteeism is very bad in my department. We got four men off sick today. . . . Those damn n——s in the CIO. They just stand around and do *so* much and that's all. No more.

Foreman Andy Hadley, a former southerner over a department two-thirds Negro, continues the same pattern with obvious race prejudice:

> My gang is fair now. It was poor during the War. *But you have to constantly stand over them.* [From the point of view of the gang, we remember, a good foreman is one who "doesn't bother you."] . . . "You're crazy to work so hard," the gang will tell a man who works hard. The colored think they're not going to get ahead very much, therefore they don't work hard. [Here Hadley puts his finger on the root cause!] They holler civil rights and discrimination. These colored are getting bold. [They are even demanding their rights as citizens!] The colored are far less efficient workers than the whites. Especially the jitterbugs and "traveling jitterbugs" [a man who came in during the War and worked inconsistently here and elsewhere]. Nobody's ever going to convince me that colored are equal to whites. They're just n——s. They come out to the plant and don't want to work.

Finally, Oliver Keighley, who is over a large department over half colored. Keighley, along with Hadley and a few others, is one of the minority of foremen who give clear evidence of race prejudice. In going about the department with Keighley, I could easily observe the rather cavalier manner he had with some of his colored workers. He says:

> Our Division is the toughest division. Look at ———— and ———— [other foremen] how nervous they are. Being a foreman is a tough job. And those B.A.I. men [government inspectors]! Three out of four of them are n———s. They're new and causing trouble. [The inspector can tie up equipment that is not clean, and thus slow down the foreman's production record.] . . . With a n———r, you can't give him any breaks. They've got no character. The only good ones are dead ones. . . . Once a colored woman slapped me in the face during a grievance hearing, during the War. Also she threw a can at a foreman. She was discharged. . . . There's no comparison between colored and white, in quality, performance, punctuality, absenteeism, neatness, attitude toward work, etc.

> *Interviewer:* Have you noticed any friction between colored and white workers?

> No, I haven't noticed any.

Foreman Keighley seemed to have nothing but contempt for his colored workers. He said that before he came to the company he didn't mind colored people, that he liked to hear them talk about themselves. But since he came to Swift, his attitudes changed. We must note that he came here in the early 1940's, during the War when the poorest type of worker had to be taken on. Undoubtedly this, plus the slapping incident are important causes of Keighley's attitude. And obviously his attitude toward colored workers largely modifies his attitude toward the gang as such.

FOREMAN VIEW OF RACE ISSUE

We have already seen that for a few foremen the race issue is a paramount one. We have also seen some examples of prejudice which make suspect the judgment of the foremen involved. But the over-all attitude of the foreman body is important. The accompanying table shows that the great majority of the foremen prefer white rather than colored employees, although many make distinctions and say that some colored workers are preferable to whites. Tables summing up such attitudes are dangerous unless used in conjunction with statements of the

TABLE 18

Attitudes of white foremen to colored and white workers
(1950)

Colored workers preferred to white	4%
No clear comparative comment	4%
Colored workers same as white	15%
White workers preferred to colored	77%

sometimes complicated, often many-faceted attitudes themselves. Hence we proceed at once to listen to the foremen.

Colored are Preferred to White. Youthful foreman, Joe Brauer, over a large department, mostly women, gives every evidence of being a very satisfied foreman. He states:

> My gang are good. The majority are *old-timers*. You can go away and not worry. As for white and colored, *I'd rather have the colored.* The white girls are too fussy. They won't wash a table and things like that. . . . Especially with the union here, you have to treat all equal or you have a grievance. . . . The DP's are good, but they try too hard. They are too eager. They raise the accident rate. And then language is a big problem. . . . But absenteeism, production, etc., with colored and white it's the same. There's no friction, no race troubles. I explain to the new whites how to get along with the colored. There's no trouble. *Often the colored will average more bonus.* [Therefore higher productivity.]

Colored Workers same as White. We have already heard Foreman George Gibravich say that colored and white are "about even." Foreman William Halloran says the same. Halloran, 50, has company allegiance, but he is dissatisfied about his advancement possibilities, and is not enthusiastic about his gang, though he sees no racial differences. His department is moderate-sized, about half white and half colored. He states:

> My gang is not too good. We got some good people during the Depression. But it's hard to get good people. That's due to the nature of the work; it's seasonal. Then it's hard to accumulate much. . . . The colored are like an ordinary person. *They're supposed to be lazy, but I don't think so.* Anyone will do a good day's work, if they're placed properly. The employment office should place them properly. I got some that are good, some fair, some poor. If I'm walking around, I always recognize the colored and say hello. Once I was going down the street with the big boss and I met one of my men and said hello. Later on he said to me: "Bill, why you recognize me when you with those big shots?" I answered, "I still know you, don't I?"

Charles Buresh whom we saw above to be satisfied with his gang says:

> Get the colored the right job and they're okay. *They're as good as the whites.*

And Ambrose Toner, of high company allegiance, states:

> I have twenty men in my gang. They're mostly *old-timers* and colored. I have two DP's who are very good, but there is trouble with the language. *I have decent colored people.* They're not foolish. They're here to do work. They are close to the age of forty and are serious family men. During the War we had floaters. . . . My gang works together well. The colored I have are *very steady workers.* We have no arguments about race. . . . I talk to the men. They ask you about their problems. I get one his check in advance. If it's days off — I say: "We'll try to give you the day you want."

White Workers Preferred to Colored. Here we must be careful to follow myriad distinctions. First, the old-timer versus the young worker. As we have seen in many interviews already, the old-timers of both races are rated over the newer men. Hugh Moriarity, for instance, 55, veteran shipping foreman, is extremely against the new colored.

> My work force? It's terrible! This began just before the War started. The CIO is the big thing. [Moriarity is not against its leadership.] . . . The crews don't take responsibility today. If something's smeared or bad, they won't clean it up. They"ll ship it out anyway. It's the type of people — mostly colored. Now the old-time colored, they're wonderful. But the war-time jitterbugs — they're the majority now — they're terrible. *The old-time colored are better than the whites we get today.* The old-time colored [I got three in my gang] say: "My God, what those guys, those jitterbugs doing? They don't get interested in the work." They make hard work out of loafing. *The B-Hour? They don't take interest.* They'd like a bonus if it was *given* to 'em for nothing! . . . The company bent over backward during the War. . . . Then the communistic influence is bad. I got one Communist instigator, ———. He went over to the Forum Hall on 43rd Street, and used to talk at Washington Park on summer afternoons. . . . To listen to colored talk is like a barnyard. . . .

Secondly, the northern Negro versus the southern Negro. The work qualities of the northerner are usually, though not always, said to be superior. This is not surprising, since the transition from a southern farm to a northern urban packing plant is a big step indeed and, incidentally, just as difficult for a so-called "hill-billy" of the white race as for a Negro. The north-south distinction can become unfairly stereotyped, of course. Veteran foreman Joe Harman, over a small department, says:

> The War brought colored up from the *south who didn't know how to handle themselves.* But our work force is improving a whole lot. The floaters taken on during World War II are mostly gone now. The DP's are helping us. They are very good workers. . . . How do I compare the colored and the whites? It all depends on the supervisor. Take the colored and be strict with 'em, and they'll go to town for you. They do appreciate a break. You got to go along with them and give them equal fair play. If they think you're prejudiced, it's no good. The old-time whites — you can tell them what to do and go away and they'll do it and look for more work. But the colored man doesn't have initiative. If he gets through, he'll stop and wait for you to come and tell him what to do.

Another veteran, Howard Frisbie, disgruntled about his chances for advancement, but with company allegiance withal, over a large department, 75 per cent colored, states:

> The *old-timers* in my gang are fine fellows. But the boys today from the *south* — well, it's a matter of education — they don't have it. There is filthy talk, especially among the young. They talk sex all the time, and about the white girls in England during the War. . . . The turnover is okay. It was higher when white and colored worked together. My department is all colored. . . . I understand the colored boys. Their rents and

groceries are higher. I send a personal Christmas card and birthday cards to the men. I send fifty or sixty cards a year.

Old-timer, Ted Plawinsky, 60:

> The colored are not as good workers as the whites. I'd give three whites for five coloreds. Especially those recently up from the south.
>
> *Interviewer:* How do you know who comes from the south?
>
> From the records. Also we ask 'em: "How long are you north?" They don't know how to handle a pick or a shovel or a tool. *For that matter the whites from Arkansas are just as unskilled!* The colored don't want to learn. They don't want to work. You have to stand over them or they won't work. You don't have to stand over a white man. The average productivity is definitely below that of the whites.

Foreman Russell Rivers, 60, expert of many years with Swift's meat production, supervisor of a large department, says:

> Some of my people are complainers. Of the colored, the southerners are less well educated. *The northerners are better workers.* The southerners have no respect for women. They're more apt to cause trouble. They like to play more and talk and laugh more. But there are agitators among *both* white and colored. With some you got to be mean, you got to use the whip. With others you got to be soft. Dealing with people is a big job. I wish the brass hats in the office got to run my department once!

On the other hand, a few foremen take the opposite view on the northern-southern issue. This is evidence that when southern inferiority is taken as a universal judgment it does become a stereotype. For example, Anton Ekberg, 46, over a small department almost all colored, says:

> My gang is the cream of the crop! But the colored are nowhere's near the white. The DP's are really workers. There's little absenteeism in my department. . . . Very few have loyalty to the company. Pride in doing a job? Yes, the *old-timers* have it. . . . The northern-born colored respect you less than the southern-born. [This foreman has never yet had a grievance he did not settle at his own level.]

Finally, Dave Phillips, 38, also over a small and skilled department, mostly colored:

> I have a good work force. I can choose whom I want — good men. My jobs are high pay, so I can pick and choose. I can tell after a forty-day trial if a man will do well. If not, I can lay him off. . . . The colored work all right, *except* the jitterbugs. You got to stand over them. The jitterbugs are *not necessarily up from the south recently. Rather, they're Chicago born,* but young and flighty.

Other foremen have different comments and distinctions about the two major races under them, but following the same general theme. For instance, Joseph Pietrowicz, 63, over a craft department:

> I got twenty men in my gang. They're pretty good. *Mostly old-timers.* Mostly skilleds. I got some apprentices, but no "labor." My men — I

raised them from the street and made mechanics out of them. But now by seniority the union almost tells you whom you can take. . . . Now the colored are coming in. They are pretty good. . . . They are never late or off. They are as good as the white. *They will never be as good mechanics as the whites though.* But they are willing and trying. [Here Pietrowicz may show prejudice.]

And Phil Kostka, also a foreman in a small craft department into which (thanks to the union), Negro workers are now able to advance, also gives the impression of yielding to stereotypes about the colored:

Most of the men are skilled. Some are very good. Quite a few intelligent men who seem to grasp the job to do. If they're not qualified, we send them back to their old gang. We get men, young, fellows from the plant and train them here. . . . We're well satisfied with the men. It's a very nice group. . . . I have two colored in my department, one janitor and one ———— a skilled job. He's an old-timer. Very few white men like that job. [Here Kostka starts to generalize not from his own experience in his department but from stereotypes.] You have to keep after the colored more than the white. That's the big complaint. You get some vicious ones, too. They live from payday to payday.

Finally, Jack Filas, 43, known as a very successful foreman for the production and morale of his small department (mostly colored women), gives an adverse judgment on the Negro workers:

The Negroes are not as healthy as the whites. They're more touchy. They want to go home more readily if sick. Their mental capacity is slower. They are lazier and less skilled. They suspect a white man that he will favor the whites. Now all this is on a proportional basis, therefore with exceptions, of course. And they're much better than during the War. Their loyalty to the company is increasing. It's better than five years ago.

The job of a foreman in the Swift-CIO plant community is far from easy. The foreman stands between the operating management, the salesmen, the staff experts, the union stewards, the workers, the other foremen. Probably no other position in the plant community carries with it more daily human relations contacts and problems than that of foreman. Ninety per cent of his time is spent in dealing with people. He is pressed from above to cut costs, raise production standards, eliminate accidents, avoid grievances, save shrinkage in the weight of meats, and so on. He is graded, and his department compared with others in this plant and in the Swift chain. He is also under pressure from his men and the union. His men are often careless with the cost of materials, too lazy or fearful to maintain standards output, cantankerous about grievances.

The foreman, as pictured in this chapter, is in an ambiguous position. According to the workers, a good foreman is one "who leaves you alone." According to many foremen, "you must stand over the workers," especially the younger colored men, if you want to get the work done. Both are doubtless right, in part. But the foreman who stands over all his men, indiscriminately, failing to see that many of them (including his Negro workers) will do better work if they are trusted, encouraged, and given responsibility rather than constantly supervised, is missing the point.

We have also seen in this and the preceding chapter that the race question in the plant, like most questions, is a two-sided one. Although some of the foremen are clearly prejudiced in their evaluation of the Negro worker, still the fact that such a majority prefer to have white workers in their gang leads us to ask whether improved interracial harmony is not partially dependent upon the Negro himself improving his own work qualifications.[8] Most of the blame falls on white shoulders in both the south and the north. There is no doubt that the American Negro is often reduced to second-class citizenry, with inadequate education and craft training, condemned to a Bronzeville ghetto, and denied the advancement opportunities which, according to the "free enterprise thesis," are the stimulant to the very initiative and ambition which some free enterprisers may find wanting in him. We see again the vicious circle that Myrdal noted in the south. "We cannot promote the Negro because he lacks ambition." But the Negro lacks ambition because he cannot be promoted. Of course, part of the blame must fall on a minority of the Negro workers themselves. They are free agents. They are not typical of all Negro workers, but the fact that some of the younger Negroes are singled out and called "jitterbugs" is not an encouraging sign. On the other hand, if many young white men were working in the Yards they might be labeled "jitterbugs" too.

All this may become more understandable when we recognize the current American crisis in morality, and add the problems of post-war youth facing an uncertain future, and add to these the special problems of Bronzeville. Evidently work remains to be done by both races toward the improvement of industrial relations in the Swift-UPWA plant community.

WORKER AND UNION IN ACTION

CHAPTER SEVEN

THE UNION AND THE MEN

UNION ALLEGIANCE

With this and the following two chapters we arrive at the second area of the Swift-UPWA plant community, the local union. In analyzing the workers' degree of union allegiance we mean simply, "general satisfaction with the union as an institution," or "an attitude of favorability toward the existence of Local 28 as a part of the plant community," or "belief in the necessity for a union in this plant," or "approval of the union as an institution." It is a concept parallel with company allegiance, though each organization is approved by the worker because it satisfies different needs.

This definition does not mean complete satisfaction with every aspect of the union, with its local and international leadership, with its handling of grievances, its contract benefits, its dues, its meetings and social events, its literature, such as the *Flash*. These are only factors which influence union allegiance, but do not constitute it. So too, the union leaders often affect a man's attitude toward the union as an institution even more than the foreman affects his attitude toward the company. Even so, the worker distinguishes between the local and its leaders.

Nor does union allegiance mean real loyalty to the trade union movement, though at times this will be included. It is simply an attitude of approval expressed in such words as "I think we ought to have a union around here." We shall discuss how the worker's attitude of union allegiance affects his behavior toward the union in Chapter Nine, for we have more complete data on the effect of union attitudes on union behavior than we have on the effect of company attitudes on company behavior.

The average worker in the Swift-UPWA plant community believes in the union half of that community. Union allegiance is not as pronounced as company allegiance, but it is there. This is the second principal finding of our research.

The presence of union allegiance in the plant community becomes almost remarkable when we consider the history of events that have militated against it: (1) Swift's tradition of fair treatment; (2) the serious failure of the union's 1948 strike; (3) the fight between Local 28 and the International, creating the impression of two unions in the plant; (4) the capture of Local 28 by the Communist party from 1949 to 1952; (5) the race issue. In spite of these forces, most of the workers believe in the union. If we had sampled the workers' attitudes in 1946 and 1947 before most of these forces had become acute, no doubt we would have found even a stronger union allegiance than we found. In view of this recent history, the clear allegiance that we did find takes on a new significance.

The average attitude of the workers toward the union as an institution is favorable, 2.14 on the scale, as shown in Table 19. This was not unexpected.[1]

TABLE 19

Workers' attitudes toward the union

(*Random, stratified sample of 192 workers, stewards, and leaders by service, sex, and race; 1950*)

Men			Women	
Negro	White		Negro	White
1.71	2.08	Short-service	1.75	2.63
1.60 (high)	2.38	Middle-service	1.81	2.13
1.85	2.46	Long-service	3.19	(low) 3.44

Totals (Weighted)		Attitude Scale	
Men	1.97	Very favorable	1.0
Women	2.17	Favorable	2.0
Negroes	1.75	Neutral	3.0
Whites	2.45	Unfavorable	4.0
Short-service	1.78	Very unfavorable	5.0
Middle-service	2.07		
Long-service	2.33		
Union members	1.70		
Nonunion workers	2.80		
Union stewards	1.00		
Union leaders	1.00		
All workers	2.14		
(Foremen	2.40)		

Table 20 shows the distribution of attitudes, with a small cluster of anti-union people at the bottom. Here the attitudes are more widely distributed than they were for company allegiance.

The outstanding fact is that nearly 80 per cent of the workers have union allegiance. Even a majority of the foremen believe in the need for a union among their employees, in spite of the forces we mentioned above. Who are those workers who are clearly unfavorable to the union?

TABLE 20

Distribution of attitudes toward the union

(Unstratified random sample of 202 workers: 1950)

Very favorable	1.0	69
	1.5	15
Favorable	2.0	65
	2.5	10
Neutral	3.0	17
	3.5	1
Unfavorable	4.0	6
	4.5	3
Very unfavorable	5.0	16

	Rank and File	Fore-men	Union Stewards and Leaders
More or less favorable	79%	57%	100%
Neutral	8%	16%	
More or less unfavorable	13%	27%	

They are especially white men of longer service and also a few colored old-timers. The long-service women are the least favorable, but they represent only a small proportion of the work force. The analysis of variance shows a significant statistical difference in attitudes between men and women, colored and white, short, middle and long service.

There is, however, "sex-service interaction," which is simply the statistician's warning bell about the length of service and the sex differences. The service difference (the old-timers have less union allegiance) is highly affected by the long-service women, both colored and white, who differ greatly from their younger coworkers. If they did not differ so greatly, it is quite possible that there would be no significant difference in union allegiance by length of service, and the service variable would be of no importance. Further analysis of the data, however, shows that among the white men there is also a significant difference by length of service. Thus we may conclude that although the service variable is affected by the sex variable, yet it does have its own independent influence at least for half of the plant community. For the Negro men, nearly 50 per cent of the community, length of service does not seem to affect union allegiance. Their slight differences shown in Table 19 could be explained by "sampling error" and are not necessarily significant.

Service and Union Allegiance. Among the colored and white women and the white men of the plant community, therefore, the old-timers tend to be less union-minded, 2.33 as opposed to 1.78 for the short-service group. The lesser union allegiance of these old-timers comes as a surprise. Our guess was the opposite. Only the old-timers worked in the plant community in the pre-union (pre-CIO) days. Only they could have the personal experience to compare pre-union conditions in the plant community with the subsequent benefits brought by the union.

Why do so many of the old-timers tend to be less union-minded? The old-timer feels secure. He remembers the good treatment he received before the CIO came along. For instance, half of those who comment on the old Employee Representation Plan favor it. He therefore feels that the company will take care of him. He feels less need of a protective union organization. As we have seen, he tends to have greater company allegiance than the younger workers. The same factors which affect company allegiance are doubtless involved in union allegiance; namely, (1) the longer opportunity for experiencing good company treatment; (2) the dropping out over the years of unfavorable workers; (3) the old-timer's greater age, maturity, conservatism.

Now let us hear Mrs. Elizabeth Washington again, whose high company allegiance we noted. She expresses well the attitude of some of the old-timers:

> The union is *especially for newcomers,* so they get seniority an' all that. The foreman just forgets who comes first sometimes. He don't meant it. . . . *Personally I don't need a union,* but I joined to keep from being the only one who don't belong. I don't want to seem obstinate. I'll support it if it means so much to everybody else.

> *Interviewer:* Has the union helped here, Mrs. Washington?

> In a way, yes. And in a way, no. The strike in 1948 made things worse. The union squandered our money then. There were two groups. One would meet in one room. The other would meet in another room. I would like to know where the union's money is going to! . . . But there's no company without unions. *You need a union to support you.* Otherwise you're not united. [Here she paused and then added an afterthought.] We're not even united *with* a union here though! [Mrs. Washington's union allegiance, of course, is affected by her attitude toward the union leadership.] The small companies had the union as we did; why didn't they stop work? [During the 1948 strike. Some did. Others were AFL and the AFL did not strike in 1948.] Somebody got paid to let them work! I came back before the end. They stopped me a couple of times. But that didn't bother me. The union office people got paid! And some not even in the union, not even in the yards. I was checking on them so I saw what was going on. Some got two helpings at the union [relief stations]; some got none. The churches would send in checks. The union would send the girl next door to cash them at the saloon and I'd never see the money again. [1948 strike relief was chaotic, because of the split between Local 28 and UPWA District One. But there was no dishonesty in Local 28's handling of strike relief funds.] . . .
>   Father, I don't like to say this, but some people in the union — of my race — are ignorant. Our steward is very ignorant. He doesn't even know the local president's phone and department. They wanted me to be a steward. Our department didn't elect our present steward. But I can't fight the company. I have nothing against it. . . . Some union leaders

and stewards got bad tempers. They are ignorant. We needs Christian people in there and they haven't got them.

Sex and Union Allegiance. There is a saying among trade-unionists that women are harder to attract to the union movement than men because they are less union-minded and take less active part in union affairs. Table 19 shows the women to have slightly less union allegiance (2.17 as against 1.97), but this is affected by the long-service women. Some of the short- and middle-service women, both colored and white, are quite union-minded. We may conclude that there are some sex differences in union allegiance, but they are not remarkable, as they were in the case of company allegiance, and they involve almost exclusively only the long-service women workers. Reasons for the lesser union allegiance of some of the women are not difficult to supply. Like the old-timers in general, they feel secure, and the factors we mentioned above apply here. In addition, the women workers may be less interested in union politics and may shy away from occasional union roughness; and the fact that they clearly participate less in union affairs (as we shall see later) doubtless affects their very attitude of union approval.

Race and Union Allegiance. The difference in union allegiance between the colored (1.75) and the white workers (2.45) is truly remarkable. We expected to find it because of the hearsay around the plant, though, of course, it represents a complete reversal from the AFL or ganizing days after the first World War. But these results must be interpreted with caution. The white workers do have union allegiance, especially the short-service men and the middle-service women. But the strike of 1948, the two unions, the Communist tactics of moving the District Headquarters to the Negro district and of constantly stressing race issues so as to make the local a race-instrument rather than a worker-instrument — these things alienated the white workers from the union leadership. Moreover, Local 28 was mostly Negro-led in 1940–1951. Some of the white workers we have found to be prejudiced. This prejudice carries over to the union itself. A man's attitude toward the leaders of an institution inevitably affects his attitude toward the institution itself, at least to some extent. Thus the whites have less union allegiance than the Negroes. But again, if this survey had been done in 1946, the whites might well have had more union allegiance, not less. It is highly probable that at the present time the whites have more union allegiance than meets the eye.

Union Membership and Union Allegiance. It is obvious that joining the union not only affects one's union allegiance but also results from it. If a man bothers to sign up and pay his $2.50 monthly dues, he will be more likely to approve the union than if he refuses to do so. The difference is clear, union members having a union allegiance of 1.7 (favorable), as opposed to 2.8 (neutral) for the "free riders."

Union Leadership and Union Allegiance. Once again, if a man becomes a steward or union leader, he is more likely to have union allegiance to begin with, and his office will in turn be more likely to increase his union allegiance partly because of the feeling of solidarity he gets at union meetings and steward educational classes, and partly because of his sense of union responsibility. The difference here is also clear: union stewards and leaders have a union allegiance of "very favorable" as opposed to "favorable" for all workers. Evidently, the leaders are the most union-minded people in the plant. (Their union allegiance must not be confused, however, with their attitude toward union leadership or their union participation, which may be different, as we shall see.) We have come to the point now where it will be fruitful to let the workers themselves illustrate and interpret these over-all statistics.

PROTECTION AND STATUS

The people of the Swift-UPWA plant community give many reasons for wanting and approving of their union. They talk in terms of the benefits the union has brought them (though some of these benefits antedate the union as can be seen in Appendix IV): holiday pay; clothes-changing time (a contract clause that really antedated the miners' portal-to-portal pay); vacation pay; improved working conditions; wage raises and back pay; "spell" time; a grievance procedure to protect them against the foreman; seniority, and so on. But the most important reason for their union allegiance is that the union gives them job-protection and status![2]

Protection and status — these are what the worker wants more than anything else and he feels that the union is necessary to provide them. The worker wants decent wages, too, and this is his second motive for wanting a union. True, the short-service workers, being more money-conscious because of their young families and lower wage-rates, want the union more for its wage-support than its job protection and status. Yet for the majority of workers, the union is primarily a social and psychological instrument, and secondarily, an economic wage instrument.

The Swift-UPWA worker thus has both company and union allegiance for almost identical primary reasons! Job security, in the case of the company, and job protection and status in the case of the union.

What do we mean by protection and status? No worker speaks of "status" and only a few of "protection," but the ideas expressed by these words can be abstracted from a significant number of interviews. The workers talk of "not being pushed around," being "able to go over the boss' head," "having seniority," "protection for our people" (colored), having "someone to talk for you." For one, it is protection against discrimination in layoff or advancement. For another, it is insurance that his foreman will not overstep himself. For another, it is the enforcement of seniority rules. But, as we shall see, all these workers have one thing in common: they want job-protection. As one Local 28 leader puts it:

> I figure that for the average guy the union is like a slot machine. It's good insurance. He throws his dough in the slot and sees what comes out.[3]

Moreover, in this concept of protection is also woven the desire for status. The worker wants recognition, respect, dignity; he wants to be listened to; he wants some say about conditions in the work life of the plant community; he wants to express the feeling of solidarity he has, in greater or lesser degree, with his fellow-workers. These are the primary reasons why he believes in the need for a union in the Swift plant.

Take George Stompert, for instance. George, we saw, has company allegiance, but dislikes his foreman. He dropped out of the union because of dissatisfaction with the strike relief administration of 1948. Yet he has clear union allegiance:

> As far as the union goes, it's okay. It's a good thing. It's given us great improvements, like clothes-changing time, work clothes, better time, etc. I'll give 'em that. I'd rather have a union than no union even if I don't support it. I won't scab even if others did. . . . I think it best to have a union. Without the union it might become a bad place to work. Even since the strike, the foremen have taken a different attitude. They're tougher than what they were before. With a union, you can get better results. If the foremen want to fire you or give you time off for no reason, the union can stand up for you. *Without a union, there's not anyone to speak for your rights.*

We have noted before that Elder Drake, veteran shipping clerk, has company allegiance, but is dissatisfied with advancement opportunities for colored. Mr. Drake is also dissatisfied with union leadership, but wants a union:

> The union did make conditions a lot better. You can't take that away from them. They got us *seniority rights*, advancement on certain jobs and the thirty-six-hour guarantee. It was quite a number of benefits, but they went to pieces after the last strike.

We have seen that Tom Wright, meat-machine-operator, feels strongly about discrimination and thinks the union has helped combat it; he says:

> The union got us eight holidays with pay. It gets you a raise. . . . But since that last strike the union lost a lot of power. It had good control before the strike. Since the strike the foremen don't respect the union as much. They were very careful before the strike. *But if the steward gets on 'em. They will be okay.* You don't want to go to the general office. You get the devil if you're wrong. . . . The union is still good. A lot of guys say the union is no good. But the union has lots of power. . . . *The union is real good. It's not because the company would do you unfair. But because of the fellows you working under.* . . . Even so, it was fair before the union. Once the foreman said in 1939: "I can't just *fire* you."

Another old-timer, Harvey Montgomery, 58, skilled butcher, dropped out of the union, yet has strong union allegiance. He tells us about the past and continues the motive of "protection":

> The colored didn't believe in the AFL union at the time of the 1921 strike. . . . Then we got the Company Representation Plan from France. It was started about 1923 [1921]. We had elections every year. Up to 1933 our department didn't have much representation. It was all on the management side. Then came the Wagner Act and the CIO. The Representation Plan was disestablished. We organized the Employees Security League on inside of plant. *The fellows got disgusted and called it a "company union."* It stopped in 1937 [1940]. Then the fellows signed up with the CIO. *Swift's Representation Plan was the best of the Big Four though.* Harold Swift talked to them once. If a man was late getting out to lunch he could come back late. About speed-up, they said: "We don't want you fellows to work too hard." . . . There was no trouble getting the colored into the CIO. There was no discrimination. . . . I am the oldest butcher in our department. Once I took up a grievance with the boss myself. Not through the union because they're split. It's not settled yet. *That's why we need a union.* I've been here thirty years. I hope to get that ――――― job; it's easy and pays the top rate. I applied for it, but I feel I've been mistreated. The boss says he can't do anything about it. I know he could.
>
> The union has done good. *A good strong union gets you consideration.* We didn't get no vacations. They'd lay you off just before vacation. And no seniority. You'd have to give whiskey to your foreman. You'd have to take a hat and give a collection to the foreman to get consideration. . . . Discrimination in the plant? It's all over. The saying is: "If you're white, you're right. If you're black, scat!" *The CIO helps against discrimination.* . . . *The union can help on speed-up.*

We saw that Mrs. Willamae Potter, middle-service, semiskilled butcher, was highly satisfied with the company and her foreman. She is also highly union-minded, although rather independent of her steward:

> I never had no reason to have the steward. I can talk for myself better than anybody else can. I go right to the foreman. . . . But we do need a union. In a large company you need a union. The first thing is: *The head people at Swift & Company don't know what's happening. The union can open their eyes.* That sixteen cent raise was a big help. . . . Maybe a man has more service — seniority rights — the union helps there, too.

We saw that Rudolph Zema, 55, has company allegiance especially because of seniority. He believes in the union for a similar reason: job-protection.

> They forced me to join the union. The colored guys got together and forced the whites to join. The steward asked me. They promised they'd break my neck. [Zema has union allegiance, but most who joined under pressure do not.] Before the strike the union was good. Twice they got us $200 or $300 back pay. . . . Union weak now. Lots don't belong.
>
> The union helps a fellow a lot. They stick up for you. If boss try to fire you, to break your seniority, *the steward protects you.* He go to general office and see big boss. . . . One good thing about the union, it

fights for the men. I remember back in 1913 and 1914, you just open your mouth and talk to other guys and foreman fire you. It was awful bad. Pressure was hard on you. They'd work hell out of you and what you get? $1.60 a day and ten hours a day! *You get break in seniority.* Just get hold on a job and get layoff! When they started the union, it helped a man. The union is good for that.

Here we come to several of the middle-service whites, in various craft and mechanical departments who were once the core of union leadership. For instance, Fred Riedl, 39, skilled mechanic, has high company allegiance and some union allegiance, though dead against union leaders. He dropped out after the 1948 strike:

> The union is all right in this way *to protect and help you* in a grievance of some kind. . . . Some men in the gang made it so miserable for me — I was nonunion — so I had to join the union. They rode me for two years. "I can't work with him," they'd tell the boss. I had to buck that. *The union is good if it is run right.* It should take the person's part for the company and for the workers. I'd belong tomorrow, but I don't want to belong to no radical group. . . . The union did good in the past. *It changed the attitudes of the foremen.* The foreman used to use very vulgar language to the men. Then the union fights for the men in grievance. The foremen talk better now. And the *partiality of the foremen — the union cut that down a lot.* I don't think I'd want the union now. If I went into any union, I'd go into the AFL. The mechanical gang is mostly out. Just a few radicals are in the union.

We see the importance of protection to the worker. These craftsmen mention the same idea in terms of "someone to speak for you," "someone to represent you." Pete Savko, for example, age 36, likes the company, his job and the union, though he is not now a member of the latter:

> Most of the mechanics don't belong to the union. I joined, but dropped out at the 1948 strike. Union benefits? I guess they did. The union is a good thing, if you got good people to run it. It got better working conditions in some departments. The CIO is mostly communistic, so I read in the papers. . . . It's all right here now, but *if there won't be a union, maybe it'd be as bad as before the CIO — from the talk I've heard; I haven't experienced it myself.* There should be a union. If you don't have one, there's nobody to fight for you.

Now for two old-timers. First, Peter Kirklauskas, 54, janitor:

> The union? It's up to the leaders. Union is all right. Get some back pay, get some overtime from it.
>
> *Interviewer:* How did you happen to join?
>
> When I was in gang I joined. I didn't want to stay out, they might beat you up. Nobody like me, if I nonunion. . . . Then, if you cut off a little too much pork, boss grab you by arm an' get sore. When union come, they changed that. Big bosses in office, they don't know. When Big Mens coming to department, bosses go an' slow down chain. Big boss see everything go nice. When Big Mens go, they speedit up again. Lotta things

bosses don't know. You are poor man. You can't go to explain to big bosses. *If you got union, you got leader. He go to see Big Mens in office.* . . . A foreman once told me: "I don't give a damn about your service. If you can't do the work, you can get out. Lotsa men outside to do your work! !"

And semiskilled mechanic, Al Suarez, 50, former steward, has company allegiance, but wants union for protection:

Our conditions were worse before the union. The union has helped a lot. Before there was more trouble with the foremen. They used to be harder than now. Men didn't have no chance before. They'd fire you for nothing. Literally. I would say your voice didn't carry far. *Now you can carry your case to the boss. Then to higher boss. That's the best arrangement.* . . . The old Employee Representation Plan didn't mean very much. If they liked you, they'd ship you. If not, they would do nothing for you. For example, in the ———— Room, the boss kept another fellow in preference to me, though I had more service. I feel bitter about it. The Employee Representation Plan fellow — I talked to him and he did nothing. If there was a union it'd be different.

Meat-packer, Mrs. Elaine Ducharme, concludes this aspect of the protection motives for union allegiance. Like not a few workers, she has been influenced by her union-minded father:

I belong to the union. *It's pretty good about helping girls if trouble comes up.* The girls should all join. They told me: "If you wanta join, you can." Dad is a union man. I asked him, and he said: "I would, if I was you. It's a big company — you need a union." He's a steam-fitter, AFL.

Protection Against Discrimination and Union Allegiance. There is another important aspect of the "protection and status" motive for union allegiance, and that is: protection against discrimination for the Negro workers. Not a great number of Negroes mentioned this explicitly, yet since Negroes did tend toward circumlocutions in race matters, I believe that the race-protection motive is a fairly significant motive, especially for the long-service Negroes who have seen the advances their race has made since the coming of the CIO. We have already noted in our discussion of Negroes and advancement that Negroes often credit the union for securing their promotion to better jobs. Arnold Lonsdale, short-service man, whom we saw to be dissatisfied with the advancement opportunities for Negroes, states:

The union is a good thing for a group of people like we are [i.e., colored]. Sometimes management wants to do differently than we want to do. It's a good things to stand together.

Several white workers, not very enthusiastic about the union for themselves, state that the union is necessary to protect the interests of the colored; long-service worker, Mary Milunas, for instance:

The union doesn't make any sense. Why should I belong? Some big colored guys stopped me on the road. I said: "Oh, gosh, I better pay the $1.50." They wouldn't let you come in unless you signed a card. I dropped out at the 1948 strike. We got nine cents and then they raised the meat prices. What good did it do? I got no help during the strike. [She said she didn't ask for help.] I know a woman though got only $5.00. . . . *But the colored have to have a union.* They don't get along. *Not treated right otherwise.* And I say: "Oh, join. It's good for you." I don't say you shouldn't join. But I don't need it. . . . The union did a lot of good to the people — eight holidays — the union got that.

Interviewer: Is the union worth having, Miss Milunas?

I don't know. I can't tell you.

Finally Tommy Zorach, 23, young mechanic dissatisfied with the union leadership, says:

I never joined the union. They pull a lot of boners. The strike in 1948 was the biggest mistake they made. It wasn't too bad for me. I was single. *The union is mostly for the protection of the colored.* The colored would have a hard time if it wasn't for the union. Some foremen don't have much use for 'em. . . . People have to have a union. In a way the foremen are afraid of the union. So they take it easy on the men. Don't push you around as if there wasn't a union. If there was no union, you either do, or pick up your time. . . . We don't need a union in our department. We have no grievances.

The second motive for the union allegiance of the Swift-UPWA workers is this: they want the union because they believe it can and will improve the contents of their weekly pay-check.

Ezra Lamb, short-service, only 39, but a grandfather with five children of his own, who pays $50 a month for two rooms in Bronzeville, wore at least seven union buttons in his hat as a sign of his clear union allegiance:

I wouldn't want to work here unless there was a union. The union done good. I got only seventy-seven cents an hour during the War. I got a sixteen cent raise. Now I get $1.27. *The union got us the raise.* They got us back pay in 1945 and 1947. The union helped us mighty good. It got us fifty cents a week for work clothes. It got us paid clothes-changing time. It got us a bracket raise. . . .

Otto Jagielski, a short-service worker in spite of his age, 50, shows how his attitude toward union leadership affects but does not destroy his union allegiance:

I'm not in the union since the strike of 1948. I wouldn't join now because of the Reds. That Peace Conference! They should make him stay there in Warsaw! [He refers to the Local 28 delegate to the Communist "peace" conference in Warsaw, in 1950.] . . . They're striking among themselves. We got two unions, one at 43rd Street and one at 48th Street. They're bucking each other. I'm not against unions. They help you to argue things out. I guess they can help you maybe. *If it wasn't for the union we wouldn't get half the pay we get.* . . . The union was good during the War. But it breaks up after the War. *I think they should have a union even though I don't belong.*

Charles Sucholdolski, also in his fifties though only recently with Swift in continuous service, continues the same theme of wages, yet we see how mixed his attitudes and motives are:

The union? I belong all time because *that's workingman's organization.* Benefits? Yes, the CIO got us better pay, clothes-changing time, fifteen-minute rests, eight paid holidays. . . . I work thirty-eight years. Before, if you work three or four years, if foreman no like you, you get laid off, and new man put on. They don't do that now.

Interviewer: Who changed that, Mr. Suchodolski?

Well, everything got changed!

Interviewer: Did the union help?

I don't know. Seniority is good!

Interviewer: Who got this seniority?

Company give it.

Charlie House, 34, proud of his skilled food-machine job, says:

The union have fought very hard for us. . . . I think the union is a great organization for the working class of people. *I don't think the company is always going to be just.* The company make a lot of profits. They should give a fellow a decent, living wage. $1.15 an hour is hard for a man with a wife and kids. [This was the common labor rate in 1950. House was making considerably more.] . . . *The union got us quite a few different things, like more money.* The union is a swell idea. After thirty days I worked here, I joined up, in 1942 or 1943. . . . I feel that if there wasn't a union, it would be very hard to work here. I talked to an old fellow and he said so. "You do this, or get out!" If there wasn't no union, we'd be right back in the old days.

Semiskilled machine-operator, Tom McClellan, whom we saw to be somewhat unfavorable to the company, perhaps largely because of an unsolved grievance, has clear union allegiance, though he thinks the union very weak:

We've gained quite a bit, thanks to the union. We got quite a few raises. And working conditions are better. They wouldn't really ride you now. They're more watchful, keep things in line. But I think the union is on its way out. That 1948 strike — they claim that outside plants forced the strike, the majority overruled us. Now the union is bickering back and forth, calling each other Communists. After the strike, very few signed cards again. . . . I'd like to see a union, if it was being handled properly without that bickering. . . . What's the use of belonging to the union if they don't know what they're doing themselves? . . . The union is through. The people are scared, so they don't join it. If it weren't for my argument with the foreman, I wouldn't have joined the union either.

Interviewer: You couldn't go to the Industrial Relations Department?

Only if it meant my job. That would be going too far. There'd be too much hard feelings. They'd always have it in for you. They'd step on your toes.

FRINGE BENEFITS

The Swift-UPWA workers give other reasons for their union allegiance, which we call fringe benefits — holidays, guaranteed time, working conditions. We should note that many of these fringe benefits actually antedate the UPWA though improvements in them have often been negotiated through subsequent collective bargaining.

For instance, short-service man James Jackson, doing unskilled work, dropped out of the union after the 1948 strike. But he says:

> The union has brought us benefits real nice. I plan to get back in. The older fellows will tell you. Now you get more *holidays,* better *working conditions* and the *foremen treats you better.*

Richard George, 24, semiskilled meat-packer, whose father was a grievance chairman of the United Mine Workers, and "was a better union man than I am," makes much of the four-hour reporting time guarantee in his own union allegiance:

> The union got us pay for all holidays. And sick benefits. Before if you were here ten years the company would pay half-pay for first day sick. Now they pay it if you're here only five years. The union has helped a lot. I wasn't here before the union. *But before the union they could call you to work and send you home and you'd lose your carfare. Now they guarantee you four hours.* They could lay you off if the foreman didn't like you. You got seniority now.

Meat-packer, Agnes Kiela, with Swift for eight years and quite satisfied, was very dissatisfied with the 1948 strike and came back before its end; yet she thinks a union necessary:

> I joined the union soon after I came here. I'd been in it about six years. . . . After the strike they asked us if we wanted to stay in. I was so disgusted, I dropped out. Only way I'd like to belong, if everybody did. 'Course it's good to have a union. It'd be worse without it. *Union brought us paid holidays, raises, help in the department.* Sometimes the girls would have arguments. Now they got a chance to say what they wanted to say.
>
> *Interviewer:* Since you're not in the union, do you think they ought to abandon the union?
>
> No, that would be terrible. We need a union. If everybody'd be in it, I'd be too. [This is a very common remark among nonunion workers!] 'Way it is, we get the same benefits even though we don't belong.

Finally, Harold Wyman, 40, skilled machine-operator, an old-timer with Swift, believes in the need for a union, though he is clearly dissatisfied with the leadership:

The CIO done some good. *Got us dressing-rooms, new lockers, and a lot of working conditions.* There's an old saying: "Swift & Company would take your last ounce of blood and ask for another drop." The union stopped that. [Curiously, Wyman has clear company allegiance, though the wage-incentive system irks him.] . . . Personally I have no use for the CIO. It's a tool of the Communist Party. Frankly, that's my opinion. When they retained ――――― [a certain international union leader], as big a Red as you will find, I got out.

The 1948 strike was a raw deal. I talked to ――――― [local union leader] the day before it. He was against it. They tried to sabotage the Marshall Plan. . . . Maybe the fellows in the local say not. But they don't know what they're being used for. They exploit the Negro. . . . The Employee Representation Plan was pretty well company-dominated. I had no grievances under it. Management had an influence over the worker. You had to keep your mouth shut. . . . *But there should be some kind of an organization.* I think basically a labor union is a fine thing. But we have very few that stick to their original ideals like the Printers and Engravers' Union.

THE MECHANICS AND ALLEGIANCE

When the CIO was first begun as "vertical" or "industrial" unionism, difficulties in getting the skilled workers to join the same organization as the unskilled and semiskilled were not infrequent. But in the Swift-UPWA Chicago plant community there was no such great difficulty. Indeed once Local 28 was under way, some of its most active leadership came from the various skilled mechanical and craft departments. But after the strike of 1948 and the seizure by the Communists, the mechanical craftsmen either dropped from the union, or failed to participate, though recently they have mostly rejoined the local. There are various reasons why the mechanics dropped out: the Negro question; the Communist question; and the sense of superiority of the mechanical crafts over the unskilled workers and even over the skilled butchers; the fact that in a packing plant, nearly two-thirds of the work force are not highly skilled, though many are semiskilled. Quite easily the mechanics build themselves a separate little "neighborhood" in the plant community. The rest of the plant is "across the tracks."

A certain union leader, himself a craftsman, explains this attitude of the mechanics to Local 28 as it is currently being run:

> The mechanics do have a legitimate beef. You can't expect craftsmen to be led by a dummy. A boy has got to have respect in Packinghouse Society. You've got to be respected. . . . The mechanics want to belong to an organization, a union, that will help them. They always talk about the butcher and the candlestick-maker.[4]

And a plant foreman says the same thing, though, unlike the union leader he is probably more inclined to a craft union for the mechanics:

> I could never figure out why the [mechanical] workers were in a butchers' union. My idea would be to have their own union, like we did years ago.

Butcher work is different. It's the same work day in and day out. Our work is always something new.[5]

Nevertheless, on the whole, the mechanics still believe in unionism. But many do not want to join up with the rest of the packinghouse workers. The result is ambivalent union allegiance. Robert Rudge, 34, middle-service wielder of a mechanical craft, explains:

I joined the union after the plant was 75 per cent unionized. I dropped out at the 1948 strike. My sister's windows were broken. A bottle of ammonia was thrown through the window. I dropped out then. The mechanical gang dropped out at the strike. There's no CIO in our gang. *We think more of the AFL.* . . . The union got us increases right along. After the start, working conditions improved. But there were two locals in Swift. That's how the trouble started. One was jealous of the other. *We should have a union. Otherwise they'd be jumping all over you.* However, we've had no grievances in our gang since 1948. But other departments need a union. We're just lucky. . . . If we got good leadership we'd go for the CIO. But the colored don't know what they're doing. They can't read some of the stuff they put out. . . . We'll wait for the electricians, to see how they get along before we join the AFL. It's just quiet now. [In 1950 the electrical department voted to join the AFL and quit the CIO.]

Craft-conscious Terry O'Boyle, once a union organizer, also dropped out. He expresses the other-side-of-the-tracks idea:

I helped organize the union in our department. But the union is strictly communistic now. We went back before the end of the 1948 strike, "scabbed," I guess you'd call it. *The union isn't interested in the skilled man, only in common labor.* The present leaders cause disruption. They have little education. They don't know how to run things. The skilled men are in the minority in the plant. It's 85 per cent common labor I guess. [By "common labor," O'Boyle probably means unskilled. The Chicago plant has about one-fifth to one-third unskilled, depending on where you draw the line between unskilled and semiskilled.] . . . *But a union is definitely necessary: we need representation of some kind.* . . . Join the AFL? No, we'd be a minority group. We'd have no bargaining rights. It would be so split up that no one would have power.

Finally, old-timer, Alex Pisarski, whose father worked long years at Swift before him, continues the same theme:

I worked in the ——— Shop and joined the AFL for awhile. When the CIO came, I was the last to join. We all went in as a group. Has the union helped us? Oh, yes. *Conditions are better. We got better dressing-rooms.* The war had a lot to do with it. Labor was hard to get. They had to consider labor. *I don't know whether the union had much to do with it or not.* As far as the union goes, the one they got in there now is no good! . . . The gang in there is all colored. . . . It's all right to be organized. I was on vacation when the gang stepped out of the union so I stayed in. But they never will come back. . . . The electricians went over to the AFL. They pay more dues, and get no special benefits. There was talk that we'd go over, but it died out. We'll just watch the electri-

cians. . . . *There should be a union.* I think we should belong to the
AFL. Then we'd be independent of the CIO. It should be split. Butchers
and producers in one union. All maintenance men in one union. We should
belong to separate groups even if it's all the CIO. *What would I have to do
with a sausage stuffer? I don't belong to the same class.* We have no business with a sausage stuffer. That's the way I feel about it. . . . The union
business is a racket. The Teamsters here and outside are in different locals,
705 and 710. The outsiders cut in on the Swift men in a strike! . . .

If anything, Pisarski brings out the complications of factors making up
an attitude, race, craft pride, leadership, an unfortunate strike, and so
on. His opinion and those of the others do not represent all the skilled
workers of the plant community, of course. But such attitudes are typical
of a significant proportion of the skilled craftsmen.

UNION LEADERS AND ALLEGIANCE

It is not surprising that the union leaders, stewards, and local officers,
should be very favorable to the union as an institution, the most union-
minded, in fact, of all in the plant community. The factors leading to the
union allegiance of these leaders are about the same as those influencing
the rest of the work force, protection, wages, fringe benefits, though the
protection-status factor is by far the most important. Because of the stra-
tegic importance of the local union leaders it will be useful to see how
they express their allegiance in their own words.

As we saw, youthful local leader Harvey Taylor is anticompany
largely because of his strong feelings about discrimination. For him the
union is an important protective agency:

People don't know about the union. When I found out the load the other
union officers had I got interested. The time of the 1948 strike — then is
when I became a steward. *The union is one of the greatest organizations
for the common working man in the world today!* . . . *The union protects
you, like a lawyer. It gives you a defense.* I'm a young man. But when you
get on in years, you get slow. Then the foreman could push you around.
But you got seniority rights, job rights. It keeps the foreman from having
"picks," and saying "I like you," to his favorites and pets. The union pre-
vents that.

For a number of the Negro union leaders the union is a protective
agency, particularly in matters of racial discrimination. Squire Stacey,
for instance, middle-service, aged around 30, has company allegiance but
even more union allegiance:

The union has made progress. I wouldn't have gotten my job without the
union. . . . *Every laboring man should be in a union.* You might get a
break sometime. But other times not! I got along okay, but some don't.
Therefore we need a union. Once in 1946 I was in a new department and
we weren't making our B-Hour. Two men and I were supposed to do it.
So we took it easy. We were fired. But we won our grievance in the first
step. . . . Take the Pipe Shop and the Steamfitters. Now you got seniority

right to go there. The union had to fight for a year or more to get men into the Fire Department. Those jobs — they're nice. They pay better. *The union did help to get colored welders, millwrights, firemen.* The union got us eight paid holidays in 1946 or 1947.

Likewise key union man, Jefferson Andrew:

Once I had a foreman who said to me three times: "I'll fire you for wasting meat." I said: "They all do it. I'm sorry. Won't do it any more." But that foreman persisted. That's why we started a union. That foreman is now a big foreman. . . . The boss if he liked you, could keep you even if you was just hired, and let a man with ten years' service go. There was no seniority in those days. . . . They drove us to unionize. The men suffered. You couldn't keep up on the job. I got out so much product. They'd say: "If you can't do it, there's a man waiting for your job at the gate." You could be fired with no redress. . . . *There was an eight-year interval when they wouldn't hire a colored girl.* Only in the Pork Trim, and Ham Room. *That was before the union.* The colored would even have to break in a new boss. Yet they could never be foremen.

The company rules are pretty good. Like the U. S. Constitution. You wouldn't need civil rights if the Constitution were enforced. But some supervisors try to be Mr. Swift. *We need to keep a union. Some supervisors won't do the right things.* He worked in the gang. Gets promoted. Then he tries to run the plant *his* way.

Another old-timer, Clara Hughes, 49, was an important woman organizer in the plant community. Though dissatisfied with Local 28's leadership, she has clear union allegiance and explains why she became active in the trade union movement:

I got in the union in 1937, right from the start. I took a lot of interest in the union. *It's great to help people out. I would like industrial relations work in the company.* The union is a wonderful thing! It's done wonders! It got a lot of raises for us. It goes according to seniority. *You got some protection behind you.* If the foreman took a liking for you, if the foreman asked you to go out with him, you'd better, or it was your job! In them days, he'd say: "You go here; you go there!" A girl might get pregnant by a foreman. There was favoritism. Today — you don't hear that today. Foremen today are very respectable. . . .

Finally, local leader Della Harris who is a loyal woman unionist:

Has the union done some good for the people?
Ooooh, 100 per cent, Father, 100 per cent!

Interviewer: What, for instance?

They could hire whoever they want and fire whoever they want. If there was a girl hired after me, an' she had more skill, the foreman could fire me an' keep the other girl. . . . An' pay rates too — used to be that the girl who puts out more work gets more money an' the girl who puts out less work gets less money. But the union fixed that. Now everybody gets the same. *Hour* work is the same. An' seniority — the union gave that. . . .

The foreman has frequent contacts with the union through his department steward. Since he is the "first line of management," we sometimes think that the union's new authority in the governance of the plant community challenges the foreman's authority and makes him antagonistic to the union. Especially with an aggressive union leadership such as Local 28 has had, we might expect the foremen to dislike it. But such are not the facts. The foremen do oppose the local leadership. But they approve the local union as an institution. The distinction is important. Of course, the local leadership influences their attitude to the union as an institution. Indeed, like the general work force, they may have more union allegiance than meets the eye. Then too, some of the younger foremen were once in the CIO, and some of the older men in the AFL.

As we saw at the beginning of this chapter, the foremen mildly approve the union, with an attitude between favorable and neutral. Putting it another way, 57 per cent of the foremen have more or less union allegiance, while 27 per cent definitely oppose the union, with the rest neutral.

Those foremen who approve the union rarely give the wage motive as a factor in their approval. Most say: The worker needs some kind of protective machinery, some representation, or grievance procedure. That the foreman himself should recognize and admit this need is significant.

Foreman Ken Robertson mentions the function of the steward as a factor in his approval of the union:

> I wouldn't want the union out of the yards. Neither do I want a radical union. *But when a guy's out of line, you can go to the steward and get him to get the guy in line.* . . . Then, too, the fact that a guy can stand up and voice an opinion, that's a good thing.

Two other foremen especially mention the steward, but in a different function. They say that many workers will go to the steward with a complaint which they would fear to present to the foreman. Thus the steward, and indeed the entire grievance procedure, acts both as a safety valve and as a communication system in that difficult direction, upwards. Veteran foreman, Joseph Herman, 50, puts it this way:

> The company had been making changes even before the CIO. I s'pose the union did get a lot of things. But the company did give a lot of things, too. . . . Through the company's efforts and the union's efforts things are much better. The boss could fire you if he didn't like you. But still he had to have a just cause to fire you, especially if you had five years' service. . . . The union doesn't hurt. If the union functions properly, it can help both. *The people will talk to their representative, the steward — things they wouldn't say to their foreman. The old-country people are shy. They won't talk. It's better to tell it.*

And George Gibravich, a well-liked foreman, says the same:

> The union has brought quite a few benefits to the workers. Better work-
> ing conditions, pay. And with the power of a bargaining unit, they get
> a lot of consideration.
>
> *Interviewer:* Do you think the union has a job to do here, George?
>
> Yes. I think it has. You can't rely on the superintendent to cover all
> grievances. The men keep troubles within themselves. They're unwilling
> to go to the supervisor. Now they can bring it out. A man may become a
> better worker. He can get it off his chest. *The grievance procedure has a
> kind of safety-valve value in quite a few cases, though not in all.* A fore-
> man can't have a perfect line of communication with all his help. In my
> department it's small. The men come to me. But newer men are afraid to
> go to the foreman. Afraid of their job maybe. But they will go to the
> union steward. . . . A man feels he has someone behind him. The union
> is not right all together. But a union with the right kind of people repre-
> senting it — not necessarily the AFL or CIO.

Some of the foremen say the worker needs some kind of representation,
and like the older employees of the general work force, some think the
old company union, the ERP, would do just as well as the CIO, while
some do not. Old-timer Philip Kostka, for instance:

> The CIO brought some benefits, like wages, longer vacations, and seniority
> rights. Do we need a union? *Well, there is needed some representation for
> the employee.* If the employee has a grievance with a foreman and if he
> gets no results, he could take it up with his representative. The old Em-
> ployee Representation Plan handled it very fair. But the employee should
> have some representation.

On the other hand, Joe Pietrowicz, also an old-time foreman, says:

> The Employee Representation Plan didn't work out so well. It was a
> company union, a lotta people say. . . . Did the CIO bring benefits? Yes.
> First of all, *you got more money.* Then a foreman can't knock a man
> around as used to be. The foreman could be pretty tough. He could beat
> you up. *You couldn't be a foreman unless you were tough enough to lick
> anyone in the gang.* Once I asked my foreman: "How much are you going
> to pay me?" He took me by the collar and gave me a kick in the tail. That
> was in 1905. . . . Is there a need for a union? *Yes. So the people can
> ask for things and defend themselves.*

We would expect this factor to influence the foremen favorably toward
the union: when the union wins a raise, the foremen (and all salaried
people) get it too, along with the entire plant. Such is Swift's policy. All
salaried people are eligible for "merit salary increases" quite independently of the union of course. This wage-motive may be important, but
it was mentioned very rarely by the foremen in the interviews. Joe
Brauer, however, does make it quite explicit:

> The plant should have a union. *It protects the foreman, too.* Otherwise the
> company could set a wage-scale any way they wanted. The foreman's

wages go down if the girls' wages go down. And hours, too, are less. *The foreman's wage goes up as the union's does.* . . . The Security League was not too effective. . . . Holiday pay is an advantage, because it gets preholiday attendance up. [Such is one of the contract requirements for the right to receive holiday pay.]

Foreman Tom Moore has high union allegiance though he is quite dissatisfied with the current local leadership:

I like the union, but I don't like the outfit in there now. . . . The Employee Representation Plan was no good. It was hit or miss. If the superintendent didn't want to give a break, he wouldn't. . . . Has the union brought benefits? Very much so. I worked in the gang and got beat around a lot at times, and overworked. You couldn't go to the foreman and gripe. I worked for a foreman who carried layoff cards in his pocket and if he didn't like you he'd pull 'em out. *I think we· need a union to keep us on the ball and keep us from thinking we are little Caesars.* The union is the best thing that ever happened in the yards. I tell the steward that, too.

Over thirty years with Swift & Company, Hugh Moriarity has both company and union allegiance, though he is dissatisfied with his work force:

The CIO done a good job. The only thing is these blame petty grievances. There were no *showers, lockers* in the old days. And you had to buy your own *frocks.* The union got these things. *And the foremen got frocks too.* . . . The old-country Irishman would push out the German, etc. Others would do the same. People were clannish. The union has done benefits for the workingman. The supervisor can get hot and fire a man. Now a fellow can go to see the steward and get a break. *It's a good thing to have a union, to have representatives.*

We saw that foreman Oliver Keighley had very little respect for his men, especially the colored, and that he showed signs of prejudice. We might expect him to be just as strongly anti-union. But he is not. He continues the protection idea:

For the worker, the union has done a lot. He wouldn't have anything otherwise. There's nothing better than a union with good leadership. [Keighley thinks the current leaders very poor.] . . . *The union is a policeman's club against the company.* It wouldn't let the company go too far against the worker. It's a stoplight. I think the union is necessary for the workers. *They should have somebody fighting for 'em. Otherwise it's too one-sided.* Too much is left up to personalities. It's some protection against the foreman.

Foreman Howard Frisbie compares the union to an industrial relations department:

The union done good. The foreman doesn't have his own way so much any more. The union is almost *another industrial relations department.*

Finally, Foreman Archie Ferris we saw to be dissatisfied about his job, his chances for advancement, and his work force, though he has company allegiance. He also believes in the union, but not its local leaders:

What do I think about the union? Well, *as a supervisor,* I don't like it! It means trouble! But *as a man,* it helped a lot. It's as necessary as an organization of supervisors. *People don't understand their problems singly. They need to get together.* The old Employees' Representation Plan was dominated by the company. I was a management member of Committee ————, and I know. I voted for the employees once! I tried to be fair and I nearly got fired for it. I think the CIO could do wonders for the men. But the leaders are a bunch of jerks.

In sum, we see that most of the foremen approve of the union as an institution and for a remarkably similar pattern of reasons based on the worker's need for some kind of protection and representation.

UNION DISALLEGIANCE

The people who have no union allegiance, who have, as it were, disallegiance, are a minority, 13 per cent of the workers and 27 per cent of the foremen. We remember that it is especially the white men of long service who are the nonunion-minded group among the men, and the white women of long service among the women.

Why is it that these people are against having a union, against the union as an institution? Four major factors emerge: (1) *leadership:* they dislike the local union leadership, the 1948 strike, or the two unions, or the Communist control; (2) *race:* they dislike the fact that the union is largely colored (this applies only to the white workers); (3) *good company treatment:* they like the way Swift treats the workers and say "We have no need of a union"; (4) *forced entry into the union:* they dislike pressure that may have been brought upon them to join the union.

The Long-service White Men. Veteran packingtown man, Charles Sukoff, 64, in the yards since 1902, where he started work at 16, is in no wise union-minded:

> The union is *all colored.* It's no good. The *strike* was not good. . . . The union makes trouble! *They wanted to make me belong.* The whites in our department say: "Let the colored run it." Join the union? For what! It's the same thing as no union.

Old-timer, John Waska, 56, who started in the yards in 1912, and seems quite satisfied, is likewise against the union:

> Did union help? Help somebody, not me. I got no grievances. I tell boss myself. He fixem up. I signed union, *they made me.* Alla time they kick on me. I say: "I sign." After I sign, no kick. . . . *I hear Communists in there.*
>
> *Interviewer:* Did the union help the men?
>
> I no see nottin'!

Long-service man, Al Montez, Mexican immigrant, and gang leader, shows mixed attitudes toward the union, indicating how, in his case at least, good company treatment seems to join with the other factors in pulling him away from union allegiance:

> *The union done a lot of good sometimes.* Helped a lot. If they put too much meat on the trucks, the union fixes it. And you got back pay and overtime after forty hours. . . . Everybody joined, so I did. . . . Right now union has trouble. *Union want too much.* They want triple time for Sundays and holidays. *Bosses treat you so good, you don't need a union.* At Armour's and Wilson's, you need a union. I had a friend who was sick there an' he was laid off.

James D. Osuch, 51, box-stitcher and wrapper, father of five, has no union allegiance:

> I don't care for the union. That's out. *We had a company-union before. It was much better.* Whatever we paid won't hurt you. There was some-body you could talk to. They would help you. *Today, the majority of the union is colored, three-fourths.* [Though he said: "I'd sooner associate with a colored person than a white person; except the colored right from the south."] *And then the strike* — I dropped the union. I came back two weeks before the end. The union gave me food during strike, $5.00 a week. Not much help. Two factions are fighting each other now. I couldn't say what's what. They were strong, but they're not strong now.
>
> *Interviewer:* What do you think will happen to the union, Mr. Osuch?
>
> I couldn't tell you and I don't care. . . . They get the DP's to sign, and they don't know what they're signing. Most of the union members are new employees. Fifteen out of forty men don't belong of the old in service, fifteen years and up. *The old-timers are not in it.*

That some white workers should fail to have union allegiance because of the race question is naturally resented. A colored union steward expresses it this way:

> The union is trying to have as much democracy as possible. But the white are not active enough. There are not enough white. For Negroes, the union is the only protection we have. But the union is for every working soul here! Some whites have a superiority complex. . . . They say: "Why should I join a union when I'm receiving the same benefits as you do!" They're narrow-minded. It makes you angry at times. They speak silly. The skilled guys, mechanics, etc., benefited at the last bracket raise, but only one-third of 'em are in the union. . . . Our problem is how we can get our white brothers and sisters together.[6]

The Long-service White Women. These women have the least union allegiance of anybody in the plant. White women of long-service, of course, represent only about 2 per cent of the work force. Mary Cibrow-ski, for instance, aged 40, a kind of gang leader in a small department, is influenced partly by the 1948 strike during which she worked, and partly by a disagreement with her steward:

> I was never much for the union. At election time, they challenged my vote. They thought I was a supervisor. I've had a lot of run-ins with the girls

on account of the union. Once I had the office job one afternoon and a dispute came up and *afterward I had to apologize to the union steward. It was unfair.* It's one reason I wouldn't join the union. . . . Some departments really needed the union and benefited by it: the beef kill, the cutting floors, the hog house. And skilled labor, they were not getting skilled labor pay and raises. *But a union in my department? I don't know what for.*

Mrs. Georgianna Pedusey, 44, a meat packer, is most influenced by the leadership and race factors:

> To be honest, *I don't care for the union. They fixed us at the last strike.* I was making $70 to $75 a week at the time of the strike. I came back after nine weeks. . . . The union wouldn't pay the E.B.A. of my girl friend. They refused. The *union helped the colored, not the white.* There are more colored than white. That's the trouble. If they had white leaders, it'd be different. . . . Everybody was disgusted at the strike. They could have taken the nine cents. I dropped out of the union at the strike. I rejoined in 1949 because I had a grievance. But the union didn't handle the grievance any good. I'm gonna drop out this summer! *The leaders are a bunch of Communists.* Tom said after the strike: "Girls, you don't need no union. *You can always go to the general office and straighten it out.* . . ." The union steward? She's no good. She's a trouble-maker. . . . At election time they wanted me to go to the hall and vote. I wouldn't. They said: "Oh, you got a good job, you're fixed." I said: "I got it myself. Not from the union." The union hasn't done nothing.

Old-timer, Mary Mikalauskas, 50, who came over from Lithuania many years ago, and who has real and evident loyalty to Swift & Company, continues the same theme we've been hearing:

> I joined union before strike for a little while. I no like union. I no pay money for that! Steward tell me: "Only three ladies don't belong in here, you and two others." They tried to stop me from going in the gates. . . . During the strike I stayed home. Then I came back for two weeks. . . . Before, we got no union. We got raise. What for I pay? If it be Catholic, I'd belong. *But they got bolsheviks and Communists in there* — lotsa those blacks are. [We saw earlier that Mrs. Mikalauskas has apparently no race prejudice. Rather she is very friendly with her colored coworkers.] It was 1000 per cent better before the union. We never go on strike then. *Now we get more pay, but everything's dear now.* We get more pay, but we can't buy anything. *I don't think we need a union.*

Other White Workers. Youthful Dave Kniznik, whose dissatisfaction about advancement and the prestige of the Yards we have already seen, is clearly anti-union with an interplay of the factors we have noted:

> I was in it, but I quit. I don't see no sense in the union, in payin' $1.50. The union got us a raise, *then they raise the dues 50¢ to $2.00 a month.* The guys are sore about that. [This dues argument may well be a rationalization for the more important factors against the union to follow.]

> *Interviewer:* How did you come to join the union, Dave?

> To tell you the truth I came out of the army and was put on the elevators. A couple of fellas asked me if I was in the union, and when I was going

to join up. One fellow called me a scab. I would have hit him too. I said:
"When I get good and ready I'll join." Then the steward asked me to
join. I said: "I might as well. *You guys are botherin' me all the time.*"
They let me in without an initiation fee.

Then there was that strike in 1948. My buddy's sister had her baby
in the crib when the strike was on and somebody took a bottle with fluid
in it and threw it through the window. It missed the baby. *That's why
my buddy says he will never join the union!* . . . We had stewards working and then they'd go over to the union hall hollering for the strike. They
were asking for too much in that strike. I came back to work. There was
no trouble. I figgered like this: If the company was willing to give eight
cents [nine cents], I'll take it. *If you ask her for a quarter, she raises her
meat.* . . . There was no money coming in at home. My father and sister
and the kids had to be fed. You can't get another job. My father went to
the union hall. They gave him a card to go to State Street and get po-
tatoes, cabbage, carrots and a loaf of bread. But no meat, no sugar or milk
for the kids. . . . The union ain't right. If the company is willing to give
you so much, you should take it. Then they won't put their meat up. A
lotta fellas are not in. What did we gain from the strike? . . . *I don't
think we need a union. Everything's going all right.* You work eight hours.
You mind your own business. You get along swell.

For short-service meat-packer, Elizabeth Nowaki, 34, of high company
allegiance, most of our factors are operating. She praises the union movement, but I think this is lip-service, not allegiance. The phrase she uses
is a common one with anti-union people: "I think a union is a wonderful
thing, *but* . . . !" Sometimes this phrase is used so the speaker may not
seem to be against a popular movement which he really opposes.

Mrs. Nowaki: I never did believe in the union. It does some good. They
wrote stories in the *Flash* that I was going out with the foreman. It was
terrible! Oh, brother, was I embarrassed! *So I joined to have peace.* . . .
*After two bad strikes I got out. We lost all that time. I think the union is
a wonderful thing,* but it's too unreasonable. For instance: "Forty hours'
pay for thirty hours' work." That's silly. It's impossible demands. They got
us holiday pay, I suppose; that's all. *Working conditions were not bad
anyway.* Personally, speaking for myself, I don't like it [the union] at all.
I wouldn't donate a dime! . . . *I'll tell you, the union is mostly colored.*
. . . When I first came here they gave me the same breaks as before the
union. Holiday pay is the only thing the union got. We always got forty
hours. The union didn't protect me. . . . Whether white or black, they
[the company] treat you alike. [This is a white person speaking.]

Finally, Mrs. Edna Stepac, 34, unskilled, short-service girl, says:

I *was* a union member. Then we had the big strike in 1948 and I lost
$500. I'm down on the union since. *Not that the union is not good, but
Swift is a good company to work for.* If somethin's wrong, you can go to
the foreman. . . . I was approached about the union — there is strength
in numbers — so I joined. Has it brought me benefits? Nothing for me.
The union didn't stand up for us during the *strike*. . . . Then they have
parties at 49th and Wabash. That's an undesirable place to go. . . . The
union has too much fighting now. 'Way I look at it, they're in it for what

they can get out of it. The future of the union? That's the least of my worries. If they drop it, it's okay with me. The foremen will be all right. *They do have an industrial relations department.*

The Long-service Colored Women. These women (from a group of less than 1 per cent of the work force) are the least union-minded among the colored workers of the plant community as the older white women were on their part. They continue the same factors for nonunion attitudes, except the race factor of course. For instance, Arbella Cooper, who has been twenty-one years with Swift and says: "I'm proud of it," was once a union steward, but in spite of that she has lost her union allegiance:

> The CIO has tactics I don't approve of: No Christianity! *Their strike practice was bad.* It is foolishness to bite the hand that feeds us. I very much don't approve of the CIO. They should help us, but not come out here and take over the company. . . . *I feel I can go to the general office, get a Division Man and talk it over.* . . . As a steward, the only case I lost was my own! The foreman wanted me to pick up cans. I was sent home three days. Had a strangulated hernia. The union lost my case. [Mrs. Cooper was very bitter about this grievance. Possibly it is the root of her anti-union views.] . . . During the strike the union was callin' for goons and radicals to go to the peoples' homes to do harm. The company didn't do so. I dropped out of the union after the strike. *The union connected themselves with communism. They're biting the hand that feeds them. That's no good.* . . . They used our money for their personal use. They say: "We're gonna fight the company." That's killing the goose that lays the golden egg. *I don't say capitalism should crush the worker, but there's always a way.* . . . Our people join the union — the Communist party, so they can get away without work, and be protected by the union. What's the future of the union? It's going now. Girls who join have no general principles!

Incidentally, Mrs. Cooper stated at the end of the interview: "*The Chicago Tribune* is my paper!" Teresa Rice, 50, another old-timer has her own special reason for lack of union allegiance. She likes the old system of department-wide seniority and dislikes the plant-wide seniority brought in by the union:

> I never did join. Something I didn't like about the union. Take *seniority.* In the old days before the union, they would send you to different parts of the ———— House, but you'd stay in that House, an' go from floor to floor. Now, you get transferred to other departments. You got to go to the employment office now. I didn't like that, and the union did it. . . . We had a bonus even before the union, and we got more then. *I've been treated fine ever since I've been here. If anything's wrong, you can go to the foreman.* They tried to get me to join the union, but I never would.

The Long-service Colored Men. We remember that as a group these men are definitely favorable to the union as an institution (1.85). They are slightly less favorable than the younger colored men. Just a few of their numbers are anti-union, but these have very pronounced views about it. Philip Elder, for example, whose company allegiance we have seen, states:

> I'm nonunion. I don't care to knock the union. But before the union I got along all right. *I was in the union up to the 1948 strike.* Then I got out. *It was such poor judgment. I felt pretty mad.* The AFL plants worked and the market didn't suffer. . . . I will sign up some day. I'm not rushing. *I don't like to fight.* After they get it settled, I may join. I never went to meetings. I been with the company too long to get messed up in something. If I get a higher wage, I'll be here. If I get a lower wage, I'll be here. . . . *They accuse the present group of communism.* If they don't get too radical, union would be all right. . . . What have we gained from the union? Eight holidays with pay, and, I suppose, higher pay. *But the old company-union worked all right.* You could go over to the office. You could get a raise. Maybe not all you asked for, but you always got consideration.

Old-timer, Art Couture, 44, has strong company allegiance, but mixed attitudes about the union. He was once a steward and loyal. But the strike plus good company treatment seem to dry up his union allegiance. Yet he utters a popular thought when he says he would join the union if a majority did. Many workers express this idea of wanting to go along with the crowd.

> *I dropped out of the union at the '48 strike. It was unpopular.* I came back to work two weeks before the end of the strike. To beat the picket line I got up at three and four a.m., took a Yellow Cab and came in at 39th Street under the fence. My family was in need! I stayed out nine weeks. But I got three kids! They grabbed me on the picket line, but I broke loose. On the L's they tried to beat me up. It was a bad strike. People were on relief. Families were broken up by it. People lost $1000 by staying out eleven weeks. It'll take five years to pay that back. . . . I was a steward. It *was* a good union. 100 per cent. It's a weak union now. Nothing to it now. They want big men in. Don't coöperate with each other now. I don't belong. They're not strong enough. I would join if they were strong. . . . *The union has done a lot of good things. Some good. Some bad.* . . . Future of the union? It doesn't affect me. They won't have no union. . . . If the majority would join, I'd join. Why? Then it would be strong. . . . *The company gives you all fair breaks anyway. We don't need a union.*

Finally, Leonard Parker, 50, semiskilled meat handler, also clearly favorable to the company, stresses good company treatment, fighting within the union, and forced entrance into the union as factors in his anti-union views:

> *The company was nice to us before the strike of 1948.* During the strike they wrote a letter to all the employees saying why they could not pay more than nine cents. They was fair. I'm not kicking. Any time you had trouble and came to the company, they'd help you. . . .
>
> *Interviewer:* Has the union brought you benefits, Mr. Parker?

No benefits. A lot of people say it. But I can't see it. Pay on holidays? Before we'd get a $7 to $10 bonus. Now we get holiday pay and *less* bonus. . . . The steward? If there's trouble I just talk to the foreman or talk to the general office. . . . I didn't have much idea of the union at first. *They kind of forced me to join. . . . The union are fighting among themselves. It's no good.*

Some Foremen Against the Union Idea. A fair minority of the foremen (27 per cent) are against the idea of having a union in the plant community. This minority does not think that the worker needs the union as a protection and source of representation. They believe that the company has given the workers good treatment in the past, and will continue to do so in the future. Most of the workers do not have grievances. So there is really no need for a union in the plant. Veteran foreman, Richard Babbit, puts it this way, with, however, a question mark:

I'm not against unions. *But the union needs to be properly run.* Upstairs — they seem not to favor the present union, Local 28, leadership.

Interviewer: Has the union helped the workers here?

No doubt it has brought benefits. It's just a question as to whether or not those benefits would have been given anyway. It's hard to answer that question. *Maybe the challenge of unions brought the benefits about. Maybe they would have been given anyway,* for instance, like pensions, and sickness and accident benefits.

Herm Shupe, a younger man, had experience in the gang, and remembers the old days of the ERP which he experienced for several years as a worker. Says he:

The union brought us a lot of grievances during the war. They've quieted down now. I'd never go through the war period again! You had to take too much from the help. . . . The Employee Representation Plan — I was in it and it worked all right. We asked for wage adjustments and got them. . . . The employees did gain through the union. *But it's hard to tell whether the company would have given the benefits or not.* [He hesitated.] Maybe I'm prejudiced. I think the union has made for poorer relations. *The union tries to sell the men: "The company is rich," etc. . . . The old Company Plan was better. There was not all this sarcasm.* If the union would say: "Do a decent day's work," I'd feel better about it. I think the company has leaned backward with the union.

Foreman, James Drucker, finds that the union's excessive claims and aggressiveness turn him away from the union itself. As for the worker's need for protection against the foreman, Drucker states an inconsistency:

The CIO takes credit for everything the workers have gotten in the last fifteen years. *Swift & Company have followed other industries in helping their employees.* The CIO is pretty radical. They don't use common sense. Don't they realize that the company pays all who are in the union. "Don't bite the hand that feeds you." They do at times. . . . Then grievances, some come up with no basis whatever. The stewards do it to kill time.

We spend a lot of money on grievances. Those colored stewards especially bring up foolish grievances. If the union would fade out on unnecessary grievances, you wouldn't have a union. The men would forget about the union. Ninety per cent of the gang have no grievances. . . . *If the foreman does his job, you don't need a union. Of course some foremen bring the union on because they are hard on their men.* . . . The new union leaders are a bad bunch in my opinion.

Younger foreman, Ambrose Toner, had nearly ten years' experience in the gang under the Representation Plan. Because of that, he feels a union is not necessary:

The CIO — they have their good points and their poor points. It helps some employees and harms some employees. It's about an even break. . . . The union does not perform any useful function now. *It's been my experience that we were treated fair and square without a union.* Maybe not 100 per cent, the majority of the time.

The main fact we have learned in this chapter is this: in spite of everything, in spite of Swift's patent good treatment, in spite of an unfavorable strike, in spite of bitter and confusing division within Local 28, in spite of Communist misleadership — and we have seen how these things work against the very institution of unionism — 80 per cent of the employees and the majority of the foremen still want a union. The workers still want to build a society around their job lives in the plant community.

We did not find the workers' desire for a union to be imposed upon them by demagogic labor leaders, as asserted by such oversimplifying and emotional observers as Westbrook Pegler. Rather we found this desire growing of the needs of the work life itself, the need for some protection, for status, for representation, for "somebody to back you up" against the giant organization, with its many levels of authority. whose primary, though not exclusive concerns are inevitably production, market competition, and profits.

CHAPTER EIGHT

THE UNION LEADERS

The local union leader is an important man in the plant community because he can interpret the union-company contract and contribute toward changing it at the annual negotiations, because he can either block or facilitate the grievance procedure, and because he can influence worker opinion. As was apparent in our treatment of union allegiance, the behavior and personality of the union leaders, especially the local leaders, play a vastly important role in determining the nature and sometimes the very existence of the workers' allegiance to the union as an institution. In this respect the local leaders are even more crucial to their institution, the union, than the foremen are to theirs, the company.

The plain fact is that during the 1948-1952 left-wing crisis period, many Swift-UPWA workers had both clear union allegiance and clear dissatisfaction with union leadership. They wanted their union, but they

TABLE 21

Workers' attitudes toward leadership of Local 28 — I

(*Random, stratified sample of 192 workers, stewards and leaders by service, sex, and race: 1950*)

Men			Women	
Negro	White		Negro	White
3.06	3.44	Short-service	2.63 (high)	3.44
3.40	3.92	Middle-service	3.00	4.00
3.40	3.96	Long-service	3.13 (low)	4.50

Totals (Weighted		Scale	
Short-service	3.02	Very favorable	1.0
Middle-service	3.62	Favorable	2.0
Long-service	3.82	Neutral	3.0
Negro	3.17	Unfavorable	4.0
White	3.93	Very unfavorable	5.0
Union leaders (right)	4.50		
Union leaders (left)	1.50		
Stewards	2.70		
(Foremen)	(4.20)		
All workers	3.45		

did not like the way it was run. By union leadership, we mean primarily the left-wing leadership and also the left-wing district leaders responsible for administering strike relief in 1948. The workers overwhelmingly disapproved of the 1948 strike. Sometimes they blamed the International who called it; sometimes the former right-wing officers who actually opposed it.

The over-all attitude of the Swift-UPWA workers toward their local leaders is between unfavorable and neutral, as shown in Table 21.[1]

This over-all average is not markedly unfavorable. Indeed, the colored short-service men and most of the colored women are simply neutral. It it especially the white men and women who are unfavorable. Once again, our analysis of variance shows a significant difference here by race, the white workers being less favorable to the union leaders. This is even more marked than the racial difference in union allegiance. But there is also a significant difference by length of service. The old-timers tend to be less satisfied. This does not surprise us since we have seen their lesser union allegiance. Partly due to their conservatism, as we shall see, they dislike radical and fighting leaders. The women workers differ from the men, but in opposite directions, the colored women being more favorable than colored men, and the white women being less favorable than white men.

TABLE 22

Workers' attitudes toward leadership of Local 28 — II

(*Random unstratified sample of 202 workers plus stewards and foremen: 1950*)

	Rank and File	Stewards	Foremen
More or less favorable	26%	53%	5%
Neutral or "I don't know"	27%	3%	20%
More or less unfavorable	47%	44%	75%

We are not surprised at the difference between foremen and stewards. The steward body as a whole favors its leadership. And as for the union leaders themselves, naturally their attitudes follow the party lines of local union politics. Note in Table 22 that only 26 per cent of the workers positively favor the union leaders. How then were the leaders elected? Because half the workers do not vote, and also because our random sample includes nonunion people. If we were to sample only union members, we would find somewhat more than 26 per cent favorable to the 1950 Local 28 leaders. Thus, though the Swift-UPWA people differ among themselves, there is some dissatisfaction with the way the union half of their plant community is being led. The effect on union allegiance itself has been shown in Chapter Seven. We will now examine the effect it has on the worker's participation in union affairs in this chapter and the next.

Those workers who are positively opposed to the union leadership (about half) give many different reasons for their views. Four factors emerge as the most important: (a) the 1948 strike; (b) leaders too anti-company; (c) too left-wing; (d) too Negro-oriented. There are other factors: "too much fighting," "too uneducated," "out for the money," "didn't handle strike relief fairly in 1948."

THE 1948 STRIKE

The 1948 strike was a tough strike for the workers and the union. We remember that Local 28 members may have voted for it, but only as a "big stick" to use in negotiating with the company, not thinking they would actually go out. It is also probable that they voted against the strike. It is certain that a majority of the workers did not vote at all. It is also certain that Local 28 right-wing leaders tried to stop the strike.

Elder Drake, for instance, aged 52, whose attitudes we have seen several times before, has both company and union allegiance of a sort. But he was so dissatisfied with the leadership that brought on the 1948 strike that he dropped out of the union. Neither is he too satisfied with the current local leaders and stewards:

> The union is timid as a baby. *I dropped membership immediately after the strike of '48.* The leadership was not right. The strike shouldn't have been. There were very few men who could understand it. . . . *Now* [in the local] *they're fighting among themselves.* It's not very beneficial to the men. Nothing constructive at all. . . . The union has very little voice in what goes on around here. ——— [a local leader] is classified as a Communist. Whether he is or he isn't I don't know. I heard maybe the CIO was suspending the UPWA? . . . I feel the *stewards* should have at least a slight amount of *education.* We got a steward around here who couldn't spell "brickbat." I don't blame 'em if they try to learn, but they don't. They're very don't-care-ish.

Old-time butcher Luke Daniels, 51, has very strong union allegiance but is outspokenly against his leaders, especially because of the strike:

> *Now that last strike* — we did vote to go out, *but* only to show our strength. The left wing tell that ——— [a right-wing leader] told 'em to go out on strike. That's stupid. Our only hope is to kick ——— [a local leader] out of the CIO. *They can't operate unless there's chaos.* If you want something, you don't try to hit people on the head! The left wing wants to control the stewards. I haven't been a steward since the strike. They said I sold them out. They would not support the PAC. March didn't agree with Murray. . . . *And that moving* [the district headquarters] *over to Du-Sable.* That's not for the union. *That's for the party.* "Let's build a strong District," they say.

Long-service craftsman Francis Connell, likewise has company and union allegiance, but as a close observer of the recent events in Local 28, voices sharp protest. The strike, communism, and the race issue are important to him. He gives evidence of some racial prejudice:

As soon as I got in the mechanical gang I joined. I was in the union whole-heartedly and for it. The union grew by leaps and bounds up to the '48 strike. ——— and ——— [right-wing leaders], good men, tried to get along with management, and the company tried to go along with them. But the belligerent attitude came in with ——— two years ago. [Here Connell mentions three local, district and international leaders.] *The strike of '48, our leaders told them at the International that they were against the strike.* The Communist party in New York pulled that strike. ——— [a right-wing leader] said that the International wanted to sky-rocket to be like Reuther's, and win the first round raise of wages. . . . I resigned from the union in full in 1949, to get peace of mind. Now I don't have any part of them. . . . That 1950 election I believe it *was* a fraud. [The right wing contested the 1950 Local 28 election, but an International committee of two dismissed their protest.] They took the meetings over to where the white man is afraid to park his car. The union used to be 50–50 white and colored. The union leaders say: "You have it pretty easy going." Supervision does go along with us. We don't have many grievances. The foreman, you can go in and talk to him.

Some of the mechanics object to being thrown in with colored butchers, and unskilled. There was some talk last year of forming a separate union. That last flat raise for all. There's no advantage of being skilled. The gap between the skills is nothing. [Bracket raises have since been given.] . . . As far as discrimination is concerned, the union should do all it can *within* the plant. They should confine it to that. *When they talk about discrimination outside, housing, etc., that has nothing to do with the union.* The colored and white eat together here. But it's an unwritten law they can't do it outside. I've no hard feeling against colored people. But I wouldn't want one to live next door to me. The CIO wants it. And I don't believe in free housing. . . . Your union dues are supporting something you're against. *The union is full of Red elements.* They're gradually taking over. The younger men who come into the plant recently. They forget it was the old officers who got clothes-changing time and paid holidays. . . . I think if the right wing won, I'd sign up again. ——— [a left-wing leader] is a figurehead, a Charlie McCarthy, I really believe. The free picnics, dances, etc., he advocated before they got in office in the summer of 1949, convinced me the Commies are in back of it. We were defeated by the new fellows in the company. . . . *"What's good for us, the company hates,"* I don't believe Swift & Company believes that saying. . . .

Butcher Walter Stuczynski, 33, Back-of-the-Yards inhabitant, talks like Connell. He has company allegiance but is violently anti-union, and anti-strike. His racial views are rigid and prejudiced. He works in a department 80 per cent Negro, which may affect his views.

I believe in the union, but not the CIO union we get. *That 1948 strike was bad. We needed help, there was a baby coming.* I went to the union for help. I don't want no charity. I want a part-time job. I don't believe in charity. Won't accept it. So I came back one week before the end of the strike. The union should take care of their members and not send 'em out on the street. *They collect money. Where does the money go to?* To break windows and stuff! I know a Mexican woman who had that done. And that man who was killed in the strike. It was not the fault of the city police. He fell off a truck. Then they had a parade on Ashland Avenue [the funeral cortège] with cars lined up from 47th and Marshfield! I believe they should have settled the strike at nine cents if the AFL did. ———— is a Communist. They made him resign. But he still has a job as a field director. Why should I be a member of a union like that? They want everything. They don't want to give anything. They know Swift's accounts, but nobody knows where *their* money is going, who gets paid. . . . My only complaint is against the CIO and the strike. If a man wants to work, let him go. It's a free country. The police were packing guns. The CIO really knocked the city police. I would have come back sooner except my wife was expecting a baby. I was afraid. I've got to show a profit, or there's no sense in working! But if ———— is fired [a certain international leader], he pays it out of the union's treasury, not out of his pocket. . . .

They try to argue out cases with the company all the time. If a man don't want to work, let him stay home. They talk about speed-up. I don't think there's any speed-up. Nobody is so pushed they haven't got another breath. You have to work hard for a living anywhere. I don't see where the union helped. They claim we got holidays. But I lived pretty good before. They got us raises. But prices go up! Who is bringing prices up but people? When I came back from service I joined the union. *I didn't want to seem not to be with the workers.* They called dirty names. Said: "We're fighting for your rights." So I joined just to keep 'em satisfied. . . . *It's a "clique" versus the "Communists."* They're fighting and men go out the window. [He refers to a recent preëlection scuffle in the Local 28 Hall.] The union is a legal racket that beats Al Capone's racket. The poor people are paying money to men who ride around and talk.

And the stewards — that's another thing. The steward don't even know how to talk English and he's going to defend you! There's two sides to every story. He goes to extremes when he hasn't got a case. Let 'em get intelligent men for stewards. Ought to have an education. The union is weak on our floor. Only about sixteen members. Most white don't belong. *The union is all colored. They preach too much about race.* They say: "The whites are trying to destroy the colored people." I don't believe that. They're hollering about a housing project. And that case at 56th and Peoria, the judge freed them. He heard the case. They didn't. You can't condemn on circumstantial evidence. The colored are moving in other neighborhoods. *They should stay where they belong and be proud of their race.* My son is a Catholic, and we'll stay that way. I'll stay in my class, my own class, and don't mix with others. They listen to the union leaders, they are their gods. . . . And that *Flash* is propaganda, baloney.

Finally, Mary Weidemann, youthful meat-packer, concludes this theme of dissatisfaction with the 1948 strike:

About our dear union — I don't belong. And I was a steward for years. *That '48 strike, I never signed after it. I came back before the strike was over.* One and one-half weeks before the end. There were three or four in the department who wouldn't speak to me. But they cheered in the cafeteria when we came in, because we were union people and came back. Two ladies to this day don't speak to me. One big fat lady I don't talk to. . . . The Polish people were afraid to strike. . . . The *Flash* said the strike vote was to go out. *The people didn't want to go out, I say.* People were crying and begging, they didn't want to go out on strike. They were scared. Didn't have work elsewhere. Have to give half your pay to the union. [This is an error!] They break your windows if you didn't. I never went near the union hall during the strike. The first strike was good and coöperative in 1946 because the *people* wanted it. . . . When the union is what I think it should be I'd join again. The union done wonders.

I wanted to see the old crowd of union leaders in. *I don't think much of the present leaders.* And 49th and Wabash — I'd never go there! I'd be scared. I've met a lot of colored fellows and they'd ask me to go out. Maybe get drinks, too much, men take you home? No. *The colored are too free with the white girls in the union. . . . Not that the whites won't join because of the colored, but because of the strike.* Also the dues are high. . . . The *Flash*? I read it and laugh. ——— [a local leader] says: "I'm goin' to run this plant!" That's silly. Communists? They're a group of people with the same kind of money and feel the same. It might be a mere name. *Hard to tell who is and who isn't.*

In sum, we can hardly exaggerate the effect of the 1948 strike on attitudes of the Swift-UPWA workers toward union leadership. Before the end of the strike, around 40 per cent of the union members, including not a few stewards, had returned to work. And, as we saw, union membership dropped from 86 per cent to 45 per cent of the bargaining unit. The marvel is that there is still clear union allegiance among most of the workers, and that Local 28 has been able to make a comeback.

ANTICOMPANY LEADERS

Another significant reason the workers give for dissatisfaction with local union leadership is central to the question of dual allegiance in the plant community; namely, "the union leaders are too anticompany." They are "too demanding," say these workers, "fighting the company," "raising voice too much," "saying gimme, gimme," or "biting the hand that feeds you." It is more often the longer-service white worker who mentions this anticompany local leadership; still, some in all groups mention it. These workers resist the class-warfare dialectic. Many of them have both company and union allegiance and do not wish the local leadership to set the two groups against each other.

We have already noted how Arbella Cooper puts this idea: " 'We're gonna fight the company.' That's killing the goose that lays the golden egg! I don't say capitalism should crush the worker, but there's always a way. . . ."

Local leader Della Harris, a right-winger, puts the issue clearly:

See, Father, I'll tell you . . . most people in packing are very ign'rant. I'm sorry to say it . . . but they are. Because they'll let anything lead 'em. You supposed to *think* — I tell 'em. Listen and then think. Don't just rush into it. The Lawd done give you five senses an' one of them is *think.* An' you s'posed to think about these things! We goin' *make* Swift an' Company do so and so! *Make* that foreman do so and so! They believe that junk. *You can't force the company to do something.* A lot of people don't want to work. If the building burn down, they goin' to get paid just to stand around and see it. . . .

Unskilled, middle-service man, Harry Bradely, 47, has lost his union allegiance. He dislikes the 1948 strike, but also radicalism:

I tell you 'bout the union. I got in in 1936 or '37. The union is all right if it's the right kind. It's all right to be organized. Organization is good. But I wished I could get out of it. I don't think much of it. We were out on strike in 1948 and the employees lost. The union didn't lose anything. I came back before the end. The CIO is on the wrong basis. In the war men were dying, and here men pulling strikes! . . . *The union got too much radicalism.* We need educated people to lead the people and the union hasn't got them. They take up cases and don't know how to talk. *You can't raise your voice. There's a way to talk to everybody.* I don't need a union for me.

Dignified old Edgar Whitcomb, a company man through and through with Swift since 1912, and skilled butcher, influenced by the old days of good treatment, especially dislikes the anticompany leadership:

Before the union we got along much better. They gave us an increase before we had a union. We had a forty-hour guarantee before the union, now we got only thirty-six! I dropped out of the union after the 1948 strike. . . . *I like a union that is agreeable with the company and with the bosses, not fighting the company all the time.* The old Representation Plan worked well. . . . Our floor is a tough floor. *Our stewards are disagreeable.* They can slow down the whole gang. Let any little thing come up, they have a meeting. Even foolish things. . . . If they'd have the Company Representation Plan and forget about the union we'd be 100 per cent better off. . . .

Short-service craftsman, Eugene Heilhecker, 47, has both company and union allegiance, but he continues this theme about the leadership:

One reason I'm out of the union is that they want to pay the same wage scale to all and the union couldn't do anything about it. The union did good for common labor, but *not for skilled crafts.* . . . And *that strike, it was very unjust.* We never should have gone out. Local 28 voted not to go out. But the International ordered 'em to go out. Now that's just hearsay. I got a job outside. I was a steward once. But the present union will never work. A union is a wonderful thing. But the almighty dollar gets in. And a union needs good leadership. This is hearsay, but they ought to get rid of the Communists. I was born in Chicago and I try to be a good American. . . .

There's too much hatred about the union now to do much. We need a union, but a good union, not one that's going around all the time with its hand out saying, "gimme, gimme." *We need a union that's going to see the company point of view, too.* It's good to have a company man to see the company's side and a union man to see the union's side. But [he shrugs] that would never work. . . . I don't know much about the left-wing leaders. But the old leaders, to tell you the truth, they were company men.

Tony Bachacci, 43, also a craftsman, has rather ambivalent union allegiance and is against union leadership because of the strike and also the
anticompany behavior. He also brings up the money and the race questions:

> *I do believe in the union and I don't believe in it.* Ain't done much for a
> man but take the poor man's money. That strike was wrong. I didn't want
> to go out. . . . *The union means "moneymakers."* They ought to have an
> inventory for the money at the end of the year. The dues are not high, if
> they show what they do with it. They sit in a chair an' you work an' they
> play. . . . Only n——rs are in the union. Then they have a dance. That's
> out. And meetings over at Indiana Avenue. The colored, you can't trust
> 'em. But they're all right in the gang. *The union is for the colored.* Forty
> per cent of the white are out. The union leaders don't do one-third what
> they promise to do. The old group was a little better, not much, but a
> little better. *In my opinion they're all Reds.* They push for things. The
> government should investigate. We got along as well in '34 as now. We
> got as fair a deal then as now. *The company-union worked out.* . . . I
> tell you, Father, a union is good to have, *but* they oughta have not pickets
> at the gates, no beats. If a man is willing to go to work, it's his privilege.
> They shouldn't try to beat him up. They oughta have votes for strikes;
> let the members decide, not the officials. And the majority wins. . . . They
> oughta give the people a fee when you're sick for your operations, etc. . . .
> *You can't go against the company. You got to give a day's work whether we
> got a union or not.*

We saw that mechanic Fred Riedl has strong union allegiance for the
motive of protection. But he dislikes the union's anticompany leadership:

> The union is good if it is run right, and takes the person's part. *It should
> be for the worker and for the company.* I'd belong tomorrow then. But I
> don't want to belong to no radical group. *They don't give the company a
> fair enough break.* They talk all union, that the company's all wrong no
> matter what they do. They say anything to get out a point. But they're not
> foolin' me or the people. The company's got to make a decent profit. The
> company is a legitimate organization. They're not goin' to do no wrong.
> I need the company more than the company needs me. . . . If you got
> the right union, run right, with the right leaders, for the benefit of *both
> parties,* workers and company, then you got a good union. *Protecting me,
> you protect the company and vice versa. 'Cause I'm part of the company
> and the company is part of me, too.* The men who have more service feel
> part of the company. For example, a friend of mine — the company is
> practically like his home. He's a twenty-five-year service man. He don't feel
> right unless he's here.
>   [Riedl then took a copy of the *Flash* of April 4, 1950 out of his pocket
> and read.] "The Company is trying to crush the union." No. I never saw
> that. The company never tried to tell me either way. No foreman ever spoke
> to me against the union. It helps the workers if Swift *does* make a profit.

Peter Rawinski, an old-timer, an elevator-operator, dislikes anticompany
union leadership. He also brings up the Red issue, showing curious misinformation:

I belong to the union but I'm not a 100 per cent union man. I'm a company man too. Company give me bread and butter and a living. . . . *I like good union, good for company and good for workers.* CIO not good for workers. Good for self. I didn't want to be steward. Didn't want to make bad for company. I get more from company than from union. . . . Communism in dere. *I no like union because communism in dere.* Union all right to ask better conditions and money, that's all right. . . . ——— [a certain left-wing local leader] is nice fellow. Talk once good for me. Only one I know. He worked same place I did so I knew him. He talked nice to me. Brought me free beer, lotta beer for nuttin' at picnic last summer at 87th Street. [Peter implied that it was such nice treatment that induced him to vote for this left-winger. Through ignorance he supported a movement which he dislikes.]

Old-timer, Joseph Kulbis, 41, we saw to have a certain amount of race prejudice. Probably this is an important factor in his lack of union allegiance. But he also mentions the Communist issue and the anticompany theme:

There are Communist elements in the union now. Especially since the 1948 strike. People were satisfied by a nine cent raise. They got orders from the Commies to strike. I came back after one and a half weeks. . . . I believe in the union very much, but on a fifty-fifty basis. *The union should coöperate with the company.* The company has some wonderful policies, but there are individuals. . . .

Long-service craftsman, Alex McLean, though an old union man in Europe, is against the CIO because of its militancy against the company:

A union is a wonderful thing. Finest thing for the workingman. For years I was in the Amalgamated Society of Engineers in Britain. I don't believe in the CIO. *The CIO has no justice for the company.* Did you ever hear of a Socialist or a Communist who was ever *for the company?* The *Flash* is a lot of nonsense. "They want this!! They want that!" They want what they'll never get. *A union should be fifty-fifty for company and union.* Now a foreman hasn't got a say. It's all in the union. If a man comes in drunk, the foreman can't send him home. The union protests. I voted against the CIO in the representation election in 1942. But we went along with the majority and joined up. Thought it was our duty. . . . *But that last strike!* It was the stupidest thing. I could have been a black-leg, but I didn't. My opinion was that we didn't vote to go out. I voted not to go out. . . . There are too many radicals in the union.

Interviewer: Did the union benefit the workers, Mr. McLean?

They done a little benefit, yes. But they took the joy out of it. I believe myself, I might be wrong, if the union acted right and had given more freedom to the foreman, it would be a strong union. The unions in the old country are better than here and still most of them were Socialists like Ramsay McDonald! . . . There are many nationalities here in the yards and many can't think for themselves. They are easily led. A radical can do it. There's an old saying: One bad apple in the barrel would spoil the whole lot. . . . The Negro element think the white man is up against them all the time.

Finally Fred Bolgar who started with Swift back in 1909, says:

> I s'pose union is all right *if working together with company.* But like two horses, they pull apart. . . .

LEFT-WING LEADERS

A fair minority of workers mention communism as a factor in their disapproval of local leadership. These remarks are much more common among the white workers than among the colored, though some of the whites may use communism as a rationalizing cloak for their antagonism to Negro leadership. There is no doubt that Local 28 leadership was dominated by the Communist party from 1949 to 1952.

Wallace Read, 25 years with Swift and partly college educated, feels strongly about discrimination. A former right-wing steward, he has both company and union allegiance, but dislikes the leadership mostly because of its communism:

> The union is too one-sided. ———— [a district leader] dictates. ————— [a local leader] is not qualified. They ought to put a man in there with a mind of his own. . . . We get no chance to speak from the floor at a union meeting. No freedom of speech. Any man who hits the floor is against him [the same local leader]. One thing, we won't have a union if he stays in. You got to have a mind of your own. . . . *The District is run by Moscow.* ———— and ———— are card carriers. There are five card carriers there. Swift wouldn't do business with ————. The union used to be 100 per cent. Now it's 60 per cent. We need a program.

Short-service man, Jim Stowa, likewise has strong union allegiance and just as strong dissatisfaction with left-wing leaders:

> The company likes to have the union split. *The Commies are in there. It's definitely Red.* It's hard to get 'em out. The white element are not interested. . . . But we need a union even if it's a Red union! . . . I'd rather see the old crowd in than the new. I've seen how the Communist Party operates. They set a special assessment to get Parks elected in the First Congressional District on the Progressive Party. . . . The company could help get the Communists out of the union.
> *Interviewer:* What about the Taft-Hartley Act?
> Even in spite of the Taft-Hartley Act!

Short-service clerk, Tom Winkowsky, who seems to want some kind of company union, began the interview quite spontaneously as follows:

> One thing — *I'd never join that union! It's a Communist front.* They were supporting a Progressive man for election — Parks. One reason I wouldn't join is all the literature they put out. The union seems to be Communist dominated. And as for Korea, they thought the same as the Russians did. They sent a delegate to the Peace Conference in London. . . . And another reason. That 56th and Peoria incident — there was a story in the *Flash* about it that was prejudiced. I was in it, and was arrested. I live near there. There were Communists involved. I don't think I'm prejudiced,

but if I say I'm not my friends ostracize me. I'm friendly with the colored. . . . That Freedom Forum the company had was grand. Trying to educate the foremen, etc., how the government is wasting too much money, etc. We should have more of them. But in the yards, 30 or 40 per cent of the people are not well enough educated to understand it. . . . I voted Republican in 1950.

Two union stewards give interesting and contrasting views on the issue of communism in Local 28 and the Chicago District of the UPWA. First, Theodore Kopcinski, semiskilled long-service man, 43, gives evidence of curious ignorance about the real affairs of Local 28. Evidently he believes the party line on "unity":

I believe the union did a lot of good. There are some things I don't like. The extreme right and the extreme left. *I'm against communism.* I come from Poland. There my sister was shipped to Siberia. . . . And my uncle, a priest, was killed in Poland by the Communists. They're taking land. Want to make collective farms. People don't know what communism is in this country. They promise a lot. People follow it unconsciously. Are there Commies in the union? It's hard to tell. I wouldn't accuse them. People have accused the union of communism. It's just some leaders. . . . When two parties run, they have a grudge against each other. *When the election is over, all should coöperate. We should not be afraid of Communists or Fascists. They all signed the affidavits.* ——— [a left-wing leader] seems to be all right.

Steward Bill Ryan, also long-service and skilled worker, is more sophisticated:

I don't care too much for the present officers of the union. ——— [the same left-wing leader as above] *has admitted to my face that he is an out-and-out Communist.* But he says he believes in the union first. He talks intelligently. Doesn't talk like a bulldozer or a radical. . . . But I'd like to see that old bunch in. They didn't even want the strike. I do believe quite a number of coloreds are Communists.

NEGRO-ORIENTED LEADERS

We have already noted that one of the reasons why some white workers in the Swift-UPWA plant community fail to have union allegiance is because they feel the union is only for the Negroes. This is a major factor in the whites' dissatisfaction with local leadership, too. These whites believe that the union has become too much a tool of Negro advancement as such, a kind of an Urban League instead of a trade union. They believe that there are too many Negro leaders and that they are talking too constantly about race questions. (More whites were leaders after the right-wing ascent to power in 1952.)

Skilled short-service man, William O. Coyne states:

I get disgusted looking at the *Flash. Negro rights is all it is.* They worry about the South and the Dixon Lines and they put the union stamp on the bottom. . . . The whites pulled away. The whites figure all the favor

is for the colored and against the whites in the union. A union is all right.
I got nothin' against the union if it's run right. The colored are 100 per
cent union. If they dropped out of the union, they'd lose their toe-hold.
They know that. *Here the white figures it's a "colored union" and he's an
outcast.*

Skilled meat-handler, Dan Hult, 40, has high union allegiance, is against
the strike and right-wingers, but continues the race theme in his attitude
to the leadership:

> The union paper? *They ought to confine their business to the union and
> leave out [interracial] housing, etc.* The *Flash* smears the company. It's
> terrible foolishness. We're working under a contract after all. The officers
> are fighting. That's another reason I got out. ——— [a defeated right-
> wing leader] had the union sewed up. Figured it was theirs. We couldn't
> touch anything. . . . And the *Flash* came out about 56th and Peoria. It
> got the guys sore. They talked about it too much. Let them stick to their
> union business.

Old-timer millwright, Alex Pisarski, admits he does not like colored
people, and so the union leadership. His prejudice is clear:

> I don't like 'em personally. They all look alike to me: black black. . . . as
> far as the union they got in there now, it's no good. The gang in there are
> all *colored.*

It is important to note that not a few colored union members are
concerned about the lack of white participation in the union, the lack of
white union leaders and the occasional stressing of race matters over
union matters. Semiskilled assembly-line machine-operator, Tom Booth,
44, has both company and union allegiance, but states:

> I know many stewards who could be better than ——— [a certain local
> leader]. I don't think much of him. *An all-colored program is no good.*
> . . . And I don't think that dances should be in union projects.

And former steward, Francis Dumas, 48, puts the same thing in his own
way:

> The union is still a one-sided affair. Part is satisfied with the leaders, part
> is not. *To build the union back, we could get whites in too.* Could give
> more consideration to the whites.

There are several other factors involved in rank-and-file dissatisfaction
with local leadership. These follow no particular pattern and are usually
interwoven with the factors we just considered.

Leaders Too Hot-headed or Dictatorial. Active unionist Laurel Jones,
31, makes this complaint:

> The union is supposed to be for the people. I don't think one man or two
> men supposed to run the union. *The new union don't give you the floor!*
> And ——— [a local officer] is wavin' his finger and sayin': "I *demand*
> this!" The union need a good sweepin' out. I'm disgusted with it. We pro-
> tested the election, we did.

1948 Strike Relief Mishandled. This complaint is directed mostly at the former right-wing leaders who were hampered because of their feud with the left-wing District Headquarters, which also administered relief. Nonunion man, George Howe, janitor, 47, says:

> I joined the union and I got out of it. My reason was after the strike of 1948. —————— [a right-wing leader] offered aid to the strikers. I witnessed several women and men who got as much as $42.43 in my presence. They told me to go to welfare station on Damen Avenue. I got no help so I came back to work. I didn't get any relief. It's unfair to give one member aid and not another. Some ladies got help and had no kids at all. [Howe has two sons and three grandchildren.] The union sent me several letters trying to get me back to hall and explain where the money goes. *If you pay for protection and then don't get it, I'd just as soon not pay for it.* [Yet Howe has strong union allegiance though he vigorously refuses to join.]

Also old-timer, Clement Orozco, 47, janitor, father of six, has strong union allegiance, but does not belong:

> I gonna tell you the truth. I was one of bes' union men in my department. I was steward. But in '48 strike I helped in kitchen at Union Hall. We had nice meat in the ice box and it disappeared. Big guys give to guys they like. Take meat home. *Big guys eat. I got nothing. Whenever they like 'em, they give 'em somp'n.* I dropped out of union after strike. I asked union for help. They sent me to relief. I didn't want no relief. To get relief you got to sell your furniture, your car to get it. I no want it. . . . They pay leaders to go to conventions. But when strike comes they don't give workers nothin'.

Union Leaders Out for Money. This is a perennial problem with the rank and file as the union gets big, just as it is a problem with the worker and management. Because the organization is big, the man at the bottom thinks it is rich. Then, too, we must remember the charge of mishandling funds leveled against the former right-wing leaders — a charge without foundation. Though he has union allegiance, short-service craftsman, Tommy Zorach, 23, is against union leadership for a number of reasons including the race issue. But the administration of union funds looms large in his mind:

> There are two outfits fighting for union leadership. One union man took $60,000. He just disappeared. I don't know what happened. [Undoubtedly Zorach is referring to an officer of Armour Local 347 who had recently run off with the local treasury and was convicted for it.] *The two are fighting not to help people, but to get money.* The union isn't run the way it should be. Not for benefit of the people but for money.

IGNORANCE ABOUT LEADERS

Any democratic organization — a local union for instance — presupposes that its members will participate at least to the extent of knowing and selecting its officers and principal policies. Without such participa-

tion, one or more cliques will sooner or later take over control and
democracy becomes an empty shell. This all-important question of participation we treat in the next chapter. Here we simply note that a significant number of the Swift-UPWA workers know little or nothing about
their union leadership.

Take Joe Dirsa, for instance, a short-service utility man. Joe dropped
out of Local 28 after the 1948 strike; yet he believes in the need for a
union. He knows nothing about the current leadership, although he is
inevitably affected by it, nonunion though he is:

> I don't bother with the union officers. I do my work. I keep away from
> them. . . . I don't know who the steward is. I don't ask questions. If
> you're in it, you're in it.

Another short-service man, a meat-cutter, Ed Slater, made a comment
that I heard frequently:

> These fellows, these officers, I don't much know one from the other. There's
> a Flash out from both sides. Each blames the other. . . . The ones in
> office now are against the ones who were in office. Each says the other is
> no good.

Harrison Wallace, 38, middle-service meat-handler has his information
precisely inverted:

> The trouble is, they's two groups. The old group was lined up with the
> International. [No, precisely the opposite. The old group opposed the
> International.] They claim one part is for the company and one part is
> for the union. . . . ——— [a left-wing leader] used to work in our de-
> partment occasionally. He's all right. Shows strength as an organizer. I
> got nothing against him. . . . Those die-hards, those old-timers — we'll
> never get them into the union.

And Tony Jablonsky, short-service butcher, 27, says:

> Our present leaders and the others, it's like the Democrats and the Republi-
> cans, that's all. . . . You hear some talk in the papers about ——— [a
> local leader] supposed to be a Communist, and some other labor leader,
> maybe in the Auto Workers? — or maybe Bridges? But I don't read about
> that stuff. I keep away from that stuff. I figger if I read about communism
> I might become one. [He laughs.] Montgomery Ward, they make you de-
> clare if you're a Communist. I think that's a good idea. . . .

Ignorance of the union's affairs and leaders seems to be more common among the women workers. Here are a few examples. Recent arrival
from Lithuania, Anna Liubauskas, 38, believes in union but says:

> I didn't like union before because they say Communists in dere. I don't
> know how true. I don't like communism. I tasted it. . . . One girl say
> one way. Other girl say other way. Everybody says union is run by Com-
> munists. Girls say Mary is a Communist. I don't know. Can't tell. Couldn't
> ask her, she wouldn't tell me. She worked at the union hall two years.

Polish old-timer, Mary Zablonski shows a curious bit of misinformation:

> The union should get together and not cut one another's throats. People who are strong, like the secretary and treasurer, they know what's going on, they should elect the people. I should go to meetings *but I have no interest. I feel I just don't want to be bothered.* To me they [the current leaders] are nice. They help you. *The present crowd* [which is mostly left-wing!] *is supposed to have thrown out the Communist party.*

Marion Hallock, 28, short-service worker, says it's "very important to have a union," but:

> I really don't know much about it. They're fighting among themselves. One side is accused of being the old clique and getting money for themselves. The other side is accused of not fighting for the worker. *I really don't know.*

Finally, old-timer, Mary Ellen Jones:

> The union? I just pay dues. You want the truth? *I don't know any more'n that about it.* I hear 'em say the union "done me good."

It will help our understanding of the rank-and-file union-leader relationship to see what the minority of workers who *favor* their leaders (26 per cent) have to say. We remember that if the worker is of short service or colored, he is more likely to favor his union leadership than if he is an old-timer or white. We shall note that many of the favorable comments contrast the 1950 union leaders with the old right-wing, anti-international group whom they defeated. Favorable remarks are: "Our officers are not afraid to stand up for the workers!" "They're working hard." "Listen to you." "Fighters." "Good speakers." "Conscientious, flexible and open to suggestions."

Frank Pine, short-service man and skilled butcher, has high union allegiance and likes his leaders, apparently for a moral reason:

> I think ———— [a local leader] is doing a fine job! He's not just against the company and for the union, *but he's for what is right.* If you're right, you're right. If you're wrong, you're wrong.

Like Pine, Stanley Stowe, skilled man with Swift eleven years, has both company and union allegiance. Along with not a few colored workers, he likes the greater amount of dances and parties the left-wing group has sponsored, frequently at the District Hall in Bronzeville:

> ———— [a local leader] and the Grievance Committee are doing a good job. Since he took over, things are a lot different. *Before, we didn't have dances, and so forth. Now we do.* He'll treat you just as well as he do others. *He lets you talk* and express your opinion. Everybody is happy now and we get along all right.

Not all who favor the union leadership are short-service men. Here are two old-timers. Allen Ludden, for example, 58, has both company and union allegiance, favors his union leaders and says:

Our officers seem to be all right. ——, that new fellow, is a little bit more warm-headed than he should be, but otherwise he's *all right*. The bunch what was in there are out. They tried to come back. Been in for four or five years, and they still didn't want to give up. *Had their hands in the dough I guess.* Didn't want to loosen up. I think our officers will get the boys together.

George Hahn, 59, does not belong to the union but approves the leaders:

There are two outfits. We got to get them together. —— [a local leader] is one of the best. *He's a fighting man.* —— was nice, but he didn't have qualifications for leadership.

Two short-service women workers comment favorably about one of the Local 28 leaders:

I think he is a good officer. *He's not afraid to stand up for the workers!* [2]

He's a good speaker. He could fix things if they wouldn't bother him. Though sometimes he doesn't know what he is sayin'.[3]

The steward body is the most favorable group to the union leaders: 53 per cent are favorable. This is understandable when we consider the high turnover among stewards and the fact that many of these recently elected stewards were supported by the current leaders. Steward Harvey Taylor, whose interesting views on discrimination we saw earlier, explains why he supports the current officers and is against the former ones:

There's a split in the union. *The ex-officers withheld the per capita tax and wanted to pull away from the UPWA and be independent.* They gave no support on the strike. They held positions so long it was a dictatorship, a clique. They must have got together and said: "Why pay the tax, we'll split the money." So they owned their own homes. I suggest these reasons. *They are company-minded.* They even hired a company lawyer to get their $3000 out of the bank. [This is a curious distortion of facts. Local 28's lawyer in its suit against the International, Mr. John Enright, has an independent practice and no connection with Swift & Company or its legal department.] Now their company lawyer wants $5000 fee for getting $3000. At the membership meeting we refused to pay. It's just rotten, when personal benefits make them forget about the people. . . . Those guys are like sick rats now.
  My job is jeopardized to an extent, because I fight the company to an extent. If they get anything on you, they'll fire you. *So it's hard on the union officers, because they're great fighters.* If the company gets anything on them, they're gone, even though they got twenty-five years' service.

Another union steward, Richard Rex, agrees with Taylor:

The present crowd are okay because they are with the International. They have to beg help from the International. What can 6500 members do off by themselves? The New Committee [the right-wingers] is really the old committee that was in before. They wouldn't pay their per capita tax to the International Union. Their president? I don't know his name. He's a Caucasian anyway. Our leaders have their little, little faults. But I'm willin' to string along with them.

52. B. Brown, candidate for alderman, addressing a rally outside the Wilson plant, just west of Swift.

53. Noon rally at "CIO corner."

54. Pickets on parade at western gate of stockyards in 1946 strike.

55. Local 28 was very militant in November, 1945.

56. UPWA stages a noon rally outside Swift offices in support of steelstrikers of 1949.

57. Another noon demonstration, March, 1951.

In sum, we see that this minority of workers likes its local leaders primarily because they are militant and say they will correct the defects of the old right-wing administration. Bold, strong talk plus the bitter charges and counter-charges in the duel between Local 28's former officers and the International leads these workers to support the 1950 (mostly left-wing) leaders.

Not all, but most of the foremen, as we have seen, have some union allegiance. They believe that there is need for a union in the plant instead of the old Employee Representation Plan. Swift higher supervision gives the impression that it is somewhat less favorable to the union as an institution than the foremen, though, of course, they accept the union as here to stay. Chicago management seems to be sincerely trying to carry out Harold Swift's instructions of 1937: "Whatever our methods of bargaining with employees shall turn out to be, we still want to maintain a cordial, coöperative attitude, with our ideals the same. . . ." As we have seen, Swift did try to prevent union organization in the AFL days and also in the original CIO days (at least at lower supervision levels); nevertheless, there is no evidence that Swift Chicago is today trying to defeat the union or hinder its activity. On the other hand, neither is management making any effort to advance the cause of the union, or to give it prestige. Management's policy is simply a hands-off, "The union is your business" attitude. For them, the UPWA is like a hot spell in the summer time. Who can do anything about the weather?

Now as for the union leadership, especially of Local 28, the foremen are unfavorable for about the same reasons the employees themselves express. Likewise, the Chicago plant higher supervision, while more cautious in their statements, definitely believe that local union leadership leaves much to be desired. Let us hear from a sample of supervisors.

Foreman, William Halloran, for instance, has union allegiance, but thinks the local leadership too anticompany:

> Has the union a function, a job to do? Yes, it has. But they still have to earn the respect of management, though. *Their aggressive leadership is too aggressive.* They ought to quit the interracial stuff in the *Flash* and start *union* policies. . . . But no matter how good a personnel policy you have, you got to give and take. We need a union. . . . I knew ———— [a right-wing leader]. I'm sorry he was defeated.

Also foreman Oliver Keighley has allegiance for the union but not its leaders:

> It was better to deal with the old [right-wing] crowd. *They weren't as radical.* Some of these boys are crazy and force themselves on people. . . .

Tom Moore continues the same theme:

I like the union but I don't like the outfit in there now. People claim they're nothing but a bunch of *Commies*. They're preaching and acting like it. *They had a planned program to upset my department and make trouble.* This is recent. ——— is our new steward and all his talk is to make trouble. I couldn't explain things to him. It was silly. Things are going along very nicely now though.

Finally foreman David Philips, exaggerating his figures, says:

The union has done good. It performs a necessary function. However, they lack good leaders. *They're about 90 per cent Communists now.*

Higher supervision in the Chicago plant also bring up radicalism and anticompany attitudes of the current local leadership. Frank Villers, for example, has had good opportunity to observe union leadership in the plant community. He says:

The union is here to stay. We'd rather have it run intelligently. It would be better for Swift & Company. So I advise people: "Why don't you join the union and get made an officer and get the union run right?" *So often the union people are just not as intelligent as they should be. Or they have something against the company.* They are not chosen because they're intelligent, as it was in the ERP, but because they are against the company. Take ——— for example. He's new to power and struts like a peacock. Is very domineering. Many men in the plant don't like him. . . . And they made a mistake when they moved their District Headquarters over to the Negro district.

Chicago plant man Philip Montgomery thinks the union is necessary because:

It established seniority rights. That was not done 100 per cent before. The foreman could put a man where he wanted him. If there was a mistake there was nothing the man could do about correcting it. . . . They did that much. But now the union goes to another extreme. They broke up the incentive to do good work. [Here Montgomery is against the union's seniority as frustrating the more ambitious man's chances for advancement.]
The union is not doing a job. It's hurting the people. They got a majority of the 5000 people on the plant. But a minority group sets the policy. Ninety per cent of the grievances are straightened out by the foreman. There's a small union group agitating to settle grievances even when the employee is wrong. To tell a man he's not wrong when he is, won't make a better employee out of him, for instance if he's been stealing. . . . *But it's always probably good to have a union here to keep the company on its toes*, on the line, to make the foremen follow things as they should. ——— [a local leader] once called me a liar. *They're hot-heads. They get less than if they were persuasive. They want to get under a fellow's skin.* They want you to say something like "Shut up!" or "Get out of here!" so they can use it in the *Flash*. They lie to such an extent that you can't even believe the truth. The foremen don't like to be bothered with the union leaders. And that's bad because Swift policy is to settle grievances as fast as possible and you can't do it that way. . . . *A Union leader has*

to be a rabble-rouser. But ———'s all right. I like to deal with him. . . .
The old [right-wing] crowd were just as militant.

Another member of higher Chicago plant supervision, Gordon Whyte, contrasts the CIO and the AFL:

We believe that unions are here to stay. And we might as well live with them as well as possible. The old [right-wing] gang was coöperative with the company. [This is a frequent comment.] And the AFL Teamsters — we get almost no grievances from them. That union is not afraid to tell its men: no.

Thomas Newcomb makes a distinction:

——— has a talent for getting under people's skin. Though I understand him better now, knowing his objectives. *His philosophy is: Fight for the worker against the company.* . . . But ——— [a UPWA International executive] is a good man and smart. He is fair to deal with.

A few of the foremen have good words to say for the current Local 28 leadership. Youthful Joe Herman is one of these exceptions, in spite of the fact that he had been criticized in the *Flash:*

The foremen would kid each other. "Did you make the *Flash* this week?" they'd say. But if they were not broadminded they would take it out on the gang. *They panned me. And my men said it was not fair.* . . . ——— [a local leader] *is fighting for the people.* I can see his angle. He'll do more good for the CIO than the former officers. *He cleaned out the liquor from the union headquarters.* They'll have good leadership.

Incidentally, Swift Chicago higher supervision does not differ very much from the foremen or even from the employees, for that matter, with respect to local union leadership. As for union allegiance itself, however, higher management has apparently less of it than foremen or workers.

Although their average formal education is only eighth grade,[4] these Swift-UPWA workers have clearly shown the ability to judge the issues, to weigh evidence, to criticize, to form conclusions. A few manifest ignorance and some emotional immaturity; but many show sharp insight, common sense, and good intelligence. On the whole, these people are by no means the ignorant dupes of either demagogues or ideologies that some editors, advertising men, columnists, and even a few labor-relations people think the average American workers to be.

One of the most interesting facts we find in this chapter is that many workers in the plant community, having allegiance to both union and company, resent the leadership of either group (in this case, the union) trying to alienate them from the other group (here, the company). Swift-UPWA people are not fodder for the class-warfare dialectic. They do not believe that there must be necessary battle between the two organizations which they support.

We recall the fact that when foreman Joe Herman was attacked in the *Flash,* his own men stood up for him. It is evident that if the workers are well treated by management, as they generally are in the Swift Chicago plant, they will not be easily turned against it. It is also just as evident that good personnel treatment does not turn the worker away from his union allegiance. We are constantly stumbling over the fact of dual allegiance, a fact which it would be well for leaders of both parties to remember.

Thirdly, one of the principal findings of this chapter is that in spite of their union allegiance, 47 per cent of the workers are plainly dissatisfied with their 1950 left-wing union leadership, primarily with their local leaders (the over-all average is between neutral and unfavorable). This is practically the only major aspect of the plant community with which the Swift-UPWA workers are dissatisfied. We will see in the following chapter how this leadership dissatisfaction affects participation in union affairs.

CHAPTER NINE

HOW THE MEN PARTICIPATE IN LOCAL 28

Participation is a vital and an all-important function for many groups. Some organizations require active participation for their continued existence or at least for their healthy existence: the family, the modern democratic state, and the local trade union. In the democratic union, if participation withers up and communication upward becomes clogged, development of leaders stops and top leadership becomes a clique or even a single ruler who finds it increasingly difficult to act with the interests of the rank and file at heart.

Participation is equally important for the person or worker himself. Since a man is not a machine, he wants to have some say, some decision, some responsibility about so important a thing as his life in the plant community. Management can, and Swift management does partly facilitate the employee's participation in his work by informing him about the company in media like *Swift News*, by the suggestion system, by the foreman's efforts to give him responsibility and to listen to his views. But no management devices or "human relations" techniques will fully satisfy the worker's desire for participation in the government and life in the Swift-UPWA plant community, for, as we have seen, the workers there also want the independent union as a means of participation. Not a few observers have noted the connection between the desire for participation and the desire for a union. Bakke, for example, states:

> Americans have absorbed . . . the desire to participate in shaping the institutions and rules within which they live. . . . The traditional organization of industrial and business enterprise did not provide for the participation of employees. . . . The union owes much of its appeal to American workers because it supplies them with an instrument of such participation.[1]

Also political scientist Frank Tannenbaum:

> If there is any meaning that can be derived from the persistent grouping of men about their tools or within their industry, it is the very clear attempt to reassert human experience, namely, that work must fill a social, a moral, as well as an economic role. The vacuum between the job and

the man has proved intolerable. . . . For the worker, the trade union has been an attempt to escape from this dilemma.[2]

Our findings agree with the theoretical statements of Bakke and Tannenbaum in that the Swift-UPWA workers want their union as an opportunity of participating more fully.[3] But, as we shall see, the workers are not at present actively using this opportunity.

What is the relationship between the attitude called union allegiance which we have found and actual behavior toward the union? In general, we call the employee's behavior toward the union his union participation. If we put the workers in their twelve "boxes" by the two sexes and races and the three service lengths (white men of middle service, white men of long service, and so forth), and then arrange the boxes in their numerical order of union allegiance and union participation, we find a high positive rank-correlation of .86. The colored men of middle service are the most active in union participation and also have the greatest amount of union allegiance. The white women of long service have the least union allegiance and also participate least in the union.

A scatter-diagram also shows moderate association between union allegiance and union participation, though in no one-for-one way, since a few workers with high union allegiance participate only slightly. Union allegiance increases participation, especially of the active union men, while participation in turn increases allegiance. Attitudes toward the local union leaders have an important influence over a worker's union participation, though again there is no one-for-one association between the two, for other factors such as race, sex, and service also affect participation.

We also have an observed fact about union behavior that is quite independent of the interviews; namely, actual membership in the union. Whether or not a man actually joins the union, signs a card, and agrees to the dues checkoff is surely an important form of behavior toward the union. Again we find a high-rank correlation between those groups which have the most union allegiance and their percentage of union members. The figure is also around .86. The colored women of short service are the most unionized and come third in their union allegiance. The white long-service women are the least unionized (13 per cent as in Table 25) and the least favorable to the idea of a union. While various motives lead a worker to join a union, union allegiance is one of the most important. Union allegiance has definite value for predicting union behavior.

THE CRITERIA FOR PARTICIPATION

Participation means nothing more complex than the UPWA worker's taking part in union affairs by going to meetings, reading, talking, co-operating, and so on. We have various criteria for judging the degree of participation, which fall into eight categories:

(1) *Attendance at union meetings,* monthly membership meetings, stewards meetings (for stewards only), departmental meetings, dances, annual picnic, rallies, etc.

(2) *Reading union literature:* the *Flash;* the International's *Packinghouse Worker;* contract; Local 28 Constitution, etc.

(3) *Talking about union* at noon hour and other times.

(4) *Doing union work:* Being an officer or steward; accepting appointments to committees and delegations; distributing handbills; signing up new members, etc.

(5) *Voting in annual election* of officers.

(6) *In grievances,* using the services of the department steward.

(7) *Wearing a union button.*

(8) *Membership* in the union.

These categories are not all of equal importance. For instance, wearing a union button (which was an important sign of participation in the dangerous days of organizing) is still a minor method of participation for the men workers. Women workers do not often wear union buttons even if they are active, simply because they wear no regular hat; and since they send their starched head caps to the laundry frequently, it is not convenient for them to wear a button. "Doing union work" is a category that applies mostly to the inner core of active unionists. "Voting" is an important category, and unless a man were very active in the other categories, failure to vote would cause him to be classified as "inactive" in participation. A deficiency in one category might be made up by greater activity in another; but if a man were active or inactive in one, he tended to be active or inactive in all.

On the basis of these eight categories, each worker is graded on his degree of participation in the union as follows: very active; active; occasionally active; inactive; very inactive; practically no current activity (nonunion). The very active union man is almost always either a Local 28 officer or a steward who attends steward and membership meetings regularly during the year, reads the *Flash* and *Packinghouse Worker,* is somewhat familiar with the contract. He may not be familiar with Local 28's Constitution, however, since few of the workers possess copies. He talks unionism and does union work. The very inactive union man may or may not wear a union badge, glances at the *Flash* occasionally during the noon hour and that is all. He attends no meetings, does not vote, and is simply "dead wood" in the local.

The average union member in the Swift-UPWA plant community simply does not take active part in the local union part of that community. This finding is not surprising in the light of what we know about many American local unions. If we take a random, unstratified sample of 133 workers who are union members, we find that the average union member is rather inactive. (The average is 3.87 on a scale of 1 to 5.) If we take all the workers including those not currently members of the union, and participating practically not at all in it, we find the average is very inactive (4.52 on a scale of 1 to 6. See Table 23).

We find further that race and sex are significant influences on participation in union affairs.[4] The white workers participate far less than the colored workers. This racial difference is much greater than it was in attitudes to company and to union. We are not surprised that the women participate less than the men because we have found that they have less union allegiance. Then too, women do not like to attend union meetings because they have work to do at home and are less likely to go out at night than men. Also the business nature of the average union meeting and literature is less to their taste. While length of service is not significant for all the workers taken together, it is significant for the Negroes, the long-service workers taking less active part.

TABLE 23

Worker participation in Local 28

(*Random, stratified sample of 192 workers, also stewards and leaders by service, sex, and race: 1950*)

Men			Women	
Negro	White		Negro	White
4.04	5.25	Short-service	4.31	5.50
3.67	5.21	Middle-service	4.31	5.56
4.63	5.21	Long-service	4.88	5.88

Totals (Weighted)

		Scale	
Men	4.47	Very active	1.0
Women	4.73	Active	2.0
Negroes	4.13	Occasionally active	3.0
Whites	5.29	Inactive	4.0
Short-service	4.23	Very inactive	5.0
Middle-service	4.49	Practically no current activ-	
Long-service	5.08	ity (nonunion)	6.0
Stewards	2.40		
Left leaders	1.00		
Right leaders	2.60		
All workers	4.52		
(Union members only on a scale of 1 to 5	3.87)		

The most active group is the Negro men of middle service. This is understandable, since old-timers lose interest and young men are too insecure or have too many family obligations to become active unionists. When whites were leaders in the union, the most active group was the white men of middle service, especially the mechanical gang. The least active group, also understandably enough, is the white women of long service.

There is a difference in activity between left-wing and right-wing union leaders because the left-wing group happened to be in power while this study was being made. Leaders who have lost power are generally less active than those now in control.

TABLE 24

Participation activity of Swift employees and Local 28 members
(*Spring, 1950*)

Category	Number	
Union		
Core* {Very active	20	
{Active	20	
Occasionally active	500	
		Average of union members "rather
Inactive	1100	inactive" (3.87)
		Average of all
Very inactive	1600	workers "quite inactive" (4.52)
Nonunion (36 per cent). (A nonunion man may participate in the union according to a few of our criteria.)	1809	
Total in Bargaining Unit	5049	

* The right-wing leaders of 1950, the "New Committee for CIO" were a very active core for several months but, after their defeat, became only occasionally active or inactive. Their activity is an example of how the participation pattern is in a state of flux.

Table 24 gives us a picture of the amount of activity in the Local in 1950. The active and very active core of the local is a very small number of people, around 40, or about 1 per cent.

TABLE 25

Percentage of Chicago plant workers unionized
(*Random, stratified sample of 192 employees by service, race, and sex: 1950*)

	Colored Men	White Men	Colored Women	White Women
Short-service	79%	58%	100%	37%
Middle-service	92%	45%	87%	37%
Long-service	62%	54%	50%	13%

All workers: 69%
(December, 1950)

Table 25 shows some striking differences in the way that service, race, and sex affect unionization. Here again we see a remarkable difference by race. There is also a difference by sex among the white workers, the white women being less likely to join the union than the white men. As for the colored women, they are as likely to join the union as colored men, though they tend to participate less once they have joined. Also length of service continues to be an important variable, the old-timers being less likely to join the union than the shorter service workers. Yet we see an interesting exception here among the white men where there is hardly any difference by length of service. The middle-service white men are less unionized, however, though they were once the stronghold of the union and may be so again.

How does nationality affect unionization? We do not have complete data, but a subsample of twenty-seven Polish men is 60 per cent unionized, while a subsample of nine Lithuanian men is only 11 per cent unionized. Because these samples are small and of unequal size, the results are suggestive only. They seem to indicate that Polish workers are much more union-minded than Lithuanians. It may well be that the Lithuanians have a more tightly knit nationalistic neighborhood life that pulls them away from union allegiance.

TABLE 26

Percentage of Local 28 membership voting in
annual election of officers

January, 1947	32% voted	
January, 1948	20% voted	(Right wing secure)
July, 1949	60% voted	
February, 1950	54% voted	(Struggle between left and right)
January, 1951	38% voted	(Left wing secure)
January, 1952	36% voted	(Right regains most positions, but left still has toe-hold)
January, 1953	48% voted	(Right wing secure. Left totally defeated)

One final point must be mentioned if we are to understand worker participation in local union activity. Such participation is obviously not static. It is constantly changing. It is affected by union contests with the company in contract negotiations or strikes, by factional struggles in the union itself, especially elections, by interest-evoking ability on the part of the union leaders, and by many other influences. Table 26,[5] for instance, shows wide fluctuation in voting participation over several years. Clearly many of the workers do not exercise their responsibilities as "citizens" of their local democratic union society, even at such a time of crisis as the Communist struggle of 1949–50. These voting figures corroborate our label "quite inactive." We must remember, though, that only 51 per cent of American voters bothered to go to the polls in the important Truman-Dewey election in 1948, though 63 per cent voted in 1952. Seventy-three per cent of eligible Americans voted in the 1900 elections. The comparable election participation of other countries is better: Belgium 90 per cent, Italy 89 per cent, Great Britain 82 per cent, and Japan 70 per cent. In the interviews, about 69 per cent of the union members indicated they had voted in the 1949–1950 period. Evidently they exaggerated a bit, as the above figures are roughly correct. In sum, we have seen that the Swift-UPWA people are not active in union life and that race, sex, service, and nationality influence their degree of activity. Now once more we let the worker tell his own story to bring these figures into life.

FIGHTING AND LEADERS

Two important and allied reasons emerge explaining the workers' inactivity in the union. Many workers state that they do not participate because they do not like the current bickering prevalent in union literature and at some union meetings. The left-right struggle, for instance, erupted into a fist fight and panic in December, 1949 at one meeting in Local 28 Hall. It seems plausible and it is sometimes stated that workers will become more active rather than less when there is a factional fight going on in a local union; they will follow the campaign literature with more interest, will talk about it and more will come out to vote. Our figures in Table 25 do show a remarkable increase in voting during the left-right struggle in Local 28. But, against this, a significant number of workers in Local 28 state that fighting and factionalism deter them from participation.

Other workers state that they do not participate because they do not like their leadership. Clearly union leaders can greatly affect rank-and-file participation. One active man in a department can organize and keep active his entire department. If he ceases to be active, or even positively turns against the union, he may turn his entire department away also. In Local 28 this happened in the mechanical departments after the left-right battle, though later key leaders among the mechanics brought them back into the union again.

We saw that a traumatic accident alienates Barney Edwards from the company and his foreman. He has clear union allegiance, although he dislikes his union leadership. His union participation is nonexistent since he is out of the union. The 1948 strike is one cause, but fighting is another: "They've had fighting once already. *Rather than have fighting, I don't go.*" Old-timer, William Thompson, 41, is occasionally active to inactive. He has high union allegiance and rather favors his leaders:

I went to four meetings last year and to dances some. But I got no time. I'm doing tailoring under the G.I. Bill. The business of the union now is to straighten things out. . . . I didn't vote in the election. Didn't bother. They hollered about the buses [to take the men to the polls] but it was all right with me; there was slop and mud. *But they were arguing and squabbling too much so I didn't vote.* We'll have to get together somehow. . . . I don't get the *Packinghouse Worker.* The *Flash* is a whole lot of propaganda. They throw the "slang" back and forth. Been hurting the union. I read part of the contract.

Polish old-timer, Fred Bolgar, 61, has only neutral union allegiance and knows nothing of his union leaders. It does not surprise us to find that his participation is very inactive partly for the fighting theme:

Meetings? Bah! [Gesture of contempt.] I never go to meetings. I didn't go to the election. I just pay my dues. *There was a fight at the union hall.* [He refers to the fight in December, 1949.] What use to go to meeting like that! Somebody cut my head! . . . The *Flash?* I don't read it much. If I want to read, I get some book somewhere. [Bolgar wears no union button.]

Another old-timer, Charles Jaworsky, 56, is neutral to the union and knows nothing of its leaders. He quit the union in anger after the 1948 strike. His participation is now zero:

I only went to a union meeting once. Why should I go. I'm tired at night. It takes me one hour to come to work. I live on the North Side. *Anyway there's too much argument in the union. I better forget it.*

Al Lamb, a middle-service shipper, was once quite active in Local 28 affairs but is now inactive because he doesn't like the way things are being run:

I was active as a steward once, for three years. I was chief steward of my division. My relations with management were always very coöperative. I had very few cases that went to the third step. Most grievances got somebody wrong. Two sides to it. The employees always want to win. I don't like clashing with management. . . . *The present union leadership is not too good.* I don't know, they don't follow CIO policy. The old heads were more business-like. I don't go to meetings now. *I get through late and I don't like their views.*

Finally, skilled pork-butcher, Art Couture, an old-timer and a very active union leader formerly, has no activity now. He dropped out of the union in anger at the 1948 strike.

I was a steward, I was a good union man, 100 per cent. I went to every meeting of the union. But it's a weak union now. Nothing to it. Want big men in. *Don't coöperate with each other now.* I don't belong. It's not strong enough. I would join if it was strong. . . . The future of the union? We won't have no union. It'll die out. *There's a fight between the leaders.* The old leaders want to be in or they won't join at all. . . . If the majority would join, I'd join. Why? Then it would be strong. The company gives you all fair breaks anyway. We don't need a union.

THE DETERRENT OF RACE

The difference in union activity between colored and white workers is the biggest difference in all our findings. Because Local 28 is now (1950) largely colored-led, has mostly colored at its meetings, holds some of its meetings in the heart of Bronzeville, white workers either do not join the union, or if they join, they do not participate actively. The whites are very inactive and the white women are either very inactive or not active at all. When a group approaches and passes the 50 per cent mark for one minority group and the former majority group now becomes a minority group, this new minority group (here the whites) will not participate very actively. Such is the story of Local 28, at least.

Interestingly enough, there were no significant race differences in company allegiance, or in attitude to foreman or job, showing that although Negroes believe their opportunities to be limited, still this does not destroy their company allegiance. But in every category regarding the union there is a sharp race difference: union allegiance, attitude toward union leaders, and union participation. As we have seen, the whites feel secure in their jobs and believe that the company would like to build up its white proportion. Either through fear or prejudice or both, the whites do not want to go to union meetings, are less likely to use the services of a Negro steward, are less inclined to follow union literature so often stressing race issues, and, in general, withdraw from union affairs.

Tom Winkowsky, a young clerk, refuses to join the union because of communism, the 1948 strike and the race issue, as we saw. As for going to union meetings, the race issue deters him. The dilemma he states is not entirely valid, for Negroes did and do participate in meetings at the Local Hall in a white neighborhood:

> As for a mass meeting, you can't have it in a white neighborhood because too many colored won't come. *You can't have it in a colored neighborhood. The whites won't attend.*

Ford Bartlett, 26, comes from the south and this no doubt influences him on the race question. He says:

> *The reason I don't go is all the meetings are at 48th and Wabash and it's all colored there.* They say it's a bigger place there. But the n——rs drink like fish. That neighborhood is too dangerous. I don't even like to *drive* through there. They say the Hall is too small at 43rd and Ashland. *I've never been to either place.* I've never been to *any* meetings. I didn't vote in 1950 and I don't want any part of social or other activities of the union. . . . I don't want to be active in the union, I just want to be *in*.

> *Interviewer:* What do you think would get the white fellows more active, Ford?

> I think white guys should be in *office* in the union. And they ought to move the meetings back to 43rd and Ashland. A fellow will say about the

meetings: "I'm not going over in a n——r neighborhood!" Or, "If you go with me, I'll go." And I'll say: "I'm not going!"

Anthony Masiello, 34, a semiskilled butcher with Swift for nine years, likewise approves the union and its leaders, but is quite inactive:

> When you go to meetings there are just four or five white and 200 colored. Well. . . . The majority in the plant are colored, *by far.* . . . The colored talk to colored "colored troubles," so the whites don't want to go to the Hall. . . . *The white fellas say: "Let the colored handle the union. I belong. But let the colored do it."* Most whites are in the union. [This is an error.] The colored in the union are always fighting for race causes. I don't think they should keep on talking about discrimination in the plant. There is none. The trouble with mixing white and colored, their [the colored] standards are so low. The white are low, too, but they try to keep their homes nice, etc. Out of every 100 colored there is one good one who has pride of family. They divorce and marry without the courts. It's better to keep 'em separated. Close is okay, but in a separate district. . . . I don't think this generation of colored and whites will get along.

Two old-timers continue this same theme. Both have strong union allegiance, disapprove of their leaders and participate inactively. Maurice Decker, 47, says:

> ——— [a local leader] protects n——rs only, and does nothing for the whites. . . . They should stand up for the rights of the worker whether he's colored or white. . . . They should have meetings as close to the plant as possible, especially afternoon meetings. But 48th and Wabash — they shouldn't have meetings there! *I know I ain't gonna go there.* Drive my car there an' have the wheels taken off!

The white women are hardly active at all, even the short- and middle-service groups. Insofar as activity involves going to union meetings, the race issue is their major deterrent. Mary Zablonski, for example, with Swift nearly fifteen years, approves both union and leaders, but fails to participate actively for both reasons peculiar to women (care of the home) and for race reasons:

> Oh, I ain't got no time to go to meetings. *After work I go shopping, or I go home an' clean house. And I like to watch television at night.* . . . I should go but I have no interest. I feel I just don't want to be bothered. People who are strong like the stewards — they know what's goin' on — they should elect the people [officers]. . . . I don't go to meetings. They might start riots, fights and mix-ups. *I used to go. But they have them over at 48th and Wabash now.* Dances and sports? I don't believe in that. They should stay in their place, the colored separate from the white. . . . Elections? I don't go. It's going to be at 48th and Wabash. I'm not interested. Let them elect who they want and do what they want. . . . In the *Flash* they call people things; I don't think they should. . . . *The union is mostly colored.* . . . They ought to get together an' make *one* union or quit. But we need a union.

Finally, Mrs. Estelle Bolduc, Slovak, 32, a semiskilled butcher with Swift for ten years is against the union though she is a member. She is very inactive:

Do I vote? I would try to. But not if you have to push through a lot of colored men. They ought to have a separate voting place for men and women. That would be all right. . . . The *Flash* is all right. It gives you the news. That's good especially since we don't go to meetings.

OTHER REASONS FOR INACTIVITY

There are many other understandable reasons for the union inactivity of the Swift-UPWA workers. As local leader Ted Kurowsky puts it:

Father, the workingman's got to have his belly-button pressing on his spine before he'll do anything. He's got to be hungry — in need. Like during the Depression, he'd come out. Now, it's the ball game or the show.

Local 28 is a small organization in a large city, whose members often live far from the stockyards in diverse neighborhoods, with all the anonymity of city life. The local must compete with neighborhood organizations and interests as well as with home interests. A worker would rather go bowling or watch a movie, game or television show than listen to a union speech. He would rather read a newspaper or magazine than union literature. He would rather stay at home than take a streetcar ride, sometimes in what he may think are dangerous streets, to the union hall. It is so easy to just pay one's dues and "let George do it."

Short-service meat-packer, Richard George, 24, attends a mechanics night school. This, combined with the fact that he finds the meetings dull, leads to his inactivity. Factionalism keeps down his reading of the *Flash*:

I used to go to meetings *but I got no time to go now. It's just talk.* But I'll take off a night from school soon, and go over to the hall and listen to both sides. . . . As for the *Flash*, I don't approve of factions. They ought to get together. If they don't agree, they shouldn't air that out.

Jonathan Jackson, short-service elevator man, has high union allegiance, dislikes his union leaders and is occasionally active in the union. We remember that his college education is a factor:

The *Flash?* It's better in the garbage can. In typing there are misspelled words. It's as if they didn't go to school. . . . Personally I don't care for union dances. *I'd rather sit at home and read a book.*

Another short-service man, Ezra Lamb, 39, used to be rather active in Local 28. Now he is rather inactive. He wears at least six or seven badges on his hat which is one way of participating in the union:

If you go to meetings at 7:30 they don't start until 9. Before the strike I went to most of the meetings, but not since the strike. But you got to go to meetings to find out what's goin' on. The *Flash* is not enough. Some don't even know when a raise is given!

Another short-service white worker also says he lives too far away to come to meetings, although he mentions other reasons for inactivity. Jim Stowa, war veteran who is bitter about Communist leadership:

> Meetings? It's inconvenient. I get off at 2:30 and the meetings are at four. *I live on the far South Side.* Anyway, I'd want another man with me at the meetings. *Why? I've seen those Communists operate.* They're like Vishinsky.

For Charles Sucholdolski, Polish immigrant, aged 54, language is a major problem in his union participation, though he has been in America since 1914:

> Meetings? I work nights. I never go. I'm workingman. I no got time. I live in three rooms an' cook because my wife dead. I bring in coal. I fix stove. *I'm so tired, nobody help me. I no go meetings.* . . . The *Flash*? *I no read English.* Polish only. . . . As long as I work I no have trouble. I no call in union.

Swift veteran, Herman Birkenhauer, 64, has strong union allegiance but does not participate mostly because he is too old:

> I don't go to meetings. When I get home I take my shoes off and put my slippers on. I got no time to go to meetings. . . . The picnics would be all right if all white people were there. I'd go with my wife. But the union is mostly colored. . . . *If I were younger I'd be more active than I am.*

The women workers of the plant community are less active than the men. Mary Winter, for example, 27, is inactive partly because of shyness:

> I very rarely go to meetings. *I don't like to go — type of girl I am. I don't like to go alone. I don't talk much,* though I like to listen.

Ellen Hall, 46, meat-trimmer, is also inactive:

> I go to meetings maybe once or twice a year. *Usually I am tired and I go home. Besides it's just business and normal routine.* As for the officers, I don't have anything to do with them. . . . *I read the Packinghouse Worker at times. The recipes in it are good.* . . . The union has helped others, but I never needed help.

Marion Hallock, short-service shipper, 28, has an interesting comment on the influence of her union steward who aroused Miss Hallock to somewhat greater activity:

> I really don't know much about the union. But I got interested after the 1948 strike. They were fighting among themselves. One side accused the old clique of getting money for themselves. The other side was accused of not fighting for the worker. *I really don't know.* But our steward, she's nice, and she was for the crowd that's now in, the left-wingers. *And she got me interested and I went to some meetings,* and what they said seemed to make sense so I cast my vote for them. . . . I don't go to dances. You

know women! Next day they'd talk about clothes: "She wore purple with yellow!"

Finally Mary Radak, 46, who participates very inactively, makes a frank admission that she should be more active:

> I didn't vote and I don't care about meetings. *Maybe we're at fault.* We don't go to meetings. The leaders are just like politics. Maybe I'm at fault.

We said that the most active group in Local 28 union activity at the present time is the colored men of middle-service. While it is true that their average is 3.67, between "occasionally active" and "inactive," still there are a number of active and very active union men in this group. Significantly, most of these activists are skilled workers, a few semiskilled, and only one is unskilled. As we have seen, this group as a whole is only 8 per cent skilled and 59 per cent semiskilled. Evidently the activists are the cream of the group in working ability, income, self-confidence, and leadership ability. One of the group is an important union leader, Jorel Byron. A number of the others either were or are union stewards. Their high union allegiance is the important factor — the highest of any group: 1.60. A further indication of this is that they are the most unionized group among the men: 92 per cent. Most of them joined the union as soon as they came to the plant, and are thoroughly convinced of its necessity. This conviction about the importance of the union, rather than the influence of any union leader on them, is what inspires them to activity.

Stanley Stowe, 41, skilled man, thinks the union is "a great thing," likes the union officers and participates with occasional activity:

> I go to several meetings a year. I don't like to argue in the debates. *But I like the dances.* There you get used to more people. Sometimes you don't know the people in the plant on the next floor. We ought to get as many people out there as possible. We're goin' to have a ball team this summer. That's a good idea. Since the officers took over, things are a lot different. Before we didn't have dances, etc. Now we do. They'll treat you just as well as others. Let you talk and express your opinion. Everybody's happy now an' we gets along all right.

Former steward, Bill Schuett, 54, is active and quite union-minded:

> *I was hired one day and I joined the union the next day.* I wouldn't want to work on a nonunion job. The union has helped: the union's worth its weight in gold! I go to meetings often. Went to every meeting in April. *There's a chance to talk.* The stewards *have* to talk. [Schuett reads union literature and talks unionism.]

Frank Dumas, a former steward and against the local leaders, was an active picket in the 1948 strike and is still an active unionist:

> *I was a steward for eleven months.* I go to union meetings once a month. But we don't have the old fellows there like we should. The fellows who could really help are fed up. A union-shop would put the union 100 per cent.

The colored men of short-service are the next most active group among the rank and file. This group also has high union allegiance and is well organized, about 80 per cent. The reasons for activity here follow little pattern. The influence of union leaders is more important than it was in the case of the middle-service men. And these men have less company allegiance than the middle group. For example unskilled meat-handler, Leo Watson, 40, likes his leaders, and feels that they are willing to listen to his opinion:

> I know ——— [a local leader] *and I believe he is conscientious.* He is open to suggestions. I go to meetings every month or oftener. *There's a chance to voice your opinion.* . . . Dances are all right for once and a while. They oughta have movies with both sides of the picture — the company point of view and the workers' point of view.

And Vincent Queen, 25, is somewhat active, partly because he likes the social life of the union:

> I go to meetings once a month. *I enjoy it. There are females there.* And the dances are pretty nice for the workingman. *It's a chance for the fellows to meet each other.* . . . The activities program in the union is good. We should have *sports.* I'd join a union team in preference to a company team.

In our entire sample of rank-and-file white workers, men and women, there is only one who is more than occasionally active — John Kulbokas: Kulbokas has a 2.5 degree of union participation, that is, between occasionally active and active. He is a skilled craftsman and a former steward, and seems to be most influenced by his strong union allegiance. He is also favorable to the company, his foreman, and his job. He states:

> I'm in the union. *The union done good, even for lower supervision.* . . . I voted this year and I go to quite a few meetings in the fall and winter. But not in the spring and summer because I get odd jobs then. As for the dances — that's a kind of touchy subject because of the colored. [Kulbokas reads union literature.] Higher supervision may not know what's going on. The *Flash* brings it out. It makes the foremen think a little. It's a real good idea.

While the Local 28 social life and dances are a natural attraction for the colored workers to make them more active, they are a deterrent to the activity of the white workers. In sum, the rank-and-file activists are outstanding workers with leadership ability and out-going personalities who have strong convictions about the function of the union in the plant community.

UNION STEWARDS

The department stewards are a kind of inner cell of union activity surrounding the small, very active leader group which is the core of the entire local. Thus the stewards exert an important influence. Along with the leaders, they make or break the local union. They are a source of union activity and information in their respective departments. If the natural leader in the department is not the steward, then the steward must get the support of that leader in order to be effective and success-ful. (There are generally one to four stewards in each department, de-pending on its size. The UPWA formula of one steward for every ten workers is not exactly followed.) Stewards sign up new members, urge members to go to meetings and especially to elections. They campaign during elections. They report to their fellow workers what goes on at the membership meetings. They can gain friends for the union if they win the grievance cases they handle.

In the Swift-UPWA plant community there are over 200 stewards. Because of the left-right struggle, most of the steward body in 1950 was new. During the struggle itself union conditions were chaotic. Sometimes a department had two sets of stewards, sometimes none, sometimes no-body knew who the steward was. The situation gradually clarified, but a highly organized, well-trained group of stewards has by no means yet been developed. Many of the older stewards who supported the right-wing leaders refused to continue as active stewards. Their replacements were sometimes elected, sometimes appointed by the left-wing union officers. There are monthly stewards' meetings and periodically there are stewards' training classes given at the union hall. Only a minority of the stewards consistently participate in these.

In union activity, the Swift-UPWA stewards are closer to their core of union leaders than to the rank and file. Their average is 2.4, that is, about "active" on our scale. Their education is slightly higher than the plant average, being first year high school. In race, they are about 80 per cent colored. They are not paid by the union. But the company pays them their regular hourly rate when they are working on grievances. If they win a grievance they may please the worker and displease the fore-man, and if they lose, they face the opposite situation. Hence it is not surprising that it is hard to get qualified men to volunteer for the job. Most of those who take the job are highly union-minded and often rather self-sacrificing.

Steward Squire Stacey, for instance, is quite active. He is tall, big, voluble, and pleasant, and likes the union especially for its help regard-ing discrimination:

> I go to meetings regularly. It's a help. You always can learn something. *It's a privilege to explain yourself.* . . I believe in givin' people free affairs [dances] for their money. Let the peoples enjoy themselves. It don't take $9000 a month to run the union. They might cut out the dues for one or two months. . . . Should they pay the steward? *No, a good union man don't need pay.* The fellas would gripe. No.

One of the few white stewards, Ricardo Mastro, 53, is also very active, even though he is against the current leaders. He says: "The union is one thing every workingman should have and work for nothing else!" This deep conviction influences his activity:

> I was a steward from 1944 to 1946. It's a hard job. You got to go around a lot; sometimes there's no time to eat lunch. I became a steward again after the strike in 1948. *We should not lose faith in the union because that strike was lost.* . . . No pay is needed for the steward. Whatever I do I do it for the benefit of my fellow workers. . . . I do go to meetings regularly. *I do like the meetings. You find out what's going on.* If I like it, I vote for it. If I don't, I vote against it. . . . Dances don't interest me. They should keep the funds for benefit of sick members more than for dances. They throw money away.

One of the most active women stewards is Lillie Leonard, 30. Miss Leonard has had a full high-school education, has a strong and attractive personality, is a natural leader, feels very strongly about the race question, and likes to help other people, since she sought a social-service job, as we saw earlier. These factors explain her high union activity. She says: "I joined the CIO as soon as I came here. . . . I have to go to the meetings. I go all the time." Not all the stewards are active. Most of those who are inactive are dissatisfied with local union leaders. Bill Ryan, for example, dissatisfied with his leaders, is only "occasionally active." He brings up our old problem, the race question, though he is not prejudiced as his other remarks show:

> *The union group that's in, they try to get meetings at 49th and Wabash* — dances and some meetings, too. *Our guys are mad about it.* We have a good Hall. You have to rent at 49th and Wabash. It's not necessary. But over there, they're among their own people.

Also steward Richard Rex is now inactive. Once he was very active, however, being a union organizer. He tells why he lost interest:

> I don't want to be a big union man. I don't aspire to office. But I was a steward. I dropped out of the stewards. Our department has not a strong union. *I resigned because the men don't coöperate, don't attend union meetings, don't worry about anything.* They offered me a steward badge five times, but I refused. . . . The fellas won't coöperate, won't go to meetings, so I don't want to be a steward. They oughta *fine* fellows. But that's unconstitutional. They give away hams, bacons and boxes of groceries, etc., to get 'em to meetings. *One of our biggest problems is gettin' fellas to go to meetings.* . . . I made all the meetings. I never misses two meetings in a row, lessen I was outa town or somp'n like that.

Finally, steward Jack Hurd, 30, who comes from a department whose foreman didn't even know whether he had a steward there or not. Hurd is also dissatisfied with union leadership saying: "There's something wrong when men drop out of the union." In addition, he is going to night school. He is inactive:

I don't like to be a steward. I got very little training. Just some things to read. I never handled a grievance. . . . *I don't go to meetings at the Union Hall because I work at night at* —————— *Trade School on the G.I. Bill of Rights.*

In sum, the Local 28 stewards are fairly active even though the turmoil of the 1948 strike and the 1949–1950 factional struggles quieted down. Yet they are doubtless not fully realizing their potentialities as an inner activity cell in the local.

LOCAL LEADERS AS AN ACTIVE CORE

Less than one per cent of the local membership, around thirty men and women, largely run the union affairs of 5000 workers in the Swift-UPWA plant community. These thirty people are the very active core of local union life. It is they who organize the local political caucuses, plan the election campaigns, raise funds, run for office or electioneer, comprise the Local Executive Board, run the local committees, such as Grievance, Bargaining, Entertainment, edit the *Flash* and faithfully attend local membership meetings. (A quorum is twenty-five members who can decide almost any local issue, such as selecting delegates for the International convention or appropriating money for some union cause, and so on.)

Clearly the power and influence of this inner core is great. We have already seen the apathy and lack of participation of the rank and file in the plant community. Rarely does a membership meeting count more than forty members present, around 1 per cent. The only exceptions are rare crisis meetings or the annual elections themselves. And precisely because of this rank-and-file apathy does the leader core possess its great power. Hence it is not surprising that a small number of disciplined and convinced Communists, well-trained in parliamentary law, electioneering, and propaganda techniques could come in and seize control of a large local union like Local 28. It is not numbers, but political ability and determined work which secure control over Local 28 government.[6]

Of course, there is another side to the picture. The very nature of the leadership is also a product of the needs of the people in the plant community themselves. John L. Lewis is as much a creature of the violent and dangerous American mines and coal pits as he is their dictator. So in Local 28, the local leaders in the long run must reflect the workers' needs for racial harmony and advancement and for dual allegiance if they are to persist as leaders.

Some observers have said men become union leaders and aggressive because they are not accepted in American society.[7] Some caricatures state that union leaders are the frustrated, neurotic, "agin' the government" fringe you find in any society, men who gravitate naturally and quickly to the trade union movement as an easy outlet for their frustrations. Are these observations valid in Local 28?

First of all, we have observed no personality type whatsoever among the Local 28 leaders, right or left, men or women, colored or white, this faction or that. It is true that all these leaders have certain leadership qualities in common. They are mostly middle- or long-service, in their forties, self-assured, out-going people who like to deal with others and who can talk convincingly about union affairs.

Secondly, their motives for becoming leaders are also highly varied, though here we have more of a pattern. Some wish to help their fellow workers secure the dignity and decency of labor. This humanitarian motive is a powerful one; it is important and must not be overlooked. Of course, it is usually mixed with other motives, and for some local leaders it may be quite subordinate.

Some other leaders wish to advance the Communist utopia on earth; they are convinced that only Marxism will help the working man and especially the American Negro. Others seek the self-expression, the chance to talk, to lead, to decide, to influence, which they find by leadership activity in Local 28 and which they could not find in the anonymous life of the assembly line, or which they could not find among the supervisory force since they happened to be born with dark skin. Some leaders seek power and prestige in their union office. Some seek to right a wrong they may have experienced in company life. Some become union leaders because their parents were.

Some men simply enjoy the politics of union leadership as a sheer engrossing game like a boxing match, or a ball game or a horse race. There is a thrill in competition and in strategy. I am convinced that this "game-mindedness" is a significant motive for many leaders. It is also significant that almost none of the Local 28 leaders is seeking personal money income by his office or seeking to vent a grudge against Swift & Company as an institution. Rather many leaders will spend more money and time than they receive, and hardly one of them, even among the left-wingers, is positively anticompany. These motives I have listed are not isolated, of course. They will be found in varying combinations among the different leaders. To understand them, let us take a brief look at the men and women who have led the affairs of Local 28 in recent years.

Take local leader *Richard Storms,* for instance. Storms is a smooth-looking, smooth-talking man of forty, college-educated, popular, with Swift since he was thirty, doing clerical work. He has several talents and outside interests, such as managing football and baseball teams. He has been a very active unionist for years and is well-informed on both local and international union affairs. He admits that he has political ambitions in the UPWA. He resents the check on advancement which he and other Negroes everywhere face. He comments:

> Swift could get better work from their employees if they had more Negro clerks, foremen, industrial relations men, etc. I went to the Swift fore-

men's school. But I had to finish with the "correspondence course." They told me: "No available space, Storms." Top management don't look at the employee as a human being. It's the office employees versus the union employees. Still, under ———— [a certain plant executive] it was like a family.

Storms has outlets for his obvious leadership ability away from the Chicago plant community. Another union leader says about him: "Dick smells hams all day. When he's away from work he coaches football teams and is a scoutmaster. If his job took all his energies he would have no interest in outside activities." [8] But Storms also wants an outlet connected with his work life and in that community where he spends most of his waking hours. Under the circumstances, that he should seek this outlet in Local 28 leadership is the most natural thing in the world.

Tom Metzger. Metzger is a heavy-set man of nearly 50 who likewise makes a good appearance. Before coming to Swift, twelve years ago, he drifted from job to job spending many years in the steelmills. He has been a trade union member all his life, but only recently an active leader. He is not anticompany, but he is aggressive toward some foremen. He has many strong ideas and convictions about economic and political matters such as the Taft-Hartley Act and is glad to expound them at length. He finished only the seventh grade. One of his pet peeves is the Bedaux wage-incentive system used in the Chicago plant. Sometimes his reasoning seems confused, but his self-assurance does not waver. His experience as a union leader is not extensive and he does not always seem to use good judgment. But his general motivation appears to be a desire to help the common workingman.

Former local leader *Philip Weightman.* Mr. Weightman (identified here, with his permission) was a former president of Local 28, rose to be Vice-President of the International UPWA, and, after his political defeat in 1948, joined the national staff of the CIO. We shall only note here Mr. Weightman's revealing statement as to why he first became active in the CIO:

> "I have never belonged to a company union and refused to vote for the Security League. And old Polish gut-snatcher, Sylvester Kaverei, began to talk to me about the CIO. I became convinced and was willing to follow in line. One evening 'Snatch' led me into a dark basement at Union Headquarters for a meeting. When we turned a corner, entering the meeting place, I saw men I had never dreamed belonged to the union. 'There he is,' they said."
>
> The men elected Phil department steward at that meeting. He accepted, but he put a challenge up to them. He was going to wear his union button the next day, and he wanted them to come out into the open with him. They agreed. The next morning, union buttons blossomed all over the hog kill. The foreman couldn't believe his eyes when he saw Phil with a union button. For Phil had been friendly with the superintendent and had always been able to get grievances settled. He kept walking past Phil and looking at the button, but didn't say a word.

Phil decided to show him that he really belonged to the union. After spell time he came back with four buttons on his cap — north, south, east and west! The foreman shook his head and said: "Phil, I never thought that *you* would join a union! The company always gave you everything you asked for." *Phil answered: "I didn't join the union because of my hatred for the company, but just for protection. One day the superintendent may die and then what happens to personal relationship?"* He pointed to another worker. "There's a fellow over there that's always getting kicked around and transferred out of turn!"

After this, the foreman began to make it embarrassing for Phil by assigning him to the worst jobs, as if to say: "What can this fellow do for you, if he can't help himself?" Phil didn't want to give in to him by complaining, so he took it without a word, and continued to present grievances for the other men. He advised union members to walk the chalk line so that the company wouldn't have the slightest excuse for discriminatory firing. Not one man was fired for union activities in his department.[9]

Frank Goff. Frank is one of the most intelligent, able and skilled craftsmen on the Chicago plant. Although his father was once a foreman, and he himself has often been offered a foremanship, he has always refused to be a foreman, saying: "I couldn't take the discipline." Goff prefers the independent life of a trade-union leader. Once he was quite radical, dallying with communism. He is still rather a Socialist at heart. Goff is not anticompany but is highly aggressive and independent. His spirit of independence makes difficult his adjustment to the necessary coöperative give-and-take of local union politics. His motivation is surely one of self-expression, but also one of bringing about social reform. Another local leader says about him: "Goff gave ten years and all his time away from his family for the good of the union movement! It was not just for money." [10]

Robert Meeker. Meeker is a quiet man in his forties, with Swift for nearly twenty years. He is a very skilled worker, and was once a foreman, but states that: "Advancement depends on who you know and having relations in the general office." It seems that when the man who was pushing him died, Meeker was demoted. He says: "I was forgotten." It is likely that dissatisfaction with advancement and recognition was one important motive that led Meeker toward the union and union leadership. He has clear company allegiance and likes his job and foreman as well. But business and capitalism look big to him: "There were only 6000 millionnaires in the U.S.A. in 1917, while there are 30,000 now." Local 28 gives Meeker both protection and a place in the sun.

Jack O'Brien. An affable, highly intelligent, well read and long-service skilled worker is Jack O'Brien. He is a professional unionist in that he knows the history and objectives of the American trade union movement and thoroughly believes it is a necessary part of our social and industrial life. In this, he has been somewhat influenced by the social philosophy of his church. He is strongly motivated by a desire to help his fellow workers and to bring about a better social and industrial order. He finds that local union leadership is a way of fulfilling this motivation.

Ethel Dodge. Miss Dodge is one of the outstanding women unionists in the plant community. She is young, 33, and only four years with the company, a good speaker, intelligent, aggressive. She lives with her mother and one child. She feels very strongly about the race question saying: "We're so used to getting pushed around!" The UPWA with its forthright stand on interracial matters is a natural outlet for the leadership ability of Ethel Dodge.

Like Miss Dodge and Jack O'Brien, a number of Local 28 leaders are motivated toward leadership by a desire to break prejudice ceilings and advance the welfare of the Negro people. Local leader *Harold Waite*, for instance, is so motivated. Waite, a well-appearing man of fifty, a highly skilled butcher who has been blocked in advancement even though he is a natural leader, says:

> I had the privilege of running the gang for a week once, when the foreman was away. There was no trouble. In fact, 100 men signed a petition to the superintendent to make me a foreman. Nothing was done. No Negro is a full foreman. Once I asked ———— [a plant officer] about it. I said: "Here you bring in a foreman and put him over a twenty- or twenty-five-year man. Why? I'm not just asking for myself." He said: "Waite, you wouldn't want Swift & Company to stick their necks out? That's a job the Federal Government should take care of first."

Also Waite very much dislikes the wage-incentive system. He fails to see why it is compulsory (as he understands it to be) to make more than the standard output, a 60 B-Hour. He has moderate company allegiance, but like the others finds leadership in the union a natural outlet for his leadership and popularity.

Durell Hunt. This man is big and good-natured. He is an old-timer and a skilled worker and a Negro. In general he is popular, so that one worker, even though a southerner, said: "I see Hunt daily. He's a swell guy. He would talk to you, and talk sense." [11] Hunt has been an active union man for many years and evidently feels dedicated to the ideals of the trade-union movement. He wants to advance Negro rights. He is cool to the wage-incentive system. Union leadership was a natural step for him.

Tom Wade. Wade is also an old-timer, having been with Swift for twenty-five years. He is a dynamic speaker and a hard worker who feels strongly about discrimination. His formal education was the fifth grade. He is very aggressive and has strong opinions. For him the bonus system is: "A stick over the worker's head! Because of it, people are dead, get fired, out on the street!" For him some foremen are all right, but many "rawhide you!" He has been influenced by left-wing propaganda and training. The forces moving him seem to be the desire for self-expression and domination, Marxian dialectics and the liberation of the Negro people from their chains.

Kenneth Gould. This man is also aggressive and an old-timer in the plant community. Gould is a skilled man and has been interested in the union from its early days. Though he has never been exactly a top local leader, he may well have ambitions to advance in the union. He tends to be hot-tempered, but can also be quite affable. Among other motives, I think he is one who thoroughly enjoys the game of union politics about which he is well informed indeed. He himself gives one other important motive for his own union participation: "My father was a union man, so I've been one too, all my life!"

Steve Forrest. Steve is smooth-spoken, intelligent and attractive in appearance. Although he is currently doing unskilled work, he has had some college education. He is with the company about seven years, and is around forty and joined the union within a week after he came to the plant. He has been strongly influenced by the Communist party and has their confidence judging by the positions of trust they have given him. He faithfully follows the party line on Peace conferences, Poland, Korea, China, and so on. When I asked him why they don't have unions, or the right to strike in Russia, he gave this interesting answer: "You don't have to strike against your boss in Russia. Your boss is one of you! . . . They give you an emblem for output." Very likely his resentment against discrimination is the basic urge leading him to the left and to union leadership. He says: "I know I can't advance, and whites can."

Alec Puttkammer. Puttkammer has around twenty years' service in the plant community, is in his forties, and a union man from the very early days of Local 28. He has a measure of company allegiance. But he is a union man, first, through and through. He says:

> Swift offered to promote me to a superintendent's job. Swift would kill you with kindness. But they're better than Armour's with the union. We got four wage cuts in 1932. That's why I wanted a union. No other reason. Swift management is good. There wasn't too much firing at Swift's. The boss told the foremen: "Treat the men nice, so they won't join the union."

Undoubtedly something of trade-union enthusiasm has entered into Alec. He is a professional union man.

Les Kearns. Les is a Swift old-timer. He is about 50 and is a skilled operator in a mechanical craft. For years he has supported Local 28 and been quite successful in organizing his part of the plant. Judging from many remarks of men in his division, he is well liked and respected as a union man and a steward able in grievance work. While he does not have dynamic leadership qualities, he is willing to sacrifice much of his time and convenience to advance the cause of the union in which he so evidently believes.

Clara Hughes. Clara is another outstanding woman leader of Local 28. She is around fifty and has nearly thirty years' service with the company. She has had only a grade-school education, but seems to have an alert mind and to be an able speaker. Although she has high company allegiance, she is aggressive and has a mind of her own, giving her evident qualities of leadership. She explains her motives for active participation in Local 28 affairs:

> I was in the union in 1937, right from the start. I took a lot of interest in the union. *It's great to help people out.* I would like industrial relations work in the company. The union is a wonderful thing! . . . A lot of people in the plant followed me. They'd do what I say. *I used to fight for the people!*

Finally, district union leader, *Jake Vickers.* While he is not a Local 28 man, Vickers' personality has so influenced local affairs that a brief description of him is pertinent here. For years Local 28 leaders fought him until the local capitulated to the party in 1949. Vickers is an orthodox Communist, convinced, and apparently sincere. He is a strong personality, a dynamic, crowd-exciting speaker and possesses a quick, retentive mind. He is courageous, ruthless, and a hard worker. So it is not surprising that he has inspired loyalty from many Chicago UPWA workers. He is anticompany, antispeed-up, anti-exploitation. In a word, he is orthodox on the class-warfare doctrine. Logic, economics, prudence, the possibility of two sides to a question — such words are not in his vocabulary. Also he is a quick fighter for Negro rights. When asked how he happened to get into a radical movement like communism, he states:

> I started thinking that way when I was 16. I was listening to a street corner talker. [Vickers came from New York's lower East Side where left-wing and radical speakers were common as fire hydrants.] Then I went up to his rooms. I heard strange talk. Words I didn't understand. . . . Then too *I didn't like the idea of the rich having all and the poor having nothing.* . . . I am of course a Communist and I have never concealed it.
> *Interviewer:* Did you hope to advance in the Labor movement, Jake?
> Not now, of course. They know I won't change now! I was told often I could have big jobs in the CIO if I would change. But I could never do that and live with myself! I could never deny what I believe! I am sincere.

We have seen sixteen key union leaders of the Swift-UPWA plant community, people of all political factions, both left and right. As a group, they are by no means the neurotic or "agin' the government" people of the caricatures. Nor are they frustrated, unless you say a Negro who tries to gain rights denied him can be so called. Of course personal ambition and craving for power strongly motivate a few, and some tend to distort the definition of "welfare of the workingman." But their basic desire to advance the cause and welfare of the workingman is the significant force that helps to explain why these men and women want to become active union leaders in the plant community.

Not all the Local 28 leaders we have discussed are equally active in union participation. We have noticed that the left-wing leaders, being in power, are more active than the right-wing leaders they have displaced. Moreover, some defeated union leaders, while active during their campaign for reëlection, may lapse into inactivity if they are not reëlected. As a matter of fact, some of Local 28's key right-wing leaders of recent years are quite inactive and refuse to have anything to do with union affairs at the moment, because they are dissatisfied either with their defeat, or with other right-wing factions or with the way the local is now being run.

It is hard to get qualified men to volunteer for leadership. It is hard to retain men as leaders unless they happen to be at the top of a wave of popularity and success. A man will begin his leadership with enthusiasm, but then the novelty will wear off and the sacrifices begin to pall. One will say: "Why go on? They throw so much mud at you!" Another will say: "I've done my bit. That's enough."

One former local union leader, an old-timer in the plant community who claims he was laid off twenty-one times for union organizing and who has engaged in many a debate and many a scuffle for his Local 28, was asked if he would still go out and work for the union. He replied:

> No, not any more. I leave that for younger men. Five times I broke down for the union. I'll do it no more. I'm a grandfather now.[12]

Several other former leaders, disgusted with their experience in the tempestuous politics of Local 28 during 1948 and 1949, now refuse to lift a finger for the union. They are bitter with the left-wing leadership but not much more satisfied with other right-wing factions. Their policy is thus expressed by one:

> What will we do about the union? We'll wait. Let ——— and his crowd of leftists get into their own trouble. They haven't even had a major break with the boss yet. They're stupid. But we won't move. We won't do a thing. Let these new officers run into the ground first. It takes time. Maybe a year. Maybe two.[13]

And another says: "The time is not ripe. Let them hang themselves!"[14]
Still another former leader was against the 1948 strike and says:

> I walked in the picket lines. I helped in the union office. I got no pay or help from the union. . . . I couldn't get work during the strike. You can't get a job. I asked advice whether I should go back. I said: "I don't want to be a scab." But my friend said: "Go back if you want." So I went back a week before the end of the strike. The company called me even though I was active in the union. Everybody said: "Look who's here! She's here to spy, not to work!" I explained. The news got to the Union Hall that one of the most active stewards was back in the plant.[15]

Understandably, this former leader dropped out of the union after the strike, along with the general exodus at that time. Another union leader

ceased to be active partly because of health, partly because of the desire
to spend more time with his wife and children.

So we see a variety of motives leading men to withdraw from the
hurly-burly life of local union leadership. These motives are understandable enough and throw into sharper relief the problems and political
hazards involved in being a local leader in the plant community. Of
course we must remember that it is only a minority of Local 28 leaders
who withdraw totally from union activity. The majority retain some degree of activity. And a few, even those who are politically displaced,
remain quite active.

Our findings are that the rank-and-file Swift-UPWA workers do not
participate in union affairs, that, even in the crucial left-wing versus
right-wing local elections of 1950, only 54 per cent voted. Yet para-
doxically, we find also that these workers definitely want the right to
participate in their local union affairs and through their union, in the
social affairs of the plant community itself. Their union allegiance is
incontestable.

Nonparticipation is typical of many local unions, of many organizations whose life depends upon participation. The activity of Swift-UPWA
workers in Local 28 is better than that of the average American in his
national or local government.

The anatomy of nonparticipation in Local 28 affairs depends primarily upon race and sex. Any improvement in local participation will
have to take account of these factors. Of course, Local 28's leader core
and much of its steward inner cell does participate. For them, union
participation is a vital means to self-expression and the "will to community." But more of this activity can be evoked from the rank and file,
partly through union education programs, activities, and steward-training
programs. Above all, labor-management committees may make an important contribution toward calling forth more participation. This is a
challenge to UPWA leadership, if it is to keep its grass roots firm and
strong. If the rank and file becomes more active, both they and Local 28
as an organization will benefit through greater self-expression, com-
munity-mindedness, union allegiance, and improved leadership. In its
turn, the company will benefit, for dual allegiance will then become more
balanced and the plant community will become a genuine community.

IV

HARMONIOUS OPPOSITION

CHAPTER TEN

GRIEVANCE PROCEDURE

When the spotlight of publicity seeks out relations between management and labor these days, it usually falls exclusively upon the differences between the two parties, especially upon their collective bargaining controversies and strikes. But the day-by-day peaceful teamwork of the mutual grievance procedure rarely rates even slight publicity, though this is one of the most important aspects of management-labor relations.

Why is it so important? We saw that the major reason for union allegiance on the part of the Swift-UPWA workers is their desire for job protection and status. The essence of job protection and status is the grievance procedure itself. The worker wants somebody to stand up for him who can go right up to the Top Boss. He wants the opportunity to voice his opinion about the circumstances surrounding his job, should there be need. It is in the grievance machinery especially that he finds this "somebody," this opportunity. Not only the workers, but also the foremen and management see and approve this protection-status value of the grievance procedure.

To the union, its grievance procedure is next in importance to its very right to exist. It is not an exaggeration to say that after the Swift-UPWA contract clause giving the union the right exclusively to bargain for the people of the plant community, next in importance are the contract clauses establishing the grievance procedure, for these clauses set up the machinery for settling almost any dispute that may arise between the employee and the company. Of course, both worker and company are helped by all the other clauses in the contract dealing with wages, hours, seniority, holidays, vacations, and so on. But even if the provisions of these clauses did not exist, the employee still has a means of protection and communication, at least for his own job, in the grievance machinery.

Thus the bilateral grievance procedure provides an opportunity for the union to fulfill a vital function of communication and settling problems that is not provided satisfactorily in any other way. In this role the union is not merely a negative antibody; it is a positive partner in the necessary governance of the plant community.

STRUCTURE AND OPERATION

The Swift-UPWA grievance procedure is fairly typical of that used in most mass-production industries in America today. In formal structure it follows naturally enough the hierarchical levels in both company and union, in a five-step procedure as shown in Table 27. Normally a grievance originates when a dissatisfied employee goes to his foreman with some complaint about conditions of work or employment. It is interesting to note that never does a grievance originate with the foreman complaining against the employee. This is natural enough, for if the foreman believes an employee to be violating a rule, he has certain company-based sanctions: later starting time, disciplinary layoff, and discharge.

The Swift-UPWA contract does not define grievances only by matters mentioned explicitly in the contract, but speaks of "differences" or "local trouble of any kind . . . pertaining to matters involved in this agreement or incident to the employment relation." [1] Swift understands by a grievance anything real or fancied that makes an employee dissatisfied. This is a broad definition of a grievance, though the arbitrator is limited

TABLE 27

Cases handled through the grievance procedure
(Chicago Swift-UPWA Local 28 plant community)

		Year ending August 11		
		1950	1951	1952
First step	No. cases presented	367	364	380
Employee and steward	No. cases settled	191	195	217
with foreman	% of all cases settled here	52	53.3	57
Second step	No. cases presented	174	168	163
Division steward, steward	No. cases settled	74	76	72
and employee with general foreman and division supt.	% of all cases settled here	20.2	20.8	19
Third step	No. cases presented	98	91	91
Grievance committee, employee and steward with plant labor relations man	No. cases settled	41	49	56
	% of all cases settled here	11.2	13.4	15
Fourth step International union's grievance man with the Swift general supt.'s labor relations man	No. cases presented	16	39	35
Fifth step Arbitrator	Charles O. Gregory 1942–46 James J. Healy 1946–48 Ralph T. Seward 1949–	About five cases a year		None

to the contract in the fifth step: "The arbitrator shall be bound and governed by the provisions of this contract, and restricted to its application to the facts presented to him in the grievance." [2]

Sometimes the employee will go directly to his department steward rather than to his foreman, and the steward alone will go to the foreman. Sometimes both will go to the foreman, or a difference of opinion will arise between the worker and his foreman, and the steward will be called into the dispute. The contract explicitly states: "In cases where the union is the aggrieved or the employee refuses to present his grievance . . . ," the grievance may originate "between the employee union representative or representatives (not exceeding three [3]), with or without the aggrieved, and the foreman . . ." [3] The grievance is still oral at this step, though an alert foreman or steward may start to gather any papers or documents that would be pertinent to the grievance.

In the second step, which may come days later, the division steward enters the scene, with or without the aggrieved worker but usually with the department steward. The division steward of the Fresh Pork Division, for example, is the superior to all the department stewards of that division. Also the general foreman, or the division superintendent review the grievance. The grievance is still orally presented; but if it cannot be settled at this step, it is then put in writing and is referred to the third step.

The people involved in the third step are the Grievance Committee of Local 28, a group not to exceed twelve members, usually including the local officers and the chief steward of the plant. The company will often be represented by two or more individuals, one of the superintendent's Labor Relations men and the foreman involved. The hearings for this third step are held several times a week in a conference room of the Chicago plant general office. The grievance is presented on a written form together with the company's answer. And "in the event said parties fail to reach a decision, both the company and the grievance committee shall have the right to call witnesses in the case and visit the department involved in order to get all the evidence concerning the case." [4]

In the fourth step, "in the event that said parties fail to reach a decision, both the Company and the grievance committee have the right to call on the General Superintendent of the Company or his designated representative or representatives, and the international representative of the Union to assist in the settlement of any dispute at the plant." [5] By this time the company will have secured an opinion from its legal department on the case.

Finally, in the fifth step, if "no decision is reached by the international representative of the Union and the General Superintendent or his designated representative or representatives, either party may submit the grievance to Ralph T. Seward, as arbitrator, whose decision shall be binding on all parties involved. . . ." [6] In this step, formal hearings are held at irregular intervals, generally in a Chicago hotel parlor suite, at which all documents and necessary witnesses are presented. When the arbitrator's decision has been presented in writing at a later date, the particular grievance is finally closed.

Informal Operation of the Grievance Procedure. The actual operation of the grievance machinery in the Chicago Swift-UPWA plant community does not exactly follow the formal structure as shown in Table 27. For instance, some of the Local 28 officers go about the plant and take up grievances at the first or second step, when formally they would not get them until the third step. This is being done partly for political reasons, and partly because of the inadequate organization of the steward body following the left-right factional war in the local, leaving some departments without stewards. This is a matter of irritation to the company. On the other hand, the foremen will sometimes defer giving any decision on a grievance or even handling it until he has presented the whole matter to his general foreman or division superintendent or even to the plant Labor Relations man. In this way, the foreman seeks to avoid mistakes and also to sew up a water-tight case. The union complains that this is really mixing the second or third step with the first and delays the procedure. It is interesting to note that Swift is not afraid to reverse its foremen if it thinks them wrong.

Especially between the third and the fourth steps is the informal routing of grievances important. The Local 28 Grievance Committee has referred many grievances to the International Representative which are not really good cases. Instead of trying to settle these grievances in formal Fourth Step Procedure, the International Representative, after studying the cases and making recommendations, refers many back to the Local 28 Grievance Committee with the instructions: "to settle them in the Third Step and win whatever you can. . . This helps the prestige of the local union officers (and strong locals make strong internationals). It also makes for better relations between the local plant management and the local union. At the local level, people tend to duck their responsibility. If they realize they will have to settle sooner or later, they will settle now." [7]

A company representative comments as follows on actual operation of the grievance procedure:

> The foremen don't like to be bothered with the union leaders. And that's bad, because Swift policy is to settle the grievance as fast as possible. And you can't do it that way. . . . When they come to the third step, they don't even know the facts. They get the company facts and then build the case. They often leave cases hanging six months in the third step. That's no good. . . . The union sends cases from the fourth to the third step to get a "package settlement." Anything they won would be gravy for the union. But they fight anyway.[8]

As far as getting the facts is concerned, the contract explicitly states that "The company will supply the necessary information from the records to the grievance committee whenever it is necessary." [9] While the company is not solely interested in winning cases, it does have better access to the more complete documentary records needed for doing so.

The current Local 28 officers have somewhat opposing views on the operation of the grievance procedure. Their major point, as we saw, is their claim that the third step is being introduced into the first. The facts indicate that when the new, left-wing leaders took over the local, they tended to increase the number of useless grievances, either because of their inexperience and that of the new steward body in handling grievances, or because of politics. Says one company representative: "Only about 2 per cent of the unnecessary grievances are introduced for their nuisance or propaganda value. The rest are just ignorantly proposed." [10]

Number and Settlement of Grievances in the Plant Community. While accurate statistics are not available except for the third step and higher, we give here estimates that are substantially correct. As indicated in Table 27, the number of grievances at the first step come in at the rate of about one a day. About 50 per cent of all these grievances are settled in the first step. This seems to be a very good record. Though ideally, both company and union would like to settle all grievances in this step, such an ideal will doubtless never be reached.

About fourteen grievances per month arrive at the second step. And one-fifth of all grievances are settled in this step. Then about eight grievances a month arrive at the third step. In other words, over two-thirds of all grievances arising in the plant never get to the third step, since they are settled in the first or second steps. This is an important asset to both worker and management, for these two steps are close to the worker and his supervisor and generally take only a short time to handle.

Third-step grievances have fluctuated widely over the years, as shown in Table 28, with the general trend downward as the company and the union get more used to living together in the same plant community under a common contract. The high number of grievances in 1944 was due to the wage-rate cases then being adjusted in accordance with provisions and recommendations of the Meat Packing Commission of the National War Labor Board. Most of those 1944 grievances were wage-rate cases. The steady decline in grievances has been reversed by the left-wing Local 28 leadership, partly because they are using the grievance procedure as a political weapon to win support for themselves and for the union, as mentioned above, and partly because with every new regime there tends to be some experimentation with the contract and hence a rise in the number of grievances. For that matter, there is frequently a rise in grievances in the experimental period after each renewal of the Master Agreement is negotiated.

TABLE 28

Number of third-step grievances

(*Chicago Swift-UPWA Local 28 plant community*)

Year	Number of Grievances
1944	518 (wage-rate cases)
1945	177
1946	173 (strike year)
1947	134
1948	52 (strike year)
1949	75
1950	98
1951	91
1952	56

About twenty-eight grievances a year get to the fourth step. Nearly 75 per cent of these grievances are settled in favor of the company and only 25 per cent in favor of the union. Evidently the company does not let such grievances get to this step unless it thinks it can win them. Many of these grievances, as we said, are sent back to the third step. About five cases a year get to the final step, the arbitrator, in the Chicago plant. Both sides ordinarily prefer to permit as few cases to go to arbitration as possible, since both prefer to settle cases themselves. Furthermore, arbitration is costly and makes for further delay in the time of settling the grievance.

Number of People Affected by the Grievances. The majority of workers do not have grievances at all. Only a minority have actually used the procedure themselves. The best estimate available is that about 756 people of the plant community are directly involved in the handling of grievances in a year. This does not mean that 756 new people are involved each year, since management people and stewards handle grievances repeatedly and some of the workers will have more than one grievance. Seven hundred and fifty-six people includes the 456 aggrieved employees and about 150 stewards and union officials, and about 150 foremen and other supervisors. This is about 18 per cent of the number of people in the CIO bargaining unit plus the Chicago plant operating management. Of course, if we were to take all those now in the plant community who had handled at least one grievance between the present and 1942 when the procedure was set up under the first Master Agreement, the number would be considerably more than 15 per cent. It would not, however, be greater than 40 per cent or 45 per cent, though no exact figures are available. It is probable, then, that nearly half the people of the plant community have had some direct participant contact with the grievance procedure at one time or another.

Moreover, the rest of the workers and supervisors have indirect contact with the procedure in this sense that they hear the grievance settlements talked about in the department or in the union hall, or they read in the *Flash* about the more important grievances that the union may have won, especially those involving back pay, discrimination, discharges, and so on. Naturally, Local 28 capitalizes on and publicizes the grievances it wins, as this is a way of proving its worth to the members of the union.

All this must not be taken to mean that the number of grievances and people affected by them in the Swift-UPWA plant community is unusually large, but simply that in so large a plant community inevitably a fair number of grievances will arise over the years, in spite of every effort to reduce them. On the other hand, a small number of grievances is by no means a good indication that plant morale is high and that industrial relations are good. On the contrary, it might mean a clogged grievance machinery which was not ventilating the complaints. As one Swift representative puts it: "Few formal grievances doesn't necessarily mean ideal relations. Grievances may then be covert and smoldering." [11] Of course, the number of grievances could be significant in judging morale, but only if taken in conjunction with other factors.

SPECIFIC GRIEVANCES

In the early days of the Master Agreement, most of the grievances concerned wage-rate cases. Once those were settled, the following classes of grievances emerged. Cases involving job assignments, discipline cases involving theft, drinking, fighting, absenteeism, tardiness, disciplinary layoffs, etc., worker complaints that the work is too cold, too hot, too heavy, etc., grievances about Sunday work, holiday pay, vacation time or vacation pay, cases dealing with the standard system of wage-incentive payments and job loads, discrimination cases, seniority cases, and so on.

Says one union representative: "Swift has tightened up on discipline since the 1948 strike." There is evidence that Swift & Company in recent years has endeavored to cut down on the amount of petty stealing of foodstuffs and that foremen have become more strict in this matter. But on disciplinary matters involved in the 1948 strike itself, Swift was apparently quite lenient. According to this same union representative: "After the 1948 strike on the Chicago plant not a single man was discharged because of the strike. (Swift wished to discharge one man, but he was finally reinstated.) As a matter of fact, the Local 28 leadership had better relations with the company. Few were engaged in rough picketing. The officers were company-minded men." [12] Swift's policy was quite different from some of the other big packers in the Chicago stockyards, especially Wilson & Company, whose 1948 strike discharge cases were a cause of friction between them and the UPWA for months and even years after the strike. But most of the grievances in the Swift-

UPWA plant community represent the rather normal social and individual problems that will crop up in any industrial community.

CONTRACT INTERPRETATION

The contract is a kind of daily guide for solution of the human relations problems that can arise in the plant community. As we have seen,
workers, union men, and foremen like this system of having such rules
down in black and white. But some human relations problems do not
exactly fit a rule book, no matter how expertly its phrases are hammered
out. At one extreme of contract interpretation we have "legalism," which
will not admit a grievance exists unless some clause of the contract
is violated, and which processes the grievance uniquely according to
the strict letter of the contract. Such an interpretation policy makes the
whole grievance procedure a strict court of law, with the rule book the
end rather than the means. Such a policy may win legal battles but it is
not likely to lead people into a happy, coöperative life in the plant community. This view does not mean to minimize the usefulness of labor law
or the company-union legal contract. On the contrary, such law is very
necessary and wanted by management, unions, and workers. But it does
deplore the fact that some people try to make law solve all industrial
human relations problems, which it obviously cannot do, an abuse which
may be called "legalism."

On the other hand, "realistic" policy of interpreting the contract
recognizes any complaint as a grievance, at least for the early stages of
the procedure, whether a clause of the contract is violated or not. Such
a policy endeavors not merely to follow the language of the contract, but
also to solve the problems of the worker.

Swift-UPWA grievance procedure is partly realistic but also tends at
times toward the legalistic. The contract, as we noted, admits anything to
be a grievance, except for the fifth step in which the arbitrator is limited
to the clauses of the contract. Generally in grievance handling, the company as well as the union try to judge a case on its merits, using the
contract, but not being slaves to its letter or to precedent cases in the
files. For instance, one company man states:

> We try to judge each case on its merits and not just regarding precedent.
> Though the philosophy of the former Local 28 leaders was: Let the com-
> pany *spell out* its policy on discharges, for instance. Thus the union there
> wanted limitation on personal judgment of supervisors for fear of dis-
> crimination.[13]

But the UPWA, like most unions, is really against legalism, and does not
prefer lawyers as arbitrators. Says one union representative:

> An arbitrator should be honest and know the field. It's better that he be
> not a lawyer, though the company prefers a lawyer. But arbitration as an

end in itself is not a stabilizing factor, for too many legal precedents are set. The arbitrator should judge each case on its merits.[14]

Swift & Company's Industrial Relations manager, Harold F. North, sees the difficulty of legalism:

> The difficulties with our current labor agreement are that it is too complicated. . . . Too often people deal with circumstances rather than with the intention. . . . There must be a sincere effort on the part of all to avoid the use of technicalities in order to gain an advantage that was not intended in the language of the agreement. As you tend to administer the agreement in terms of law rather than in terms of common sense and justice, you tend to create labor difficulties in the interpretation of an agreement.[15]

Should time spent on grievances be paid for? If so, by whom? If a man has to take up grievances on his own time, the chances are he will be less likely to take them up, which is not necessarily a good thing. And if he is paid for his grievance time, the organization that pays him will doubtless gain some prestige in his eyes.

In the Swift-UPWA plant community time spent on handling grievances during working hours is recompensed by the company. There is precedent for this from the days of the Employee Representation Plan under which grievances were handled on company time. Swift is the only one of the Big Four who now pays this bill.

One company representative discusses this grievance time expenditure as follows:

> It costs us around $1000 a week or $50,000 a year for one plant! The men get paid not only their hourly pay but their average premium output too. . . . We'd get less grievances if we didn't pay for them. People would keep them harbored. It's better to get them in the open air though. If I couldn't see my boss on company time I wouldn't like it. I'd vote for paying for grievance time.[16]

A union representative has the following opinion which is not a stated policy of the UPWA, of course.

> Swift pays for grievance time, including premiums. They're the only one of the Big Four that does. But I think it's better for the union to pay. This way there's a psychological effect. The employee feels more bound over to the company.[17]

Doubtless Swift's policy does improve its prestige with the workers and is one more factor in their high company allegiance.

STEWARDS AND FOREMEN

The effectiveness of the grievance procedure in furthering good industrial relations in the plant community is very dependent upon the two key performers, the foreman and the steward. At once we run into a fundamental difficulty. It is easy for the company to train its foremen on how to prevent grievances or handle them once they arise. It is much more difficult for the union to train its stewards. Swift & Company has an efficient foreman training program, done on company time and during work hours. In addition to the optional night school courses and YMTC (Young Men's Training Course) offered by the company, the foremen have regular classes and discussion groups on all phases of their jobs: safety, production methods, plant organization, time study, job instruction, conference techniques, human relations, employee relations. The Employee Relations course is specifically aimed at the analysis, prevention, and handling of grievances. Incidentally, some of this course is based on the findings of the Roethlisberger-Dickson Western Electric study. Thus the Swift foremen are unquestionably well trained in grievance procedure.

One company man puts it:

> The foremen have now achieved considerable experience in handling grievances, since 1942. Whereas at the start, they made mistakes, they make much fewer now.[18]

At various supervisors' meetings the foremen are told of any changes in the contract or its interpretation. If some problem comes up, they are all advised of it. For instance, a new case arose when a foreman was challenged for promoting a man to be gang leader without following seniority in so doing. Since the job of gang leader is not a supervisor's job and is subject to the contract, promotion to it must follow seniority, and thus this promotion was in violation of the contract. Since all the plant supervisors were simultaneously and clearly alerted to this contract violation, its repetition would not be likely.

Local 28, on the other hand, periodically conducts well-planned steward-training classes at the Union Hall. But the steward who attends is not paid. He must often make a trip back to the Hall at night in order to attend. It is not surprising that union steward classes are not fully and regularly attended by all the stewards. In fact, if 10 per cent of the steward body attend an evening class it is a good attendance. In addition, there is a higher turnover among stewards than there is among foremen. The conclusion is that while the Swift foremen are well trained for efficient participation in the grievance procedure, the Local 28 steward body is not so well trained, with the result that in the Chicago plant community, the grievance procedure is not doing in fact the job it could do on paper. Could some program of steward training on company property and perhaps on company time (but handled by the union) be worked out? This program might actually mean less money-time spent for grievances, but it would meet the opposition of union leaders. To return to one leader whom we quoted above:

> *Interviewer:* Do you think it would be a good idea to have steward training on company time?

Leader: No. It would be too close to the company. It would be company-dominated. The union would be called a company-union by the rest of the unions. I can't help but feel that a man is controlled by where his money is coming from. Paid grievance time is bad enough. Swift is the only one of the Big Four that pays it. A Swift steward could walk around and do no work. The company winks at it if the steward is not too aggressive. . . . Have a hall on company premises, where we alone do steward training? No. Sometimes people can't be trusted even in our own halls as to what gets back to the company. It's our own responsibility to train our stewards. It's not the responsibility of the company, although it is in their interest.[19]

TWO-WAY COMMUNICATIONS

While the primary function of the grievance procedure is to settle the worker's problems, it fulfills another closely allied function almost as important, that of providing a ready channel of communication not only downward but, also, upward. Communication is inextricably bound up with status. The right to talk to somebody is a partial criterion of your equality with him. If you cannot talk to him, it is generally because he is higher up, and you have a lower status than he has.

In the large industrial plant community, communication is all important. As both company and union get larger, and the distance widens from the worker to the top, communication becomes a problem for each. People are commonly talking about communication these days but not always with the right solution. Peter Drucker brings this out well:

> During the last few years industry as a whole, and management in particular, have become aware of the communications problem. . . . But awareness is not in itself a solution, nor are the measures which management have taken so far to establish communications particularly effective. By and large, they consist of flooding the plant community with information material. But the worker is neither willing nor able to accept and to understand the information management pelts him with. . . . *The solution . . . lies in the sphere of institutions rather than in that of information. Top management will have to develop an organ for listening,* so that it knows what the worker and middle management want to be informed about. . . .[20]

Such an organ for listening is the institution of the grievance procedure.

The workers in the Swift-UPWA plant community have already told us how much the grievance procedure as a means of communication and status signifies to them. It is the primary reason for their union allegiance. "But the Grievance Committee gives you a chance to prove whether you are right or wrong." "Without a union, there's not anyone to speak for your rights." "But if the steward gets on 'em, you will be okay." "Everytime somethin' goes wrong, you can go to the union." "The head people at Swift & Company don't know what's happening. The union can open their eyes." "Now you don't have to worry about what the boss thinks of you." "They can't push you around. You can make a case out of it." "You gotta have somebody to represent you." "If you got union you got leader. He go to see Big Mens in office." "Now you can carry your case to the boss. Then to the higher boss. That's the best arrangement."

Many union stewards and leaders say the same thing. For instance, steward Joe Calder:

> I likes bein' a steward fine. I been one six months. You got a contract to go by. The foreman can't deny it. If he does, *I can go see his boss. I can go to the top.*

And steward Edward Hassett:

> The Supervision Department over there in the general office, they didn't know the things that was did by the foremen. They didn't know anything about it. *Because you had no way of gittin' to 'em to explain your problem.* Because if you went over the foreman's head there was a possibility that you'd be fired. *So when the union came in, you had a steward, you had representatives.*

Even many Swift foremen single out the representation aspect of the union as one of their reasons for approving its presence in the plant community. "If the union functions properly, it can help both. The people will talk to their representative, the steward — things they wouldn't say to their foreman. The old-country people are shy. They won't talk. It's better to tell it." "The grievance procedure has a kind of safety valve value in quite a few cases, though not in all. A foreman can't have a perfect line of communication with all his help." "Well, there is needed some representation for the employee."

While it is true that the old Employee Representation Assembly saw the need for worker representation and sincerely tried to provide it, nevertheless that Assembly was undoubtedly company-dominated and not a true bilateral grievance procedure. While it often did good work, we have seen that half of the workers and foremen who comment on it were dissatisfied with it.

Without the bilateral route from the bottom to the top of the plant community, neither a worker, nor a foreman, nor, for that matter, a middle management executive, is inclined to go over the head of his boss in a controversial matter that finds his boss on the opposite side. The "open door policy" is no doubt a fine ideal and does work to some extent with some personalities. But as one foreman said: "If you open your mouth, they'll open the door!"

The Chicago plant Industrial Relations Department also provides an alternative communication route upward. It is a kind of listening post for the wants and needs of the workers and foremen. While it is in no sense a substitute for a union-company grievance procedure, it is a valuable communication adjunct to that procedure.

The grievance procedure, as mentioned above, also provides communication downward. At the first step, it gives the foremen a chance to explain some company policy to the worker which the worker might never have known. Likewise, it gives the steward a chance to explain to the worker something in the contract which the worker might not have understood. A good steward will be courageous enough to dissuade a worker from continuing with a grievance that is in reality no violation of contract at all. Likewise in the higher steps, the Grievance Committee or the plant Labor Relations man will discuss a case, often in the presence of the aggrieved employee himself, and give him the reasons *pro* and *con* for the decision which affects him. Finally, the fourth step and also the arbitrator's written decision proclaim to the aggrieved employee or employees and all others who hear about the case what top union, management, or neutral people have to say about this particular problem of the Chicago plant community.

This is a very vital means of communication downward, sometimes oral, sometimes written. The employee will usually be present to hear the decision orally in the first, second, and third steps. Not always, however. Witness this announcement in the *Flash:*

> The Grievance Committee urges all members of Local 28 who have grievances pending in the 3rd step to stop by the Union Hall, 4306 So. Ashland and receive information as to what has been done about *your* grievance.[21]

The worker usually hears the results of the fourth step from his steward who may know about it before his foreman does. The same holds true for the rare decisions of the arbitrator.

As we said, Local 28 publicizes the more important grievance cases that it wins. Such advertising is of considerable political importance to the local and its leadership. Some typical articles in the *Flash* read like these:

UNION WINS BACK PAY FOR SWIFT EMPLOYEE

> The Grievance Committee of Local 28 reports that Swift & Co. has finally indicated a willingness to completely settle the long pending grievance filed by Violet Hudnall Ross of the Sliced Bacon Department. . . . This case was sent to arbitration where it was ruled that Violet be reinstated with full seniority rights. . . .[22]

UNION PAYS OFF AGAIN

> Many Swift workers will again collect substantial back pay checks in the near future as a result of an arbitrator's decision on the case presented to him by the UPWA-CIO. The case is an old one on wage inequalities which was decided by the War Labor Board in 1945. . . . This case is another proof of the determination of the Union to protect the interests of our members no matter how long it takes.[23]

There is one final and important aspect of the grievance procedure as a method of communication: the question of how long it takes to get a decision with reasons to the aggrieved employee. For many grievances, speedy settlement is almost as important as settlement itself. Even an adverse decision with plausible reasons will be more likely to satisfy many employees than months and even years of no decision at all. Does the Swift Local 28 grievance machinery turn fast enough to do the best kind of communication job?

We saw that 68 per cent of the Chicago plant grievances never even got to the third step. Settlement is usually quite speedy in the first two steps — a week or two. That means that two-thirds of all Swift Local 28 grievances are handled with excellent speed. What about the other third? Here there are often unfortunate delays. There is some evidence that the current Local 28 grievance committee has sometimes brought a number of cases up to the third step for political reasons, cases which it never hoped to win, and then let the cases rest there for as long as six months. At times the company may have concurred with this delay, since by it one grievance can be bargained against another. Further delay has occurred while the cases took the circuitous route to the International Union Grievance man and were returned by him to the third step. In addition, sometimes a case might be over a year old before it ever got to the arbitrator. The Ross arbitration case, cited above, originated in August, 1948, and was not finally settled until July, 1950. Such a delay in decision seems excessively slow, whatever the reasons for it might be. For a minority of Swift Local 28 grievance cases, then, it would seem that the procedure is far from operating at the ideal speed for doing the communication job it is designed to perform.

DUAL GOVERNMENT

The grievance procedure is indeed an important link between company and union in the Swift-UPWA plant community. As a matter of fact, operating the grievance procedure is the only major job Local 28 has to do in the plant community at present. The Local Bargaining Committee usually meets only bi-monthly with the company and does bargain on the terms of the Master Agreement, but discusses local interpretations and applications that are not ordinarily vitally important. Safety is only a minor work for the local at the present time. And the local has nothing to do as such with negotiating the various annual changes in the Master Agreement. Its big job is to handle grievances.

But as unions get larger and power becomes more centralized in their internationals, increased by industry-wide collective bargaining and the concentration of experts and staff functions, the need for retaining some local autonomy and for recognizing that the local plant community cannot be absentee-governed becomes more urgent. Nothing is better calculated to keep some power in the local and offset this centralization process of unions than the local grievance machinery. After all, if grievances are to be adequately handled, they must be handled primarily by people close to them and belonging to the plant community itself. Nearly three-fourths of all Swift Local 28 grievances are handled right in the Chicago plant community. In this way, both Local 28 and the Chicago plant management retain their importance in the vast network of which they are a part.

Finally, we see in the grievance machinery of the plant community that dual government of which we spoke in Chapter One. In the Chicago Swift-UPWA plant community a two-in-one government is actually operating, even though haltingly, for the common good of that community. The most important aspect of that government, the grievance procedure, is not perfect. But the important thing is that dual government of the plant community exists and works daily, providing a bond between company and union which is not a fiction, but a practical link.

CHAPTER ELEVEN

STOP WATCH AND SLIDE RULE

THE WAGE-INCENTIVE SYSTEM

The importance of the Swift wage-incentive system became steadily more apparent in our investigation of the human relations in the Swift plant community. What do the people of the plant community, so close to the incentive system, have to say about it? Our global study of the community must inevitably come to this question, sooner or later. Is the wage-incentive system a factor in the company or union allegiance of the Swift-UPWA workers or not?

In the 1920's the French engineer Charles E. Bedaux had developed an efficiency system of wage payments which fast became popular in the United States.[1] Bedaux' staff were invited by Swift & Company in 1923 to train engineers so they could introduce the plan to the great chain of Swift plants. So in 1923, workers, foremen, and departments of the Chicago Swift plant were put on the Bedaux system. Later the system was modified by Swift engineers and therefore we shall call it here the Swift Standards System.

In the Chicago plant, as the company puts it:

> The Standards System is administered by a local Standards Department. . . . The first duty of this department is that of making technical time and motion studies of jobs performed on the plant. These . . . studies make it possible to determine accurately how much production it is proper to expect from a *normal* employee working at a *normal* rate of speed for a *given* length of time. [By "normal," we should point out, Swift does not mean "average," but a set work pattern that does not deviate from some rule. How you arrive at what is "normal" is obviously one of the debatable issues in this or any wage-incentive system, as Gomberg well says.[2]]
>
> The Standards System defines a "Work Unit" as the amount of work done by the normal worker working a normal rate for one minute, plus an allowance for personal needs. Such a worker will produce sixty Work Units in one hour. . . . If he works nine hours, he should normally produce 540 Work Units.
>
> Every job requires the performance of a definite amount of work. . . . The number of basic Work Units credited to a worker for any particular job

will always be the same, no matter how often the performance is repeated, *provided there has been no change in the equipment, raw material, process, or conditions under which the work is done.* [This important matter is incorporated into the Swift-UPWA contract. Whether or not it allays the workers fear of rate-cutting we shall see in the interviews later.] For example, the time and motion studies might show that a worker of normal ability should pack 12 cartons of some product in one hour. Since a normal hour's work represents 60 Work Units, it is evident that packing one of these cartons will represent 1/12 of 60 or 5 Work Units.

Now suppose that workman packs 110 of these cartons in an 8-hour day. He will then have produced 110 × 5 or 550 Work Units. In eight hours he is required to perform only 480 Work Units, however, in order to equal normal production. Our workman will, therefore, he credited with 550 − 480 = 70 Work Units' production in excess of what is considered normal. These are called *Premium* Work Units which are converted to Premium Hours and recorded on the Posting Sheets.

The Employee's Premium Hours . . . are always equal to 75 per cent of the Premium Work Units expressed in hours. For example: If in one day an employee has produced 180 Premium Work Units, they would be converted to Premium Hours by dividing 180 by 60 and multiplying the result by 75 per cent to obtain 2.25 Premium Hours [instead of 3 Premium Hours, if 100 per cent were used]. . . .

[A fair percentage of the difficulties union leaders had with the Standards System concerned the 75–25 split. Such difficulties were happily ended during the 1952 Swift-UPWA contract negotiations, when Swift spontaneously suggested a change as follows: "Standard Premium earnings shall be computed on the basis of 100 per cent of the applicable hourly rate."]

A checker records the results of each day's production for every employee in the department on checking sheets. A comptometer operator computes the Premium Hours and records the results on the Posting Sheets. The Posting Sheets are then placed in the department where every employee can see them. The Posting Sheet shows the number of Premium Hours earned each day by each employee and the total for the week.

One of the important provisions of the Standards System is that premiums earned on any day of the week are not forfeited by the employee no matter how much his production may fall below normal on other days of the same week. [There are some exceptions here, especially in the Mechanical Department.][3]

Such is the Swift Standards System. It applies to workers on an individual basis, or in small groups or on a large "gang" bonus. It also applies to the entire department. The worker is guaranteed his basic hourly rate of pay. And once he has learned his job, he is expected at least to maintain the standard: an average of 60 Work Units per hour. But more, the company hopes he will produce well over the standard, by reason of the financial incentives explained above, making not merely a 60 B-Hour (B standing for Bedaux), but a 65, a 70, even an 80 B-Hour or more, according to his ability.

The Standards System has four basic objectives: the System is (1) a management tool for production control; (2) a method of labor accounting; (3) a method to increase the employee's output over the minimum standard and thus lower the labor cost per unit of product; (4) a means for the employees to increase their earnings. For our purposes, the first two objectives may be considered together. Probably the most important value of Standards to Swift is that it provides management with an effective means for controlling production and labor costs. It helps eliminate waste and ineffective effort. Said one Chicago plant representative: "Before the system was put in I can remember one department, the sweet-pickle cellars, where there were men all over the place, and nobody knew exactly what each man was doing. After the system, there were far less men, and the same production was achieved." Thus a very important benefit of the system is that it sets a definite minimum standard for nearly every job in the plant, and for every department in the plant.

A worker or a foreman may fall behind for a while. But they must not fall behind consistently or they will "hear about it." The foremen are competing against each other, and also against departments similar to their own in all the other plants of the coast-to-coast Swift chain. For instance, in the spring of 1950 the Chicago plant had a plant-wide B-Hour, or standards output of 68, while the South St. Paul plant had 71 and the leading plant of the entire chain had 72. This cost and production value of the Swift Standards System in setting production standards for a man, a foreman, a plant, undoubtedly makes for greater efficiency and productivity and thus benefits all who are concerned with the meatpacking industry.

The third objective of the system, however, is apparently not being achieved with any such efficiency. That is, the Standards as a true psychological incentive urging on the worker to do more and better work, over this minimum standard and rewarding the superior worker who does so, does not seem highly effective in the Chicago plant community. This will become clear from the interviews later on. Of course we are not measuring incentive output directly. We are inferring the frequent ineffectiveness of the incentive from the expressed attitudes of the workers concerning it.

On paper, the Standards System as a psychological incentive may sound plausible to some. The company states:

> Money is the universally recognized symbol of . . . power. The opportunity to obtain it is naturally the most powerful incentive there is to stimulate workers to give their best productive efforts to their employers, for it is by these efforts that they earn the money they receive as wages and salaries.[4]

The Harvard-Western Electric studies at the Hawthorne Plant in Cicero found other incentives sometimes more powerful than money; namely, the working harmony of a small social group. The company theory goes on to say:

In order that maximum production may result from the use of these incentives, *it is necessary for employees to be fully satisfied that the amount of pay they receive really does reflect their productivity accurately.*[5]

Here is the rub. Many Swift-UPWA workers do not understand the complicated Standards System, or do not fully trust in its accuracy and fairness. It is doubtful that for these employees, the majority, the system is doing any urging on to greater productivity. The ignorance and distrust of the worker is not surprising, however. Most of the instruction he gets about the Standards System is from his foreman and sometimes in a very sketchy manner. On the other hand, Swift has recently intensified and modernized its foreman training program on Standards. The Standards Department does not deal directly with the worker, except in the casual contacts the checker has with him. The new worker starting at Swift & Company often picks up more information about and attitudes toward the Standards System from his fellow workers than from his foreman. Some foremen, usually with Standards Department experience, succeed in giving their employees a pretty good idea of the system, but many do not. We must remember that the system is not simple to explain and it has such knotty questions as: How do you determine what is normal, and (up to 1952) why the 75–25 split, and how are standards set?

THE MANAGEMENT VIEW

Operating management's view of Standards is expressed by the following company representative (above the foreman level), who is apparently convinced that both of the basic objectives of the Standards System are being achieved. He defends the system against some objections as follows:

As far as falsification [of output records] by the worker is concerned, there is very little of it. The checker gets all the data from the department. There's not much falsification if the checker is on the ball. But if the checker takes the worker's word for it, maybe. . . . Does the system set worker against worker [as the union claims]? Not too much. There's some kidding. Maybe a fellow will drop his pay stub in front of his locker. They'll compare bonuses, especially in the mechanical gang. Or they'll say: "I better give the checker a cigar." . . . [As we shall see, the mechanics are often against the system because the variability of their work makes time study difficult.] As for the millwrights, we do a weekly application because of the variation. Our time-study men know the normal conditions and the worst conditions. If there's a bad job the checker will know it. All mechanical standards are set up on *average* conditions. They won't send a mechanic on a bad job every day. [The implication is that these mechanical jobs are satisfactorily time studied.] . . . We've had only one grievance case on the bonus go to arbitration and the company won that! [6]

But another company representative, also higher than the foremen, is less enthusiastic about the Standards System and thinks there are still some large hitches in it. Management thinking in these matters is not monolithic, it is good to remember, and neither is union thinking. Leaders of both organizations can and do freely differ so that it is dangerous to say: "The company thinks this." "The union thinks that." This company man says:

> The Standards System is primarily a system to measure the costs of doing business and only secondarily to pay a bonus, let's admit it! When I was in the gang, I'd rather not have made a bonus. . . . Standards men *can't* check on falsification. For instance, did the machine break down five minutes, or ten minutes. You can falsify delays. The checkers don't know the tricks. . . . In the shipping departments, there's not a man that can make an honest B-Hour. There's no company law or rule that can operate perfectly by the law and still get the production out. There were examples of falsification during the war. For instance a general foreman might hint [regarding Standards reports]: "You wouldn't want to put luncheon meat through as hams?" . . .[7]

The Foremen. Since we did not discuss the Standards System in any methodical way with the foremen, the following comments must be taken as suggestive only and not necessarily representative of the entire supervisory body of the Chicago plant. It should be noted that foremen get a premium payment based on their department B-Hour output. Foreman Jack Filas has one of the highest Standards output of any department in the plant. Evidence indicates that he is a very successful foreman in other ways. He likes the Standards System:

> I've had wonderful success with the bonus system. You're here to make the most money in the easiest way you can possibly get it. It's good to take the waste motions out of jobs. . . . If they make a bonus, they're happy. . . . My men are on individual bonuses. . . . Standards experience is good for a foreman. [It is significant that Filas was once a Standards Department man himself.]

Foreman Hank Dame, while less enthusiastic, in general likes the Standards System:

> Speed can lead to wasteful cuts [of meat]. Those Standards men should work on with the practical men. But the system is very good. It's helpful to the foreman. Especially with a big gang — it's a check on the slow guys.

A younger foreman, Joe Comiskey, does not like the way the system operates. He voices a complaint very frequently mentioned by the employees: wide bonus differentials in the same department:

> It's the worst system. It's not equalized. In my department, some get $5 or $6 while others get only 50¢ or no bonus at all. Of course, it's up to the Standards Department if a man is not producing. But it makes for gripes.

We may recall that foreman Howard Frisbie is not too well satisfied with his job. Neither does he like the way that the bonus system is run:

Our biggest problem is when the Selling Department gives you an order and your job is to get out the product in good shape. Now quality is a problem. But there's too much speed-up for quality. The *system* is okay. But the standards are set too high.

We shall hear more of this objection among the employees. It is not surprising. Naturally no standard will be free from debate. And foreman Archie Ferris describes why the Standards System does not work as an incentive in his department:

My gang doesn't want to make a 70 B-Hour. They will do a 60 B-Hour only. I don't like to force it down their throats. [The theory of the system, on paper, we remember, should not require the foreman to do more than get out the 60 B-Hour standard production. Theoretically, the psychological inducement of premium pay should itself be enough to incite the worker to a 65 or a 70 B-Hour. Here the foreman apparently has to insist on a premium production. Evidently, the incentive aspect of the Standards System has broken down in this department.] . . . Their only gripe is that we're getting out too much product. This complaint goes way back. We've had it again and again, for years. "Speed-up!" They say. It's all based on coöperation. One man for another. *But they haven't got trust in the company or the Standards.* If I said: "Now we'll just get out so much in eight hours. That's all I'm going to require of you," — they'd say: "The next day, you'd ask for more. And the next day, more. Where in the world are you going to stop. If we got to make bonus and extra time, we don't want any part of it." That's what they'd say. Why they could make $20 a week bonus on my floor if they wanted to, I don't tell this to my bosses, but it's true. But they slow down. It's all coördinated. . . . *It's fear, that's what it is.*

THE OFFICIAL UNION VIEW

The International UPWA has long been concerned with the Swift Standards System. It has never tried to have the system removed, but it has managed to gain some control over its actual operations. Beginning in 1945, the bilateral grievance procedure has jurisdiction according to the following clauses of the Master Agreement: Once set, no standard shall be changed unless "through error, insufficient credit is being given" . . . "or the operation is changed," and that "the new standard will permit the same opportunity for earning premium. . . ." (These had been current practice, but were now subject to bilateral definition of "same opportunity," instead of unilateral.) It also agrees that "the foreman shall inform the union steward of the new production standards. When an operation is to be time studied, the foreman will inform the operators of that fact." It puts down a rule for handling a worker's premium when he is not working on his "regular job." Finally (a company point), it lays down very specific limitations on the arbitrator's powers to adjudicate Standards System grievances: "The arbitrator shall have no power by his award to establish, discontinue, or change any production standard.[8]

Local 28, on its part, has consistently opposed the methods of the

Standards System. Both the former right-wing leaders and the current left-wing leaders opposed the operations of the system. For instance, a *Flash* of the former leaders stated in 1949:

> We would rejoice if the evil system which Bedaux fastened on the workers of Swift & Company were to die. . . . It's greatest evil is that workers who try to compete under the Bedaux system eventually commit industrial suicide themselves. Thus workers, who should be in their prime of life at 50 years of age, are worn out and broken down in health from constant speed-up and overexertion.
>
> Another evil of the Bedaux system is that it is an anti-social force. It sets worker against worker. It sets worker against foreman and foreman against worker because the foreman has to make a "showing" of high departmental "B" Hours. The worker is set against his foreman when he gets a red "B" Hour.
>
> The Bedaux System is a wage-cutting system. It is supposed to give you 75 per cent of your hourly rate for every extra hour of operating the system. In other words, the company gets all the benefits and the workers pay the company's bill. There are honest bonus systems where the workers get 100 per cent of what they make over the standard. . . . It takes 25 per cent out of the bonus dollar to maintain the Standards Department. We say that this 25 per cent should not be charged to the worker but should be paid out of the general administrative fund of Swift & Company. . . .
>
> The harder you work, the less you get, when the sliding scale standard is applied. [The union charged that some job standards were figured on a sliding scale.] At least, that the way we get it. You work on a fairly good "B" value until a certain "B" hour is reached, 70. Then the value tightens, you work like ———— and don't get the carrots! We figure a "B" value should be constant. . . .[9]

It is not our purpose here to test the validity of such strongly phrased charges against the Swift Standards System. We simply note that they exist as the policy of many local leaders and are therefore an influence in the plant community.

Likewise Local 28's current leadership, along with that of District One, approved a resolution and publicized it in a 1950 *Flash* against the operation of the Standards System and other incentive systems as follows:

> Speed-up affects the health of the workers; results in accidents, and helps to bring about more layoffs. It results in cuts in wages due to failure of the companies to pay for the increased work. . . .
>
> In all plants where incentive systems exist, we shall seek the following contractual safeguards against the use of the incentive system to cut wages:
>
> a. Any incentive system established must give a 100 per cent return to the workers on the number of units above standard produced. The sliding scale in practice in the incentive systems in Swift and Libby must be altered. . . .[10]

Clearly Local 28 leadership has been very openly critical of the Swift Standards System.

In view of the clash between the company view of the Standards System and the union view, we might ask: What efforts have been made to try to talk a common language, to try to improve communication between the two organizations so that some common ground of understanding might be reached on the system? Some unions, like the International Ladies' Garment Workers, actually have their own time- and motion-study department with expert engineers who will, on occasion, jointly study jobs with the garment employers' time-study men. Swift & Company recently invited the UPWA to offer several union men whom the company would then train in time study so that they could check on the Standards System themselves. The UPWA nearly accepted this proposal, but then, in suspicion, rejected it. Said one union representative in frank answer to the question, "Why didn't you accept the company's offer to study Bedaux?":

> Because I might have to tell someone to work faster. And that's no good. The bonus system is okay in general. I always tell the workers: "You're going to have a minimum standard anyway. Why not get paid for what you turn out over that:" . . . The union has never made the Standards System a bone of contention in negotiations.[11]

The International UPWA at both its 1949 and 1950 international conventions took a strong stand against the training of union time-study men. The following resolution was adopted by the Resolutions Committee in 1950 and still represents the policy of the International UPWA today:

RESOLUTION XV
TIME-STUDY MEN

Whereas some packing companies are attempting to entice local unions to have members of the United Packinghouse Workers of America participate in speed-up systems by becoming union time-study men,

Whereas such participation tends to make proponents of time-study systems out of active union members,

Therefore Be It Resolved, that this convention go on record as determining that time-study men shall be regarded as supervisory personnel ineligible for membership under our International Constitution. . . .[12]

As we shall see presently, the attitudes of the union leaders and stewards closely follow this official union view.

THE WORKERS' VIEW

In view of Local 28's repeated criticism of the Swift Standards System, we might imagine that the average worker would be critical also. As a matter of fact, a slight majority of the Swift-UPWA people distrust and misunderstand the Standards System, as Table 29 indicates, but almost none mention the union as a factor in their attitude, and very few (16 per cent) are really against the system as such.

TABLE 29

Attitudes toward the Swift Standards System

(Unstratified sample of 104 employees, 14 union leaders, and 16 stewards: 1950)

	Men	Women	Total Rank and File	Union Leaders	Stewards
Understanding-trust	23%	36%	25%	14%	6%
Neutrality	19%	28%	20%	0%	13%
Misunderstanding-distrust	58%	36%	55%	86%	81%
Want System Abolished	16%	21%	16%	43%	13%

This sample is not small, as statistical samples go, for it comprises over 100 employees, about two per cent of the population. It comprises those workers with whom there was time and opportunity to discuss the Standards System. Therefore the sample is not mathematically random. But I do not think it is biased because in practically no interview did the subject of Standards come up entirely spontaneously. It was usually brought up by the interviewer and then followed by nondirective discussion. Whether or not the subject of Standards came up at all, and during what part of the interview, seemed to be entirely a matter of time and chance as each interview progressed. I discussed Standards with about every other employee.[13]

Since our sample of 104 is not stratified by sex, and the number of women in it is small (14), our comparison between the men and the women must be used with caution. It suggests, however, that the women employees are more favorable to the actual operation of the Standards System than the men. Such a conclusion seems very plausible from other facts and conversations in the plant community. Many women work in the Sliced Bacon Department or similar departments where at times high premium pay is made, sometimes up to $25 or $30 a week. It is quite possible that on the average the women make more premium pay in proportion to their hourly pay than the men do. Also, no women have mechanical jobs, and as we shall see, the mechanics are mostly unfavorable, thus influencing the average score of the men. Finally, the women are less likely to be on large department gang bonuses, such as the men in the pork, sheep, and beef kills who tend to be more critical of the system.

If we compare equal samples of colored and white, we find some racial difference in attitudes toward the system, involving those who want the Standards System abandoned. More white workers are against the system as such, chiefly because more white workers are mechanics. Likewise, if we take equal samples of the service groups, we find a difference, with the middle-service group being the least favorable. This group is partly influenced by the mechanics, yet the middle-service colored men (mostly not mechanics) are also definitely distrustful of the system.

The over-all figures in Table 29 have important meaning for both Swift & Company and for the UPWA. To the company they say: Only 25 per cent of the people in the plant community really possess an understanding trust of your system. It is not essential that the worker grasp the mathematical fine points of the system, but he must understand its basic arithmetic if he is to believe that the system rewards his extra effort. As we shall see in the interviews, a great many workers do not seem to have this minimum understanding. If it be objected that the workers do understand the system well enough to know when their bonus is not computed properly and to complain of it to their foreman, the answer is that such action may assume a lack of understanding, especially if the bonus *has* been computed properly. Above all, it indicates a lack of trust.

To the union, Table 29 says: If you want to banish all time study and incentives you will find only 16 per cent of the workers agreeing with you. The great majority of the workers are not against the system as such. Indeed, it is unlikely that the 16 per cent who are against the system have in mind any substitute plan. Quite possibly if they were on a flat hourly rate they would prefer going back to incentives.

Those workers who distrust the Swift Standards System say things like: I can't figure it out; I don't make enough bonus, it's not fair; I figure that they just give you what they think is right; you work yourself out of a job; when I sweat I don't make any bonus, and when I take it easy I can make good bonus; why is it I only make $1.50 bonus and that guy makes $7? The harder you work, the less bonus you get; that bonus system is just speed-up! But not many workers complain, as the Local 28 leaders do, that the system sets worker against worker.

Robert Jackson, for instance, likes the company, his foreman and his job. But he does not like Standards:

> That bonus system — I don't think much of it. *The B is only to speed up.* That's why the company wants it. The scalers and checkers make a bonus. The women sausage-ropers make a bonus, sometimes $20 or $30 a week. But I'm in the middle. I make little bonus. It's not fair. *You're doin' their work, yet you get less bonus.* And on a gang bonus some guy is not doin' anything. That's no good!

Young Vincent Queen, who had three years of high school and is with Swift for four years, objects to the system as being too complicated:

> I doubt whether any employee on our two floors can figure the B-Hour out. It's complicated. The company give you what they want. And they don't, if they don't want to. I don't make no bonus at all, much. My job is just as tedious as the others. It pays the company as much. *I should have a better bonus.*

Semiskilled drum-filler, Willie McCormick thinks the system cut down his rate. He too thinks he should get more:

> I used to get $6 a week bonus. Now for the same stuff I get $2 or $3. But fillin' is fillin'! *They cut out a man and retimed the job. I think I should get more bonus after them cuttin' a man out.* I talked to the foreman and the time-study man. But there's nothin' I can do. *They didn't explain why they cut me down.* I don't know — *I think they give you what they want to give you.* Even with all of that, I'm not disgusted with my job.

Harrison Wallace, 38, is on an unskilled job, to which he is neither favorable nor antagonistic. The bonus is part of it:

> Well, our bonus system is not so good. The reason we don't make bonus is a few men hold us back on the elevator. *There's nothing standard about our bonus.* If we work over 42 hours, the bonus fades out. *We don't know how much work we have to do for a B-Hour.* We've had no time-study for a year in our department.

Silas Wilson is a semiskilled meat-trimmer in a large department on a gang bonus. He brings out the problems in the gang bonus:

> The gang is fine. We work so as to put out a certain amount each day. . . . The bonus is sump'n I never could understand. I never make over $2 a week. *And easier jobs than mine, they make more bonus.* . . . The standard is set too fast. Some men do two men's jobs. Others lie down.

Butcher Ed Slater, short-service man, is fairly well satisfied with both union and company, but not with Standards:

> The Bonus System? It's bad! Like on my job — you can't hardly figure it out. We're at a different bench, on a group bonus. We works together, we get little bonus, our bench is the lowest bonus; three, four, or five dollars. Why? They start new men at our bench and that slows us down. How could they improve it? Keep a steady gang of fellas there. . . . Butt-pullers have to cut the butt out and take out the lean. They get less bonus than before. The bonus would probably run too high. Different chutes would check against individual gang members [The chutes carry the meat to the floor below.] But the company don't want to spend a little money for four chutes. Two fellas spoil the bonus for the whole gang.

Elevator-operator Jessie Moorhouse, 38, likes his job, but appears to have little understanding or confidence in his premium pay:

> I makes $1.50 to $1.60 a week. How they figure that bonus? Tha's what I don't understand! I have nine flo's. They's work on four flo's. I have to keep runnin' or their work stops. Even if I goes to the washroom I have to have relief man. In one day of six hours, I makes 91 trips. They's no chart for the bonus now. *To save my life I couldn't figure it out.* I do feel I should get more bonus.

The following two men are in the same department and have a special grievance about their premium. John Wambuck, a middle-service man and semiskilled operator, has endorsement for both company and union, but he says:

> The bonus is my big grievance with the company now. My job was re-timed. They put in a new system and schedule. It means more work and less bonus. I get no bonus now. It's my one pet peeve against the company. *We put out more product now and get no bonus. I don't understand it.* It started last November, an' still going. It's the union's fault; they been handling it very bad. It's in the third step — "downtown" or not, I don't know. My own foreman told me I got a chance to win it and get back pay. I'm getting disgusted.

Tom McClellan, 33, shares the sentiments of Wambuck, though he is neutral to the company:

> I like my job. It's a good job — the best in the department, but I make no bonus at all, not even ten cents since 1948! The bonus has been really awful. Before the War, we had less production, but we had three men [on his particular job]. *Then they changed the set-up.* The cooks asked for a separate standard. They claim we got too many cooks. If there was less cooks we could make more bonus. That's not true. It's too much for one man! We've had grievances on it. We work consistently in the red. The other cook — he's a go-getter. He tried to handle the job himself. He got some help — part-time. But the guy is killing himself and he averages sixty cents, seventy cents [bonus]. *It's not worth it.* He is stubborn. Or maybe he's afraid because he's got three kids? We have two men on the job and one on the side job. We're just riding now, until the new guy gets disgusted.

Now let us listen to three men, mostly old-timers, from three of the mechanical craft departments. Night-worker Fred Riedl says:

> The bonus is not so good on my job. Mine is a set standard. They time-studied me three times in a week. Funny — I don't figure it out. *They give me what they give.* Sometimes, I wonder where it comes from. You work hard and you get nothing. You work easy and get big bonus.

Paul Gedansky is a skilled man, no longer in the UPWA bargaining unit, who likes his work and says, "As I get older, I enjoy it more. We move around a lot. Our work never gets boring." As for Standards, Mr. Gedansky says:

> *They give what they feel like giving you.* I don't think they give an honest bonus. It's rather what they want to give you, than what you earn. For example, if you go up to an 81 [B-Hour], they drop you to a 72. That's too much difference in two weeks' time. . . . The majority would prefer a flat-rate to a bonus. You can figure better on it by the end of the week. Sometimes you get $17 [bonus] at the top, and $4 at the bottom. You can't estimate it.

Finally, Theodore Pitluk, a long-service mechanic, though he is only 39, likes his work and the company, but says:

> The bonus has been dropping since the War. Been a 75 per cent cut in Standards. I install and repair machinery. If I get stuck on a job, they

call it day work. [A flat rate, without premium pay.] *My work varies — how are you going to time-study it?*

As we shall see later, women workers are often more favorable to Standards than men. Some women, however, lack either confidence or interest in it. For instance, Mrs. Edna Stepac, is an unskilled tally girl. But she likes the job and would not prefer a more skilled (and responsible) one, partly because of the Standards she would have to make on it:

> My job is suited for my need; I'm active. Packing is too monotonous. Mine has change. To me, packing is too nerve wracking. You wanted to make that rate! *Bonus? Maybe I make a dollar.* I have money. *It's not important.* I'm fresh when I go home at night.

To return to the men, Jasper Hartford has high company allegiance, and likes most of his supervisors. One or two he dislikes, and he says:

> The bonus has a lot to do with the trouble. You see the foremen drive the men. *Bonus is slave driving.* It builds the foreman's record. And the company gets a profit on it.

Because the system is mathematical and remote, it arouses suspicion in the mind of Allen Ludden, an old-timer:

> I can't tell how they figure it out. *'Cause they have to run a scale themselves to figure it out.* They put it in a book. *And only they have the "book."*

Rare among the craftsmen is Tom Schlos, short-service man. For he is merely unfavorable to the operation of the Swift Standards System; he is not positively against the system as such. He is very frank about the chances for cheating:

> *Funny thing — I don't know how it works.* You have to burn so many welding rods per hour. You turn in more than you do. It's a white fib but all do it. I'm satisfied with the bonus system. If a man does five or six pipes, for instance, instead of four, he will ask the other guy: "Why not get out six?" So he kills it for the others. If you're in the red, you pull out orders. Here's what I did. . . . *The old-timers say it was better before the bonus system. You could go to sleep for four or five hours!* I guess that's why the company brought it out. And also to find where their material was going, etc. I don't see where the company profits on the bonus system. To do a job and then cut it out is a waste of money. . . . You work hard for Christmas to get more bonus. *But it seems to me, the harder you work, the less you get. And the more you give on a lying basis, the more you get.*

An old-timer craftsman, Bill Voorhis makes a curious comparison between the Standards System and the race track:

> *The bonus is like playing the horses.* You work hard an' you expect him. You get nothing. You work easy. You get a lot.

About 16 per cent of the workers, we said, are so unfavorable to the Standards System that they would like to see it abolished. This minority is largely to be found among the mechanical gang and craftsmen, though some production men and butchers also feel this way. The craftsmen say that exact time- and motion-study is simply not applicable to their kind of varying work, makes cheats out of them and interferes with quality.

Old-timer Alex McLean, for instance, has high company and union allegiance (though he is against the CIO). But he has no use for Standards:

> I'll tell you! I don't approve of Bedaux System at all! In 1919 Mr. Bedaux' representative came to the Scotch gun shop where I worked. The union got it thrown out right away. *There's never a millwright on bonus on all the jobs I've ever worked at except here at Swift's.* Straight-time, that's what it should be. Confidentially [I wouldn't want this to get any further], *we couldn't make any bonus in the mechanical gangs if we didn't tell a lie!* Suppose you take a machine apart. On one day it takes a man fifteen minutes. On another day it takes him one and a half days! The machine might be "frozen" with rust. . . . *We don't take time to do a perfect job today, as we used to, because we gotta make bonus.* If you don't make bonus they get after you. The B System means *both* hands are supposed to be working. If you stop to look at the job, that's lost time.

Terry O'Boyle, whose great pride of craftsmanship we noted earlier, brings up the quantity *versus* quality argument:

> The bonus is the rottenest system in the world, we think! It's the only shop I've ever been in where we had a system like this. A flat rate would be better. *The system gets more work done but at very much poorer quality. The foremen have been told to keep still. The Standards System dominates over all. But ——— our foreman, knows it's a bad set-up.*

And Dave Kniznik, who is dissatisfied with his job, as we may remember:

> The bonus system is no good! Suppose you get a shaft here and you work on it six hours. Then you work on a motor two hours. There's eight hours. Next day you move a fan. It takes one and a half hours. Then the boss says: "Go into the mill." Then you unload a lumber car and when half the car is done you've lost your bonus. You can't unload a car in four hours with four men. *At the end of the week you're forty-five in the red.* . . . I want no bonus system at all. All the fellas say: "It's too much trouble." Cut out the bonus and you'd get much more work done. . . . *The checkers will erase off some of your work up in the cafeteria. I know it.* They blame the girls in the office. If they get a bonus or if they don't get a bonus, the fellas don't care. *If there was no bonus system not everybody would be hollering at you.*

Tony Bachacci is one of the few men to mention the competition element in the system as something he dislikes:

> The bonus is up to the company. It's kinda mixed up. You work your head off and you don't make money. You take it easy and you make more.

It's hard to figure out. . . . Sometimes up on a tank where it is 150 degrees, you can't do a job just as you would on the ground. A flat rate'd be better. Be less arguments between a man and his foreman. *They put up sheets to show your bonus more or less. They shouldn't put it up on the board what you made. They should do it individually, not to show what the other man gets.* . . . I'd prefer a nickel more and no bonus. But the men do try to make more bonus.

Here is a long-service, skilled worker, 40, and a high-school graduate, Harold Wyman, who gives us interesting insights on the workman's-eye-view of the Standards System. His opinions follow the pattern of many of the mechanics:

I was in the —————— Department but didn't see eye-to-eye on the Standards. So I went to school and now I'm a craftsman. I overhaul machines. . . . The Standards comes out and says: "One man is enough." So I'm still in the red. I've told the time-study men that the standards won't work. But they put a standard on the work anyway. *The office wants it.* I would have been fired long ago but for my foreman. They got new "time and method and motion." *Now it's what they think you should do, instead of what you do do.*

One time-study man quit in disgust in ——————. Jackie tried it a half-day and then he tore up the standard. *The Standard System is all right on the production line, but on a maintenance crew, it's no good.* It might be okay on a lathe where you got the same piece months on end. But in *our* shop we got different problems every day, like patch work, etc. The most bonus I make is $1.86 a week. . . . The Standards has done more to make liars out of Swift Employees! If a Standards checker is not a company man, he will lie like a trooper. *Other fellows in the mechanical gangs also feel the same way about it.* The Standards checkers better never get in the gang they're checking!

Not many women employees of the Swift-UPWA plant community are against the bonus system as such, but those who are give us further insights into the system. First, Louella Scott, who is semiskilled and has both company and union allegiance. She brings up most of the objections to the system and mixes in the idea of a Christmas bonus with it:

I'm in favor of throwing the bonus system out. I work harder because of the bonus system. *If I make $3 for me, Swift & Company makes $5.* It's two to one. . . . It puts other people out of a job. . . . At the end of the year they could give all a bonus. . . . Some are sick and die in the plant because of working themselves to death on the job. . . . *I know a little about mathematics.* [She has had some college education.] *But I can't understand the bonus.* . . . If I must say so, Negroes don't work as hard as whites because they don't see a reason to! . . . *They're sacrificing quality for quantity.* Better to be a steady worker and work so many days and earn your bonus that way. Better to get a bonus at Christmas. I believe they'd get better work put out, better production. . . . *If they'd come an' tell us: "We got 70,000 pounds of meat to get out, girls." I believe they'd do better work.* Christmas is at the end of the year. People want money when they need it.

Since the union's publicity and leaders have important influence on the acceptance of the Standards System in the plant community it is important to know what they think about the system and why. One International UPWA Representative says that it was largely because Swift put in the Standards System that he got interested in the union. Other things were going all right, but he did not like Standards:

> We were very well treated. We hardly needed a union at Swift's until they started the Standards incentive system. I didn't like it. It makes cheats out of the men and sets man against man. Though I admit that stopping it now would create a squawk.[14]

We remember UPWA District One leader Jake Vickers saying that under the Swift Standards System the worker is exploited:

> The Bedaux System is worse than incentives. They all say: "Last week I worked harder and I got less bonus than this week." Why did the union refuse to have time-study men? Because then you got to accept *their* premises for a unit of work. Then a union man must go on *company* postulates, and you end up by speeding up your own people! . . . We are against the system. The sliding scale must be abolished. The worker must get a 100 per cent return. [The discussion then turned to the frequent stoppages in the "kill" departments of the various packing plants.] On those kills there is speed. Especially in hot weather. When the mercury hits 90 degrees, I always expect stoppages. When that chain starts to go, it's bad! It's speed-up!

Jorel Byron is another union leader who has an objection:

> The bonus? I don't know how to figure it. It means a decrease on the work force and an increase on the supervision. In the last few years, they press the workers so hard, so they have to have more assistants. The foreman always wants the gang to get out more product. . . . Some of these things come from supervision, personnel department. They get a bonus for so much production. They're always pressin' the worker under the bonus system. . . . Swift & Company as a company is fair. *But the bonus system makes the company rawhide a man to get all that's in him.*
> They deduct 25 per cent for the cost of administration of the bonus system. *Why take that 25 per cent from us?* We make the output. [We recall that beginning with 1952, standards are based on 100 per cent of the hourly rate.] It'd be better to drop it. We don't gain anything from it. We're putting it out at a cut rate. You work a normal day. Then they compensate you for extra effort, they say. *But this is compulsion!* You're threatened to be fired or sent home or some disciplinary action. They work less men. But they get all out of them that they can. You can't even do that with a car!

Harold Waite is a right-wing leader and therefore labeled (according to Communist stereotypes) as a "company man." But Mr. Waite is no "company man" so far as Standards is concerned:

They all know how I feel about the B-Hour. They can throw it out! *It is set too high.* The Big Boss told one of our union guys: "Waite is going around the Chicago plant keeping the B-Hours down!" They set the Standards when the men are rushing to get out to dinner and working fast. But you can't keep that up! . . . Then too, it's compulsory to make over a 60 B-Hour. *Why is it compulsory?* . . . The men don't enjoy their jobs. No pride. It's just push-rush. They say: "To heck with it now." The company wants quantity more than quality now. In the old days if you made a "black eye" [a tear in the blue meat] you'd almost get fired. Not now. . . .

Finally, Ted Kurowsky, another local leader from the right-wing group:

The bonus system? A foreman asked me that once. I said: "Ever see the Boric Mule Team? The driver and whip and twenty mules?" "Yes," he said. "Well," I said, "the mules, that's us. The driver, that's you. *And the whip, that's the Bedaux System!*" *It's speed-up and slidin' scale.* If you make a 95 B-Hour, you get only 70. You're always in the red.

Interviewer: What about the beef-boners, don't they make a lot of bonus?

They're on a different system. It's not a sliding scale.

Since their leaders are so outspokenly against the Standards System, we are not surprised to find the union stewards critical. Not all the stewards are against the use of the system, but most of them find something or other in its operation that they clearly do not like. Frequently they mention differences between the bonuses, where the jobs do not seem to warrant such differences. Almost universally they mention the complexity of the system. And many, echoing labor's traditional fear of rate-cutting, feel no security in their bonus. Some, like Paul Gedansky, Tom McClellan and John Wambuck, fear that once they are making a good bonus, the company will simply rearrange the production line or the men in order to justify retiming the job, and then cut their bonus. Sam Couch brings up his fear of "technological unemployment":

It was a pretty smart fellow that worked it out [the Standards System]. . . . *But one guy's goin' to pitch in harder and that makes it harder for the other guy.* The work he did in three days, if he worked regularly he could have it in a week. *He works himself out of a job and shortens his pay, though he doesn't know it.* In Dry Sausage, for instance, they make $10 to $15 bonus. And look how they work! They could use more girls and pay 'em out of the bonus! You come to work for six days for less than forty hours to make a few dollars bonus!

Richard Rex is a strongly union-minded steward who is against the company and his foreman and dislikes his job. That he is strongly against the wage-incentive system does not surprise us:

A man has to do two men's work, you know, for one man's pay. It's not a fair system. It means fast production. [Rex is in a conveyor-belt department.]

Interviewer: Would you want to give it up?

Yes, I would. They could give up the Standards System. Then there wouldn't be so many fellows gettin' ruptures.

Finally Joe Calder who gets a gang bonus while operating a machine on a production line. He dislikes the Standards changes and complexities:

> Our bonus used to be pretty good, $5 or $6 a week. *But now for the same production we only get $2 a week. They moved up the standard a year ago and the bonus came down.* The workers feel bad about it. I don't know if the union got a man who can figure it out. *I think the bonus is on the end of the checker's pencil.* . . . We get 48,000 cans in eight hours. That's the standard. Sometimes we run 53,000 cans. That's all right when we got $5 bonus. But we don't now. *They took off two operators and cut the bonus.* The bonus should go up when they take off operators. There should be more B-Hours among less people. The foreman agreed we should get more bonus. But his foreman didn't agree. The Stuffing Gang get more bonus than we do! The system is okay. It's just the way it's worked. The standards are too high. There's no strain at work, though.

No doubt the Standards Department men could give many answers to the objections put almost unanimously by Local 28 leaders and stewards against either the operation or even the existence of the Standards System. It is not our purpose to debate the technical perfections or imperfections of the system, but simply to point out that the system is not understood, not accepted, not trusted, by key union people in the plant community and by the majority of the rank and file. There is a psychological problem here fully as important as the technical one.

A sizable minority, about 25 per cent of the Swift-UPWA workers are favorable to the existence of the Standards System and also are clearly confident in its operation. For these people the system is fulfilling the company's objectives: control against inadequate work and waste, and an effective incentive to greater output. For these people it fulfills the worker's objectives: more pay if you want to work for it. The workers who are favorable to the system do not have as much to say about it as the unfavorable ones. In general, their comments are: "You can make some extra pay." Since the system is, after all, primarily a wage-incentive system, naturally the primary worker-reason for liking it is that it does put more money in the pay envelope.

We may remember that youthful Frank Pine, skilled butcher, is very satisfied with his advancement at Swift & Company. He likes the bonus:

> The bonus is improved. It's fine. *It's going up.* It's really good. *I'm making $5 a week.* And I make a 70 B-Hour.

Butcher Upson Torpey compares the Swift system wih Armour's piece work:

> I'd rather have the bonus system than the piece work they have at Armour's. They got to work harder. The bonus system is okay.

Short-service butcher, Tony Jablonsky, 27, in general likes the system:

> We made $10 to $14 bonus. Now we make $2 or $3. They raised the gang. The bonus is a sucker for the workingman. It benefits the company as well as the man. I work steady anyway, bonus or no bonus. In the cooler you got to work or you get cold. I'd do it anywhere. If I walk out of my job I'd do it with a clear record. . . . Piece work is too dangerous. I wouldn't like it. You couldn't do it with the different cuts of meat in our gang. I think the bonus system is pretty good. We're on a gang bonus. We have to carry an old fellow. If we didn't have bonus, they'd have to give us more money. It's up to the company. . . . *Swift & Company is the best of the packers* — my friends tell me of Armour and Wilson — *because they pay for the bonus system.*

Semiskilled butcher, Tom Stacewicz, with Swift for thirteen years, indicates that the system is a real incentive for him. His comment is rare.

> I make a good bonus: $5 a week. *The system is a stimulant. It keeps you on your toes.*

Also with Swift thirteen years, skilled butcher Walter Stuczynski, is against union leadership and dropped out after the 1948 strike. He dislikes the union's opposition to the Standards System:

> They talk about speed-up. *I don't think that there's any speed-up.* Nobody is pushed so they haven't another breath. *You have to work hard for a living anywhere.* They claim we're killing too much. . . . I make $3 or $4 bonus.

And a Swift old-timer, Clarence Ussher, 48, says the same:

> The bonus system works all right. A lot say it's a joke. But you hear that in the packinghouse all year round. A lot are dissatisfied. *But if you don't work, why kick? If you do work, you do get the bonus.* . . . I like my job. The chain doesn't bother me. If you can't do it, they throw the meat in trucks and let others do it. *That's what I like about the joint — there's nobody pushin' you.*

Edgar Whitcomb, 56, whose company loyalty and whose critical views about the union we have heard, likes the Standards System and is irritated at the union's opposition to it:

> The bonus system would be okay if the boys would work along with the bosses. But we're on a gang bonus and one guy can slow down the bonus of the whole gang. We used to make $8 or $10 under the old gang. [It is not clear whether he means the old right-wing local leaders, or simply the earlier days in his department.] Now we make $2 or $3.

Finally, we must note this union steward, Frank Daniels, 35, significantly enough a right-winger, who does not criticize Standards, but praises the system. He is unusual in the steward body. He is an unskilled truckman, yet he owns his own home. He expresses himself briefly: "The bonus system is very nice!"

Some of the women workers make good premiums indeed. Mrs. Ella

Robinson, for example, a meat-trimmer, likes the company and her job very much. She finds Standards easy:

> It's fine. We don't work hard. *They don't rush us. The B-Hour is not hard at all.* I'm a fast worker. I made 432 B's by last Wednesday. Everybody looks at the chart. It's up on Wednesday and Friday.

Elizabeth Washington, with Swift for twenty-six years, says the bonus is one thing that makes Swift an outstanding company:

> Swift is one of the top rank concerns. It's a leading company. They pay more. *There's no bonus elsewhere. Yet they work as hard as we do.* Other companies don't have it.

In departments like the Sliced Bacon Department, the girls are highly satisfied with Standards. Doubtless, short-service packer, Joanna Haywood, expresses the opinions of many such workers:

> I'm satisfied if I make $10 bonus. I've made up to $15. Last week I made only $2. *Naturally the girls like the bonus system in Sliced Bacon! The graders and some other girls make big bonus.* Naturally there's some friction, but you can't take away from one girl what she makes.

Finally, we shall hear two important union leaders, both women, who are quite favorable to Standards. Union leader Jenny Lee, for example. Jenny is a pleasant person, seven years with Swift, a wrapper and sealer. She says:

> We make almost no bonus. We go in the red now. But it's a new job and not well timed as yet. *They will fix it up.* [She is doing a new sealing and packing operation, not yet standardized.] The bonus system is pretty fair. *We should have it.*

Significantly, local leader Della Harris, a well-adjusted Swift veteran, is in a small department whose foreman is a Standards expert making one of the highest outputs in the Chicago plant:

> *Interviewer:* How is your foreman?
>
> Oh, he's nice! Real nice. You can set down as long as you want to. He'll let you be there a year before you got to put out the day's rate. But the other foremen give 'em only ninety days. Some, only a week or two. We're on the Bedaux System. You s'posed to make the rate for that day. . . . What you get over that — that's extra. *Evvybody understands that system.* You make this an' this an' this. *Then you get a little extra money on your pay check.* . . .

We have seen that the slide rule and the stop watch are a point of misunderstanding between many workers and the company, and especially between the union and the company. In sum, we have found that: (1) Many workers simply do not have that minimum understanding of the system necessary for confidence in it as a method of real reward for extra effort; (2) the majority do not know why they make more bonus or less; (3) the workers are afraid of working themselves out of a job; (4) they are afraid of new standards, afraid that changes will only mean a reduction in their bonus and an increase in their work load. As one Standards man points out, "There is always resistance to change. Moreover, after a change, the worker's inexperience in the new movements often does make his Standards output go down for awhile, with temporary loss in earnings. The employee remembers this, so when changes come, his fears arise"; (5) A number of people, especially union leaders, distrust the system because of the debatable 75–25 slope of the premium payment curve and wonder why they are not paid 100 per cent for what they do. This problem has ceased to exist; (6) some, especially union men, say the standards are too high and make for speed-up; (7) almost to a man, the mechanics say that Standards System cannot be applied to their variable type of work, makes cheats out of them and impairs quality work.

Yet, in spite of these findings, the wage-incentive system does not seem to be a major factor in the workers' dual allegiance in the plant community. There is no very important association between the Standards System and either company allegiance or union allegiance, except in the case of the union leaders and stewards. We might expect the workers who are most violently against the system to be strongly pro-union or pro-union leaders, since those have fought Standards so openly. Some are, but some are not, and so it is with company allegiance. Many of those who strongly distrust Standards trust the company and supervision nevertheless.

For the union leaders, it is another story. There is a definite connection between their allegiance to the union and their distrust of Standards. We recall that one key leader began his union career precisely because Swift put in the Bedaux System.

But for the average worker, the Standards System is rather a minor factor in his dual allegiance. Other things are more important to him: steady work, job security, seniority, fair treatment, basic wages. It is significant that there have been very few grievances on Standards, and that most have been settled within the third step. While we found that many workers misunderstand and distrust the Standards System, we must not think that they constantly think about it or are greatly disturbed about it. Rather, they accept the system as one more condition of employment, like wearing white coats or punching a time clock.

While we must not exaggerate the importance of the Standards System in the plant community, neither must we minimize it. The system is close to the daily and weekly work lives of both employees and supervision and their mutual misunderstanding about it definitely merits our analysis. To the engineer, concerned as he is with the logic of mathematics, the efficiency of production, and the reasonableness of gain, the

Swift Standards System is a technically accurate tool. It has, as Roethlis-berger might put it, all the "logics of efficiency." But to the worker, con-cerned as he is with the protection of his job, the security of his earnings, his dignity and status as a man of skill, envious at times of his fellow-workers, aware of his engineering ignorance and his position as one who must obey in the community, the Standards System is simply a complex mathematical formula imposed upon him (by a benevolent company it is true) with neither his consent, his coöperation, nor his understanding —a system therefore often to be distrusted, and sometimes to be de-spised. Here we have the "psychologics of job dignity."

But in the author's opinion, there is a deeper reason for the Swift-UPWA people's misunderstanding and distrust of the Standards System: their inarticulate dissatisfaction with the tacit assumptions of the mass-production itself, upon whose logics the Standards System is built. This deeper reason is perhaps without compelling support in our research data. But I believe that when all the findings of this book are put to-gether they strongly suggest it. Standards are rather a symbol and a symptom.

We recall that it was here in this very plant that the "second indus-trial revolution," namely, the mass-production revolution, was spawned in the eighty's and ninety's. This was an entirely new system of produc-tion with minute task-specialization, whether on a conveyor chain or at a work bench, requiring men to be machine tools or robots to serve its needs and giving them the highest standard of living the world has ever seen.

By 1911, this revolution was so well under way that it was classed as a special branch of the new science (also having its own revolution), for in that year the phrase "scientific management" was popularized by F. W. Taylor's new book of that title. Taylor, Frank Gilbreth, and their dis-ciples brought the rationale of the laboratory and the engineer right on to the work benches and assembly-lines of Chicago, Detroit, and Pitts-burg. Likewise the psychologists were busy. Münsterberg published his *Psychology and Industrial Efficiency* in 1913, and Cattell began his workers' intelligence tests.[15] Organized labor did not like all this new "efficiency" and was suspicious of it. But organized labor, in the mass-production industries, in packing, autos, steel, was struggling for its bare existence until the CIO days many years later.

Today the mass-production system is here to stay. It may indeed de-mand a rather skilled bodily movement from the worker, like cutting pork loins out with a draw-knife, a movement too difficult and variable for a machine, but it demands nothing more, no other movement, no other skill, and above all, no judgment, no inventiveness, no planning, no thought. These latter are handled for the worker by somebody else far above in another world: the time-study engineer, the sales executive with a bright idea for a new product, the laboratory man, the manufacturer of conveyor belts and packing machines, the foreman. As a reward to the worker for fitting himself into the system, he is free to talk, tell stories, sing, joke, day dream, brood, or just to be numb, though never letting his eyes or muscles wander far from that one movement demanded of him.

But the Swift-UPWA worker does not like to be taken for a machine tool. That is one reason why he does not like to have his every motion plotted on a blueprint and then timed, as one would measure the revolutions of a wheel or the thrust of a piston. We recall how much he valued being let alone by his foreman so he could exercise some responsibility of his own. We saw in Chapter Five that, although he does not complain overtly of monotony, neither does he show great pride of work (except for the craftsmen) and that he finds job satisfaction in being on his own. We recall that he does not want his children to come here to work in coolers or be truck pushers. Thought, judgment, inventiveness, planning, cannot be time-studied because they involve no external motion and the time needed may be quite unpredictable. We recall the remark of craftsman Alex McLean: "The B-System means both hands are supposed to be working. If you stop to look at the job (that is, to think about it and plan it), that's 'lost time.'" Time study implies thought-free bodily motion that is repetitive and often so uncomplicated as to suggest machine-like motion. But the worker does not think of himself as a machine.

But the folklore of The Happy Machine Tool goes deep. More than one management man, both at Swift and elsewhere, believes it. His objections and their answers may be grouped under six main headings. (1) Q: Is it not true that the worker often does not like to be transferred out of his department to another — thus proving that he likes his assembly line, since he does not want to leave it? A: Yes, it is true, but it proves rather that he does not want to leave the social group he has come to know, or lose his departmental seniority, and not that he has creative satisfaction with his job. (2) Q: Is it not true that the worker dislikes changes in production methods that would give variety to his work? A: Yes, he is lazy; he sees little to be gained from changing from one sort of machine-tool action to another. It is easier to keep your muscles in the old groove. (3) Q: But the worker does not want to take responsibility and take a job that requires initiative. A: The old-timers do not. Most cannot. But most of the young men do. That is why some try to be transferred into the mechanical gangs. (4) Q: The worker can satisfy his desire for creativity off the job, at home, in some sport or hobby. A: To admit that, is to admit defeat to the machine age. A man spends one-third of his life on his job, he must also have job satisfaction if he is to be a balanced personality. (5) Q: The worker is really quite happy with his mass-production role. You are just projecting the discontent of an intellectual into these happy, simple people who are not really capable of being more than machine tools. A: Rather, we are finding our conclusion strongly suggested by the total interview and other data of this book. (6) Q: But the workers rarely complain of monotony; they hardly even mention the assembly line. A: Correct. The Swift-UPWA worker, like most mass-production workers, no doubt, is inarticulate about his dislike of being a machine tool. Some workers may not even be aware of it. But the basic work frustration is there, nonetheless, and may be inferred from the other things the workers say and do: their desire for independence, their lack of work pride, their wish for their children to go elsewhere, the mechanics' belief that quality craftsmanship is not desired, and so on.

And why should we expect the worker to be articulate? The mass-production system is here to stay, and people soon learn not to protest against the inevitable. Then, too, it gives the worker the highest standard of living the world has ever known — far higher than he knew on the Carpathian foothills or the Mississippi Delta. There is an opium in the assembly line, giving the worker the pleasant sensation of a fair income with a minimum expense of creative effort. Drug addicts rarely complain of their drug; they come to like it, to need it. This is not to say that the assembly line must necessarily be a drug, but simply that, with all the prosperity it has brought, it has raised the problem of the worker's non-creative participation in his work, a problem still largely unsolved.[16]

We recall how the Swift foreman came to work in Richard Babbit's department during the 1948 strike, saying: "How much money, and where is the toilet, and when do we go to spell?" And Babbit's dry comment: "Maybe that's the view of the worker, often enough." We recall how the foremen say a good number of their men "just stand around," "don't work hard," "don't take responsibility," "take no interest in the B-Hour." Are we really surprised at this? The mass-production system demands only that the worker be a machine, and can we then expect a machine to show creative interest in the job?

Does this mean that the mass-production system to which we are inevitably committed, with its frequent expression in time study, wage incentives, and assembly lines will forever make trouble in our new industrial era? Not if dignity, responsibility, and understanding can somehow be injected into the mass-production idea. Labor-management committees can evolve that will solicit the worker's ideas. We have seen again and again in these interviews that he knows his job far better than the foremen could ever know it. The worker could make many suggestions for saving money, for brilliant work simplification, but he will never do it. He will never trust the "suggestion system," if he is afraid that he will work himself out of a job, or have his rate cut, or see the company take all the benefits. Labor-management committees for joint time study might come to be feasible. As Golden and Ruttenberg well say in their *Dynamics of Industrial Democracy:*

Give workers as a formally organized group a say-so in setting wage rates, work standards, job evaluations, and in making time and motion studies, and they will produce all they can within the limitations of physical endurance, health and fatigue; deny workers such a say-so and they will engage in restrictive practices out of self-protection.[17]

There is one proviso. An insecure union will never participate in joint time study. To quote Golden and Ruttenberg again:

The adamant refusal of unions to adjust downwards any rates found to be too high is only partly related to the absence of the union shop form of recognition. A basic part of organized labor's program is to resist wage cuts on any grounds. . . . But certainly a union is not free to adjust a member's rate downwards when, as a consequence, he can immediately quit the union and agitate for other members to follow his example.[18]

Gomberg speaks of the necessity for union security as a condition of such coöperation. He has also said as much to one Swift Standards man. The UPWA will doubtless never change its decision to reject joint time study with Swift until it is given recognition as a necessary institution in the plant community by additional union security provisions. Indeed, if labor-management committees based on mutual trust, confidence, and respect will come into being, if they will study job methods not only with the "logics of efficiency," but also the "psychologics of job dignity," then great vistas of increased company productivity, of worker satisfaction and participation, of union satisfaction and importance will open up before them. This is no more utopian than the union leaders' dream of bilateral government in the plant community, fifty years ago in the days of Mike Donnelly, but it will take more than either a psychologist's or an engineer's format to provide it. It will require a generous measure of justice and charity as well. But the mass-production revolution gives the challenge to provide it, a challenge to all the people in the Swift-UPWA plant community.

CHAPTER TWELVE

DUAL ALLEGIANCE AND THE FUTURE

THE PLANT COMMUNITY AND DUAL ALLEGIANCE

The very concept of the plant community, our definition of it, the verification of our definition in the Swift-UPWA Chicago plant and our description of its anatomy, especially its curious dual government — these are highly important for an adequate understanding of industrial relations in American mass-production industries of today. Many are disturbed at the growing tendency toward centralization in world civilization. Centralization can bring benefits, and this is one reason why it has come upon us. We need not fear it, provided the smaller groups in our society retain their vitality and perform the jobs which only they can do best. The only danger is that the growing centralization of government in economic matters and the growth of the mammoth corporation and labor union, with stress on top-level, often industry-wide collective bargaining, will cause the plant community, comprised of local union and local plant, to be overlooked or to atrophy.

But now the local plant and union are more important than ever, for the job they have to do cannot be done by centralized powers or bureaucracies. The problem is to integrate the plant community with the company and union power centers above it, without letting them completely absorb it.

What job have we seen performed by the local plant community? It provides a plant manager with a manageable amount of men and production problems so that his job of supervision is not too big. It provides the union with a political, social, and economic unit of manageable size, the local union, in which politics may be close to the workers, status may be achieved, leaders may be developed and find an outlet for their ability, the opportunity for participation may be presented and welfare, economic, social, and neighborhood activities may practicably be exercised. Finally, the local union and the plant management together have the dual job of governing the plant community in many social, economic, and disciplinary matters, primarily those mentioned in their mutual contract.

This job can best be done on the plant, by the people concerned, and not by absentees. Most of it is done by that newly evolved and excellent institution for communication and government, the bilateral grievance procedure. Since it does not bargain collectively, the plant community, if it is to thrive, must have something else to do. Aside from actual production, the grievance procedure is its important function. Labor-management committees, about which we shall talk later, are another. Where we shall precisely draw the line between the functions to be performed by the plant community and those functions to be handled by higher union and management executives, will depend on the type of industry, community, and personalities involved. The point is that the line should not be drawn so as to withdraw functions from the plant community which it is perfectly able to perform.

There is a good principle of social philosophy that a larger group should not seize for itself functions that can be just as well or better performed by a smaller group. This is the important "principle of subsidiarity" as put by the papal social encyclicals:

> It is indeed true, as history clearly proves, that owing to the change in social conditions, much that was formerly done by small bodies can nowadays be accomplished only by large corporations. Nonetheless, just as it is wrong to withdraw from the individual and commit to the community at large what private enterprise and industry can accomplish, so too, it is an injustice, a grave evil and a disturbance of right order for a larger and higher organization to arrogate to itself functions which can be performed efficiently by smaller and lower bodies. This is a fundamental principle of social philosophy, unshaken and unchangeable, and it retains its full truth today. *Of its very nature the true aim of all social activity should be to help individual members of the social body, but never to destroy or absorb them.*[1]

It is a major conclusion of this book that the principle of subsidiarity must be applied in our American mass-production economy to the industrial plant community.

As a matter of fact, we have seen that the Chicago Swift-UPWA plant community is not absorbed or destroyed by the power centers above it. We remember, though, that tension did arise between Local 28 and the UPWA International. Local 28 felt itself strong enough and autonomous enough to lead a revolution against the International and win a lawsuit to control its own funds. The problems arising from malintegration of this smaller group with the larger were handled at the subsequent UPWA Constitutional Convention in 1949 as follows: The UPWA Constitution was changed by the delegates from the locals and all UPWA local unions were shorn of some of their powers. For example, if a local now withholds per capita tax, the International may revoke its charter, take over its funds and property, and act in its place.[2]

Probably such centralized constitutional power in the hands of the

UPWA International is necessary. But the point is: The locals must retain some power, too. Indeed the UPWA locals do have more powers than some other CIO unions, and vastly more power than some of the AFL locals or United Mine Workers' locals. But the trend toward centralized efficiency of the UPWA or any International must not go too far.

As for Swift Chicago plant management — they apparently have sufficient autonomy. Of course, the Chicago plant is unique in that its offices share the same building with the General Offices of the Swift chain, and hence its executives are more under the eye of top management than in another Swift plant. At times doubtless this is irritating to local management. Yet it also has advantages in getting advice and quicker decisions from the top. There seems to be no antagonism to the proximity of the two managements.

In a word, we see that the Chicago Swift-UPWA plant community exists, performs an important function, and retains its identity and powers. The important thing is that the role of such an industrial plant community become fully realized and conserved.

One of the questions we had to ask in deciding whether the Chicago Swift-UPWA plant was a plant community was this: Have the people there, both management and labor, actually accepted the common ends and community means of the plant community? In other words, do they really have allegiance to the objectives of the two organizations sharing

TABLE 30

Dual allegiance in Chicago Swift-UPWA plant community — I

(*Random, unstratified samples of 202 employees, 31 foremen, and 34 stewards: 1950*)

Employees	Per cent
Unfavorable to both company and union	0
Neutral to both	½
Favorable to company and unfavorable to union	13
Favorable to union and unfavorable to company	13
Positively favorable to both — dual allegiance	73

Stewards	
Unfavorable to both company and union	0
Neutral to both	0
Favorable to company and unfavorable to union	0
Favorable to union and unfavorable to company	12
Positively favorable to both — dual allegiance	88

Foremen	
Unfavorable to both company and union	0
Neutral to both	0
Neutral to company and favorable to union	3
Neutral to union and favorable to company	12
Neutral to union and unfavorable to company	3
Favorable to company and unfavorable to union	25
Favorable to union and unfavorable to company	0
Positively favorable to both — dual allegiance	57

that community? The critical answer has already been shown by the data: dual allegiance is a fact.

We have seen that dual allegiance means acceptance of the company as an institution (and therefore acceptance of its existence and primary objectives), and acceptance of the union as an institution. Here we simply bring the data together and clarify it:

The most important figure in Table 30 is that 73 per cent, nearly three-fourths of the men and women of the plant community, do have positive allegiance both to Swift & Company and to the UPWA. This is all the more remarkable, as we have said before, in view of the crisis through which Local 28 was passing.

For most of those who fail to have dual allegiance, allegiance fails in the union half of the plant community. These are predominantly white or long-service or women, as will be seen in Table 31:

TABLE 31

Dual allegiance in Chicago Swift-UPWA plant community — II
(*Random, stratified sample of 192 employees, by sex, race, and service: 1950*)

Employees	Men	Women	Negro	White	Short Serv.	Middle Serv.	Long Serv.
Unfavorable to both	0%	0%	0%	0%	0%	0%	0%
Neutral to both	½%	0%	0%	1%	0%	2%	0%
Neut. to Co., fav. to U.	4%	0%	4%	2%	5%	4%	2%
Neut. to U., fav. to Co.	8%	4%	3%	10%	5%	5%	11%
Neut. to U., unfav. to Co.	½%	0%	1%	0%	2%	0%	0%
Fav. to Co., unfav. to U.	12%	24%	10%	20%	7%	10%	27%
Fav. to U., unfav. to Co.	½%	0%	1%	0%	2%	0%	0%
Dual allegiance	74%	71%	80%	67%	79%	79%	60%

The workers' allegiance to the union as an institution, as we saw, was much affected by their dissatisfaction with the 1948 strike, local factionalism and left-wing leadership, along with the race problem for the white — all of which are adjuncts to, but not the essence of the union's existence as an institution. Change some of these adjuncts and you will find more union allegiance and more dual allegiance among the people of the plant community. All this will seem more possible when we note that even now 86 per cent of the plant community favor one organization and are at least neutral to the other.

It is not surprising that the stewards should have more dual allegiance than the work force generally, when we remember that the stewards are much more union-minded but not much less company-minded than the rank-and-file workers. Eighty-eight per cent of the stewards positively favor the company as opposed to 91 per cent among the work force, while 100 per cent of the stewards favor the union as an institution, as opposed to 79 per cent among the rank and file.

We see that a slight majority of the foremen have dual allegiance — 57 per cent. Again, the problem is mostly concerned with the union half of the community. We remember that 27 per cent of the foremen and probably a larger proportion of plant higher management are opposed to the union as an institution, seeing no real need for it. Evidently among a sizable minority of supervision, dual allegiance does not exist, primarily because the union is not accepted as a necessary and important component in the plant community. The company, on the other hand, is accepted by almost everybody, at least as a necessary and valid institution.

It is important that a significant minority of Swift management do not yet see in the union a vital and necessary part of the plant community. This fact adds to the union's occasional insecurity and distrust of management. We recall the penetrating comment of one UPWA leader:

> I often ask myself the question: How far has Swift really accepted unionism as a *good* thing? Maybe they say: "If it is an evil, let us try to control it." Swift people are of high calibre, honest and honorable. But they have an *esprit de corps*, unconscious maybe, that "the company can do no wrong." Their judgment is "better" than ours as to what is good for the employees. In a sense they say: "We don't need a union around here. We'd be better off without it." They do not accept the union as an equal. Are they bargaining just because the law requires it? [3]

Perhaps these comments do not apply to more than a minority of Swift management. But it is a large minority, I think. This is not surprising. UPWA leadership has at times been imperfect, and it is hard for a man to distinguish between an institution as such and its leadership. Furthermore, Swift has always had a very advanced and successful personnel policy, as proved by the high company allegiance we have seen. But, as one executive said: "Some of our people say, what good was our personnel policy? It failed to keep unions out!"

In other words, some management leaders think that unions are a penalty for bad management or at least a penalty for an inadequate management, one with insufficient human-relations skill to defeat them. Such a view corroborates the fears of some union leaders, Solomon Barkin, for example, that the human-relations approach, made famous by the Harvard Business School, is simply a tricky tool to make unions unnecessary. The study of Human Relations, of course, is just as necessary for unions as it is for the companies, especially as the unions become larger. Indeed, this entire research project aims to prove that both organizations can be benefited by the human-relations approach.

We may recall another Swift executive making this comment:

> I don't understand why the workers have gone back to the union in such numbers after the [unsuccessful] strike of 1948! *What is it about the company that they don't like?* [4]

This man apparently sees the union as a foreign body in the plant community. The men want it because there is something wrong in the company. He fails to see, as the evidence in our chapter on union allegiance brings out, that the main reason the workers want the union is because it gives them protection, status, and basically, dignity. They want the union not because there is something positively inadequate about the company, but because there is something negatively inadequate. In other words, the Swift-UPWA worker has wants and needs which he believes a union and not the company can satisfy. He is not thereby against the company for something it cannot do. He simply says in effect: "The satisfaction of my wants here requires two organizations, not one. My dual allegiance is not a contradicition in terms!"

Since dual allegiance exists in the Swift-UPWA plant community, neither union nor company will build secure organizations there unless they build on this foundation found in the workers themselves. I refer again to Peter Drucker's penetrating analysis of this foundation:

> Above all, the solution of the problem of unionism depends on the resolution of "split allegiance" into "twin allegiance." In the last analysis every union problem hinges on this. Make it possible for the union to function *within* the enterprise and yet to discharge its opposition role, and all the other problems of unionism become solvable. The basic insecurity of the union would then disappear or at least become a subordinate rather than, as at present, the compelling motivation of union action.[5]

While Mr. Drucker may exaggerate the opposition role of the union, the role does exist, and his theory of twin allegiance is highly valuable.

In sum, we find that most of the Swift-UPWA employees possess dual allegiance, but only a slight majority of management have it. And since dual allegiance is so important to the plant community if the full possibilities of harmonious opposition are to be realized within it, we might wish that these figures were higher.

Dual allegiance can grow. It will be a point of wisdom for both company and union to see their need for it and to encourage its growth. A higher amount of dual allegiance, even of dual loyalty, is clearly possible, as the interview evidence in this book has demonstrated.

THE THREE QUESTIONS ANSWERED

In the first chapter, we said that the purpose of this research was "to see how the dual presence of company and union affects the work attitudes and motivations of the worker as member of both, of his immediate superiors in each, and thus to find what basis the worker offers for harmonious opposition." Of the three basic questions that we formulated, the first two were the most important:

> I. Will the average worker actually have dual allegiance to, or satisfaction from, both company and union?

II. Will the worker have allegiance which is necessarily dual, in that he says his wants can be satisfied only by both organizations?

These questions inquire whether the worker at the plant level will be favorable to both his company and his union as institutions. The second goes beyond the first to ask whether or not the worker is convinced that both organizations are necessary to satisfy his needs in the industrial plant community. We saw the answers to these questions gradually evolve as we listened to the men and women of the plant community, and we found that most of the workers say they want both company and union. We saw who has dual allegiance and who has not.

The third question helps us focus more sharply on the nature of dual allegiance and the possible threats to its existence in the plant community:

III. Will the worker's allegiance to one of the two organizations in the plant community pull him away from the other organization, thus straining his dual allegiance, or will the allegiance he gives to one organization not noticeably affect the allegiance he gives to the other?

The purpose of this question, as we said, is to help us find out whether one or the other of the two organizations competing for the favor of the worker may be pulling him away from the opposite one, even though the over-all fact is the existence of dual allegiance. We want to know whether or not dual allegiance in the Swift-UPWA plant community is under stress and strain and whether or not the two parties are pulling it apart to any degree.

The facts do not support completely either alternative presented in this question. In other words, dual allegiance is not under a strain for many workers, but it is for some. We have seen that the two groups of people in the plant community officially identified with the two organizations, the foremen on the one hand, and the stewards and union leaders on the other, are among the least favorable people in the community to the opposite organization. These men have strong allegiance to the organization they represent and this, along with the official role they play, tends to draw them away from the opposite organization. For them we can say: Their allegiance to company (or union) tends to diminish their allegiance to union (or company). For them, their "mother" organization tends to alienate their favor to the other. I say "tends," because most of them do have allegiance to both organizations.

For example, the comments of some of the foremen with unequal allegiance are like this: "It's been my experience that we were treated fair and square without a union." "If you have good supervision, a union is not necessary. When I worked in the gang I was well treated." "Swift is a good company; they would give those benefits anyway." These men have strong confidence in the company and its good intentions, but their company allegiance is no greater than the average of the work force.

Why is their union allegiance less than this average? Not because of their greater favorableness to the company but because of the official role they must play as foremen, a role that occasionally brings them in conflict with union officials.

The stewards and union leaders, though they have company allegiance, are the most union-minded and the least company-minded of anybody in the plant community. Their strong union identification undoubtedly holds in check their favor toward the company. For example, steward Richard Rex, a staunch union advocate and antagonistic to the company, makes much of the fact that "Our foreman has fought the union in every way possible. . . . It's company policy to fight the union because the company backs up the foreman." . . . If Rex were not such a union man, he would not resent so much the alleged action of the company. His strong union allegiance leads him to lesser company allegiance. He does not want challenged the organization that is dear to him.

As to whether the rank-and-file work force is affected by the competition of company and union for their allegiance, the answer is that the pull of the company seems to attract a few workers, but not most, from full allegiance to the union. Likewise, the pull of the union affects the company allegiance of some.

Our evidence for this answer is based first on rank correlations of worker subsamples. Secondly, it is based on the influence of the sex and service variables (shown to be significant in many cases by our analysis of variance) which seem to influence attitudes toward company and union in opposite directions. Thirdly, the individual interviews will help to clarify the whole matter.

The Rank Correlations. Here we arrange the workers in their twelve "boxes" by the two sexes and races and the three lengths of service — for instance, white men of middle service, white men of long service, etc. We put the groups in the numerical order of their company allegiance and then compare their order of union allegiance to see if it is the same order, or opposite, or related. The result is a moderate negative correlation: — .48. This means that the order of company and union allegiance of the twelve groups moves moderately in opposite directions — the group most favorable to the company tending to be the least favorable to the union. The colored and white women of long service are the most company-minded and the least union-minded of all twelve groups, and the colored men of short service are the least company-minded and next to the most union-minded. This rank correlation, while not high, is meaningful. At least for the three groups or clusters just mentioned, their position at the extremes of the rank order is reasonably explained by their high attraction for the union pulling them away from the company and vice versa. The long-service women, both colored and white, however, are hardly 3 per cent of the work force. If we simply eliminate them, and do a rank correlation with the remaining ten groups, we get a coefficient of only —.11, which is very low.

We saw that the race variable is not important in affecting attitudes toward company, though it is important regarding the union. If we disregard race and classify the work force only by sex and length of service into six sub-samples: men of short, middle, and long service; and women of short, middle, and long service, we find that the rank correlation of these groups is —.65. The extreme groups here are the short-service men and the long-service women. This correlation is also rather significant. It simply underlines what our analysis of variance has already told us: namely, that sex and service tend to affect attitudes to company and union in opposite directions.

Influence of Sex and Service Variables. We remember that there is a statistical interaction between sex and service in attitudes toward the union and that the figures must be interpreted with certain distinctions. If you are a long-service woman worker, your greater company allegiance tends to make you much less union-minded, or vice versa. If you are a short-service male worker, your greater union allegiance tends to make you less company-minded, or vice versa. On the other hand, if you are a colored man, your service will not much affect your views toward the union; and if you are a white man your service will not much affect your views toward the company. Apparently length of service makes much more difference among the women than it does among the men.

Individual Interviews. If our analysis of the opposing attractions of company and union is correct so far, we ought to find some evidence for it in the individual interviews, especially in those extreme clusters we mentioned. As a matter of fact, we do not find a great many individual cases (among those most union-minded and least company-minded) where it is clear from the interview data that the worker's union allegiance tends to diminish his company allegiance. There are a few such cases. For instance, Amos Maker has less company allegiance than the average worker because he feels that "the company is working against the union," and Maker is a loyal union man.

But we often find cases in which company allegiance tends to diminish union allegiance, especially among the old-timers. This difference between the union and company capacity to attract allegiance has already become apparent. While there is dual allegiance in the plant community, there is somewhat more allegiance to the company (1.58) than to the union (2.14). Swift has a somewhat greater pull on the work force than the UPWA.

This pull of the company is exemplified in at least two ways. First, some employees, especially the old-timers, feel that good company treatment makes the union unnecessary. Edgar Whitcomb says: "Before the union we got along much better . . . I could go to the general office and get what I wanted." And Al Montez: "The bosses treat you so good, you don't need a union."

Secondly, some workers, with strong company allegiance, are not against the union because of their company allegiance, but because they dislike the union attacks on the company. We heard Arbella Cooper put it this way: "Swift is supreme to a lot of companies in packing . . . It's foolishness to bite the hand that feeds us . . . The union should help us, but not come out here and take over the company . . ." And Alex McLean: "I think Swift & Company is one of the finest packinghouses . . . But the CIO has no justice for the company . . ." We recall that one reason for dissatisfaction with Local 28 in 1950 leadership was that it was too anticompany. For this minority, dissatisfaction with the leadership carries over to the institution of the union itself.

Bill Schuett, a middle-service worker with both company and union allegiance himself, makes this illuminating comment about those workers, especially the old-timers, who let their company allegiance cool their zeal for the union:

> Since the strike of 1948 quite a few fellows refused to come back in the union. They say: "Swift treats me all right. I been here twenty-seven years! Swift never did me nothin' wrong!" They love the company more than the union. *It's those kind of fellows who pull the union apart!*

Mr. Schuett expresses a common attitude: The worker does not want to see split allegiance in the plant community.

We must therefore conclude that dual allegiance is under some strain for the foremen and local union leaders and stewards, but for the work force in general, we find that certain clusters of workers give evidence that their allegiance to one organization tends to pull them away somewhat from the other — more away from the union than from the company. These clusters are especially the long-service women and the short-service men (therefore of opposite sex and length of service). They represent about one-third of the work force. There may be others so affected. We estimate that at least one-third, but not more than one-half of the Swift-UPWA people are affected by the opposing pulls of company and union.

IMPLICATIONS FOR SOCIAL AND INDUSTRIAL PSYCHOLOGY

It is time to make explicit the meaning of our findings for the psychology of industrial relations. As a science concerned with people in their social relationships, social psychology asks two key questions: "What do people think about each other and why?" "Why do they act the way they do?" Social psychology is principally concerned with peoples' attitudes and their formation, and their motivation. We shall apply our findings to these two theoretical categories, principally to check the validity of accepted theory against the concrete detail of people in everyday work situations not always reached by psychological test, experiment, or clinic.

The Complexity of Attitudes. We saw that the worker's attitudes toward an institution, a race, a job, a fellow-worker, or a foreman may be at times quite definite and simple, yet often they are highly complex. Sometimes they are contradictory, like those of the man who said: "I like the union and I don't." Sometimes they include real loyalty, or emotion or ego-involvement; sometimes they are simply dry approval. Sometimes they affect behavior greatly, depending on their volitional and emotional content; sometimes they affect it very slightly; but always they have some effect upon it, and always they are important.

Influences on Attitudes. We are as interested to know why a man thinks the way he does, as what he thinks. The influences affecting the work attitudes of Swift-UPWA people are intriguing and limitless. We have isolated a few of the most important ones. We have seen how the worker's company allegiance affects his union allegiance, and vice versa, in the data referring to our third question. We have seen how the past history of social relations in the plant community, and how the neighborhoods, wages, contract, production methods, and so on, affect attitudes.

We have seen other attitudes influence allegiance to the company, such as one's attitude to his foreman, his job, pay, gang, working conditions, but just as important, we have seen that the worker's attitude toward the company as an institution is a distinct attitude which the worker himself distinguishes, for instance, from his attitude toward his foreman: "It's not the company, it's the people." We saw a similar pattern for the union.

The influences of sex, race, and service over the attitudes of working people we have studied in detail. We are not surprised that these variables, differentiating a man's personality and social environment, should also influence his attitudes. We were especially interested to see how these variables actually work, and how they are inevitably related to other variables. Do Negroes want a union that protects their racial status? Of course. But not all Negro workers are union-minded. We have seen that other factors influence their attitudes. The long-service colored women, for instance, are quite indifferent to the union as an institution. Indeed, if we do no more here than bring out the fact that not all the people of any group think alike, that neither union, management, men, women, colored nor white are monolithic in their attitudes, we have helped a bit to dispel the stereotyping that the lazy human race likes to stamp upon itself.

Attitudes and Motivation. The relationship between attitudes and motivation or the needs, wants, fears, and ambitions of the worker comes strong in our findings. Because of the ebb and flow of work, the worker needs the security of steady employment in order to support his family and live decently without fear of creditors. A primary reason for his favorable attitude toward Swift & Company is that the company provides him with a secure and steady job. And because the American worker is a human being and needs recognition, status, a say in things, and dignity, like anybody else, he has a favorable attitude toward the union primarily because it gives him the protection, status and, more fundamentally, the dignity he wants.

Attitudes, Perception, and Learning. Clearly the Swift-UPWA worker does not take his attitudes out of the sky. He learns them as he perceives the world and the people about him. These psychological processes of perception and learning which organize our attitudes through experience are likewise influenced by our wants and needs and fears and ambitions and desire for meaning. We saw for instance what different attitudes some management people and some workers have toward the same wage-incentive system. We saw how they see it differently. We saw how they perceive it in terms of their personal interests and needs. Do we want to know why they don't agree, why they have different attitudes about it? Our analysis of their differing needs influencing their very perception of the wage-incentive system gives us the answer.

Attitudes and Behavior. We saw especially the influence of work attitudes on behavior toward the union, toward joining the union and toward participating in it. We found that the union allegiance attitude of the Swift-UPWA people has a definite influence on their union behavior. But we also found that their union allegiance and behavior toward the union are not the same thing. We found a variety of attitudes from very favorable to very unfavorable among people who participate slightly in the union. And among those who have union allegiance we found many degrees of actual participation-behavior in union affairs. Yet we also found some definite association between union allegiance and union participation.

Finally we might ask: How does the dual allegiance that we found affect "dual behavior" toward company and union, when leaders of each are in sharp opposition? If that opposition arises because one organization challenges the existence or basic objectives of the other, then the workers will either strike or scab. For dual allegiance does not necessarily mean exact obedience to the commands of either organization but rather approval of the existence, basic objectives, and over-all policies of both. The workers do not want to see their dual government threatened. They will strike if the company tries to put the union out of business. They will scab if the union tries to put the company out of business.

Strikes or scabbings over "immediate" collective bargaining issues (not involving the existence or objectives of either institution) may arise from time to time. Dual allegiance will not entirely prevent nor perfectly predict them. The workers of the Swift-UPWA plant community very probably had dual allegiance when they struck in 1946 over issues they believed in. They certainly had dual allegiance in 1948 when many of them scabbed over issues they did not believe in. Today in 1953 they are generally satisfied with conditions and would oppose a strike. What might happen in 1963 is anybody's guess. Of course the relative amounts of company and union allegiance possessed by the workers would influence them to strike or to scab, though factors quite apart from allegiance would have a more important influence: the workers' opinion of these "immediate" issues, their fear of picket lines, reprisals or scorn of fellow-workers, or their fear of losing their seniority or jobs.

But to repeat, the main behaviorial fact flowing from the dual allegiance which we found is that the workers want their two-in-one government intact and will act accordingly! They want management to give their union its right to equal voice in determining working conditions. "Without a union, there's not anyone to speak for your rights. . . . If you got union, you got leader. He go to see Big Mens in office." They want the union to give their management its right to manage. "The union should be fifty-fifty for company and union . . . the foremen should have a say too!" They will oppose either one in its attempt to undermine the other. They strongly resent a struggle for existence between the two organizations they support. It would be well for both management and labor leaders to recognize this dual allegiance if industrial peace is to be advanced.

Attitudes and Rationality. In our listening to the people of the Swift-UPWA plant community we remarked at frequent intervals how reasonable, fair-minded, dispassionate, and objective the workers could be in their perceptions, judgments, and reasoning. We also noted that emotional, nonlogical motivation at times does influence and distort their attitudes and judgments. But the point is — and it needs to be said — the workers are often very rational indeed in their attitudes. By "rational" we mean simply that emotion, bias, prejudice, motivational need do not greatly distort or twist the worker's perception, judgment, or attitude from a close connection with objective fact and objective evidence.

Some psychologists and sociologists have exaggerated the very real influence of "drives," "urges," and "unconscious motives" to the denigration of man's capacity and desire to reason logically. But men like Bartlett have well brought out man's striving after meaning. And Pareto puts as one of his strongest "residues" the residue to make "derivations," that is, to make sense.[6] Our findings agree.

For example, when a man joins Local 28 not because he has something against the company, but because he wants protection against being "kicked around by the foreman," because he wants some say in the governance of the community in which he works, because basically he wants to express the dignity he believes he has — then the words nonlogical, emotional, are inadequate to describe his behavior, though some emotion may enter into it. Quite possibly in his mind the worker even makes a syllogism about his decision to join the union, as he did implicitly in more than one interview: "I want job protection, the help of someone to look out for my interests, and some voice around here. The union is a help in that. Therefore, I want the union."

Even if the worker joins the union from fear of scorn or violence, as a minority do, he is doing something not only emotional, but also rational. He wants to live with the people of his department in peace. If he has to pay union dues to get that peace, he will pay.

The Manifest and Latent Content of Attitudes. The distinction between what appears on the surface of a worker's attitudes and what may sometimes lie beneath, was well brought out by Roethlisberger and Dickson. It is a basic part of psychological theory and we came across it from time to time in the plant community. Many complaints about the operation of the Standards wage-incentive system, as we developed them at length, rest basically on the worker's dissatisfaction with being a machine tool of mass production. This distinction between the manifest and latent content of attitudes must be made cautiously. Analysis of the total interview helps to make it.

Implications of Our Findings for the Theory of Motivation. As we listened to the people in this book, we asked as we went along: What are their basic work needs, fears, wants, ambitions? The answer should help us to clarify psychological motivation theory, and also to understand better the nature of harmonious opposition in the American plant community. Here is what we found:

SOME WANTS of some or many workers:	SOME FEARS AND AVERSIONS of some or many workers:
Steady work, without layoffs or reduction of hours.	Being out of a job with almost no savings and constant expenses.
A foreman "who leaves you alone," "who doesn't stand over you," "who listens."	Arbitrary discipline by foreman, "getting pushed around."
A clean job, not too wet, nor too cold, nor too hot, nor too dusty.	"Arthritis" or ill health allegedly caused by working conditions.
More pay.	A cut in the wage rate, or more commonly a cut in hours worked.
A chance to be a skilled butcher or a craftsman.	The frustration of doing a routine unskilled job all their lives.
A chance to be a foreman.	Advancement ceilings due to race.
Their children to go elsewhere and get a "better" job.	Constant rising prices, especially food and rent.
Recognition for work well done.	The subtle "superiority attitude" of some whites.
Answers to their requests for a raise.	The "aggressiveness" of some colored.
Advancement for the Negro race through themselves or even through another.	"Not the company, but the people."
	Radical union leadership that will "kill the goose that lays the golden egg."

Better understanding of wage-in-centives.

A union.

A chance to go to the "Big Boss" through the grievance procedure.

A steward who is "intelligent."

Union leaders to "work along" with company.

Company to "work along" with union.

Dual allegiance to be had in the plant community.

The company really to accept the union.

Scorn of fellow-workers if they do not join the union.

That company is not primarily concerned with their interests — so they belong to union.

That dual allegiance will be spilt.

That they'll "work themselves out of a job."

That the union is getting too strong [Supervision].

These wants and fears are more or less reciprocal. Our lists are neither complete nor logically arranged. They are simply a brief suggestion of the basic forces exerting a directive and dynamic influence upon the people of the Swift-UPWA plant community. These are real wants and not fictitious ones. And the worker will strive to gratify them, by one means or another. The industrial relations and institutions of the community must take account of these wants and build upon them. In turn, the worker's fears and aversions are highly real to him. Sound industrial relations and union policy will try to reduce such fears as far as possible.

Throughout this book we have seen how peoples' wants differ from each other. We have watched the influence of race, sex, and service, the influence of the foreman and steward roles. We saw the high morale of Swift top management so conscious of the Swift family spirit and Swift leadership. We saw the desire of the assembly-line worker for a steady job, some security and dignity. Occasionally we saw conflict in motivations: "As a foreman I'm not so favorable to the union, but as a man I am." We saw the worker who wants to be a loyal union man cross the picket line because the 1948 strike is long and his family in need. We have seen how these motivations are affected by attitudes, and affect them in return, how they influence behavior — behavior that sometimes seems incomprehensible to the man with different needs. Finally, we have seen how reasonable many of these wants and fears really are. Of course it is not easy to put one's self in another fellow's shoes and take on his wants and fears. No one can do it perfectly. But understanding those wants and fears is the first step. Understanding plus a measure of empathy will go a long way toward a betterment of social relations of the plant community.

Finally, while we have analyzed the people of the plant community into their attitudes, motivations, allegiances, for the sake of scientific understanding, we realize that no analysis gives a perfect picture. That is why we have always tried to show the interrelationship of these psychological abstractions.

AREAS FOR FUTURE CONSIDERATION

Our investigation of the past and present industrial relations in the Chicago Swift-UPWA plant community leads us toward certain observations which may promote greater dual allegiance, loyalty, and harmony in the plant community. These are made with full awareness that it is the people of the plant community who would have the practical task of working them out. They may be tabulated as follows:

For the Company

(1) *Basic Attitude.* With trust and good faith, let all management grow in full internal acceptance of the union as a good and even as a necessary institution in the plant community.

(2) Accept the union as a legitimate partner in the plant community, and give its affairs normal place in company publications.

(3) Consider giving additional union security (perhaps of the compromise type in the GM-UAW contract), as a practical demonstration of the company's acceptance of the union.

(4) Consider joint labor-management committees with the union for study of wage-incentives, work-simplification, etc., giving full access to the facts and agreeing to protect the worker's position by contract guarantees.

(5) Provide a company meeting-room, or time off, or pay to the union stewards for their own program of steward training.

(6) Consider advancement of qualified Negroes into Chicago plant supervision and office.

(7) Revise Standards payments so that the employee is paid on 100 per cent of the work units he produces over 60, instead of on 75 per cent. [Beginning with the 1952 contract this was done.] Continue the present foreman-training in the Standards System and extend it as far as possible to hourly-paid.

For the Union

(1) *Basic Attitude.* Let the union rid itself of its minority of Marxist, left-wing leaders [Local 28, at least, did this in the 1953 elections], and with trust and good faith, view the company as a partner and not an enemy or a threat.

(2) Periodically stress the members' obligation toward the comany to do a fair day's work, etc.

(3) Encourage steady, responsible leadership by reducing factionalism.

(4) Agree to form with the company joint educational committees for time study, work simplification, etc., with the contract guarantees [building on the safety committees already set up].

(5) Accept the company hall and/or time for union-steward training programs, without charging company paternalism, thanks in part to union security.

(6) Encourage white participation in the local by maintaining balance of white officers [attained in 1953 elections], and by less frequent and more persuasive talk about Negro rights.

(7) Consider moving the UPWA District One Hall back near stockyards in a neighborhood equally acceptable to whites and colored.

The mutual dependence of these observations is nowhere more complete than in the first basic attitude necessary for both union and company, an attitude of trust and good faith. Without this, none of the other practical ideas are likely to be made operative.

On management's part, the growth of this attitude will mean acceptance of the union as a legitimate and even a necessary partner, and not merely a *de facto* power group. On the union's part, this growth will certainly mean ousting its Communist minority for whom good faith in the company is a denial of dogma. Moreover, it will mean for the unionists no more suspicion and fear that the company is trying to undermine the union allegiance of their fellows when it takes an interest in its employees and even in the union. The plant community is much influenced by the International UPWA, and unfortunately the UPWA in recent years has been beset by factionalism, communism, and distrust. Until the International UPWA can rectify and stabilize itself, the rest of the suggestions are simply ephemeral.

Without a doubt observation (3) on additional union security is controversial. There are many forms of such security. Perhaps the compromise form adopted by General Motors and the United Auto Workers might be considered here. Under this arrangement, present members of the union must continue in the union, as a condition of employment. Nonmembers shall not be required to join, though anyone who does join must remain in. New employees must join the union for one year. After this time, they may withdraw from the union, during a two-week period. If they do not withdraw, they must remain in the union from then on.

Many conditions of employment are now set unilaterally by management: a man may not work in the Swift-UPWA plant community unless he has a certain degree of health, unless he wears a white coat if his job requires it, and so on. The various forms of union security may be considered as other conditions of employment. If the union is a legitimate bargaining agent for the workers, possesses good leadership for the most part, does not discriminate against its members, and if the majority of its members want the union shop, there can be, on principle, no valid argument against it. The argument against it in practice might become valid, if one of the above conditions were not verified.

The need for a reasonable degree of union security in the Swift-UPWA plant community emerges out of the findings of this book, for again and again our data point to it. The union leaders complain frequently of the "free riders," employees who are glad to get the benefits of collective bargaining, raises, fringe benefits, but who are unwilling to pay dues to and support the union which is in part responsible for their benefits. To the union man, this disloyalty is a constant irritation. He will never be at peace with it. In addition, the considerable turnover in the plant community and in the packing industry also leads to free riders.

The steady influx of new employees means that Local 28 must constantly sell itself and the union movement to these people. Therefore it will stay in the somewhat insecure state of perpetual organization with much of the aggressiveness of its old organizing days of the late thirties, when the local was struggling for its existence. Can we expect a high degree of industrial harmony under these circumstances? Some people complain that union leaders are not mature, that they behave like aggressive organizers instead of administrators. The answer is that employee turnover forces them to remain organizers.

Our data have shown us the clear and pronounced union allegiance of the Swift-UPWA workers. We have seen that this allegiance grows out of the needs of the worker and is not just imposed by demagogues. If some women and old-timers fail to have this allegiance, the GM-UAW compromise formula exempts them from joining the union. The union allegiance of the great majority of the workers indicates that a union has a definite place in the plant community.

What about our finding of low worker-participation in Local 28's affairs? Would the GM-UAW formula increase participation? Generally when people pay dues to an organization they are more likely to take part in it. The nonparticipant free riders lead the way toward encouraging general nonparticipation.

Some of the insecurity of Local 28 and UPWA leaders may well arise because they wonder whether Swift has really accepted their union. Union-management coöperation in the fields of steward training and time-study may be facilitated under some more tangible form of union security.

When we asked a certain UPWA leader about steward training on company time, we recall his answer: "No. It would be too close to the company. It would be company-dominated. The union would be called a company-union by the rest of the unions. I can't help feeling that a man is controlled by where his money is coming from." This brings out the interdependence of the above observations. Steward training (5) depends on union security (3), and this in turn depends on trust and good faith (1), especially with respect to the left-wing element of the UPWA.

Observation (4) recommending joint union-management committees of time study and work simplification is also merely utopian without additional union security. We recall that Swift made this offer, and the offer was rejected by the UPWA. We heard another UPWA leader say that he would not accept Swift's offer to study the Bedaux System because: "I might have to tell someone to work faster. And that's no good!" And we recall the wise comments of Golden and Ruttenberg of ten years ago regarding wage rates, and applicable just as well to incentive payments: "Certainly a union is not free to adjust a member's rate downward when, as a consequence, he can immediately quit the union and agitate for other members to follow his example."

Above all, additional union security might help the UPWA to realize that it has "arrived," and that it is wanted. Such union security might well win real labor-management coöperation from the UPWA. We realize that such security is a matter for national bargaining as it affects the entire Swift chain and not simply the Chicago plant community, and that it is subject to various state laws. Only the two parties involved will know best the time and manner of its implementation.

Labor-management committees (4), merits special comment. The possibilities for fruitful coöperation by joint UPWA-Swift committees for work simplification and time study are tremendous. The mere fact that in many industries during the second World War such committees did not work is no proof that they cannot work. The fact that Swift and the UPWA have just established joint safety committees in their 1952–1954 Agreement is a hopeful sign for the future.

As we said in Chapter Eleven on time study, one of our findings is that the mass-production revolution is a covert cause of discontent and frustration in the plant community. An important step toward the solution of this twentieth-century American problem can be taken through labor-management committees, in which the worker has a chance to participate, to contribute his finger-tip knowledge of the job toward plans for incentive payments, for job simplifications and method of improvements. It is possible that the worker will develop a creative interest in his work and in his department through these committees, that will offset the repetitive machine-tool work now being demanded of so many Swift-UPWA men and women.

Furthermore, the chance for increased productivity through these committees is great. As we saw, nobody knows the job better than the man doing it, not even the foreman. The workman can see short cuts, time-saving and work-saving methods undreamed of by the engineer. Let us put it bluntly: Swift has not even begun to tap the talent of its workers, including its unskilled common labor. But with an insecure union and an insecure worker, such coöperation must remain forever untapped. That is why, in addition to growth in trust and good faith, guarantees will need to be written into the Swift-UPWA contract. A man who makes a labor-saving suggestion needs to be guaranteed that he will not suffer through downgrading and less hourly pay as a result. Possibly the guarantee would be that his successor in the job would receive the lower rate, but that his rate would be preserved. Admittedly, there are many practical problems involved in the spelling out of such guarantees. But mutual good-will should solve them.

Finally, we shall discuss only three other observations, those involving racial relations, (6) for the company, and (6) and (7) for the union. We can be brief here, since we have treated this subject earlier. For Swift management, surely a more aggressive and far-sighted program of trying to improve interracial relations would be wise. An important part of this program will be the full incorporation of qualified Negroes into the ranks of supervision, and into foreman-training programs. The *Swift News* from time to time could explicitly treat interracial questions in the effort to educate both white and colored people to live and work together as the UPWA *Packinghouse Worker* has done. The *News* for years has been trying to educate Swift workers against socialism, so this would not be something entirely new.

For Local 28, observations (6) and (7) are simply two of many possible explicit measures that might increase white participation in union affairs. Since the field work was done for this book, the new right-wing officers of Local 28 already have a better balance of white and colored. While it is not desirable, by any means, that the union give up its talk about Negro rights and interracial relations, if this talk is less constant than it was under the Communist aegis in 1950, and persuasive rather than aggressive, it will probably have greater success. Both colored and white union leaders should be aware that there are two sides to the race question, with faults on both sides, though the predominant unfairness must be laid at the door of the whites. Racial relations in Local 28 and the plant community are greatly affected by the general race and housing picture in Chicago. Local 28 and the UPWA cannot be expected to solve all the problems in Chicago. There are other organizations for that. But if the union can go on improving the interracial work relations of its members, it will be doing a good service.

Finally, we can hardly overstress the mutual interdependence of these suggestions. They are like a circle. They can become a vicious circle unless both company and union are daring enough to apply several of the ideas at the same time. Fearfulness will not conquer the throttle grip of a vicious circle; only courage on both sides can transform these conflicts into the state of harmonious opposition which is at present the highest aim of the industrial plant community.

As we come to the end of this book, after watching and listening to the people of the Swift-UPWA plant community, we find that they have told us that they do comprise a true industrial community, a "stable union of working people seeking common goals and using community means, and under an authority." They have told us that, on the whole, they want and approve the two-in-one nature of that community, with its dual government by company and union. They have told us in their own words that dual allegiance is something they have, something they want, something that must not be threatened. They have made it clear to that harmony and coöperation in the plant community are something that they strongly desire. And so these men and women give us hope that the great social upheavals of our times need not mean the disintegration of our modern society. For we see in the molecule to which we may liken the industrial plant community, a buffer between the individual in his small work group and the great industry or state. Composed of differing elements, primarily the union and the company, this unit has its own harmony, and the anatomy of its harmony now lies revealed for all who wish to understand and utilize it.

APPENDICES

APPENDICES

AN INTERVIEW WITH EDWARD HASSETT

Hassett is a Negro right-wing union steward who has twenty-three years' continuous service with Swift & Company and began with the company in 1930. He is forty-six, has four dependents, and owns his own home (not yet paid for). He had a number of jobs before coming to Swift, and during his twenty-three years, has had three layoffs. He is a skilled butcher and makes $1.45 an hour. He grosses about $51 a week. His wife works to help pay for their recently bought home. His son also works at Swift in the ———— Department. He has had a grade school education.

This interview with Edward Hassett (not his real name, of course) was chosen because it is among the more interesting interviews and because Mr. Hassett has general attitudes of allegiance to the company and to the union. It is typical in this sense that Mr. Hassett has dual allegiance.

We began with some generalities and quickly got into a discussion of Hassett's new house he had just bought on South Park Avenue:

I'm considered one of the top-paid men in the whole Division . . . Make $51 a week . . . but after taxes, and so on, after you take all that out, you take home about $42 . . . I just bought my home . . . I live on South Park Avenue, 4400 south.

I: Is that so? I live near you, then, at Oakwood and Vincennes, at Holy Angels' Parish.

H: Oh I've heard about it . . . Well I just bought a home over there . . . ah . . . last Tuesday.

You really had to save up for that?

Yes, I did, I had to save quite a bit. That's one of the reasons my wife works . . . because out of the $40 I save a quarter a week and I'm still broke . . . You see what responsibility you have working . . . Due to the fact of the sacrifice and also that I'm off on my vacation — all I can do is sit on the back porch and smoke my pipe . . . because I had to sacrifice to save up the money and finish the time on it . . . And then I had to borrow $1000 from the credit union to make the down payment. Now you see the responsibility I got on account I got to keep those payments up . . . see what happens if I happen to stalk my toe?

Yes, it's a responsibility.

Yeah. Well, now what is it that you're interested in?

Well, whatever you're interested in, Mr. Hassett, for instance about the company and the union. Is the company a pretty good place to work or is it a kind of tough place, or how do you feel about that?

Well I've worked for . . . I'd say I've had about seven jobs since I been in Chicago. I worked for Swift & Company for twenty-three years.

Have you really? You've got a lot of service, haven't you?

And honestly . . . in my honest opinion, Swift is just about one of the best companies to work for in its day for its employees. They give you all kind of consideration unless'n you are completely outa line altogether. And even then they will talk with you about it.

That's good, so they seem to be pretty fair, I guess?

Yeah, they are pretty fair.

How about your foremen and all that?

Well as far as I'm concerned, about my own foreman personally, he's a nice fella.

Makes a lot of difference if you got a good foreman, I suppose.

Yeah, well he's the kind of fella you can sit down and discuss your problems with him and talk with him. 'Cos he's just like anybody else. Sometimes comes down in the mornin' an' doesn't feel good, just like me or anybody else. Might raise his voice, that's another thing . . . But if he gets outa line, he's man enough to come back an' say: "I'm sorry, I had so much on my mind I didn't intend to holler at you." Well, that means a lot! We have a pretty good guy.

How about the crowd up there, Mr. Hassett? Get along pretty well with the gang?

Yes, we have a pretty good gang. We works together.

And you said your son was working over here, didn't you?

Yes, he is.

Well that's good, what department is he in?

He works in, ah, ——— Department.

——— Department? Is there a good chance for advancement there?

We-e-ll, there's some chance. Doesn't go so fast. But for colored people, not so much.

What do you mean? Is there discrimination there?

Well. To a certain extent.

To a certain extent?

Yeah. I been workin' for the company . . . twenty-two, ah, or twenty-three years — been so long I really can't keep up! [laughs]. But anyway I have broke in at least — I would say ten . . . fellas who have started in at that dock. I've taught 'em how to butcher. An' they got to be foremen.

Is that right? You broke in ten men, and taught them how to do the job?

An' they went to supervision! That's facts. I'm sayin' just exactly how I feels about it.

You taught them how to do the job and now they are foremen? Do you feel there's a chance of a foremanship for you?

No, I don't. Because one more — six cents more, raise — an' I'll be the top. Far as I can go in this department, as much as I know about the ———— Division.

You know that Division well?

Oh yeah! I started all the way in the cellar and worked up all the way.

Do you think you could handle the department?

Well, I wouldn't say that, but with a little schoolin' I could do what the rest o' them do.

They had schooling, did they?

They send other fellas to school. They don't send colored fellas over there though.

The schooling is not open to colored?

No, it's not open to colored . . . I'm just goin' by what is felt, and I feel they *are* showin' discrimination in that department — the supervision departments. I know everybody is not qualified for that job in education and in intelligence, but . . .

How about advancement, let's say to a higher job or skill in a department, could you get that if you wanted it?

Oh yes, you go by seniority. Like last week — they had two gangs, the oldest men come up in the $1.51 an hour [bracket]. I got practically that all the time.

Yes. Well maybe there will be a change someday?

Yes, I think there will. You know those things — you got to work themselves out. An' the only way you can work 'em out is by the way you're doin'. You comin' in, an' talkin' and findin' out. Because you know you can't *bull* your way into those tactics. As long as you goin' to protest against those things, there's hope. You have a problem, an' *some*body will come in an help you to solve it.

And there has been a lot of improvement, I guess?

Oh yeah!

Did the union help?

Oh yeah! That's 75 per cent of it.

About how did they help you, for instance?

Well befo' we had a union, the foreman could tell you, if you didn't want to work, you could go home. And on top of that, company had half-hour rule. If you came in one half hour late — it depended on how he felt about it — if you were one of his boys — in other words if he like you — you could go to work. If he didn't — it was the rest of the day off — or two or three day's off. Well there wasn't nobody, in other words, to go to the bat for you, to speak for you. So the foremen did just whatever they wanted. The Supervision Department over there in the general office — the things that was did by the foremen, they didn't know anything about it. Because you had no way of gittin' to 'em to explain your problem. Because if you went over the foreman's head there was the possibility that you'd be fired. So when the union came in an' you had a steward, you had representatives, and they draw up a contract and the company and foremen were a party to that contract an' had to keep it.

And so befo' we had the union we had to buy our own knives an' steel, and ah, we had to buy our frocks ourselves, and we didn't have — I think its 12½ minutes — to change our clothes. And so the possibilities after the union, ah, came in, was around 75 per cent better.

And I'll have to give the company credit on that, because they have been coöperating with the union — I would say — the same as the union did coöperate with the company.

They have coöperated with the company?

That's right.

You remember the days before the union, of course.

Oh yes! I can tell, I know all about it!

That goes back to 19 . . . what?

1926. We didn't have a union. You had a company — what you call it?

Security Plan?

No.

Representative?

Yeah. See, the company had a Representation Plan. You take it to the representative. Nine chances out of ten that they give him, there was a company man on top of it. You come up to him [the representative] with a case. He wouldn't take you to the foreman. He would go up an' talk to the foreman and come back an' say: "Well there ain't very much we can do about it, but next time come up." But whatever the case was — you know — there wasn't much you could *do* about it.

So the union has helped out. You were a steward weren't you? Some time?

I'll be a steward — this makes the second time. The majority are younger. We want to get younger men to be stewards. We want to *school* them to it. We older guys, we know the score, so we want the younger fellas to know when they got a case and when they haven't got it.

Is being a steward a hard job?

No, it's not a *hard* job — but most everybody put their finger on you. If somethin' goes wrong with the foreman an' a guy comes to you an' sees red, an' you don't go to the foreman, an' the guy jumps on you, say — it's a pretty hard job. Says you're not a good steward. It depend a lot on the opinion of the men. Sometimes it's a pretty hard job. Then again, there's nothin' to it. Depends on how your foreman coöperates. So far we have a foreman that *will* give his men all kinds of consideration. I will have to give him that. Because if a guy do something wrong, he will absolutely warn him about it, 'most two or three times. And if he gives you a day off, he's really got you by the neck. [Laughs.] Well if he does give a guy time off — 'most thing I can do is come to him and tell him about this guy's large family, how he bought a house, or sump'n like that. It's not easy to be a steward. No, nobody wants that responsibility. See, even the majority of guys — if something go wrong, then he wants the steward. As long as things is goin' along smooth, he don't care about the steward . . .

How is the union getting along?

Some time ago we got a raise. In some departments, a lotta departments, say 25 per cent, 50 per cent of 'em don't belong to the union. And the majority of 'em say: "Why should I join the union. If I get the same benefits — about $2 raise — an' without payin' $2 [union dues], so why should I pay $24 a year union dues? I can get the same benefits you get!" We have quite a bit of this. That makes you warm! "Free riders" — that's what we call 'em.

The union went down a bit, didn't it? A little earlier?

The union went off — let's say — in 1948. After the strike. The peoples was out on strike. I'd say about only 25 per cent came back in. We dropped in numbers then. Some foremens told some of the employees as long as they didn't belong to the union they would get the same consideration as the union men was getting, and in the meantime those wouldn't stay out [on strike] an' went to work. They s'posed to have more consideration than the fellows who stayed out till the strike was over with. I would say only around 25 per cent of those fellows still don't belong.

Did many scab during that strike?

Well, around 30 or 35 per cent of 'em came back. Most of 'em was young, or younger boys. The foremen — the Supervision Department — promised them they wouldn't be laid off. Under the contract they couldn't be, of course — we got a contract.

Has the union been coming back at all since then?

Yes, we came back. The year before we were about 1700. Last year I think we had an average of about 2400. Today, at present, I think we got a little more than 3400.

Is that so? That's double.

That's right.

Do you get over to union meetings much, Mr. Hassett?

I used to go. All the union people did. But not now. The Executive Board — I haven't got anything against them *personally*, but the company they keep. They let other people tell us how to run our union, other different organizations — you know what I mean — that I don't think very much of. So I don't go much.

You mean they're kind of being run by the outside?

That's right . . . As far as union men, I think they're all right, but —

Do they have social gatherings and dances?

They used to have a bowling team. 'Course I don't go to dances. I disapprove of my union givin' dances for one reason that if I want to be a social worker to some extent I'd join a social club. But I think from my point of view that if a union *want* to do something, it should do something so *everybody* would benefit by it. We have a lotta people who don't dance and I think from my point of view if they should spend on the average $1500 or $1000 a year and have a large picnic and serve whiskey and beer an' ice cream and candy — *every*body would be happy.

They don't have a picnic like that?

No. They could have a picnic for the whole family. So you could take your own kids an' everybody be happy. [UPWA District One does have an annual picnic for the Chicago locals.]

A picnic would be better than dances?

See, you know we get four or five dances a year. Frankly, the dances you go to — most people there are the lowest type — it always works up into an argument. There's no security in a dance. Now insurance is more important. You spend 50–50 with the company. Suppose now you get down with the TB or sump'n like that. This thing will work. Company give me $65, $75 a month to carry me over till I pass [die] or till I get help from relatives. Insurance is better than dances.

As for the union meetings you said they were being run by outsiders?

Yes. The majority are practically outsiders. Our union [local] president [1950] is a progressive young fellow, but he's got the idea if you don't agree with him, you wrong. Why even with my wife — we've been livin' together for thirty years — and even we don't agree on *every*thin'! [Laughs.] If he raises up something on the agenda you disapproves of, an' if you get up to oppose it, then you are a "rabble-rouser."

A rabble-rouser?

Yes. Confusin' the meetin' . . . Then our Executive Board — they have discrimination. There are thirteen or fourteen men on the Executive Board and three are white [1950]. We disapprove of that, as a whole. Same like as we're all mixed up workin' together. If we work together, we want the board one and one, all the way down, one and one. We tried to put a Mexican on. But they have an inferiority complex, you know, that they don't know how to talk well enough to be on it. We got one or two trustees on it . . . It's why the majority of the old-timers white and colored is against the Executive Board we got now. One reason the whites are out of the union — they feel they're being shoved to one side. They're outnumbered over there about 10 per cent. It's what we have coming up in the next election. [Annual election of local officers of February, 1950.]

It's going to be quite an election, isn't it? Do you think you have got a pretty good chance?

Yes we have at least a 75 per cent chance to reëlection . . . The old officers were bad too, but better'n ————. They didn't pay no per capita tax. Still, I'd rather have them than ————. In my department, I got the majority . . .

How about the grievances, Mr. Hassett? How have they been going?

They're in bad shape.

What's the trouble? Going through too slow?

Let's put the blame where it belongs. It's on ————. As I said before he's the type of fellow who tries to run the whole show. ———— is the grievance chairman. He's got no chance to take care of cases right. ———— wants to run everything. He takes over cases hisself, lotta times. Just wants to run everything. [Hassett then recounted an anecdote how a certain grievance was almost won by ————, one of the grievance committee, when ———— burst in and aggravated the plant superintendent, Mr. Armstrong. The union lost its argument and the case was postponed.] That ———— is a dictator. We don't go to meetings because of him. We got a lot of grievances layin' over. Some just fades out. You got to know how to handle other people . . .

Have you got any suggestions on working conditions, Mr. Hassett? How are the working conditions?

Well working conditions is fair. Only — Tuesday and Thursdays are gen'lly short days [on hours]. Wednesday and Saturday, that's the day you make schedule. We work six days . . . on Saturday we gets four hours. If we could do it in five days, forty hours in five days, instead of six days, it'd be lots better. We have brought that up several times. It happens mostly in pork. We come down here Saturday. Get up at 5:30. Come down here and start workin' at 7:00. Go home at 11:00. Well, you come out to make only four hours. An' say you already got thirty-five. An' four hours gives you thirty-nine. Clothes-changing time gives you forty hours and fifteen minutes. If we came during the week, we could get that in five days . . . Maybe you want to go to school on Saturday. Make some outside change. Somethin' you wanted to do. Maybe take the weekend off, go fishin'. There'd be a chance if we was gettin' through for the weekend. But in the pork department we handle hogs. Orders come in Friday and Friday evening and Saturday morning for Monday. That's the reason why we're buttin' our heads up against the wall, see, just like . . . [In the 1952–1954 contract, Swift agreed to pay time and one-half for Saturday work. This will probably mean less such work in the future.]

I see what you mean. There are some other things I'd like to get your opinion on. The *Swift News,* for instance. How is that? Do you read it?

It's real nice. They lets you know what happens in the plants all over the country. Greatest thing Swift could do. To let the employees know what's goin' on. How much money they make, profits an' all that. If you go off on a vacation, you got the opportunity of havin' your picture in the paper. Or you can get pictures of your grandbabies in it, and so on.

Then there's the *Packinghouse Worker.* How about that?

No, I don't read that much. You know — it comes in the mail. I put it out and half the time I just don't get to it.

Do you find it interesting?

Yessir. I find it awful inter*e*stin' when I do get a chance to read it. But sometimes I don't. An' sometimes I do.

And how about the *Flash?*

Yes, I read that. Well, the *Flash* now — it's nothing what I might call educational or helpful to it. I don't know — I really can't put the words exactly — there's nothin' to get out of it. Nothin' that any person with any intelligence would want to read and get anything out of it. That's the best I can do . . .

Well, it's a big help to me to get all your ideas and suggestions, Mr. Hassett. You know it all adds up to something. So things are going pretty well?

As a rule. When you familiar with it. When a man works for Swift & Company for twenty-three years, he gets to know the score. I been workin' for 'em a long time. But one thing that gets on a man's nerves: when you been workin' a long time for the company — they bring up some young guy from the supervision department — says he went to Chicago University or wherever he went — put him in school. He goes to school for six months. Then he comes into your department an' he tells you what to do!

You've been there longer than him.

Right! You know all the tough jobs. He takes that slide rule an' slides off. An' he tells him he's s'posed to get out so much an hour! Buckies! That's what we called 'em in the army. Buckies.

Buckies?

Yes. He wants to get up to the top. Well there's no use in puttin' your foot on someone's head and climbin' over up on their shoulders. If you can't climb up by yourself, you're no good. Other than that he's a nice kid. He means good. He gets that stuff out faster than the old foreman can. In the long run we do it much faster. In that ———— department when you works fast, the men work just like the chain.

Does that get on your nerves sometimes?

No. It don't bother them. The bes' thing to do is work right. See, because they're doin' their work right . . . Say you got seven men doin' on an average ———— an hour. You have to have two more men there downstairs . . . [Here the discussion became technically involved.] . . . But you can't explain *that* to 'em . . .
Oh there's another suggestion I want to make about cuttin'. Over on the killin' floor there's a counter. See — the hogs come down on the chain. They got a counter on the chain and as the trolley passes by, it clicks. In other words if you want to know how fast you goin', all you got to do is look at that counter. But on our floor, we haven't been able to get that. It's one of the things I think the company is unfair about. "The foreman wouldn't tell a lie about it?" they say? Well I don't think he would lie. But if it's for the good of the company and the foremen and the men, therefore why not put a counter there?

[Here the interview veered into the Standards System.]

We used to have the bonus system so you'd get so much an hour, $1.50 or a $1.40. A guy could go to the bonus sheet and figure out his own bonus. The way they got it now — you don't know how much rate you gonna get. At the end of the week you get your bonus check. Maybe 68 bonus or 70 bonus. Next day — 62 bonus. If the bonus is fair for the employee he should know *exactly* how much you s'posed to make; how many pieces of meat you s'posed to trim. If you goin' to make a certain amount of bonus, you could add it up, an' it'd be as good as your bonus check. In other words, you don't know what you're doing. What the foreman gives you, it's right.

You think there should be some kind of a counter, or . . .

Yes, a counter. Some kind of a standard. If he's s'posed to make 70, he should know it. I don't say the company is cheating or anything, or taking away bonus — but we'd just like to know! But we don't know just what we're doin'. A man has a right to know what he's doin'! I don't know how much we're doin' to get a bonus. Kinda got us workin' in the dark . . .

And how do the fellows like the bonus system?

We been on it so long. I'll tell you, we're used to it. They did have it at Armour's and they cut it out. Got piece work. We do the same work, an' it gives us more bonus — $4, $5, $7, $8, some fellows as high as $25 a week more bonus. We'd rather have it than to take it out. We do the same amount of work an' get a bonus with it. I think the bonus system is a good system. I have nothin' against it. Only thing I have against it is: I don't know how it works . . .

Well, I'm glad to know what you think. Is there anything else now?

I think I've just about covered it all.

I think this whole thing will be useful. I hope to publish a book later, if it goes well, about the company. So you'll be in there. Though people won't know who you are.

I'm one of those fellows I just tell the truth about it. I'm proud to be able to help you. I want to read your book.

I appreciate your coming in, Mr. Hassett.

I'm glad I was some help to you. Maybe in the future we'll have a chance to set down and talk again. Anytime I can help you, I'll be glad to.

Thanks. If you're ever over by Holy Angels' parish, stop in and say hello.

I will. Well I'm awful glad I had the opportunity to talk with you. So long . . .

APPENDIX II

FIVE QUESTIONS ABOUT METHODS

Here are five questions I have frequently been asked about this research, together with my answers:

1. *Question:* Would you get a valid report of employee attitudes? Would not employees magnify their statements knowing they had a ready listener, so that, as the interviews proceeded, they would influence each other, or the company or union would influence them, to "present a case" thus leading to a distortion of their true attitudes?

Answer: (a) By our system of random sampling, the employees did not know in advance who was to be asked for the next interview. It is rather incredible that either by the grapevine or by positive company or union propaganda 7000 employees should be briefed on "what to tell to Father Purcell."

(b) Even assuming such attempts, however, I do not believe that the majority of the employees would or did accept it. The average person resents being instructed what to say, but likes to express his own opinions, provided he can do so without fear of censure.

(c) Finally, even assuming some employees would distort their statements, they could rarely do so throughout an entire hour of interview so as to deceive the interviewer. The experience of Roethlisberger and Dickson expresses perfectly my own findings: "It was the experience of the interviewers that the genuine hypocrite was rarely encountered. In order to play the role of hypocrite, it is only necessary to realize that if a person is to disguise completely his feelings and sentiments, he must be aware of them explicitly and to an extent which few people can achieve (pp. 276–277).

2. *Question:* If you were to interview a few and not all, would not the others become jealous and perhaps foment trouble?

Answer: Jealousy was avoided because the workers understood that the interviewer would not possibly have time to interview all, and that those chosen had been randomly selected without favoritism. As a matter of fact, in one department, which was largely colored, the random numbers (chosen from the entire plant list) turned up mostly white. There was some resentment by some of the colored workers in the department. At once I invited the dissatisfied workers in for interviews and explained that the random numbers were not based on their department only, but on the entire plant and that such an unusual number drawing would happen occasionally by chance. The workers seemed satisfied and the incident was closed.

3. *Question:* How did your role of priest affect the interviews? Would not the workers feel restrained from using their easy profanity, from expressing a spontaneous critical attitude, and might they not resent your religious role?

Answer: Of course they were affected by my role. They undoubtedly polished up their language compared with the way they might talk in a tavern. But this does not mean distortion. A man's basic attitude can be perceived whether he uses his full complement of adjectives and exclamations or not. As for criticism of what the worker disliked, the interviews themselves show plentiful evidence of that. I could perceive no resentment of my role, despite the fact that the majority were not Catholics. Religion was not mentioned unless the worker himself brought it up. Indeed, my role seemed to put me in a position of confidence and neutrality which facilitated rather than hindered open discussion.

4. *Question:* As a priest how could you get at the attitudes of any Communists or fellow-travelers in your sample?

Answer: The Communists and fellow-travelers whom I interviewed all seemed glad to talk. Frequently their ideas would be party-line, but not always. There are various possible reasons for their wishing to talk to me: (a) most of the Communists do their best to avoid all reference to the Red issue; they pretend to talk as mere trade unionists. (b) All concerned had my assurance that I was there not to interfere, but simply to get everyone's point of view. The Communist is anxious to get his point of view heard. (c) Some might have thought that they might make a new convert to the party.

5. *Question:* Would not the fact that the interviews were done in the plant rather than in the worker's home or elsewhere create a company-slanted situation in which the worker might hesitate to express his real criticism of the company for fear of endangering his job?

Answer: This is a good objection. If I had been a layman in ordinary business clothes, it would have been quite possible for the workers to identify me with management, even though I assured them I was from an outside university. But since I was a priest I was clearly not identifiable with management, especially in view of the fact that several priests had been recently quite openly sympathetic to the union. There were only two or three men whom I found to be lying or at least seemed to be distorting the truth. In each of these cases, the worker told me that he belonged to the union when the records show that he did not. If anything, this means that the worker thought I was union-biased rather than management-biased. In other words, in the only cases in which distortion apparently occurred, it seemed to be caused rather by a union-slanted than a management-slanted interview situation. I offer this as additional evidence that interviewing in the plant did not cause distortion. Moreover, in those interviews which I made at the union hall and in the workers' homes, I found no difference attributable to location. I do not deny that for some investigators, it might be difficult to overcome the bias of in-plant interviewing.

APPENDIX III

HOW WELL ARE THEY PAID?

Wages, of course, are an important aspect of the workers' life in the Chicago Swift-UPWA plant community. There are at least four significant questions we can ask about wages: (1) How do Swift wages compare with those in other industries? (2) How much money do the production workers actually make in a year's time, and what standard of living does this annual income give them? (3) How successfully does the system of wage levels (from common labor to top skills) operate within the plant community? (4) How much have real earnings and labor's share of Swift's total costs varied

TABLE 32

The comparative wage position of the Chicago Swift-UPWA plant community with other industry

Chicago Swift-UPWA plant community[a]	All meat packing[b]	All manu-facturing[b]	Illinois meat products[c]	Illinois food and kindred products[c]	All Illinois manufactur-ing[c]
AVERAGE TOTAL HOURLY EARNINGS					
1950 $ 1.49	$ 1.465	$ 1.465	$ 1.46	$ 1.43	$ 1.52
AVERAGE TOTAL WEEKLY EARNINGS					
1950 $60.84	$60.94	$59.33	$60.25	$59.26	$62.34

[a] Swift figures.
[b] *Monthly Labor Review*, January, 1952.
[c] *Non-Agricultural Hours and Earnings in Illinois* (Revised Series), Release of the Research and Statistics Section, Illinois State Employment Service and Division of Unemployment Compensation, September, 1951.

in these last years since the UPWA appeared in the plant community and annually pressed for wage raises? These are four highly interesting questions. We shall treat them but briefly, simply giving the facts, with a mimimum of comment.

(1) HOW DO SWIFT WAGES COMPARE? We have at hand only two bases of comparison that are significant: average hourly earnings and average weekly earnings. The second of these is more important. Table 32 shows Chicago Swift-UPWA's comparative position.

Swift workers' earnings are somewhat below those of the heavy-goods industries in the Chicago industrial area, such as U. S. Steel and International Harvester. They are above all national manufacturing, but below Illinois manufacturing. Swift weekly earnings compare favorably with the meatpacking and food industries.

(2) HOW MUCH MONEY DO THEY MAKE IN A YEAR'S TIME AND WHAT LIVING STANDARD DOES THIS GIVE THEM? Annual income is important. People do not live by the hour or the week, but through all the seasons of the year. Hence their annual income is a more significant figure than their hourly or weekly income. Of course people also live through many years. But we shall not take a longer unit, say triennial income, for this involves less predictable variations like business cycles and wars. But a year has only recurrent seasonal changes, especially in meatpacking, and so it is a time-unit that is both significant and manageable.

Secondly, annual income is important to us because the UPWA is now in the forefront of those unions seeking the guaranteed annual wage — along with the Steel and Auto workers. One reason the UPWA seeks annual wages is this: In 1945 national hog slaughtering was half that of 1944 with resulting loss of income for workers in hog departments. In 1946 and again in 1951 the fight over price controls led to a decrease in cattle slaughtering with loss of income for workers in cattle departments. The UPWA for many years has had a very successful "annual wage" plan with the Hormel Company. (See Working Agreement between UPWA Local 9 and Hormel Co., Article III.) Moreover, the UPWA has recently negotiated important new annual wage contracts with the Revere Sugar Company in Boston, and with the National Sugar Refining Company in New York. Annual income is "in the air." It will probably become more common.

Thirdly, annual income is interesting to us because the UPWA was one of the first to use the annual budget approach so intensively in the crucial wage negotiations with the Big Four in 1948. (These negotiations ended in a strike, we remember.) The Bureau of Labor Statistics' "City Worker's Family Budget" was a central point of controversy in these negotiations. We are curious to see how actual income compares with this budget. What are the facts about annual income in the Chicago Swift-UPWA industrial plant community? We have two samples of the actual gross income made by the workers in the year 1949. (While the workers' sex, race, and service are revealed, their identity is not known to me. It was kept confidential.) These samples — of men and of women — are not small as samples go. They are about 3 per cent of the populations from which they are drawn. Table 33 gives us the results.

This 1949 annual income is not necessarily dated, for since that date wages and prices have varied (and doubtless will continue to vary) together. Now what standard of living does this income of $3,154.71 provide for the Swift-UPWA worker? Table 34 gives us the budget amount for Chicago.

The City Worker's Family Budget is an extensive effort to discover the contemporary American urban worker's living cost in thirty-four of the prin-

TABLE 33

Average annual total gross income of Chicago Swift-UPWA workers working fifty-two weeks

(*Random unstratified samples: 1949*)

127 men	$3,154.71
20 women	2,624.84

cipal American cities. It is prepared by the U. S. Bureau of Labor Statistics and is designed "to describe a 'modest but adequate' standard of living for an urban worker's family of four persons — an employed father, a housewife not gainfully employed, and two children under fifteen years of age. Costs of

TABLE 34

City worker's annual family budget

(*Total cost of budget, goods, rents, and services Chicago, Illinois[a]*)

June, 1947	$3,369.
October, 1949	3,605.
October, 1950	3,745.
November, 1951	4,185.

[a] First presented in the *Monthly Labor Review* of February, 1948; revised and carried ahead in the *Review* of February, 1951, and May, 1952.

goods, rents and services, payment of personal taxes, Social Security deductions and nominal allowances for occupational expenses and life insurance are included." [1]

We see that the average Chicago Swift-UPWA male worker was $450.29 or 12 per cent below this "modest but adequate" budget of 1949. In addition, our sample shows that 57 per cent of the male workers made less than the plant community male average of $3,154.71. In other words, a majority of the Swift-UPWA workers are more than $450.29 below the budget. The lowest income in our sample was $2,517.72. This man, who worked the full year, was probably on the common labor rate of $1.15 an hour, at that time, and made low premium earnings or overtime. He was a long-service white man and may well have been a janitor. His income was $1,087.28 below the budget, or just 70 per cent of the budget.

While the majority of the Chicago Swift-UPWA workers are living anywhere from 30 per cent to 12 per cent below this City Worker's standard, we estimate that over a third of American urban families are also below the budget.[2] We shall not debate here whether or not the City Worker's Family Budget ought to be a minimum for all workers, or whether it is too high or too low. We simply note that it is a scientific effort to arrive at one "modest but adequate" standard of living, and that the average Swift-UPWA worker lives at another, and definitely lower, standard.

Let us get a brief picture of what standard of living the City Worker's Family Budget provides. It claims to be neither a "subsistence" budget nor a "luxury" budget. It attempts to measure and describe a "modest but adequate" standard of living. It is not "ideal," but represents the actual choices of American families. The family lives in a separate house or apartment, rented, of five rooms. The wife does all the cooking, cleaning, and laundry without paid assistance. The home has a gas stove, refrigerator, washing machine. The diet approximates the recommendations made by the Food and

Nutrition Board of the National Research Council. Meat can be served at dinner several times a week. Clothing allows one heavy suit for the husband every two years and one light one every three years, five shirts and two pairs of shoes each year. For the wife, a heavy coat every four years, four dresses, and three pairs of shoes each year. The budget provides a used automobile, for some, but not all. A trip out of town every three or four years for a vacation is provided. In Chicago, most of the travel is assumed to be by public transportation. A small radio, one daily newspaper, and movies once in two or three weeks are provided. A telephone is not considered essential. Taxes, dues, some private insurance and contributions to churches, and welfare organizations are included.

As for the use of the budget in wage negotiations, we quote the findings of the Presidential Board of Inquiry, Nathan P. Feinsinger, Walter V. Schaefer and Pearce Davis in the Big Four-UPWA wage negotiations of Spring, 1948: "The budget approach involves a consideration of the amount of money necessary to achieve and maintain a particular standard of living. This consideration is a basic premise of the labor movement. Such an approach has been used as a criterion in the enactment of various state minimum wage laws. The same or a related concept lies behind the minimum wage provisions of the federal Fair Labor Standards Act. The union is in part seeking to carry over this governmentally recognized principle into the area of free collective bargaining.

"The Union's approach is not novel. Although wage scales in the United States have not often been tied directly to specific budgets, there has been widespread recognition of the principle, enunciated in 1920 in the Award of the Bituminous Coal Commission, that every industry must support its workers in accordance with the American standard of living. In the present dispute the UPWA has selected the City Worker's Family Budget as its immediate goal in seeking to achieve an 'American standard of living.' " [3]

The Board found that the UPWA's specific demand for a twenty-nine cent general wage increase as necessary to achieve the budget was not supported by conclusive evidence. But the Board did approve of the budget approach in helping determine what a just wage should be.

One final aspect of annual income is worth examining: How do our three variables of sex, race, and length of service affect it? Table 35 gives a suggested answer.

These figures must be interpreted cautiously since the samples for the women

TABLE 35

Estimated average annual total gross income of Chicago Swift-UPWA workers working fifty-two weeks

(Random, stratified samples of 178 employees by sex, race, and service: 1949)

Men			Women	
White	Colored		White	Colored
(25)	(37)	Short-service	(5)	(5)
$3220.63	$2900.02		$2515.12	$2479.87
(20)	(17)	Middle-service	(4)	(5)
$3526.25	2988.60		$2537.43	$2409.39
(34)	(16)	Long-service	(5)	(5)
$3271.19	$3234.67		$3198.63	$2500.88

workers are small and since there is variability in subsample sizes. The numbers in parentheses indicate the size of the subsamples (not proportional since we take only those who worked fifty-two weeks a year). The most obvious difference in this table is between men and women. This is not surprising since (by 1951) the common labor rate for women was ten and one-half cents below that for men, and since women rarely get highly skilled jobs. This differential is quite common, of course, in American industry. We also note that in many cases the white workers make more than the colored. No doubt this difference is partly due to the fact we have already seen; namely, the whites tend to have the more skilled (and higher paying) jobs. Finally we note a difference by length of service. It is quite natural that the older employees, having more time to work up, should have the higher-skilled, and therefore higher-paying, jobs. There is an exception here, though, for the white men of long service. Some of these men are either too old or too infirm to carry the responsibility and work often involved in the highly-skilled jobs (mostly in the mechanical crafts) held by the white men of middle service. This latter group is the highest skilled and highest paid group in the plant community.

(3) HOW SUCCESSFULLY DOES THE INTERNAL SYSTEM OF WAGE LEVELS OPERATE WITHIN THE PLANT COMMUNITY? First, a brief history and description of the system.

Before 1923, in the Swift Chicago plant there was really no system at all. The thousands of different jobs (specialized operations) were haphazardly evaluated and paid for. Often a job rate was the result of a personal agreement with the foreman. An older employee might get more because of his age and service. There was great variation between departments and within departments.

1923. When the Bedaux System was installed in 1923, Swift, operating through the Employees' Representation Plan, also set up an elaborate system of job evaluation. Every job was studied as to the skill, length of training time, manual dexterity, amount of responsibility and working conditions that it required. Then the job was given a value, as a certain percentage of the common-labor jobs in the same department. For instance, in the Hog Dressing Department, the splitter was evaluated at 150 per cent of common labor there. The result was around 1000 job evaluations.

1942–1943. As stated in the first contract between UPWA and Swift & Company: "In accordance with the Directive Order of the National War Labor Board . . . the parties will negotiate . . . with a view towards eliminating intra-plant inequalities between wage rates for individuals and between job classifications . . ." [4] The UPWA felt that in spite of Swift's Job Evaluation System, there were inequities and over-complications. So it pressed for adjustments and Swift agreed to negotiate changes. Differences were to be submitted to the arbitrator.

1945. Wage-rate adjustments were slow and few under the first Directive of the NWLB. So in February, 1945, the NWLB set up a special Meat Packing Commission, under the chairmanship of Clark Kerr, to complete the review of internal wage structures for the Big Five. The Commission tried to be largely advisory. Its purpose was to (a) simplify the existing complex rate structures; (b) standardize the rates (between departments, but also between plants and between companies); (c) eliminate "personalized" rates, preferential rates for single individuals; (d) reëxamine contested rates. The Commission did its job well and 90 per cent of the rates in the entire industry were voluntarily settled by the companies and unions involved. The Commission was dissolved in 1947. Swift and the UPWA agreed in their third contract of 1945–46 to continue their efforts to work out a satisfactory structure and to submit their differences to the Meat Packing Commission. A uniform labor grades system (brackets) was established with approximately twenty-five grades and two and one-half cents intervals. Then the UPWA and Swift began to fit all the many jobs into one or other of these twenty-five grades. A wage increase not to exceed an average of two cents an hour was permitted as a kind of pool on which to draw in adjusting the old rates up or down. By a year or so the entire new bracket system was finally set up. In the future, of course, there will always be some negotiated changes and adjustment, as new jobs in the plant are developed and old jobs abandoned.

1946–1949. A series of flat wage raises were agreed upon by Swift and the UPWA, thus tending to close the accordion of pay between common labor and skilled labor to the dissatisfaction of the latter.

1949. A bracket raise increased the spread between brackets from two and one-half cents to three cents, thus spreading the accordion.

1950. Another flat raise contracted the accordion.

1951. Another bracket raise increased the spread between brackets from three cents to three and one-half cents. The current male labor rates begin at $1.35 an hour for common labor and go up at three and one-half cents intervals through twenty-five steps to $2.19, the top skilled pay.

1952. Around 800 individual job classifications were raised into higher wage brackets.

Secondly, some questions about the Swift-UPWA Internal Wage System:

I. *Are most of the inequities in job rates now settled?* The answer is: Yes. Both union and company representatives are fairly well satisfied. And the workers as shown in our interviews had few complaints. There will always be some dissatisfied people, of course. A cattle "floorsman" might say: "I don't see why that beef-boner should make more than I do," etc., or a loin-puller might say the same about a ham-smoker. Some of these misunderstandings must be related rather to the wage-incentive system, as we have seen, rather than to the bracket system as such. Also due to the constant changes in production methods and jobs, there will always be some alleged inequities to debate about. These are settled by Swift and UPWA Wage Rate Department and at annual contract negotiations, rather than through the grievance procedure.

II. *Is the span of the Bracket System broad enough?* In other words, are the skilled men at the top brackets satisfied that their greater skill and responsibility is being sufficiently rewarded compared with skilled men in other plants and trades and compared with the unskilled work in the Swift plant? This is an important question, for the internal wage system is an essential determinant of status levels. In general, the span does seem broad enough — eighty-four cents in 1951. (We might compare this with the span of $1.55 of thirty-one brackets at five cents each in the steel industry, and the span of seventy cents of fourteen brackets at five cents each in the auto industry.) While the skilled craftsmen were well aware that their rates are below those in the building trades outside, for instance, they were also aware that they work every day in the year with no bothersome layoffs due to bad weather. Also they knew that they had various "fringe" benefits such as an excellent pension program. In general, the skilled men seemed satisfied. The low turnover among them would seem to confirm this. The bracket adjustments of 1949 and 1951 apparently made the skilled men feel that the differential between them and common labor is sufficient. Ideally, if the present differentials are reasonable, every future raise would be also on a bracket, or proportional, basis, and never simply a flat raise. Of course the common laborer does not always understand this reasoning. He may not see that a flat raise gives him a greater proportional raise than it gives the skilled man. And since nearly a third of the work force is unskilled, it has not always been easy for union leaders to sell their membership on the necessity for bracket raises. Then, too, the UPWA has been very much concerned about raising the position of the unskilled workers. But the pattern of all raises being also proportional raises seems to be forming. We recall that the skilled men, especially, the mechanical gangs, have recently been antagonistic to the union. In my opinion, the contracting of the wage accordion due to the UPWA's lesser concern with bracket raises, was one factor (though a minor one) in this antagonism.

III. *Is the number of wage brackets too great or too small?* It is a vast simplification from the old days when half-cent and even quarter-cent steps were not infrequent. Even so, there are many plants with fewer levels, though they doubtless also have simpler operations and less job types. There is no concerted effort on the part of Swift, UPWA or workers to change the number of brackets.

(4) HOW MUCH HAVE REAL EARNINGS AND LABOR'S SHARE OF SWIFT'S TOTAL COSTS VARIED IN THE RECENT UNIONIZED YEARS? We see in Table 36 that in spite of the UPWA's annual presure for wage increases and the frequent raises obtained since the unfreezing of wages after the second World

TABLE 36

Comparative movements of profits, money wages, real wages and labor cost percentages[a]

(*Swift & Company: the entire chain*)

	Profits as per cent of gross sales	Profits as per cent of net worth	Weekly earnings in dollars	Weekly earnings real[b]	labor cost per cent of total sales dollar
1938	.4 (Loss)	1.48 (Loss)	30.35	27.87	12.8
1939	1.1	4.13	30.19	27.87	11.8
1940	1.4	4.28	30.17	30.11	13.1
1941	1.7	6.80	31.80	30.23	11.45
1942	1.2	6.28	35.04	30.05	9.8
1943	1.2	6.23	42.00	33.95	10.3
1944	1.0	5.48	49.66	39.51	11.0
1945	.9	4.29	49.08	38.16	12.3
1946	1.3	5.61	48.05	34.44	12.6
1947	1.6	10.95	57.83	36.23	9.7
1948	1.2	8.56	60.86	35.40	9.6
1949	1.2	7.63	59.65	35.05	10.7
1950	.7	4.77	61.44	35.74	11.1
1951	.5	3.63	70.95	38.23	10.6
1952	.8	6.29	74.47	39.30	11.4

[a] Figures taken from Swift's annual *Report to Employees* and other wage releases and also from the *Monthly Labor Review*. It is important to note that profits here are given after taxes, but earnings before taxes.

[b] Real earnings are based on a comparison with legitimate prices. We should note that some Swift workers, such as Negroes, have had to pay illegitimate, black-market rent prices. For such people these real earnings figures are somewhat inflated.

War, the workers' part of the total cost to the consumer has not increased. If anything, it has declined. But we note an upward trend of real earnings. The war period with its large amount of overtime work is atypical. Profits have declined since the War. This is partly due to the fact that Swift uses the "Lifo" system of accounting. (One effect of Lifo is to lower profits during inflation and raise them during deflation.) Higher taxes, and less cattle slaughtering due to confusion in the administration of price controls, and higher livestock prices, thanks in part to government subsidies to cattle raisers, are also factors in this decline of profits.

In view of the fact that real earnings have risen throughout the Swift chain, we may well ask: Has the UPWA pressure for higher wages stimulated Swift management to more extensive labor-saving methods and machinery through "work simplification" insofar as this is possible in meat processing? The answer, for the Chicago plant at least, seems to be: No. Chicago, being an old and therefore a high-cost plant, has been trying to reduce costs for many years. The best evidence is that UPWA pressure for raises has not greatly affected this trend.

APPENDIX IV

WHAT COMPANY AND UNIONS HAVE DONE FOR THE WORKERS

A historical outline of the principal personnel advantages and their major variations given by Swift & Company either independently or jointly under collective bargaining with the AMC&BW and especially later with the UPWA. Primarily applicable to the Chicago plant community.

1900——1. MEDICAL SERVICE AND HEALTH PROMOTION. Medical treatment office for the occupationally disabled.

1903——2. COLLECTIVE BARGAINING WITH INDEPENDENT UNION. The Amalgamated Meat Cutters and Butcher Workmen is recognized as bargaining agent for the workers and a contract is negotiated.

1904——3. HOURLY WAGES. After panic of 1903 and the strike of 1904, hourly pay cut two and one-half cents to ten cents an hour. AMC&BW grows weak.

1907——1. MEDICAL SERVICE aids EBA with medical examinations.

4. EMPLOYEES' BENEFIT ASSOCIATION (EBA). Low cost accident, health and death benefit insurance protection for employees and families. Entirely contributory.

1910——5. COMPENSABLE ACCIDENT POLICY. Swift pays compensation benefits immediately from date of accident, not waiting seven days as permitted by the new Illinois Workmen's Compensation Act. (This advantage was bargained into the Swift-UPWA contract of 1950.)

1911——6. SAFETY PROGRAM installed to reduce accidents.

1912——7. GUARANTEED PAY-TIME. Forty-five hours of pay guaranteed as 75 per cent of the work week of sixty hours (the ten-hour day for six days).

1913——8. EMPLOYEE PUBLICATIONS. The *Buzzer* published for salaried workers.

9. SICKNESS AND ACCIDENT PAY PLAN. This sickness and accident plan provides one-fourth pay for those employees not occupa-

tionally disabled, in order to wipe out the inequity between those occupational cases and the nonoccupational cases. This plan is entirely noncontributory and was later codified in the Swift-UPWA contract of 1943.

1915——3. HOURLY WAGES. Raise of eight and one-half cents, bringing hourly-rate to eighteen and one-half cents.

10. EMPLOYEE RECREATION PROGRAMS. Financial assistance for employee activities such as clubs, sports, picnics, etc. Also occasional "open house" or family parties on the plant.

11. LEAVE OF ABSENCE POLICY. Leave without pay under certain conditions. (Codified into Swift-UPWA 1942 contract.)

1916——3. HOURLY WAGES. Raises of four cents bring rate to twenty-two and one-half cents an hour.

12. PENSION PLAN. A company-financed, noncontributory pension program put in applying equally to salaried and hourly-paid employees, who have sufficient length of service — at least twenty years before the age of sixty (changed to sixty-five in 1949).

13. PART-PAY FOR EMPLOYEES IN ARMED SERVICES, during annual military training period.

14. EMPLOYEE TRAINING PROGRAMS. Superintendents', sales, employee education courses, such as the Young Men's Training Course, tuition free.

1917——2. COLLECTIVE BARGAINING. The AMC&BW revives and, though not officially recognized, threatens strike for more pay and the eight-hour day.

3. HOURLY WAGES. Raises of five cents bring the common labor rate up to twenty-seven and one-half cents an hour.

15. CENTRALIZED EMPLOYMENT. A specialized recruitment and placement program precluding favoritism.

16. MILITARY SENIORITY POLICY. Maintenance of jobs and seniority for men in the armed services. Later codified in the Swift-UPWA 1942 contract.

1918——2. COLLECTIVE BARGAINING. Judge Alschuler, Federal Administrator for the packing industry appointed by the President of the United States, began here a series of awards affecting the personnel advantages given to the workers in the Chicago plant of Swift & Company.

3. HOURLY WAGES. Alschuler gives awards of twelve and one-half cents raises, brings hourly rate for common labor up to forty cents an hour. Overtime pay granted.

7. GUARANTEED PAY-TIME. Alschuler reduces the guaranteed pay time from forty-five to forty hours a week. This is 83 per cent of the forty-eight hour week, that is the eight-hour day for six days. The work week was reduced from sixty to forty-eight hours.

17. SUNDAY AND HOLIDAY EXTRA PAY POLICY. This is another part of Alschuler Award.

1919——3. HOURLY WAGES. Alschuler award gives more raises of ten cents bringing common labor rate to fifty cents an hour.

18. INDUSTRIAL RELATIONS DEPARTMENT FORMED. Social service and welfare work now begun under the direction of this Department.

1920——3. HOURLY WAGES. Alschuler Award gives further raise of three cents bringing hourly rate to fifty-three cents an hour.

1921——3. HOURLY WAGES. Judge Alschuler ends his term as Federal Administrator. During the Depression of 1921, Swift wishes to cut wages. The AMC&BW strikes and loses. The common labor rate is reduced from fifty-three cents to thirty-seven and one-half cents an hour.

8. EMPLOYEE PUBLICATIONS. The *Swift Arrow* is established, a magazine for all employees to report the proceedings of the ERP and to acquaint the employees with company affairs.

19. EMPLOYEE REPRESENTATION PLAN. This is an effort (experimentally begun at Jersey City in 1916) to obtain collective bargaining, employee representation, and grievance procedure on a company-union basis. Many subsequent personnel advantages will be handled through the ERP.

1923——3. HOURLY WAGES. Raise of five cents an hour brings common labor rate up to forty-two and one-half cents per hour.

20. VACATION POLICY. Vacations with pay for hourly-rated employees came into existence through the ERP. Later this policy was codified in the Swift-UPWA Contracts.

21. SPELL-TIME POLICY. Paid relief periods were begun in many departments of the Chicago plant.

1924——22. SENIORITY POLICY. A plan for departmental and divisional seniority for layoffs is begun. An employee with five years' service cannot be laid off without superintendent making every effort to find another job for him in the plant.

1925——23. SUGGESTION PLAN. Cash awards for those work ideas of the employees that are used.

1926——24. GROUP LIFE INSURANCE PLAN. The EBA members wanted more death benefit protection, so they contracted with the Aetna Life Insurance Company for additional group insurance available only to members of the EBA. The cost is divided between company and employee.

1927——25 JURY AND COURT TIME PAY. Employees serving as jurors or court witnesses receive pay during such service.

1929——3. HOURLY WAGES. Raise of two and one-half cents bringing labor rate to forty-five cents an hour.

26. GROUP HOSPITALIZATION. Blue Cross established in Chicago plant.

1931——1. MEDICAL SERVICE. Further health research on working conditions, silicosis, undulent fever, etc.

3. HOURLY WAGES. Reduction of five cents an hour to forty cents an hour.

27. CREDIT UNIONS. A credit union for the Chicago plant is started with Swift providing free space and time.

1932——3. HOURLY WAGES. Reduction of four cents bringing labor rate to thirty-six cents an hour.

28. SEPARATION ALLOWANCE. Extra pay is given for employees laid off because of the closing down of a department or unit. Later put into Swift-UPWA contract of 1949.

1933——3. HOURLY WAGES. Raises of ten and one-half cents, bringing labor rate up to forty-six and one-half cents.

7. GUARANTEED PAY-TIME. Under the NIRA the forty-hour guar-

anteed pay-time is reduced to thirty-two hours and work week reduced from forty-eight to forty hours.

1934——3. HOURLY WAGES. Raise of three and one-half cents bringing labor rate to fifty cents.

1936——3. HOURLY WAGES. Raise of three and one-half cents bringing rate to fifty-three and one-half cents.

1937——2. COLLECTIVE BARGAINING. The ERP is abandoned and the employee Security League is begun. Likewise, Local Industrial Union #340 (later UPWA Local 28) is chartered by the CIO for Swift-Chicago, has informal dealings with Chicago management, and presses for improvement in seniority provisions.

   3. HOURLY WAGES. Raise of nine cents bringing common labor rate up to sixty-two and one-half cents an hour.

   26. GROUP HOSPITALIZATION PLAN for Chicago plant improved.

   29. AID FOR DEPENDENTS OF NONPENSIONERS. Financial aid is given to families and dependents of deceased employees who are not eligible for pensions.

1938——3. HOURLY WAGES. In compliance with the Fair Labor Standards Act, overtime pay at time and a half is given for work over a forty-hour week or an eight-hour day.

   22. SENIORITY POLICY. Rehiring now on a seniority basis. Plantwide seniority for employees of five years' continuous service and over.

1939——7. GUARANTEED PAY-TIME. A change is made in this plan so that if an employee comes down to work at all on Monday morning, he must be given at least thirty-two hours of pay-time for the week.

   22. SENIORITY POLICY. Plantwide requirement reduced from five years to two years.

1940——30. MILITARY WELFARE PROGRAM. Certain pay benefits, insurance premiums, gift packages, magazines, etc., are supplied to employees in the armed services.

1941——3. HOURLY WAGES. Raises of ten cents, bringing rate up to seventy-two and one-half cents an hour.

   10. EMPLOYEE RECREATION PROGRAM. Additional "open house" and family party programs adopted.

1942——2. COLLECTIVE BARGAINING. The Packinghouse Workers' Organizing Committee of the CIO wins its election in the Chicago plant, is now certified as the exclusive bargaining agency for the employees in place of the old Security League which had been previously abandoned. (*From now on most employee personnel advantages, except pensions, are jointly bargained for by Swift and the UPWA.*)

   3. HOURLY WAGES. Previous overtime pay practice codified. An improvement of five cents an hour extra pay for night work added.

   7. GUARANTEED PAY-TIME. Existing practice codified in contract.

   16. MILITARY SENIORITY POLICY. The practice of 1917 is now codified in the Swift-UPWA 1942 contract.

   17. SUNDAY AND HOLIDAY EXTRA PAY POLICY. Double time is granted for work on Sundays and eight specified holidays.

   20. VACATION POLICY. Existing practice codified in 1942 contract.

   22. SENIORITY POLICY. Existing practices are codified with these

improvements: Seniority is now applied to promotions, and plantwide seniority is more effective, with divisional seniority eliminated.

31. WEDDING PRESENT POLICY. Wedding presents for all employees, hourly-paid as well as salaried, are given to employees with the required length of service.

32. BILATERAL GRIEVANCE PROCEDURE.

33. NO DISCRIMINATION POLICY. While this codifies a clause of the 1921 ERP, it gives additional sanctions for enforcement by the bilateral grievance procedure.

34. REPORTING TIME POLICY. Employees called to work must be provided with four hours of work at least, or equivalent pay in lieu of work.

35. RECALL TIME POLICY. After going home, employees called back to work on the same day get time and a half for all time worked and a minimum of four hours' work.

36. MEAL TIME PAY. Employees required to work more than five consecutive hours without meal period are paid time and a half for time worked in excess of five hours and until meal period provided.

1943——9. SICKNESS AND ACCIDENT PAY PLAN. The existing plan, dating from 1917, improved to give half-pay, and codified in contract.

22. SENIORITY POLICY. The second (unpublished) Swift-UPWA contract added important "waiting list clause" for applicants desiring to enter a certain department from other departments.

36. MEAL TIME PAY. Employees furnished a second meal free under certain conditions of long work.

37. CLOTHES-CHANGING-TIME PAY. Employees paid at regular rate for twelve minutes working time per day allowed for changing clothes.

38. CLOTHES ALLOWANCE PAY. Employees allowed fifty cents a week for furnishing work clothes.

1944——20. VACATION POLICY. Minor improvement in pay.

1945——3. HOURLY WAGES. Intraplant bracket-wage raises made under NWLB.

7. GUARANTEED PAY-TIME. Guaranteed time raised from thirty-two to thirty-six hours per week under NWLB.

20. VACATION POLICY. Improvement in pay.

26. GROUP HOSPITALIZATION. Blue Shield added to Plan for Chicago plant.

39. TOOL AND EQUIPMENT ALLOWANCE. Company to provide knives, hooks, etc., and to allow sharpening, etc., on paid company time.

1946——3. HOURLY WAGES. Two raises totaling twenty-three and one-half cents bring common labor rate up to ninety-six cents an hour. Night work extra pay increased to seven cents an hour.

17. SUNDAY AND HOLIDAY EXTRA PAY POLICY. Improvement so that employee receives pay on the holidays even though he does not work then.

22. SENIORITY POLICY. Layoffs are no longer to interrupt seniority. (No *plantwide* seniority unless employee has two years' seniority, instead of former thirty days.)

1947——3. HOURLY WAGES. Six cents raise bringing rate to $1.02 an hour.

1948——3. HOURLY WAGES. Thirteen cents raise bringing rate to $1.15 an hour.

    12. PENSION PLAN. Certain improvements. Credit for past service and minimum pensions increased.

    17. SUNDAY AND HOLIDAY EXTRA PAY POLICY. Improvement: Pay for work performed on holidays increased from "regular rate" to "double rate" in addition to holiday pay.

1949——3. HOURLY WAGES. Bracket-raises increased spread between job rates from two and one-half cents to three cents thus giving raises to all employees above the common-labor rate.

    9. SICKNESS AND ACCIDENT PAY PLAN. Length of service requirements for immediate sick benefits reduced.

    12. PENSION PLAN. Further improvements in qualification requirements to receive pension.

    27. SEPARATION ALLOWANCE. Codification in the 1949 contract of existing practice dating from 1932.

1950——3. HOURLY WAGES. Raise of eleven cents bringing rate to $1.26 an hour.

    5. COMPENSABLE ACCIDENT POLICY. Swift's practice beginning in 1910 is codified in the 1950 contract.

    20. VACATION POLICY. Improvement of length-of-service requirement.

1951——3. HOURLY WAGES. Raise of nine cents brings hourly rate up to $1.35 an hour. Also a bracket raise makes spread between wage classifications three and one-half cents.

1952——3. HOURLY WAGES. Raises of six and four cents bringing common labor rate to $1.45. Female starting-rate brought up to $1.40, five cents below male rate. 1700 individual job classifications given bracket-raises. Improvements in night premium and vacation pay.

    25. JURY AND COURT TIME PAY. Swift policy of 1927 now put into contract.

    40. STANDARDS OUTPUT PREMIUMS. Premium earnings now computed on the basis of 100 per cent of the applicable hourly rate (instead of 75 per cent).

This historical outline finds forty major personnel advantages coming to the workers of the Swift-UPWA industrial plant community. We have given only the major advantages and their most important changes, omitting details.

Most of these advantages were given independently by Swift & Company. Many were wrought out jointly in collective bargaining. The first UPWA-Swift contract of 1942 did codify many benefits previously existing. On the other hand, it (and the subsequent contracts) also added many advantages. It is difficult to see how many of these advantages Swift would have given completely on its own initiative, and how many were stimulated by the challenge of the AMC&BW, the UPWA and other unions or by the persuasion of government legislation. All these factors have been at work together over the last fifty years. There is one outstanding benefit, Swift's noncontributory pension program, that was far ahead of its time, dating from 1916. This was spontaneously given and is not in the Swift-UPWA contract, or any other labor union contract.

This outline shows us clearly how much the position of the packinghouse worker has improved since 1900.

APPENDIX V

Statistical tables

TABLE A

F-ratios*

Source of variance	Degrees of freedom	Attitude toward the					
		Company	Foreman	Job	Union	Union leadership	Participation in union
Between sexes	1	[6.78]† 10.0757	(3.90)‡ 6.1581	[6.78]† 16.5535	(3.90)‡ 5.9242	0.1707	(3.90)‡ 4.7270
Between races	1	0.0570	0.6107	0.7079	[6.78]† 10.8411	[6.78]† 14.1770	[6.78]† 47.8867
Among service length	2	(3.05)‡ 3.5464	0.2004	0.2517	(3.05)‡ 3.4117	(3.05)‡ 3.5905	2.9224
Sex-race interaction	1	1.5431	1.0306	0.0074	0.0710	2.2236	0.0086
Race-Service interaction	2	2.5965	1.6127	0.5338	0.0862	0.2363	2.0087
Sex-service interaction	2	0.2013	1.1484	0.4822	(3.05)‡ 3.2444	0.3189	0.1564
Sex-race-service interaction	2	0.4177	0.9830	0.4435	0.6032	0.0943	0.3050
Residual	180	0.3646	0.5458	0.4708	1.3751	1.3447	1.2569

* F-ratios from Snedecor, G. W., "Statistical Methods" (see his Chapter 11 for a discussion of analysis of variance.)
† = 1% level or 99% F-ratio
‡ = 5% level or 95% F-ratio

TABLE B

Company allegiance
(*Analysis of variance table*)

Source of variance	Sum squares	Degrees of freedom	Mean square
Between sexes	3.6736	1	3.6736
Between races	0.0208	2	0.0208
Among length service	2.5859	2	1.2930
Sex-race interaction	0.5626	1	0.5626
Race-service interaction	1.8933	2	0.9467
Sex-service interaction	0.1468	2	0.0734
Sex-race-service interaction	0.3045	2	0.1523
Residual	65.6250	180	0.3646
Total	74.8125	191	

TABLE C

Attitude toward the job
(*Analysis of variance table*)

Source of variance	Sum squares	Degrees of freedom	Mean square
Between sexes	7.7934	1	7.7934
Between races	0.3333	1	0.3333
Among length service	0.2370	2	0.1185
Sex-race interaction	0.0070	1	0.0035
Race-service interaction	0.5026	2	0.2513
Sex-service interaction	0.4540	2	0.2270
Sex-race-service interaction	0.4176	2	0.2088
Residual	84.7499	180	0.4708
Total	94.4948	191	

TABLE D

Attitude toward the foremen
(*Analysis of variance table*)

Source of variance	Sum squares	Degrees of freedom	Mean square
Between sexes	3.3611	1	3.3611
Between races	0.3333	1	0.3333
Among length service	0.2188	2	0.1094
Sex-race interaction	0.5625	1	0.5625
Race-service interaction	1.7604	2	0.8802
Sex-service interaction	1.2535	2	0.6268
Sex-race-service interaction	1.0730	2	0.5365
Residual	98.2499	180	0.5458
Total	106.8125	191	

TABLE E

Union allegiance
(Analysis of variance table)

Source of variance	Sum squares	Degrees of freedom	Mean square
Between sexes	8.1463	1	8.1463
Between races	14.9076	1	14.9076
Among length service	9.3828	2	4.6914
Sex-race interaction	0.0976	1	0.0976
Race service interaction	0.2370	2	0.1185
Sex-service interaction	8.9227	2	4.4614
Sex-race-service interaction	1.6589	2	0.8295
Residual	247.5104	180	1.3751
Total	290.8633	181	

TABLE F

Attitude toward local union leaders
(Analysis of variance table)

Source of variance	Sum squares	Degrees of freedom	Mean square
Between sexes	0.2296	1	0.2296
Between races	19.0638	1	19.0638
Among length service	9.6563	2	4.8282
Sex-race interaction	2.9901	1	2.9901
Race-service interaction	0.6354	2	0.3177
Sex-service interaction	0.8576	2	0.4288
Sex-race-service interaction	0.2535	2	0.1268
Residual	242.0520	180	1.3447
Total	275.7383	191	

TABLE G

Participation in the union
(Analysis of variance table)

Source of Variance	Sum squares	Degrees of freedom	Mean square
Between sexes	5.9414	1	5.9414
Between races	60.1888	1	60.1888
Among length service	7.3464	2	3.6732
Sex-race interaction	0.0108	1	0.0108
Race-service interaction	5.0494	2	2.5247
Sex-service interaction	0.3932	2	0.1966
Sex-race-service interaction	0.7667	2	0.3834
Residual	226.2395	180	1.2569
Total	305.9362	191	

TABLE H

Sample of the analysis of variance design and attitude scores for union allegiance

	Negro						White					
	Male			Female			Male			Female		
	Short	Med.	Long	Short	Med.	Long	Short	Med.	Long	Short	Med.	Long
	1	1.5	4	1	2.5	5	3	5	1.5	2	1.5	2.5
	2	1	1	1	2	2	2.5	2	5	5	2.5	4
	2	2	1	2	5	4.5	1	2	2	1.5	2	3
	1.5	2.5	1	2	1	4	2	1	1	4.5	2	5
	2.5	2	1	2.5	1	5	2	3	3	2	2	1
	2.5	2	2	2.5	1	1	1.5	3	1	3	1	5
	1	1	1.5	1	1	2	2	1	3	1	4	2
	1	5	3				2	1.5	3	2	2	5
	3	3	4				4	2	2			
	1	1	1.5				1	1	4			
	2	1	1				1	2	1			
	2	2	4.5				2	5	5			
	2	1.5	1				2	5	2			
	1	2	1				1	3	1.5			
	1.5	2	1				2	2	2			
	2	2	1				1	2	2			
	2	1	2.5				2	2	2			
	2	1	1.5				1	1	1			
	2	2	2				5	1	5			
	3	1	5				1	2.5	1			
	1	1	1				5	4	3			
	1	1	1				2.5	2	3			
							1.5	2	1			
								2	4			
	41.0	38.5	44.5	14.0	14.5	25.5	50.0	57.0	59.0	21.0	17.0	27.5
	1.71	1.60	1.85	1.75	1.81	3.19	2.08	2.38	2.46	2.63	2.13	3.44

NOTES

CHAPTER ONE: BACKDROP AND PROPS

1. See St. Thomas Aquinas, *On the Governance of Rulers*, trans. Gerald B. Phelan (New York: Sheed and Ward, 1938).

2. The department is not a real governing unit since the grievance procedure cuts across departmental lines and since plant-wide seniority puts the department in some state of flux. The department as a "primary group" is an important social unit in the plant community, for it is here that individuals make their friends, have their cliques, and achieve their status, but it is not really a governing unit.

3. *Census of Manufactures, 1947*, U. S. Government Printing Office (Washington, D. C., 1950), vol. I, General Summary. Dividing the total number of production workers by the number of establishments (plants) we arrive at a figure for the size of the average plant community. Supervision and some management employees should be added to give a more accurate picture. The average number of production workers per plant for all manufacturing was around 60 employees; for the food industry, 27 employees; for food plants "adding most value per product" (because of the extent of their manufacturing operations), 100–250 employees; for wholesale meatpacking, 80 employees; for wholesale meatpacking "adding the most value," 1000–2499 employees (35 plants); for basic metals, 180 employees; for basic metals "adding the most value," 2500 and over.

4. *Swift & Company Master Agreement with United Packinghouse Workers of America*, 1950–1952, paragraph 10.

5. Peter F. Drucker, *The New Society* (New York: Harper and Brothers, 1950), p. 146.

6. John Holmes, *Message to Swift & Company Shareholders* (January 20, 1949), Company pamphlet, p. 9.

7. Constitution of Swift Local 28, UPWA-CIO, 1943.

8. E. Wight Bakke, *Mutual Survival, The Goal of Unions and Management* (New York: Harper and Brothers, 1946).

9. Drucker, *op. cit.*, pp. 146–148.

10. Solomon Barkin, "A Trade Unionist Appraises Management Personnel Philosophy," *Harvard Business Review* (September, 1950), p. 63.

11. Company Executive E. See Note 15.

12. Carroll R. Daugherty and John B. Parrish, *The Labor Problems of American Society* (Boston: Houghton Mifflin Co., 1952), p. 494.

13. Robert Wood Johnson, "Human Relations in Modern Business," *Harvard Business Review*, vol. XXVII, no. 5 (September, 1949), p. 533.

14. Statistical Tables, see Appendix V.

15. In all the interviews fictitious names are used, except for a few union and management leaders who have given permission to be identified. Moreover, details that might identify the workers have been changed. The italics are sometimes ours, sometimes the workers' emphasis. These unpublished coded interviews are deposited in the files of the Department of Psychology of Loyola University of Chicago. Permission to inspect them should be sought from the author and the department chairman.

16. There is no strict, equal-unit continuum between "very favorable" and "very unfavorable," as the use of the numbers might imply. "Very favorable" does not necessarily differ from "favorable" by exactly the same "distance" (namely, "one") as "unfavorable" differs from "very unfavorable." Although the interviewer must do his best to achieve exactness in his evaluation and treat the scale as if it were a mathematical continuum, it cannot of course be taken as a precise evaluation. In conjunction with the qualitative evaluation of the interviews, however, the scale can give new insights into the meaning of the data. We have used it in the analysis of variance, in scatter-diagrams and in rank correlation.

17. Talcott Parsons and E. A. Shils, editors, *Towards a General Theory of Action* (Cambridge: Harvard University Press, 1951), p. 372.

CHAPTER TWO: PARENT PLANT AND WORKER POPULATION

1. For the dramatic story of Swift's role in the "refrigerator car revolution," see C. E. Russell, *The Greatest Trust in the World* (New York: Ridgway-Thayer Co., 1905), pp. 23–25. (First published in serial form in *Everybody's Magazine.*)

2. Interview with Harold H. Swift, Summer, 1950.

3. Louis F. Swift, *The Yankee of the Yards* (Chicago and New York: A. W. Shaw Co., 1928), pp. 36–37.

4. Cf. R. A. Clemen, *American Livestock and Meat Industry* (New York: The Ronald Press, 1923), p. 803.

5. Swift & Company figures.

6. This is my estimate. As will be seen in Table 8, *Chicago Plant Turnover*, p. 35, 35 per cent of the hourly-paid employees got layoffs during 1951. Hence we might say that not more than 65 per cent nor less than 40 per cent received fifty-two pay-checks a year. Some men, however, choose to take a layoff rather than a job offered in another department, hence they could have received fifty-two pay-checks. Thus we could raise the figure 65 per cent. On the other hand, some of the 65 per cent are those who quit or were discharged or who retired or died and were not eligible to receive fifty-two paychecks a year. From this, we could lower the figure 65 per cent. 1951 was an atypical year because of the cattle shortages due to price control confusion. Our estimate of two-thirds to three-fourths is fairly good.

7. Cf. Charles R. Walker, *Steeltown* (New York: Harper and Brothers, 1950), p. 72.

8. U. S. Bureau of Labor Bulletin, No. 56 (January, 1905) letter of Commissioner to the President on Influence of Trade Unions on Immigrants.

9. Eleventh Census of the United States, 1890, i, pp. 650–651.

10. *The Chicago Tribune,* July 15, 1894, p. 3. *The Chicago Herald,* July 17, 1894, p. 8. *The Chicago Record,* July 18, 1894, p. 2. Gunnar Myrdal, *An American Dilemma* (New York: Harper and Brothers, 1944), p. 1123. (This book is the most comprehensive study done on the American Negro.)

11. *The Negro in Chicago,* The Chicago Commission on Race Relations (University of Chicago Press, 1922), p. 430. Myrdal, *op. cit.,* p. 1123.

12. *The Negro in Chicago,* p. 79.

13. St. Clair Drake and Horace R. Cayton, *Black Metropolis* (New York: Harcourt, Brace & Co., 1945), p. 58.

14. Statement to Chicago Commission on Race Relations, MS, August 16, 1920, pp. 59–61.

15. *The Negro in Chicago*, pp. 363–364.

16. These proportions are subject to some sampling error, but they are substantially correct.

17. Tardiness is no great problem and a study of it is not useful to us here. Excessive tardiness is controlled by penalizing the employee a certain amount of time and pay.

18. Because the subsample sizes in this table vary, these subgroups are not strictly comparable. These percentages are to be taken as suggestive only. They show the percentage of those who worked any period less than fifty-two weeks (including paid vacation) during the year. Almost none of these absences can be accounted for by layoffs since all these workers have at least two years' seniority and as such are almost immune from layoffs. Likewise the number of disciplinary layoffs is small. Most of these absences are due to sickness, a few to leaves of absence requested (without pay) by the employee, and the remaining are just unexplained failures to report for work.

19. Jack Filas.

20. G. W. M. Hart, "Industrial Relations Research and Social Theory," *The Canadian Journal of Economics and Political Science*, XV, February, 1949.

21. For a description of the former social conditions back-of-the-yards, see C. J. Bushnell, *The Social Problem at the Chicago Stock Yards* (University of Chicago Press, 1902); S. P. Breckinridge and E. Abbot, "Housing Conditions in Chicago, 1911, III: Back of the Yards," *American Journal of Sociology*, XVI, 433–468; H. E. Wilson, *Mary McDowell Neighbor* (University of Chicago Press, 1928), chaps. ii, iii, iv; Mary McDowell, "A Woman's Story," *Official Journal*, AMC & BWNA, April, 1904, V, no. 11, p. 25.

22. J. B. Martin, "Certain Wise Men," *McCall's Magazine*, March, 1949, p. 20.

23. Joseph Meegan, "A Decade of Progress," pamphlet of BYC, Chicago, 1950, p. 1.

24. Interview with Agnes E. Meyer, as published in a series of articles in *The Washington Post*, June 4–9, 1945.

25. "Urban League Told Negro Rent Woes," Article in the *Chicago Daily News*, February 8, 1951.

26. Drake and Cayton, *op. cit.*, p. 790. (This is the best study on Bronzeville.)

27. Elected President of the Chicago Chapter of left-wing National Lawyers Guild, 1951.

28. Neighborhood Leader B.

CHAPTER THREE: UNIONS PAST AND PRESENT

1. H. A. Millis and R. E. Montgomery, *Organized Labor* (New York: McGraw-Hill Book Co., 1945), p. 66.

2. Samuel Gompers, *Seventy Years of Life and Labor* (New York: E. P. Dutton and Co., 1925), p. 178.

3. John R. Commons, *et al.*, *History of Labor in the United States* (New York: Macmillan Co., 1926), p. 419. Also see Selig Perlman, *A History of Trade Unionism in the United States* (New York: Macmillan Co., 1923), pp. 97–98.

4. Powderly was said to have been influenced by a Catholic priest, Rev. P. M. Flannigan, to call off the strike. Powderly himself denied this. For a discussion of the issue, with pertinent references, see Henry J. Browne, *The*

Catholic Church and the Knights of Labor (Washington, D. C.: Catholic University of America Press, 1949), p. 206.

5. Alma Herbst, *The Negro in the Slaughtering and Meatpacking Industry in Chicago* (Boston: Houghton Mifflin, 1932), p. 17 n.

6. Herbst, *op. cit.*, p. 18. Also see accounts in *The Chicago Tribune, The Chicago Record, The Chicago Herald,* and *The Chicago Times* during July and August 1894, which give substantially the same report as Herbst.

7. *Ibid.*

8. *The Chicago Times,* July 19, 1894, p. 1.

9. *The Daily Inter-Ocean,* July 2, 1894, p. 12.

10. Harper Leech and John C. Carrol, *Armour and His Times* (New York: Appleton and Century Co., 1938), p. 230. See also Swift's strike strategy as seen through the eyes of his eldest son: Louis F. Swift, *The Yankee of the Yards* (Chicago and New York: A. W. Shaw Co., 1928), pp. 180–183.

11. Commons, *op. cit.*, p. 504.

12. *Official Journal,* vol. II, no. 35.

13. *Ibid.*

14. Mary E. McDowell, "How Casual Work Undermines Family and Neighborhood Life," *Proceedings of National Conference of Charities and Correction* (Buffalo, 1909), p. 150.

15. *The Chicago Daily News,* July 29, 1904, p. 3.

16. *Ibid.*, August 4, 1904, p. 1.

17. *The Chicago Tribune,* July 25, 1904 and July 26, 1904, p. 2. *The Inter-Ocean,* July 30, 1904, p. 2. *The Chicago Tribune,* July 24, 1904, p. 2 has the following account: "RUSHING MEN TO STOCKYARDS. PACKERS MAKING ELABORATE PLANS TO OPERATE PLANTS WITH NON-UNION FORCE. At the Stockyards yesterday, preparations for a long struggle were being made by both sides. . . . The Armour and Swift plants had forces of carpenters working all day putting up bunks in four tiers for the accommodation of the strikebreakers. . . . At noon a train containing 185 strikebreakers arrived at the Yards and the men were distributed among the Swift, Armour and Morris plants. . . . Shortly before midnight last night, four trains loaded with Negroes came from the South where they had been engaged by the Packer's agents. There were 1400 men on the cars. In addition to the laborers, there were 200 butchers picked up at various towns along the way.

"When the trains bearing the non-union men reached Chicago, they were switched to the tracks of the Lake Shore Railroad and taken into the Yards in old cars in anticipation of an attack that might damage the rolling stock.

"All the Companies affected by the strike shared the expenses of the enterprise, and the men were equally divided between the plants." (A picture of Negro workers escorted by police is on page three.)

For other accounts of Negroes in this strike see also Herbst, *op. cit.*, p. 25, and John R. Commons, "Labor Conditions in Meat Packing and the Recent Strike," *Quarterly Journal of Economics,* XIX, no. 1, November, 1904, p. 30.

18. John R. Commons, *Trade Unionism and Labor Problems* (Boston: Ginn and Company, 1905), p. 222.

19. *Monthly Labor Review,* February, 1921, p. 23 and March, p. 41.

20. William Z. Foster, "How Life Has Been Brought Into the Stock Yards," *Life and Labor,* April, 1918.

21. R. A. Clemen, *The American Livestock and Meat Industry* (New York: The Ronald Press, 1923), pp. 716–717. (Italics ours.)

22. Arthur Kampfert, "History of Meat Packing, Slaughtering and Unionism," MS, Part II, p. 35.

23. Lewis Corey, *Meat and Man* (New York: Viking Press, 1950), p. 287. (Corey seems well-informed regarding the affairs of the various packing unions.)

24. St. Clair Drake and Horace R. Cayton, *Black Metropolis*, p. 304.

25. S. D. Spero and A. L. Harris, *The Black Worker* (New York: Columbia University Press, 1931), p. 272.

26. Excerpts from letters and messages as investigated from Swift files by the Federal Trade Commission in 1919.

27. Swift figures. See also, *The Negro in Chicago*, The Chicago Commission on Race Relations, p. 361, which gives a 1920 figure for Swift of 2278 Negroes.

28. Clemen, *op. cit.*, p. 740.

29. Kampfert, *op. cit.*, Part II, 92.

30. Clemen, *op. cit.*, p. 741.

31. *The Chicago Daily Tribune,* December 8, 1921.

32. Kampfert, *op. cit.*, Part II, p. 93.

33. *The Chicago Daily Tribune,* March 13, 1921.

34. Spero and Harris, *op. cit.*, p. 281.

35. Kampfert, *op. cit.*, Part III, p. 38.

36. Copy of a letter sent to all Swift managers and superintendents by Harold Swift, at that time Vice-President of Industrial Relations.

37. *People's Press*, Packinghouse Workers Edition, November 6, 1937.

38. Interview, Summer, 1951.

39. *People's Press*, November 13, 1937, p. 10.

40. Interview, Spring, 1952.

41. Kampfert, *op. cit.*, Part II, pp. 6–8.

42. Interview, Spring, 1952.

43. National Labor Relations Board, Case No. XIII–C–1187, Swift and Local 28 of the PWOC-CIO, April 17, 1940. The Board took no action here, but the "parties . . . determined to adjust amicably the matter without further action."

44. The important certification election was held on January 9, 1942. There were 5787 eligible to vote, and a high proportion (80 per cent) or 4628 people voted. The results were: CIO, 2662; Independent Union, 1180; neither, 660; challenged ballots, 58; void ballots, 45; blank ballots, 23.

45. Interview, Summer, 1951.

46. Interview, Summer, 1951.

47. *The Butcher Workman,* May, 1948, p. 13. Also recorded by Labor Detail of Chicago Police.

48. Swift release. See *The Chicago Daily News* and *The Chicago Daily Tribune,* March 15, 1948. On March 15, 1948 the UPWA proposed that the dispute be arbitrated by the U. S. Conciliation Service. Swift refused this and countered with the suggestion that an impartial vote be taken, in which the employees would be able to express a preference either for accepting the Company's 9-cent offer, or for striking. This the UPWA refused. Incidentally, as far as arbitration is concerned, it is interesting to note that the shoe was on the other foot in 1904. Swift attorney, A. F. Evans, stated at the outbreak of the 1904 strike: "We offered arbitration. . . . That was a fair proposition certainly, and there should be no objection to it by the Union men." Donnelly was at first cool to arbitration. See *The Chicago Tribune,* July 13, 1904, p. 2.

49. *The Chicago Tribune,* March 16, 1948.

50. "Report to the President on the Labor Dispute in the Meat Packing Industry by the Board of Inquiry," April 8, 1948, Chicago, Ill., MS.

51. The union had used the BLS City Workers' Family Budget in the presentation of its case. The Packers did not want to accept this. But the Board found that "a budget approach to wage determination is not invalid or unprecedented. The Union could properly offer it for consideration as a criterion for resolving this dispute." See Appendix III, "How Well Are They Paid?"

52. "Report to the President . . . ," op. cit., p. 92.

53. Joseph Gallista, 1937; Owensby Lee, 1938–1942; Philip Weightman, 1942–1944; Sol Hawkins, 1945; Stanley Piontek, 1945–1946; Andrew Pitts, 1947–1949; John Lewis, 1949–1952; Howard Pratt, 1952–   .

54. Ted Kurowsky.

55. UPWA-CIO Local 28 v. Richard Criley, Educational Director of the District, Manuscript of trial reporter, Chicago, September 25, 1946, p. 123.

56. Proceedings, Illinois State Industrial Union Council, CIO, Seventh Constitutional Convention, December 9–11, 1949, Chicago, Illinois, p. 147.

57. The Cleaver, issued by Local 347, UPWA-CIO, November 4, 1949.

58. Most of the organizations listed here can be found in pamphlets of the United States House of Representatives' Un-American Activities Committee on Subversive Organizations and Current "Peace" Movements, and also in the U. S. Attorney General's subversive organizations lists.

59. The Flash, June 6, 1950.

60. The controversial Resolution no. 18 was passed by the Convention. It read as follows:

Whereas: On many occasions the Congress of Industrial Organizations has pointed out that the Communist Party is attempting to take over and control the Trade Union Movement in all countries; and

Whereas: The Congress of Industrial Organizations in convention assembled has taken action to expel those unions affiliated to it, who have allowed themselves to come under the domination and control of the Communist Party:

Therefore be it resolved that this Seventh Constitutional Convention of the UPWA go on record as endorsing the actions of the CIO; and

Be it Further Resolved that we pledge our full support to all CIO sponsored unions in the jurisdiction of the expelled organizations whose purpose it is to reorganize our brothers into free democratic trade unions.

— Proceedings, Seventh Constitutional Convention, UPWA-CIO, Minneapolis, May 25–28, 1950, p. 222.

61. The Negro in Chicago, op. cit., p. 424.

62. See Wilson Record, The Negro and the Communist Party (Chapel Hill, N. C.: University of North Carolina Press, 1951). Also, William A. Nolan, S.J., Communism vs. the Negro (Chicago: The Henry Regnery Co., 1951).

CHAPTER FOUR: THE COMPANY AND THE MEN

1. The psychological thinking of this and the following chapters focuses on two important areas of social psychological theory: "attitudes" and "motivation." Since we are not trying to reformulate basic social psychological theory in this research, but rather to test present theory by field observations, we shall not go into any theoretical detail at this point. We simply call attention to the fact that this study is based on a more or less eclectic synthesis of

such writers on attitude and motivation as: Allers, Allport, Bartlett, Bruner, Krech and Crutchfield, Herr, Lewin, T. V. Moore, and Woodworth. For us, Allport's definition of attitude is useful: "An attitude is a mental and neural state of readiness, organized through experience, exerting a directive or dynamic influence upon the individual's response to all objects and situations with which it is related." (See G. W. Allport, "Attitudes," in *The Nature of Personality* (Cambridge: Addison-Wesley, 1950).

2. See Tables A, B, Appendix V for analysis of variance data.

3. Washington Hubbard, Potter Treadwell and Bunny Roberts.

4. Swift began a seniority plan in 1924, improved it in 1938 and again in the first contract of 1942. (See Appendix IV.) However, the UPWA stimulated other improvements in seniority and made the plan more effective. Henry Schoenstein remarks that seniority was the local's major objective. In an interview in the Spring of 1951 he said that seniority was not too effective in the old days because it could be abused at the plant level. He states that the union stimulated the important plant-wide clause of 1938:

"The foreman who had a pet would tell him to take off a week sick, instead of being in the plant on the day of the layoff. *In that way, the foreman could avoid laying off by seniority one of his pets. There were no published lists.* You just took their word. Though the E.R.P. would check. It happened all the time. Why we had men of 8 and 10 years' service but no seniority or vacations because they would get a layoff for 31 days or more. The foreman would do that to keep certain men from vacations or building up seniority.

"Departmental seniority was on paper only. There were no transfers that I remember from one department to another in the same Division following seniority — which would be divisional seniority. Instead you got a layoff. You would come the next day and get rehired like anybody else. They would come and holler at the Employment Office: 'Got any coopers here?' 'Got any butchers here?' If you had your layoff slip you would get first choice — provided the foreman hadn't given somebody a special letter privately. There was lots of 'letter hiring' and 'telephone hiring': 'Fix this guy up,' etc.

"In 1937, our PWOC Committee (Local #340) won a seniority policy. *Now we got notices put on the bulletin boards, at least in the Pork Block.* We wanted the company to keep butchers there even on non-butcher jobs, so you would have them around. So divisional seniority was now practiced for the first time."

Interviewer: What about Swift's plan of plant-wide seniority put in by the company in 1938?

Schoenstein: It worked for those who did have five years' continuous service. *But, because of the 31 day breaks, few got up to five years' service.* There were many colored on the cutting and trimming floors who did not have seniority although they were on the plant for as much as 8 years . . . *Then that seniority requirement about rehiring was stimulated by our PWOC Committee.* If people like Vic Kustush hadn't been raising cain, they wouldn't have done it. You'd have to be in the Employment Office to see it. It worked all right. But you had to supervise it close . . . *Then too that "transfer clause of seniority"* (a clause entitling a worker to get his name on a waiting list for a job in a better department), *that was due to the PWOC.* It was the instrument of getting the colored into the mechanical gangs.

5. We shall see Mr. Hahn's views on these ceilings in the next chapter.

CHAPTER FIVE: THE WORK AND THE MEN

1. See Tables A, C, Appendix III, for analysis of variance data.
2. John Wambuck.
3. Pete Savko.
4. With his permission, Mr. James Johnson is identified here.
5. It is important to distinguish policy at top-management level from practice at the plant level. They are by no means the same thing. A foreman or a higher supervisor could discriminate without the top levels knowing anything about it. That some discrimination has occurred at the plant level is irrefutable. Even as late as 1950 a grievance involving employment office discrimination in hiring was decided in favor of the union by Arbitrator Seward.
6. Company Executive D. He means that the directors would just as soon fully integrate Negroes, but that white employees would not accept them.
7. Agnes Kiela.
8. Estelle Bolduc.

CHAPTER SIX: THE MEN AND THEIR FOREMEN

1. Thus F. L. Roethlisberger considered the average wartime foreman. "The Foreman: Master and Victim of Double Talk," *Harvard Business Review,* XXIII, no. 3, Spring, p. 283.
2. While the Swift-UPWA contract prescribes a grievance procedure channeled through the foreman and steward, it does not explicitly forbid other channels made possible by the so-called "open-door policy."
3. See Tables A, D, Appendix V, for analysis of variance data.
4. Charles Sucholdolski.
5. Francis Duma.
6. Sam Chavez.
7. B stands for Bedaux, a time-study engineer whose system forms the basis of the Swift Standards System. Swift Standards will be explained in Chapter XI.
8. The Chicago Commission on Race Relations found the following results in 1920. Interviewing 101 Chicago-area employers, they found 71 who considered the Negro equally as efficient as the white worker, 22 who considered the Negro less efficient, and 8 who had no comment. *The Negro in Chicago,* p. 374. The Commission concludes: "Despite occasional statements that the Negro is slow or shiftless, the volume of evidence before the Commission shows that Negroes are satisfactory employees and compare favorably with other groups." P. 378.

CHAPTER SEVEN: THE UNION AND THE MEN

1. See Tables A, E, Appendix V, for analysis of variance data.
2. Here we are using "status" in a broader sense than the anthropological usage we took for discussing the status system of the Chicago plant in Chapter Three. Here we mean not only the worker's formal and informal level of authority, but also his importance and his value as seen by himself and others.
3. Frank Goff.
4. *Ibid.*
5. Philip Kostka.
6. Harvey Taylor.

CHAPTER EIGHT: THE UNION LEADERS

1. See Tables A, F, Appendix V, for analysis of variance data.
2. Bernice Callaway.
3. Shirley Tisdell.
4. A random, unstratified sample of 104 workers gives 8.1 average years of formal education.

CHAPTER NINE: HOW THE MEN PARTICIPATE IN LOCAL 28

1. E. Wight Bakke, *Obstacles to Labor and Management Peace*, Reprint no. 6 (New Haven: The Economic and Business Foundation, 1947), p. 8.
2. Frank Tannenbaum, "The Social Function of Trade Unionism," *Political Science Quarterly* (New York: Columbia University, June 1947). See also Tannenbaum's stimulating, *A Philosophy of Labor* (New York: Alfred A. Knopf, 1951).
3. Our thinking in this chapter has been influenced by Gordon Allport's chapter: "The Psychology of Participation" in *The Nature of Personality* (Cambridge: Addison-Wesley, 1950). However, we are not taking "participation" here in Allport's sense of real "ego-involvement."
4. See Tables A, G, Appendix V, for analysis of variance data.
5. Based on figures published in the *Flash* of "total ballots cast," and also on the number of men on union checkoff. Voting percentages may be slightly inflated.
6. Since we have discussed how the union members participate in the union part of the plant community, it is relevant to inquire about the participation of the shareholders in their part, namely, in the management. Neither numbers nor political ability, but rather managerial ability and determined work secure control over Swift management. Of the 64,000 owners of Swift & Company including individuals, institutions, associations and 5100 Swift employees, 75 per cent of the proxies were voted for the directors in the annual election of 1950. However, this is hardly a political election since there was no opposing slate of candidates or managerial platform. Nor did the stockholders probably vote in an informed way. If dividends are being paid steadily, the average stockholder does not concern himself with the policies of the men who manage his property. Swift & Company has paid good dividends for the past fifty years, omitting payment only once during the depression year of 1933. Hence, it is doubtful that many Swift stockholders, in 1950, bothered to inform themselves about either the men or the policies supported by their proxies. Such proxy voting is usually a mere formality. In fact, often a bank investment trust or broker will vote the owner's proxy for him, he paying no attention whatsoever. Only if dividends were to cease or markedly diminish would the stockholder electorate rekindle its interest and begin to exercise an informed responsibility over the administration of its property.

As far as stockholder participation is concerned, about 600 people, or nine-tenths of one per cent attended the annual stockholders' meeting of 1950. The thirteen Swift directors may be said to be the "inner cell" of management control. They are two-hundredths of one per cent of the number of stockholders. Top management, or the "leadership core," is about the same. All this, of course, is typical of most large modern American corporations. I simply mention it here, because if we are talking about participation in the union, it is pertinent to talk about participation in management too. Clearly the union and the company are not the same kind of societies. But does the corporation's lack of real stockholder participation and peculiar political structure without political parties and popular suffrage indicate the need for the union to provide the political structure demanded by the plant community?

7. See A. A. Imberman, "Labor Leaders and Society," *Harvard Business Review,* XXVIII, no, 1, January 1950, p. 52. Among others, Patrick Gorman, Secretary-Treasurer of the Amalgamated Meat Cutters AFL, wrote sharp disagreement with some of the conclusions of this article. For an interesting description of the personalities, activities, and problems of local union leaders, see George Strauss and Leonard R. Sayles, "The Unpaid Local Leader," *Harvard Business Review,* XXX, no. 3, May–June, 1952, pp. 91–104, and also their recent book published by Harper and Brothers.

8. Harold Waite.

9. Arthur Kampfert, "History of Meat Packing, Slaughtering and Unionism," MS, Parts III and IV.

10. Philip Weightman.

11. Ford Bartlett.

12. Ted Kurowsky.

13. Philip Weightman.

14. Stanley Koslasky.

15. Clara Hughes.

CHAPTER TEN: GRIEVANCE PROCEDURE

1. *Swift & Company Master Agreement with United Packinghouse Workers of America,* CIO, 1950–1952, p. 49.

2. *Ibid.,* p. 52.

3. *Ibid.,* p. 3.

4. *Ibid.,* p. 51.

5. *Ibid.,* p. 51.

6. *Ibid.,* p. 52.

7. Union Leader G.

8. Philip Montgomery.

9. *Swift-UPWA contract, op. cit.,* p. 49.

10. Thomas Newcomb.

11. Thomas Newcomb.

12. Union Leader G.

13. Thomas Newcomb.

14. Union Leader E.

15. Excerpts from "Changing Concepts of Industrial Relations," a talk at University of Chicago, December 13, 1948, and "Negotiating and Administering the Labor Agreement," a talk at the University of Illinois, March 27, 1947. Mr. North also made the following interesting comment on the annual contract negotiations:

> Today, in negotiations — and this is not intended as a matter of criticism either of labor or of management — we are going through what I call the "legalistic" phase of human relations. It is an evidence of a lack of confidence on the part of management in labor and on the part of labor in management which has tended to cause labor agreements to become too much like legal documents which attempt to cover all the possible human situations that may arise. Dealing with something as unpredictable as is human behavior, it is a practical impossibility to reduce to legal language

and legal contract those things which will make for the best human relationships among people at work. It will take time for us to pass through this phase, but as sure as I am standing before you, I am confident that the time will come when we shall develop a mutual confidence in and respect for each other on the part of labor and management that is necessary to remove this problem in the negotiation of labor agreements.

16. Thomas Newcomb.
17. Union Leader G.
18. Company Executive B.
19. Union Leader G.
20. Peter F. Drucker, *The New Society* (New York: Harper and Brothers, 1950), p. 195. (Italics ours.)
21. The *Flash*, October 31, 1950.
22. *Ibid.*
23. *Ibid.*, November 6, 1950.

CHAPTER ELEVEN: STOP WATCH AND SLIDE RULE

1. This popularity became obscured in the light of M. Bedaux' later Nazi affiliations.
2. See William Gomberg, Chapter XI, "The 'Normal' Worker," in *A Trade Union Analysis of Time Study* (Chicago: Science Research Associates, 1948).
3. Swift & Company's Training Courses, *The Standards Department*, Series M, Lesson IV, August, 1948. Unpublished notes. (Italics ours.)
4. "Financial Incentive Plans," Swift & Company's Training Courses, *Employees' Earnings for Services*, Series O, Lesson IV, August, 1949. Unpublished notes, p. 2.
5. *Ibid.* (Italics ours.)
6. Company Executive C.
7. Company Executive A.
8. *Swift & Company Master Agreement with United Packinghouse Workers of America,* paragraph 68, pp. 60–63.
9. The *Flash*, vol. III, no. 67, February 23, 1949.
10. The *Flash*, vol. III, no. 127, April 18, 1950.
11. Union Leader I.
12. Unpublished notes distributed at UPWA Seventh Constitutional Convention, Minneapolis, 1950.
13. If there were any bias by race, sex or length of service as associated with attitudes toward the Standards System, one would expect our sample of 104 also to be biased by one of these characteristics, so that it would have more men in it or more short service people, etc. As a matter of fact, there is almost perfect correspondence between the small sample of 104 and the large random sample of 202 in every one of the twelve "cell" combinations of the three key variables, race, sex and length of service. This fact should indicate that if race, sex or length of service have any influence on attitudes toward Standards, then our sample is not biased. It was not apparent to the interviewer that any other factor crept in to cause bias.
14. Union Leader G.
15. For an early psychological treatment of the reasonable use of time and motion study, see Charles S. Myers, former director of the Psychological

Laboratory at Cambridge University, *Mind and Work* (New York and London: G. P. Putnam's Sons, 1921).

16. A recent interesting study of the workers on an automobile assembly line finds conclusions similar to our own: C. R. Walker and R. H. Guest, *The Man on the Assembly Line* (Cambridge: Harvard University Press, 1952).

17. C. S. Golden and H. J. Ruttenberg, *The Dynamics of Industrial Democracy* (New York: Harper and Brothers, 1942), p. 183. Gomberg, whose union, the ILGWU, has had signal success in joint time study, comments on Golden and Ruttenberg's optimism with general agreement. Gomberg, *op. cit.*, pp. 178-180.

18. *Ibid.*, p. 174.

CHAPTER TWELVE: DUAL ALLEGIANCE AND THE FUTURE

1. Pius XI, *Quadragesimo Anno*, 1931, quoted by Oswald Von Nell-Breuning, S.J., in *Reorganization of Social Economy* (Milwaukee: The Bruce Publishing Co., 1936), pp. 194–195. (Italics ours.)

2. See *International Constitution* of the UPWA, 1949, Article IX, Section H, and Article XVII, Section E.

3. Union Leader D.

4. Company Executive E.

5. Peter F. Drucker, *The New Society*, p. 150.

6. For an interesting and lucid discussion of the theoretical questions we are trying to clarify here, see Crane Brinton, *Ideas and Men* (New York: Prentice-Hall, 1950), especially chapter 14, "The Twentieth Century: the Anti-Intellectual Attack."

APPENDIX III: HOW WELL ARE THEY PAID?

1. *Monthly Labor Review*, February, 1951, LXII, no. 2, 152.

2. For example 34 per cent of American four-person, nonfarm families received less than $3000 income in 1948. See *Low Income Families and Economic Stability*, Materials on the Problem of Low Income Families Assembled by the Staff of the Subcommittee on Low-Income Families, Joint Committee on the Economic Report. U. S. Government Printing Office, September 15, 1950. Incidentally, if it be argued that Chicago Swift-UPWA families are smaller than the four persons of the budget and have more than one wage earner per family, such an argument is highly vulnerable from a sociological point of view. If the average worker is not paid enough to support a family of more than four, he ought to be. And as for mothers of families as supplementary wage-earners, this is a well-known contributory cause of juvenile delinquency.

3. Report of the Presidential Board of Inquiry appointed under Executive Order No. 9934A, March 15, 1948, dated April 8, 1948. Typescript, p. 86. While it is true that Ewan W. Clague, Commissioner of the Bureau of Labor Statistics, said: "The budget total should not be compared directly with industrial wages or wage rates" (Press Release, December 16, 1948, p. 11), it is clear that Mr. Clague does not want the budget directly compared with specific hourly and weekly earnings of hourly rates, etc. He is surely not disclaiming a comparison of the budget with gross annual earnings.

4. *Swift & Company Master Agreement with the PWOC-CIO*, August 20, 1942, p. 11.

SELECTED BIBLIOGRAPHY

BOOKS, ARTICLES, JOURNALS, PAMPHLETS AND NEWSPAPERS

Abbot, Edith, *Women in Industry,* New York: Appleton, 1919.

Adams, Kate J., *Humanizing a Great Industry,* pamphlet of Armour and Company, Chicago, 1919.

Alinsky, Saul D., *Reveille for Radicals,* Chicago: University of Chicago Press, 1946.

Amalgamated Meat Cutters and Butcher Workmen of North America, AFL, *The Butcher Workman,* official magazine; *Official Journal; Fifty Progressive Years.*

American Meat Institute, various pamphlets on the meat industry such as "Meat — How It Serves You, the Soil and the Nation," etc.; *The Packing Industry,* Institute of American Meat Packers (former name of the American Meat Institute), Chicago: University of Chicago Press, 1924.

Andrews, Wayne, *Battle for Chicago,* New York: Harcourt Brace & Co., 1946.

Aquinas, Thomas, *On the Governance of Rulers,* translated by Gerald B. Phelan, New York: Sheed and Ward, 1938.

Armour, J. Ogden, *The Packers, the Private Car Lines and the People,* Philadelphia: Henry Altemus Co., 1906.

Armour and Company, *The Armour Star,* Company magazine, and many pamphlets.

Allport, Gordon W., *Personality,* New York: Henry Holt & Co., 1947.

———— *The Nature of Personality,* Addison-Wesley, Cambridge, 1950.

Allport, Gordon W. and Leo Postman, *The Psychology of Rumor,* New York: Henry Holt & Co., 1947.

The Back of the Yards Journal.

Bakke, E. Wight, *Mutual Survival,* New York: Harper and Brothers, 1946.

———— *Bonds of Organization,* New York: Harper and Brothers, 1950.

———— *Obstacles to Labor and Management Peace,* Reprint no. 6, The Economic and Business Foundation, New Haven, 1947.

Bakke, E. Wight and Clark Kerr, *Unions, Management and the Public,* New York: Harcourt, Brace & Co., 1948.

Barbash, Jack, *Labor Unions in Action,* New York: Harper and Brothers, 1948.

Bartlett, F. C., *Remembering,* Cambridge, England: Cambridge University Press, 1940.

Barkin, Solomon, "A Trade Unionist Appraises Management Personnel Philosophy," *Harvard Business Review,* September, 1950.

Bogart, E. L. and C. M. Thompson, *The Industrial State,* vol. IV of *The Centennial History of Illinois,* C. W. Alvord, Editor, Springfield, Ill.: Illinois Centennial Commission, 1920.

Breckenridge, S. and Edith Abbot, "Chicago Housing Conditions: III. Back of the Yards," *American Journal of Sociology,* vol. XVI, no. 11, Jan. 1911.

Brinton, Crane, *Ideas and Men,* New York: Prentice-Hall, 1950.

Brown, Leo C., S.J., *Union Policies in the Leather Industry,* Cambridge: Harvard University Press, 1947.

Browne, Henry J., *The Catholic Church and the Knights of Labor,* Washington, D. C., Catholic University Press, 1949.

Bruner, Jerome S. and Cecile C. Goodman, "Value and Need as Organizing Factors in Perception," *Journal of Abnormal and Social Psychology,* vol. XLII, 1947.

Business Week, "More Work from Workers — Labor's Way," April 22, 1950.

Bushnell, C. J., *The Social Problems at the Chicago Stock Yards,* Chicago: University of Chicago Press, 1902.

Carver, A. H., *Personnel and Labor Problems in the Packing Industry,* Chicago: University of Chicago Press, 1928.

Cayton, H. R. and G. S. Mitchell, *Black Workers and the New Unions,* Chapel Hill, N. C.: University of North Carolina Press, 1939.

The Chicago Daily News, The Chicago Tribune, The Chicago Daily Record, The Chicago Herald, The Chicago Daily Drovers' Journal, The Chicago Sun-Times.

The Chicago Commission on Race Relations, *The Negro in Chicago,* Chicago: University of Chicago Press, 1922.

The Cleaver, weekly newssheet of Armour Local Union #347, UPWA-CIO.

Clemen, Rudolph A., *The American Livestock and Meat Industry,* New York: Ronald Press, 1923.

———— *By-Products in the Packing Industry,* New York: Ronald Press, 1923.

Collective Bargaining in the Meat Packing Industry, Bulletin no. 1063, U. S. Dept. of Labor, Bureau of Labor Statistics, Feb. 27, 1952.

Commons, John R., *Trade Unionism and Labor Problems,* Boston: Ginn and Company, 1905.

Commons, John R. *et al., History of Labor in the United States,* New York: Macmillan Co., 1926.

Corey, Lewis, "Human Relations Minus Unionism," *Labor and Nation,* vol. VI, no. 2, Spring, 1950.

———— *Meat and Man,* New York: The Viking Press, 1950.

The Daily Inter-Ocean.

Davey, Harold W., *Contemporary Collective Bargaining,* New York: Prentice-Hall, 1951. (Contains an analysis of the 1949–50 Swift-UPWA contract.)

Dempsey, Bernard W., S.J., "The Roots of Business Responsibility," *Harvard Business Review,* vol. XXVII, no. 4, July, 1949.

Donnellan, E. A., "The Back-of-the-Yards Neighborhood Council," unpublished thesis, Loyola University, Chicago, 1940.

Drake, St. Clair and Horace R. Cayton, *Black Metropolis,* New York: Harcourt, Brace & Co., 1945.

Drucker, Peter F., *The New Society,* New York: Harper and Brothers, 1949.

Dunlop, John T., *Wage Determination Under Trade Unions,* New York: Macmillan Co., 1944.

———— "The Development of Labor Organization: A Theoretical Framework," Chapter 7 in *Insights into Labor Issues,* ed. R. A. Lester and Joseph Shister, New York: Macmillan Co., 1948.

Dunlop, John T. and James J. Healy, *Collective Bargaining,* Chicago: Richard D. Irwin, 1953.

Encyclopedia of Social Sciences, "Meat Packing and Slaughtering," by E. R. A. Seligman and A. Johnson, vol. 9, New York: Macmillan Co., 1937.

Faulkner, H. U., *American Economic History,* New York: Harper and Brothers, 1924.

Federal Trade Commission, *Report on the Meat Packing Industry,* U. S. Printing Office, Washington, D. C., 1921.

The Flash, weekly newssheet of Local 28, UPWA-CIO.

Foster, William Z., "How Life Has Been Brought into the Stock Yards," *Life and Labor,* April, 1918.

Foster, William Z., *From Bryan to Stalin,* New York: International Publishers, 1937.

Frazier, E. Franklin, *The Negro Family in Chicago,* Chicago: University of Chicago Press, 1932.

Golden, Clinton S. and Ruttenberg, Harold J., *The Dynamics of Industrial Democracy,* New York: Harper and Brothers, 1942.

Gomberg, William, *A Trade Union Anaylsis of Time Study,* Chicago: Science Research Associates, 1948.

Gompers, Samuel, *Seventy Years of Life and Labor,* New York: E. P. Dutton & Co., 1925.

Goodspeed, T. W., *G. F. Swift,* University of Chicago Biographical Sketches, vol. I, reprint, 1922.

Harbison, Frederick H., *Patterns of Union Management Relations,* Chicago: Science Research Associates, 1947.

Hart, G. W. M., "Industrial Relations Research and Social Theory," *The Canadian Journal of Economics and Political Science,* XV, February, 1949.

Hayes, Samuel P., Jr., "Some Psychological Problems of Economics," *Psychological Bulletin,* vol. XLVII, no. 4, July, 1950.

Herberg, Will, "Bureacracy and Democracy in Labor Unions," *The Antioch Review,* III, no. 3, Fall, 1943.

Herbst, Alma, *The Negro in the Slaughtering and Meat Packing Industry in Chicago,* New York: Columbia University Press, 1932.

Hinsman, Robert B. and Robert B. Harris, *The Story of Meat,* Chicago: Swift & Company, 1939.

Homans, George C., *The Human Group,* New York: Harcourt, Brace & Co., 1950.

Homans, George C. and Charles P. Curtis, *An Introduction to Pareto,* New York: Alfred A. Knopf, 1934.

Hope II, John, Preliminary Report: "United Packinghouse Workers Union of America, CIO, Self Survey of Human Relations," typescript, May, 1950.

Hoslett, Schuyler D., *Human Factors in Management,* Parkville, Missouri: Park College Press, 1946.

Human Relations in Modern Business, A Guide for Action Sponsored by American Business Leaders, New York: Prentice-Hall, 1949.

Imberman, A. A., "Labor Leaders and Society," *Harvard Business Review,* vol. XXVIII, no. 1, January, 1950.

Illinois State Industrial Union Council, CIO, *Convention Proceedings,* 1949.

Jimerson, Earl W., "Fifty Golden Years," *American Federationist,* vol. LIV, no. 4, April, 1947.

Josephson, Matthew, *The Robber Barons,* New York: Harcourt, Brace & Co., 1934.

Kampfert, Arthur, *History of Meat Packing, Slaughtering and Unionism,* unpublished typescript, Chicago, 1949.

Krech, David and Richard S. Crutchfield, *Theory and Problems of Social Psychology,* New York: McGraw-Hill Book Co., 1948.

Life, "The CIO Loses Its Meat Strike," vol. XXIV, no. 21, May 24, 1948.

Leech, Harper and John C. Carroll, *Armour and His Times,* New York: D. Appleton and Century Company, 1938.

Lytle, Charles W., *Wage Incentive Methods,* New York: Ronald Press, 1943.

McCarty, Harold and C. W. Thompson, *Meat Packing in Iowa,* Iowa University Studies in Business, vol. XII, Iowa City: Iowa University Press, 1933.

McDowell, Mary E., "How Casual Work Undermines Family and Neighborhood Life," *Proceedings of the National Conference of Charities and Correction,* Buffalo, 1909.

Malott, D. W. and B. F. Martin, "The Livestock and Meat Packing Industry," Chapter III of *The Agricultural Industries*, New York: McGraw-Hill Book Co., 1939.

Martin, John B., "Certain Wise Men," *McCall's Magazine*, March, 1949.

Mayo, Elton, *Human Problems of an Industrial Civilization*, New York: Macmillan Co., 1933.

———— *Social Problems of an Industrial Civilization*, Harvard Graduate School of Business Administration, Division of Research, 1945.

Meat, an operation and management magazine.

Meegan, Joseph, "A Decade of Progress," pamphlet of the Back-of-the-Yards Neighborhood Council, Chicago, 1950.

Meyer, Agnes E., "Orderly Revolution," articles in the *Washington Post*, June 4–9, 1945.

Millis, Harry A. and Royal E. Montgomery, *Organized Labor*, New York: McGraw Hill Book Co., 1945.

Monthly Labor Review.

Moore, Thomas Verner, *Cognitive Psychology*, Philadelphia: J. B. Lippincott Co., 1939.

———— *The Driving Forces of Human Nature*, New York: Grune and Stratton, 1948.

Mosteller, Frederick and Philip Nogel, "An Experimental Measurement of Utility," *The Journal of Political Economy*, vol. LIX, no. 5, October, 1951.

Myers, Charles S., *Mind and Work*, G. P. Putnam, London, 1921.

Myrdal, Gunnar, *An American Dilemma*, New York: Harper and Brothers, 1944.

National Labor Relations Board, Case No. XIII–C–1187, Swift and Company and Local 28 of PWOC-CIO, April 17, 1940.

The National Provisioner, a management magazine.

Von Nell-Breuning, Oswald, S.J., *Reorganization of Social Economy*, translated by Bernard W. Dempsey, S.J., Milwaukee: Bruce Publishing Co., 1936.

The New Majority, formerly the official magazine of the Chicago Federation of Labor.

Nichols, W. H., *Labor Productivity Functions in Meat Packing*, Chicago: University of Chicago Press, 1945.

Nolan, William A., S.J., *Communism vs. the Negro*, Chicago: The Henry Regnery Co., 1951.

Northrup, Herbert R., *Organized Labor and the Negro*, New York: Harper and Brothers, 1944.

Perlman, Selig and Philip Taft, *History of Labor in the United States*, New York: Macmillan Co., 1935.

Record, Wilson, *The Negro and the Communist Party*, Chapel Hill, N. C.: University of North Carolina Press, 1951.

Report of the Commissioner of Corporations on the Beef Industry, Washington, D. C., U. S. Government Printing Office, March 3, 1905.

Roethlisberger, Fritz J. and William J. Dickson, *Management and the Worker*, Cambridge: Harvard University Press, 1947.

Roethlisberger, Fritz L., "The Foreman: Master and Victim of Double Talk," *Harvard Business Review*, vol. XXIII, no. 3, Spring, 1945.

Rogers, Carl R., *Counselling and Psychotherapy*, Boston: Houghton Mifflin Co., 1942.

Russell, C. E., *The Greatest Trust in the World*, Ridgway-Thayer Company, New York, 1905. (First published in serial form in *Everybody's Magazine*.)

Selekman, Benjamin, *Labor Relations and Human Relations*, New York: McGraw-Hill, 1947.

Seidman, Joel, Jack London, and Bernard Karsh, "Leadership in a Local Union," *The American Journal of Sociology*, vol. LVI, no. 3, November, 1950.

Shiel, Roger R., *Twenty Years in Hell with the Beef Trust*, Indianapolis: privately printed, 1909.

Shister, Joseph, "Locus of Union Control in Collective Bargaining," *Quarterly Journal of Economics*, LX, August, 1946.

———— "Trade Union Government," *Quarterly Journal of Economics*, vol. IX, no. 1, November, 1945.

Sinclair, Upton, *The Jungle*, New York: Doubleday, Page and Co., 1906, and Alfred A. Knopf, 1946.

———— "Is the Jungle True?" *Independent*, May 17, 1906.

Slichter, Sumner, *The Challenge of Industrial Relations*, Ithaca: Cornell University Press, 1947.

———— "The Social Control of Industrial Relations," Industrial Relations Research Association Second Annual Meeting *Proceedings*, Champaign, Illinois: IRRA.

Smith. A. D. H., *Men Who Run America*, New York: Bobbs-Merrill Co., 1935.

Snedecor, George W., *Statistical Methods*, Ames: Iowa State College Press, 1946.

Spero, S. D. and A. L. Harris, *The Black Worker*, New York: Columbia University Press, 1931.

Staley, Eugene, *History of the Illinois State Federation of Labor*, Chicago: University of Chicago Press, 1930.

Swift, Helen, *My Father and Mother*, Chicago: Privately printed, 1937.

Swift, Louis E., *The Yankee of the Yards*, Chicago and New York: A. W. Shaw Company, 1928.

Swift & Company, *The Swift News*, a company magazine; *The Meat Packing Industry*, and other pamphlets.

Tannenbaum, Frank, *A Philosophy of Labor*, New York: Alfred A. Knopf, 1951.

———— "The Social Function of Trade Unionism," *Political Science Quarterly*, New York: Columbia University Press, June, 1947.

Taft, Philip, "Opposition to Union Officers in Elections," *Quarterly Journal of Economics*, LVIII, February, 1944.

United Packinghouse Workers of America, CIO, Convention Proceedings; *The Packinghouse Worker; The Meat of It; Minorities in the UPWA; Eighty Years of Packinghouse Workers' History; Early Unionism in Packing*.

U. S. Bureau of Labor *Bulletin*, no. 45, 1905.

U. S. Bureau of Labor Statistics, *The Meat Industry and Trade*, 1917.

U. S. Congress, *Conditions in Chicago Stockyards*, Neill-Reynolds Report, 59th Congress, 1st Session, Document No. 873, U. S. Government Printing Office, Washington, D. C., 1906.

U. S. Census of Manufactures.

U. S. Census, *Eleventh Census of the United States*, 1890.

Walker, Charles R., *Steeltown*, New York: Harper and Brothers, 1950.

Warner, W. L. and J. O. Low, *The Social System of a Modern Factory*, New Haven: Yale University Press, 1947.

Weld, Louis D. H., "Private Freight Cars and the American Railways," *Studies in History, Economics and Public Law*, New York: Columbia University Press, vol. XXXI, no. 1, 1908.

Whyte, William F., *Pattern for Industrial Peace*, New York: Harper and Brothers, 1951.

Williams, Whiting, *Mainsprings of Men*, New York: Charles Scribner's Sons, 1925.

Wilson, H. E., *Mary McDowell Neighbor*, Chicago: University of Chicago Press, 1928.

Wilson and Company, *Wilson's Certified News*, a company magazine.

Worthy, James, "Organizational Structure and Employee Morale," *American Sociological Review*, April, 1950.

Wright, Carroll, "Influence of Trade Unions on Immigrants," *Bulletin of the Bureau of Labor*, X, January, 1915.

Yoder, Dale, *Personnel and Labor Relations*, New York: Prentice-Hall, 1938.

INDEX

Swift family, present status in Swift & Company, 19

Swift News, 9, 88, 99, 193, 280, 291

Swift Standards System, wage incentives, 236–237; objectives of, 237–239; management view, 239–241; union view, 241–243; workers' view, 243–250, 253–255; union leaders' and stewards' views, 251–253; reasons for dissatisfaction with, 256–260; comment in Edward Hassett interview, 292–293

Swift-UPWA contract; quoted on rights of company and of union, 4–5. *See also* Contract

Swift-UPWA plant community. *See* Plant Community

"Table ready meats," 20, 22

Taft-Hartley Act, 64, 65, 182

Tannenbaum, Frank, quoted on participation, 193–194

Tarbell, Ida, 18

Tarbuck, William, interview, 95

Tardiness, 317

Taylor, F. W., *Scientific Management,* 257

Taylor, Harvey, interview, 98–99, 160, 188

Textile Workers, 8

Thompson, Alexander, interview, 91, 113, 114

Thompson, William, interview, 104, 199–200

Time, influence on worker attitudes of, 14–15

Time and motion study, UPWA attitude toward, 243. *See also* Swift Standards System.

Toby, Jack, interview, 97

Toner, Ambrose, interview, 138, 172

Torpey, Upson, interview, 253

Tribune (Chicago), 56, 57, 169

Truman, President Harry S., action in 1946 strike, 60; action in 1948 strike, 61

"Trust busters," influence on packers, 18

Turnover of Chicago plant workers, 34–35, 316; compared with other plants of Swift & Company, 35

Union, history in packing industry of, 43–73; internal troubles, 49; and the workers, 145–172; participation, 193–217; grievance procedure, 221–235; and the Standards System, 241–243, 245, 251–253; need for security before full coöperation, 260; areas for greater dual allegiance, 276–281; accomplishments for the worker, 302–307. *See also* Local 28, United Packinghouse Workers of America

Union allegiance, 111, 145–150, 310; effect of protection and status, 150–157; effect of fringe benefits, 157–158; of mechanics, 158–160; of union leaders, 160–161; of foremen, 162–165; disallegiance, 165–172; effect on union participation, 194; little effect of Standards System on, 256; effect on company or dual allegiance, 269; shown in Edward Hassett interview, 285–293

Union disallegiance, 165–172

Union inactivity, various reasons for, 203–206

Union leaders, company allegiance of, 80–81, 93–97; attitude toward foremen of, 124, 132–134; union allegiance of, 150, 160–161; attitude of foremen toward, 164–165, 172; attitude of workers toward, 165, 167, 310; and 1948 strike, 175–178; anticompany leaders, 178–182; left-wing leaders, 182–183; Negro oriented leaders, 183–184; ignorance about leaders, 185–189; management and union leadership, 189–192; union participation of, 195, 197, 209–217; influence of, 206

Union leadership, motives for, 209–210, 215; motives against, 216–217

Union-management committees, 278–279

Union membership, 64; effect on union allegiance, 149; effect on union participation, 194, 195–196

Union participation, criteria for, 194–199; effect of fighting and leaders, 199–200; race deterrent, 201–203; other deterrents, 203–206; of stewards, 206–209; of local union leaders, 209–217; statistical table of, 310

Union security, 63–64; need for, 277–279

Union stockyards, concentration of packing industry plants, 85

United Auto Workers, 277, 278

United Food Processers' Union, 52

United Mine Workers, 263

United Packinghouse Workers of America (CIO), International, 3; objectives, 5–6; areas of coöperation with company, 6–7; rebellion of locals against, 14; early support of BYC, 39–40; early Negro support, 42; establishment, 59; growth after World War II, 60–62; Communist struggle for control, 64–72; good relations with company, 73; partial credit for seniority benefits, 87; company allegiance of, 95–97; accomplishments for Negroes, 110;